"This book is an impressive feat. Bounegru and Gray have put together a truly global and diverse collection that greatly enriches our understanding of the politics of data and what it means for journalism. In the wake of the Covid-19 pandemic, this contribution is more important than ever."
– Lina Dencik, co-founder of the Data Justice Lab, Cardiff University; co-author of *Digital Citizenship in a Datafied Society*

"Ostensibly focused on data journalism, this handbook is so much more, providing an overarching analysis of much of the emerging field of critical data studies. Journalists and others interested in how to assemble, work with, make sense of, apply, and critically reflect on data and their uses will revel in the extensive theoretical and practical insights."
– Rob Kitchin, Maynooth University; author of *The Data Revolution: Big Data, Open Data, Data Infrastructures and Their Consequences*

"*The Data Journalism Handbook* is an indispensable resource for students, researchers, and journalists who want to understand how data are translated into information, information in knowledge and, ultimately, wisdom. That itinerary all starts with a full comprehension of how data reflect, construct and shape our social reality. Jonathan Gray and Liliana Bounegru have collected and presented an impressive number of illuminating practices in this Handbook."
– José van Dijck, Utrecht University; author of *The Culture of Connectivity* and *The Platform Society*.

"By providing a wealth of living testimonies from practitioners and academics from different countries, this book gives a rich overview of practices that have become key in contemporary journalism. By cautioning the reader against overconfidence in technology, the main virtue of this book is to give a set of practical insights to help journalists not only to better cooperate with their peers, through computational tools, but also to establish more fruitful relationships with researchers and publics."
– Sylvain Parasie, Sciences Po; author of *Sociologie d'internet*

"A professional and academic field reaches maturity when it begins to cast a light on itself and becomes capable of self-criticism, asking not only descriptive questions such as *how* we do things, but analytical ones, such as *why* we should—or shouldn't—do those things. The new edition of *The Data Journalism Handbook* signals that we might have reached that point with the use of digital data to do news reporting and inform audiences. The variety, diversity, and depth of the contributions to this collective effort make this book a required reading for beginners and professionals alike."
– Alberto Cairo, University of Miami; author of *How Charts Lie: Getting Smarter About Visual Information*

The Data Journalism Handbook

Digital Studies

The *Digital Studies* book series aims to provide a space for social and cultural research with and about the digital. In particular, it focuses on ambitious and experimental works which explore and critically engage with the roles of digital data, methods, devices and infrastructures in collective life as well as the issues, challenges and troubles that accompany them.

The series invites proposals for monographs and edited collections which attend to the dynamics, politics, economics and social lives of digital technologies and techniques, informed by and in conversation with fields such as science and technology studies and new media studies.

The series welcomes works which conceptualize, rethink and/or intervene around digitally mediated practices and cultures. It is open to a range of contributions including thoughtful interpretive work, analytical artefacts, creative code, speculative design and/or inventive repurposing of digital objects and methods of the medium.

Series Editors:
- Tobias Blanke, University of Amsterdam
- Liliana Bounegru, King's College London
- Carolin Gerlitz, University of Siegen
- Jonathan Gray, King's College London
- Sabine Niederer, Amsterdam University of Applied Sciences
- Richard Rogers, University of Amsterdam

The Data Journalism Handbook

Towards a Critical Data Practice

Edited by
Liliana Bounegru and
Jonathan Gray

Amsterdam University Press

Cover design: Coördesign, Leiden
Lay-out: Crius Group, Hulshout

ISBN   978 94 6298 9511
e-ISBN   978 90 4854 207 9
DOI   10.5117/9789462989511
NUR   813

Every effort has been made to obtain permission to use all copyrighted illustrations
reproduced in this book. Nonetheless, whosoever believes to have rights to this material is
advised to contact the publisher.

Table of Contents

Working With Data

Experiencing Data

Investigating Data, Platforms and Algorithms

Organizing Data Journalism

Learning Data Journalism Together

Situating Data Journalism

Introduction

Jonathan Gray and Liliana Bounegru

Abstract
An introduction to the book as a collective experiment in accounting for data journalism practices around the world, providing an overview of its sections and chapters and twelve challenges for critical data practice.

Keywords: data journalism, critical data practice, critical data studies, digital methods, science and technology studies, Internet studies

Data Journalism in Question

What is data journalism? What is it for? What might it do? What opportunities and limitations does it present? Who and what is involved in making it and making sense of it? This book is a collective experiment responding to these and other questions about the practices, cultures, politics and settings of data journalism around the world. It follows on from another edited book, *The Data Journalism Handbook: How Journalists Can Use Data to Improve the News* (Gray et al., 2012). Both books assemble a plurality of voices and perspectives to account for the evolving field of data journalism. The first edition started through a "book sprint" at Mozilla Festival in London in 2011, which brought together journalists, technologists, advocacy groups and others to write about how data journalism is done. As we wrote in the introduction, it aimed to "document the passion and enthusiasm, the vision and energy of a nascent movement," to provide "stories behind the stories" and to let "different voices and views shine through" (Gray et al., 2012). The 2012 edition is now translated into over a dozen languages—including Arabic, Chinese, Czech, French, Georgian, Greek, Italian, Macedonian, Portuguese, Russian, Spanish and Ukrainian—and is used for teaching at many leading universities and training centres around the world, as well as being a well-cited source for researchers studying the field.

Bounegru, L. and J. Gray (eds.), *The Data Journalism Handbook: Towards a Critical Data Practice*. Amsterdam: Amsterdam University Press, 2021
DOI 10.5117/9789462989511_INTRO

While the 2012 book is still widely used (and this book is intended to complement rather than to replace it), a great deal has happened since 2012. On the one hand, data journalism has become more established. In 2011 data journalism as such was very much a field "in the making," with only a handful of people using the term. It has subsequently become socialized and institutionalized through dedicated organizations, training courses, job posts, professional teams, awards, anthologies, journal articles, reports, tools, online communities, hashtags, conferences, networks, meetups, mailing lists and more. There is also broader awareness of the term through events which are conspicuously data-related, such as the Panama Papers, which whistleblower Edward Snowden then characterized as the "biggest leak in the history of data journalism" (Snowden, 2016).

On the other hand, data journalism has become more contested. The 2013 Snowden leaks helped to publicly confirm a transnational surveillance apparatus of states and technology companies as a matter of fact rather than speculation. These leaks suggested how citizens were made knowable through big data practices, showing a darker side to familiar data-making devices, apps and platforms (Gray & Bounegru, 2019). In the United States the launch of Nate Silver's dedicated data journalism outlet *FiveThirtyEight* in 2014 was greeted by a backlash for its overconfidence in particular kinds of quantitative methods and its disdain for "opinion journalism" (Byers, 2014). While Silver was acclaimed as "lord and god of the algorithm" by *The Daily Show*'s Jon Stewart for successfully predicting the outcome of the 2012 elections, the statistical methods that he advocated were further critiqued and challenged after the election of Donald Trump in 2016. These elections along with the Brexit vote in the United Kingdom and the rise of populist right-wing leaders around the world, were said to correspond with a "post-truth" moment (Davies, 2016), characterized by a widespread loss of faith in public institutions, expert knowledge, and the mediation of public and political life by online platforms which left their users vulnerable to targeting, manipulation and misinformation.[1]

Whether the so-called "post-truth" moment is taken as evidence of failure or as a call to action, one thing is clear: Data can no longer be taken for granted, and nor can data journalism. Data does not just provide neutral and straightforward representations of the world, but is rather entangled with politics and culture, money and power. Institutions and infrastructures underpinning the production of data—from surveys to statistics, climate science to social media platforms—have been called into question. At the

---

1   For a critical perspective on this term, see Jasanoff, S., & Simmet, H. R. (2017). No funeral bells: Public reason in a "post-truth" age. *Social Studies of Science, 47*(5), 751–770.

time of writing, as the COVID-19 pandemic continues to roll on around the world, numbers, graphs and rankings have become widely shared, thematized, politicized and depoliticized—as exemplified by daily circulating epidemiological charts referred to by the now ubiquitous public health strategy to "flatten the curve." At the same time, the fragility and provisionality of such data has been widely reported on, with concerns around the under-reporting, non-reporting and classification of cases, as well as growing awareness of the societal and political implications of different kinds of data from sources—from hospital figures to research estimates to self-reporting to transactional data from tracing apps. The pandemic has broadened awareness of not just using but also critically reporting on numbers and data.

Thus one might ask of the use of data in journalism: Which data, whose data and by which means? Data about which issues and to what end? Which kinds of issues are data-rich and which are data-poor, and why? Who has the capacity to benefit from data and who doesn't? What kinds of publics does data assemble, which kinds of capacities does it support, what kinds of politics does it enact and what kinds of participation does it engender?

Towards a Critical Data Practice

Rather than bracketing such questions and concerns, this book aims to "stay with the trouble," as the prominent feminist scholar Donna Haraway (2016) puts it.[2] Instead of treating the relevance and importance of data journalism as an assertion, we treat this as a question which can be addressed in multiple ways. The collection of chapters gathered in the book strive to provide a richer story about what data journalism does, with and for whom. Through our editorial work we sought to encourage reflection on what data journalism projects can do, and the conditions under which they can succeed. This entails the cultivation of a different kind of precision in accounting for data journalism practice: Specifying the situations in which it develops and operates. Such precision requires broadening the scope of the book to include not just the ways in which data is analyzed, created and used in the context of journalism but also the social, cultural, political and economic circumstances in which such practices are embedded.

The subtitle of this new book is "towards a critical data practice," and reflects both our aspiration as editors to bring critical reflection to bear on

---

2   Alluding to this work, Verran's chapter in this book explores how data journalists might stay with the trouble of value and numbers.

data journalism practices, as well as reflecting the increasingly critical stances of data journalism practitioners. The notion of "critical data practice" is a nod to Philip E. Agre's notion of "critical technical practice," which he describes in terms of having "one foot planted in the craft work of design and the other foot planted in the reflexive work of critique" (Agre, 1997, p. 155). As we have written about elsewhere, our interest in this book is understanding how critical engagements with data might modify data practices, making space for public imagination and interventions around data politics (Gray, 2018; Gray et al., 2018).

Alongside contributions from data journalists and practitioners writing about what they do, the book also includes chapters from researchers whose work may advance critical reflection on data journalism practices, from fields such as anthropology, science and technology studies, (new) media studies, Internet studies, platform studies, the sociology of quantification, journalism studies, Indigenous studies, feminist studies, digital methods and digital sociology. Rather than assuming a more traditional division of labour such that researchers provide critical reflection and practitioners offer more instrumental tips and advice, we have sought to encourage researchers to consider the practical salience of their work, and to provide practitioners with space to reflect on what they do outside of their day-to-day deadlines. None of these different perspectives exhaust the field, and our objective is to encourage readers to attend to different aspects of how data journalism is done. In other words, this book is intended to function as a multidisciplinary conversation starter, and—we hope—a catalyst for collaborations.

We do not assume that "data journalism" refers to a single, unified set of practices. Rather it is a prominent label which refers to a diverse plurality of practices which can be empirically studied, specified and experimented with. As one recent review puts it, we need to interrogate the "how of quantification as much as the mere fact of it," the effects of which "depend on intentions and implementation" (Berman & Hirschman, 2018). Our purpose is not to stabilize how data journalism is done, but rather to draw attention to its manifold aspects and open up space for doing it differently.

A Collective Experiment

It is worth briefly noting what this book is not. It is not just a textbook or handbook in the conventional sense: The chapters do not add up to an established body of knowledge, but are rather intended to indicate interesting directions for further inquiry and experimentation. The book is not just a practical guidebook of tutorials or "how tos": There are already countless readily available materials and courses on different aspects of data practice (e.g., data analysis and data visualization). It is not just a book of "behind the scenes" case studies: There are plenty of articles and blog posts showing how projects were done, including interviews with their creators. It is not just a book of recent academic perspectives: There is an emerging body of literature on data journalism scattered across numerous books and journals.[3]

Rather, the book has been designed as a *collective experiment* in accounting for data journalism practices of recent years and a *collective invitation* to explore how such practices may be modified. It is collective in that, as with the first edition, we have been able to assemble a comparatively large number of contributors (over 70) for a short book. The editorial process has benefitted from recommendations from contributors during email exchanges. A workshop with a number of contributors at the International Journalism Festival in Perugia in 2018 provided an opportunity for exchanges and reflection. A "beta" version of the book has been released online to provide an opportunity to publicly preview a selection of chapters before the printed version of the book is published and to elicit comments and encounters before the book takes its final shape. Through what could be considered a kind of curated "snowball editorial," we have sought to follow how data journalism is done by different actors, in different places, around different topics, through different means. Through the process we have compiled and trawled through many shortlists, longlists, outlets and data sets to curate different perspectives on data journalism practices. Although there were many, many more contributors we would have liked to include, we had to operate within the constraints of a printable book, as well as giving voice to a diversity of geographies, themes, concerns and genders.

It is experimental in that the chapters provide different perspectives and provocations on data journalism, which we invite readers to further explore through actively configuring their own blends of tools, data sets, methods, texts, publics and issues. Rather than inheriting the ways of seeing and ways of knowing that have been "baked into" elements such as official data sets or social media data, we encourage readers to enrol them into the service of their own lines of inquiry. This follows the spirit of "critical analytics" and "inventive methods" which aim to modify the questions which are asked and the way problems are framed (Lury & Wakeford, 2012; Rogers, 2018). Data journalism can be viewed not just in terms of how things are *represented*, but in terms of how it organizes *relations*—such that it is not just a matter of producing data stories (through collecting, analyzing, visualizing and narrating data), but also attending to who and what these stories bring together (including

3   https://www.zotero.org/groups/data_journalism_research

audiences, sources, methods, institutions and social media platforms). Thus we may ask, as Noortje Marres recently put it: "What are the methods, materials, techniques and arrangements that we curate in order to create spaces where problems can be addressed differently?"[4] The chapters in this book show how data journalism can be an inventive, imaginative, collaborative craft, highlighting how data journalists interrogate official data sources, make and compile their own data, try new visual and interactive formats, reflect on the effects of their work, and make their methods accountable and code re-usable. If the future of data journalism is uncertain, then we hope that readers of this book will join us in both critically taking stock of what journalism is and has been, as well as intervening to shape its future. As with all works, the success, failure and ultimate fate of this book-as-experiment ultimately lies with you, its readers, what you do with it, what it prompts and the responses it elicits.

The cover image of this book is a photograph of Sarah Sze's *Fixed Points Finding a Home* in the modern art museum Mudam Luxembourg, for which we are most grateful to the artist, her gallery and the museum for their permission to reproduce.[5] While it might not seem an obvious choice to put a work of sculpture on the cover of a book about journalism, we thought this image might encourage a relational perspective on data journalism as a kind of curatorial craft, assembling and working with diverse materials, communities and infrastructures to generate different ways of knowing, narrating and seeing the world at different scales and temporalities. Rather than focusing on the outputs of data journalism (e.g., with screenshots of visualizations or interactives), we wanted to reflect the different kinds of processes and collectives involved in doing journalism with data. Having both serendipitously encountered and been deeply absorbed by Sze's exhibitions at the Mudam, Venice Biennale, ZKM, the Tate and beyond, we thought her work could provide a different (and hopefully less familiar) vantage point on the practice of data journalism which would resonate with relational perspectives on information infrastructures and "data assemblages."[6] Her installations

---

4   A question that Noortje Marres asked in her plenary contribution to EASST 2018 in Lancaster: https://twitter.com/jwyg/status/1023200997668204544

5   Sarah Sze, *Fixed Points Finding a Home*, 2012 (details). Mixed media. Dimensions variable. Mudam Luxembourg Commission and Collection. Donation 2012—Les Amis des Musées d'Art et d'Histoire Luxembourg. © Artwork: Sarah Sze. Courtesy the artist and Victoria Miro. © Photo: Andrés Lejona/Mudam Luxembourg.

6   For relational perspectives on data infrastructures see, for example, the seminal work of Susan Leigh Star: Star, S. L., & Ruhleder, K. (1996). Steps toward an ecology of infrastructure: Design and access for large information spaces. *Information Systems Research*, 7, 111–134; Star, S. L. (1999). The ethnography of infrastructure. *American Behavioral Scientist*, 43, 377–391. For more recent work on "data assemblages," see, for example: Kitchin, R. (2014). *The data revolution:*

embody a precise and playful sensibility towards repurposing found materials that visually paralleled what we were hoping to emphasize with our editorial of different accounts of data journalism for the book. Bruno Latour recently wrote that Sze's approach to assembling materials can be considered to affirm "compositional discontinuities" (Latour, 2020) —which sits well with our hopes to encourage "critical data practice" and to tell stories both *with* and *about* the diverse materials and actors involved in data journalism, as we discuss further below, as well as with our editorial approach in supporting the different styles, voices, vernaculars and interests of the chapters in this book.

An Overview of the Book

To stay true to our editorial emphasis on specifying the setting, we note that the orientation of the book and its selection of chapters is coloured by our interests and those of our friends, colleagues and networks at this particular moment—including growing concerns about climate change, environmental destruction, air pollution, tax avoidance, (neo)colonialism, racism, sexism, inequality, extractivism, authoritarianism, algorithmic injustice and platform labour. The chapters explore how data journalism makes such issues intelligible and experienceable, as well as the kinds of responses it can mobilize. The selection of chapters also reflects our own oscillations between academic research, journalism and advocacy, as well as the different styles of writing and data practice associated with each of these.

We remain convinced of the generative potential of encounters between colleagues in these different fields, and several of the chapters attest to successful cross-field collaborations. As well as exploring synergies and commonalities, it is also worth noting at the outset (as astute readers will notice) that there are differences, tensions and frictions between the perspectives presented in the various chapters, including different histories and origin stories; different views on methods, data and emerging technologies; different views on the desirability of conventionalization and experimentation with different approaches; and different perspectives on what data journalism is, what it is for, its conditions and constraints, how it is organized and the possibilities it presents.

Big data, open data, data infrastructures and their consequences. SAGE; Kitchin, R., & Lauriault, T. (2018). Towards critical data studies: Charting and unpacking data assemblages and their work. In J. Thatcher, A. Shears, & J. Eckert (Eds.), *Thinking big data in geography: New regimes, new research* (pp. 3–20). University of Nebraska Press.

After this introduction, the book starts with a "taster menu" on doing issues with data. This includes a variety of different formats for making sense of different themes in different places—including tracing connections between agricultural commodities, crime, corruption and colonialism across several countries (Sánchez and Villagrán), mapping segregation in the United States (Williams), multiplying memories of trees in Bogotá (Magaña), looking at the people and scenes behind the numbers for home demolitions in occupied East Jerusalem (Haddad), mobilizing for road safety in the Philippines (Rey) and tracking worker deaths in Turkey (Dağ). The chapters in this section illustrate a breadth of practices from visualization techniques to building campaigns to repurposing official data with different analytical priorities.

The second section focuses on how journalists assemble data—an important emerging area which we have sought to foreground in the book and associated research (Gray et al., 2018; Gray & Bounegru, 2019). This includes exploring the making of projects on themes such as knife crime (Barr) and land conflicts (Shrivastava and Paliwal) as well as accounts of how to obtain and work with data in countries where it may be less easy to come by, such as in Cuba (Reyes, Almeida and Guerra) and China (Ma). Assembling data may also be a way of engaging with readers (Coelho) and assembling interested actors around an issue, which may in itself constitute an important outcome of a project. Gathering data may involve the modification of other forms of knowledge production, such as polls and surveys, to the context of journalism (Boros). A chapter on Indigenous data sovereignty (Kukutai and Walter) explores social, cultural and political issues around official data and how to bring other marginalized perspectives to bear on the organization of collective life with data. As well as using numbers as material for telling stories, data journalists may also tell stories about how numbers are made (Verran).

The third section is concerned with different ways of working with data. This includes with algorithms (Stray), code (Simon) and machines (Borges-Rey). Contributors examine emerging issues and opportunities arising from working with sources such as text data (Maseda). Others look at practices for making data journalistic work transparent, accountable and reproducible (Leon; Mazotte). Databases may also afford opportunities for collaborative work on large investigative projects (Díaz-Struck, Gallego and Romera). Feminist thought and practice may also inspire different ways of working with data (D'Ignazio).

The fourth section is dedicated to examining different ways in which data can be experienced, starting with a look at the different formats that data journalism can take (Cohen). Several pieces reflect on contemporary visualization practices (Aisch and Rost), as well as how readers respond to and participate in making sense with visualizations (Kennedy et al.). Other pieces look at how data is mediated and presented to readers through databases (Rahman and Wehrmeyer), web-based interactives (Bentley), TV and radio (de Jong), comics (Luna), and sketching with data (Chalabi and Gray).

The fifth section is dedicated to emerging approaches for investigating data, platforms and algorithms. Recent journalism projects take the digital as not only offering new techniques and opportunities for journalists, but also new objects for investigation. Examples of this are Bellingcat and *BuzzFeed News'* widely shared work on viral content, misinformation and digital culture.[7] Chapters in this section examine different ways of reporting on algorithms (Diakopoulous), as well as how to conduct longer-term collaborations in this area (Elmer). Other chapters look at how to work with social media data to explore how platforms participate in shaping debate, including storytelling approaches (Vo) as well as affinities between digital methods research and data journalism, including how "born digital" data can be used for investigations into web tracking infrastructures (Rogers) as well as about apps and their associated platforms (Weltevrede).

The sixth section is on organizing data journalism, and attends to different types of work in the field which are considered indispensable but not always prominently recognized. This includes how data journalism has changed over the past decade (Rogers); how platforms and the gig economy shape cross-border investigative networks (Cândea); entanglements between data journalism and movements for open data and civic tech (Baack); open-source coding practices (Pitts and Muscato); audience-measurement practices (Petre); archiving data journalism (Broussard); and the role of the #ddj hashtag in connecting data journalism communities on Twitter (Au and Smith).

The seventh section focuses on learning about data journalism as a collaborative process, including data journalism training programmes and the development of data journalism around the world. This includes chapters on teaching data journalism at universities in the United States (Phillips); empowering marginalized communities to tell their stories (Constantaras; Vaca); caution against "digital universalism" and underestimating innovation in the "periphery" (Chan); and different approaches for collaborations between journalists and researchers (Radcliffe and Lewis).

Data journalism does not happen in a vacuum. The eighth and final section focuses on situating this practice in relation to its various social, political, cultural and economic settings. A chapter on the genealogies of data

7   https://www.buzzfeednews.com/topic/fake-news, https://www.bellingcat.com/

journalism in the United States serves to encourage reflection on the various historical practices and ideas which shape it (Anderson). Other chapters look at how data journalism projects are valued through awards (Loosen); different approaches to measuring the impact of data journalism projects (Bradshaw; Green-Barber); issues around data journalism and colonialism (Young and Callison); whether data journalism can live up to its earlier aspirations to become a field of inspired experimentation, interactivity and play (Usher); and data journalism and digital liberalism (Boyer).

Twelve Challenges for Critical Data Practice

Drawing on the time that we have spent exploring data journalism practices through the development of this book, we would like to conclude this introduction to the book with twelve challenges for "critical data practice." These consider data journalism in terms of its capacities to *shape relations* between different actors as well as to *produce representations* about the world. Having been tested in the context of our "engaged research-led teaching" collaborations at King's College London and the Public Data Lab,[8] they are intended as a prompt for aspiring data journalists, student group projects and investigations, researcher–journalist collaborations, and other activities which aspire to organize collective inquiry with data without taking for granted the infrastructures, environments and practices through which it is produced.

1. How can data journalism projects tell stories *both with and about data* including the various actors, processes, institutions, infrastructures and forms of knowledge through which data is made?

2. How can data journalism projects tell stories about big issues at scale (e.g., climate change, inequality, multinational taxation, migration) while also *affirming the provisionality* and *acknowledging the models, assumptions and uncertainty* involved in the production of numbers?

3. How can data journalism projects account for the *collective character of digital data, platforms, algorithms and online devices*, including the interplay between digital technologies and digital cultures?

4. How can data journalism projects *cultivate their own ways of making things intelligible, meaningful and relatable through data*, without simply uncritically advancing the ways of knowing "baked into" data from dominant institutions, infrastructures and practices?

---

8   https://www.kcl.ac.uk/research/engaged-research-led-teaching and http://publicdatalab.org/

5. How can data journalism projects *acknowledge and experiment with the visual cultures and aesthetics that they draw on*, including through combinations of data visualizations and other visual materials?
6. How can data journalism projects make space for *public participation and intervention* in interrogating established data sources and re-imagining which issues are accounted for through data, and how?
7. How might data journalists cultivate and consciously affirm *their own styles of working with data*, which may draw on, yet remain distinct from, areas such as statistics, data science and social media analytics?
8. How can the field of data journalism *develop memory practices to archive and preserve their work*, as well as situating it in relation to practices and cultures that they draw on?
9. How can data journalism projects collaborate around transnational issues in ways which *avoid the logic of the platform and the colony, and affirm innovations at the periphery*?
10. How can data journalism support marginalized communities to use data to *tell their own stories on their own terms*, rather than telling their stories for them?
11. How can data journalism projects develop their own *alternative and inventive ways of accounting for their value and impact in the world*, beyond social media metrics and impact methodologies established in other fields?
12. How might data journalism *develop a style of objectivity which affirms, rather than minimizes, its own role in intervening in the world* and in shaping relations between different actors in collective life?

Words of Thanks

We are most grateful to Amsterdam University Press (AUP), and in particular to Maryse Elliott, for being so supportive with this experimental project, including the publication of an online beta as well as their support for an open access digital version of the book. AUP is perhaps also an apt choice, given that several of the contributors gathered at an early international conference on data journalism which took place in Amsterdam in 2010. Open access funding is supported by a grant from the Netherlands Organisation for Scientific Research (NWO, 324-98-014), thanks to Richard Rogers at the University of Amsterdam.

The vision for the book was germinated through discussions with friends and colleagues associated with the Public Data Lab. We particularly benefited from conversations about different aspects of this book with Andreas

Birkbak, Erik Borra, Noortje Marres, Richard Rogers, Tommaso Venturini, Esther Weltevrede, Michele Mauri, Gabriele Colombo and Angeles Briones. We were also provided with space to develop the direction of this book through events and visits to Columbia University (in discussion with Bruno Latour); Utrecht University; the University of California, Berkeley; Stanford University; the University of Amsterdam; the University of Miami; Aalborg University Copenhagen; Sciences Po, Paris; the University of Cambridge; London School of Economics; Cardiff University; Lancaster University; and the International Journalism Festival in Perugia. Graduate students taking the MA course in data journalism at King's College London helped us to test the notion of "critical data practice" which lies at the heart of this book.

Our longstanding hope to do another edition was both nurtured and materialized thanks to Rina Tsubaki, who helped to facilitate support from the European Journalism Centre and the Google News Lab. We are grateful to Adam Thomas, Bianca Lemmens, Biba Klomp, Letizia Gambini, Arne Grauls and Simon Rogers for providing us with both editorial independence and enduring support to scale up our efforts. The editorial assistance of Daniela Demarchi and Oana Bounegru has been tremendously valuable in helping us to chart a clear course through sprawling currents of texts, footnotes, references, emails, shared documents, version histories, spreadsheets and other materials.

Most of all, we would like to thank all of the data journalism practitioners and researchers who were involved in the project (whether through writing, correspondence or discussion) for accompanying us, and for supporting this experiment with their contributions of time, energy, materials and ideas without which the project would not have been possible. This book is, and continues to be, a collective undertaking.

Works Cited

Agre, P. E. (1997). Toward a critical technical practice: Lessons learned in trying to reform AI. In G. Bowker, S. L. Star, B. Turner, & L. Gasser (Eds.), *Social science, technical systems, and cooperative work: Beyond the great divide* (pp. 130–157). Erlbaum.

Berman, E. P., & Hirschman, D. (2018). The sociology of quantification: Where are we now? *Contemporary Sociology, 47*(3), 257–266. https://doi.org/10.1177/0094306118767649

Byers, D. (2014, March 19). Knives out for Nate Silver. *Politico.* https://www.politico.com/blogs/media/2014/03/knives-out-for-nate-silver-185394.html

Davies, W. (2016, August 24). The age of post-truth politics. *The New York Times*. https://www.nytimes.com/2016/08/24/opinion/campaign-stops/the-age-of-post-truth-politics.html

Gray, J. (2018). Three aspects of data worlds. *Krisis: Journal for Contemporary Philosophy, 1*. https://krisis.eu/three-aspects-of-data-worlds/

Gray, J., & Bounegru, L. (2019). What a difference a dataset makes? Data journalism and/as data activism. In J. Evans, S. Ruane, & H. Southall (Eds.), *Data in society: Challenging statistics in an age of globalisation* (pp. 365–374). The Policy Press. https://doi.org/10.5281/zenodo.1415450

Gray, J., Chambers, L., & Bounegru, L. (Eds.). (2012). *The data journalism handbook: How journalists can use data to improve the news*. O'Reilly Media.

Gray, J., Gerlitz, C., & Bounegru, L. (2018). Data infrastructure literacy. *Big Data & Society, 5*(2), 1–13. https://doi.org/10.1177/2053951718786316

Haraway, D. J. (2016). *Staying with the trouble: Making kin in the Chthulucene*. Duke University Press. https://doi.org/10.1215/9780822373780

Latour, B. (2020) Sarah Sze as the sculptor of Critical Zones. In B. Latour & P. Weibel (Eds.), *Critical zones: The science and politics of landing on earth* (pp. 158–159). The MIT Press.

Lury, C., & Wakeford, N. (Eds.). (2012). *Inventive methods: The happening of the social*. Routledge.

Rogers, R. (2018). Otherwise engaged: Social media from vanity metrics to critical analytics. *International Journal of Communication, 12*, 450–472. https://dare.uva.nl/search?identifier=e7a7c11b-b199-4d7c-a9cb-fdf1dd74d493

Snowden, E. (2016, April 3). Biggest leak in the history of data journalism just went live, and it's about corruption. Twitter. https://twitter.com/Snowden/status/716683740903247873

About the Authors

Liliana Bounegru (@bb_liliana) and **Jonathan Gray** (@jwyg) are Lecturers at the Department of Digital Humanities, King's College London, co-founders of the Public Data Lab, and Research Associates at the Digital Methods Initiative, University of Amsterdam. They contributed equally as editors of this volume.

Doing Issues With Data

1. From Coffee to Colonialism: Data Investigations Into How the Poor Feed the Rich

Raúl Sánchez and Ximena Villagrán

Abstract
How we used data to reveal illegal business practices, sustained environmental damage and slave-like conditions for workers in developing countries' agroindustries.

Keywords: cross-border investigations, agriculture, colonialism, data journalism, environmental damage

At the beginning of 2016, a small group of journalists decided to investigate the journey of a chocolate bar, banana and cup of coffee from the original plantations to their desks. Our investigation was prompted by reports that all of these products were produced in poor countries and mostly consumed in rich countries.

Starting from those reports we decided to ask some questions: What are the labour conditions on these plantations like? Is there a concentration of land ownership by a small group? What kinds of environmental damage do these products cause in these countries? So *El Diario* and *El Faro* (two digital and independent media outlets in Spain and El Salvador) joined forces to investigate the dark side of the agroindustry business model in developing countries.[1]

The resulting "Enslaved Land" project is a one-year cross-border and data-driven investigation that comes with a subheading that gets straight to

---

[1]   https://www.eldiario.es/ (Spanish language), https://elfaro.net/ (Spanish language)

Bounegru, L. and J. Gray (eds.), *The Data Journalism Handbook: Towards a Critical Data Practice*. Amsterdam: Amsterdam University Press, 2021
DOI 10.5117/9789462989511_CH01

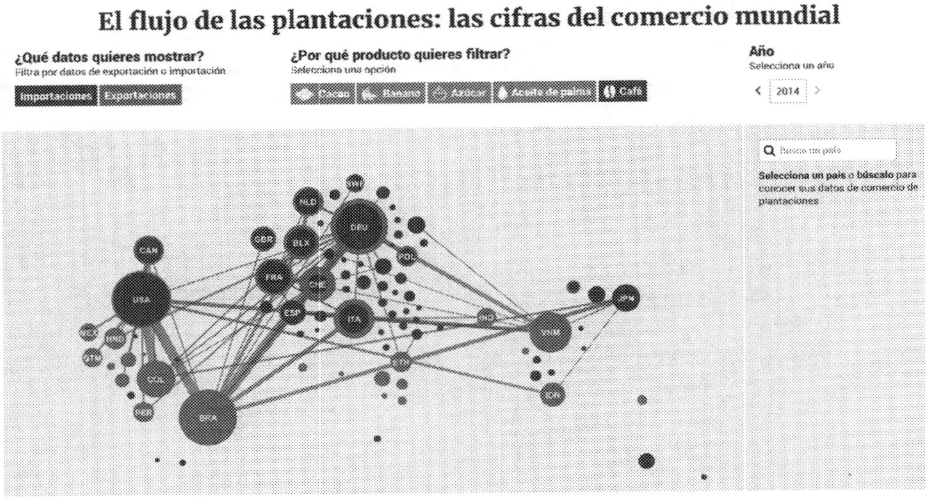

Figure 1.1. Network graph showing world imports and exports of coffee in 2014.
Source: eldiario.es.

the point: "This is how poor countries are used to feed rich countries."[2] In fact, colonialism is the main issue of this project. As journalists, we didn't want to tell the story of the poor Indigenous people without examining the more systemic picture. We wanted to explain how land property, corruption, organized crime, local conflicts and supply chains of certain products are still part of a system of colonialism.

In this project, we investigated five crops consumed widely in Europe and the United States: Sugar, coffee, cocoa, banana and palm oil produced in Guatemala, Colombia, Ivory Coast and Honduras. As a data-driven investigation, we used data to get from pattern to story. The choice of crops and countries was made based on a previous data analysis of 68 million records from the United Nations' World Trade Database (Figure 1.1).

This investigation shows how the balance of power between rich and poor countries has changed from the 15th century to the present and proves that these crops are produced thanks to exploitative, slave-like conditions for workers, illegal business practices and sustained environmental damage.

The focus of our stories was shaped by the data we used. In Honduras, the key was to use geographic information to tell the story. We compiled the land use map of the country and overlaid the surface of palm plantations with protected areas. We found that 7,000 palm oil hectares were illegally

2   https://latierraesclava.eldiario.es/ (Spanish language)

planted in protected areas of the country. As a result, our reporter could investigate the specific zones with palm plantations in protected areas. The story uses individual cases to highlight and narrate systemic abuse, such as the case of Monchito, a Honduran peasant who grows African palm in the Jeannette Kawas National Park.

This project is not only about land use. In Guatemala, we created a database of all the sugar mills in the country. We dived into the local company registry to find out the owners and directors of the mills. Next we used public business records to link these individuals and entities with offshore companies in Panama, Virgin Islands and the Bahamas. To find out how they create and manage the offshore structure, *El Faro* had access to the Panama Papers database, so we used that information to reconstruct how one of the biggest mills of the country worked with the Mossack Fonseca law firm to avoid taxes.

A transnational investigation aiming to uncover corruption and business malpractice in poor countries is challenging in many ways. We had to work in rural areas where there is no governmental presence, and in most cases the reporting posed some risk. We dealt with countries where there is a considerable lack of transparency, where open data is absent, and, in some cases, where public administrations do not know what information they hold.

Honduras and Guatemala were only one aspect of our investigation. More than 10 people worked together to produce this material. All this work was coordinated from the offices of *El Diario* in Spain and *El Faro* in El Salvador, working alongside journalists in Colombia, Guatemala, Honduras and Ivory Coast.

This work was undertaken not only by journalists, but also by editors, photographers, designers and developers who participated in the development and production process to develop an integrated web product. This project would not have been possible without them.

We used an integrated scrollytelling narrative for each of the investigations. For us, the way that users read and interact with the stories is as important as the investigation itself. We chose to combine satellite images, photos, data visualizations and narrative because we wanted the reader to understand the link between the products they consumed and the farmers, companies, and other actors involved in their production.

This structure allowed us to combine personal stories with data analysis in a compelling narrative. One example is the story of John Pérez, a Colombian peasant whose land was stolen by paramilitary groups and banana corporations during the armed conflict. To tell this story we used a zoomable map that takes you from his plantation to the final destination of Colombian banana production.

This project showed that data journalism can enrich traditional reporting techniques to connect stories about individuals to broader social, economic and political contexts.

Our investigation was also published by *Plaza Pública* in Guatemala and *Ciper* in Chile, and was included in the Guatemalan radio show "ConCriterio." The latter led to a public statement from the Guatemalan Tax Agency asking for resources to fight against tax fraud in the sugar mill business.

About the Authors

Raúl Sánchez is a Spanish data journalist covering stories of inequality, gender and corruption despite everything at *elDiario.es*.

Ximena Villagrán is a Guatemalan data journalist who co-founded *El Intercambio*.

2. Repurposing Census Data to Measure Segregation in the United States

Aaron Williams

Abstract

Visualizing racial segregation in the US with census data.

Keywords: programming, mapping, racial segregation, census, data visualization, data journalism

How do you measure segregation by race? In the United States in particular, there has been a historical effort to separate people since its founding. As the country changed, and racist policies like segregation were outlawed, new laws emerged that aimed to keep African Americans as well as other groups separate from White Americans. Many Americans have experienced the lingering effects of these laws, but I wanted to know if there was a way to measure the impact based on where people live.

I was inspired after reading *We Gon' Be Alright: Notes on Race and Resegregation* by Jeff Chang, a book of essays where the author explores the connecting themes of race and place. I was struck by chapters that talked about the demographic changes of places like San Francisco, Los Angeles and New York City and wanted to work on a project that quantified the ideas Chang wrote about.

Many maps that show segregation actually don't. These maps often show a dot for each member of a specific race or ethnicity within a geography and colour that dot by the person's race. They end up showing fascinating population maps about where people live but do not measure how diverse or segregated these areas are.

How do we know this? Well, segregation and diversity are two terms that have wildly different definitions depending on who you talk to. And while many people may perceive where they live as segregated, that answer can

Bounegru, L. and J. Gray (eds.), *The Data Journalism Handbook: Towards a Critical Data Practice*. Amsterdam: Amsterdam University Press, 2021

DOI 10.5117/9789462989511_CH02

Figure 2.1. Dot-density population map of race in the United States from census estimates, 2018.
Source: *The Washington Post*. https://www.washingtonpost.com/graphics/2018/national/
segregation-us-cities/

change depending on how one measures segregation. I didn't want to act
on anecdote alone. Thus, I looked for ways to measure segregation in an
academic sense and base my reporting from there.

I interviewed Michael Bader, an associate professor of sociology at
American University in Washington, DC, who showed me the Multigroup
Entropy Index (or Theil Index), a statistical measure that determines the
spatial distribution of multiple racial groups simultaneously. We used this
to score every single census block group in the United States compared to
the racial population of the county it inhabited.

This project took roughly a year to complete. Most of the time before then
was spent exploring the data and various measures of segregation. During
my research, I learned that there are several ways to measure segregation.
For example, the Multigroup Entropy Index is a measure of evenness, which
compares the spatial distribution of populations within a given geography.
And there are other measures like the Exposure Index, which measures
how likely it is that two groups will make contact with each other in the
same geography. There is no single measure that will prove or not prove
segregation, but the measures can work together to explain how a community is comprised. I read a lot of research on census demographics and
tried to mirror my categories to existing literature on the topic. Thus, I chose
the six race categories included in this project based on existing research

about race and segregation that was commissioned by the Census Bureau, and chose the Multigroup Entropy Index because it allowed me to compare multiple racial groups in a single analysis.

I decided to compare the makeup of each census block group to the racial makeup of its surrounding county. Then, my colleague Armand Emamdjomeh and I spent months working on the pipeline that powered the data analysis. In the past, I've seen a lot of census demographic research done in tools like Python, R or SPSS but I was curious if I could do this work using JavaScript. I found JavaScript and the node.js ecosystem to provide a rich set of tools to work with data and then display it on the web. One challenge was that I had to write several of my analysis functions by hand, but in return I was able to understand every step of my analysis and use the same functions on the web. Mapbox and d3.js both have very powerful and mature tools for working with geospatial data that I leveraged at each stage of my analysis.

About two months before the story was published, we went back and forth on the story design and layout. An early version of this project implemented the scrollytelling approach, where the map took over the entire screen and the text scrolled over the map. While this approach is well established and used heavily by my team at the *Post*, it prevented us from including the beautiful static graphics we generated in a holistic way. In the end, we opted for a traditional story layout that explored the history of segregation and housing discrimination in the United States, complete with case studies on three cities, and then included the full, historical interactive map at the bottom.[1]

The story is the most read project I have ever published as a journalist. I think letting readers explore the data after the story added a layer of personalization that allowed readers to situate themselves in the narrative. Data journalism allows us to tell stories that go beyond words, beyond ideas. We can put the reader directly into the story and let them tell their own.

About the Author

Aaron Williams is an investigative data reporter who specializes in data analysis and visualization for *The Washington Post*.

---

[1]   https://www.washingtonpost.com/graphics/2018/national/segregation-us-cities/

3.   Multiplying Memories while Discovering Trees in Bogotá

María Isabel Magaña

Abstract

How we used data about trees to create memories, promote transparency and include citizens in storytelling in Bogotá, Colombia.

Keywords: data journalism, citizenship, transparency, open government, multimodal storytelling, trees

Bogotá holds almost 16% of the population of Colombia in just 1,775 km². You get the idea; it is crowded and furious. But it is also a green city, surrounded by mountains and inhabited by many species of trees. Most of the time, trees go unnoticed by its residents in the midst of their daily lives. Or at least that is what happened to the members of our data team, except for one of our coders. She loves trees and can't walk down the street without noticing them. She knows all the species and the facts about them. Her love for nature in the midst of the chaos of the city is what got us thinking: Has anybody, ever, talked about the trees that are planted all over town?

And that simple question was the catalyst for so many others: What do we know about them? Who is in charge of taking care of them? Are they helping to clean the city's pollution? Do we need more trees in the city? Is it true that only the rich neighbourhoods have tall trees? Are there any historical trees in town?

We began our investigation aiming to do two different things: Firstly, to connect citizens with the green giants they see every day; and secondly, to understand the reality of the city's tree planting and conservation plans.[1]

---

1   http://especiales.datasketch.co/arboles-bogota/

Bounegru, L. and J. Gray (eds.), *The Data Journalism Handbook: Towards a Critical Data Practice.* Amsterdam: Amsterdam University Press, 2021
DOI 10.5117/9789462989511_CH03

To do so, we analyzed the urban census of tree planting in Bogotá that the Botanical Garden conducted in 2007, the only set of information available, and which is updated every month. The Botanical Garden refused to give us the full data even after we submitted multiple freedom of information requests filled with legal arguments. Their position was simple: The data was already available in their DataViz portal. Our argument: You can only download 10,000 entries and the database is made up of 1.2 million entries. It's public data, just give it to us! Their answer: We won't give it to you but we will improve our app so you can download 50,000 entries.

Our solution? Reach out to other organizations that had helped the Botanical Garden collect the data. One of those entities was Ideca, which collects all the information related to the city's cadastre. They gave us the whole data set in no time. We, obviously, decided to publish it so that everyone can access it (call it our little revenge against opacity). The Botanical Garden realized this and stopped any further conversation with us, and we decided not to continue a legal battle.

In addition, we included public data from the Mayor's Office of Bogotá and the National Census, to cross-reference information that we could analyze in relation to trees. Finally, we conducted interviews with environmental experts and forestry engineers that allowed us to understand the challenges the city faces. They had done so much work and so many investigations analyzing not only the reality of tree planting schemes, but also the history behind the trees in the city. And most of this work was largely unnoticed by authorities, journalists and many others.

The final product was an eight-piece data project that showed the reality of the tree planting plans of the city. It mapped every single tree—with information about its height, species and benefits for the city—debunked many myths around tree planting, and told the stories of some of the city's historical trees. We used Leaflet and SoundCloud for the interactive elements. The design was implemented by our talented group of coders. We also used StoryMapJS to allow users to explore the historic trees of the city.

We decided how and which pieces were important for the story after researching many other similar projects and then partnered with a designer to create a good user experience. It was our first big data project and a lot of it involved trial and error as well as exploration.

More importantly, we involved citizens by inviting them to help us build a collaborative tree catalogue and to share their own stories about the trees we had mapped. We did so through social media, inviting them to add information about tree species to a spreadsheet. Bogotá's residents continue to help us enrich the catalogue to this day. In addition, we shared a WhatsApp number where people could send voice notes with their stories about trees. We received almost a hundred voice messages from people telling stories of trees where they had their first kiss, that taught them how to climb, that protected them from thieves or that were missed because they were cut down. We decided to include these audio files as an additional layer in the visualization app, so users could also get to know the city's trees through people's stories.

The main article and visual was then republished by a national newspaper (both in print and online), and shared by local authorities and many residents who wanted to tell their stories and transform the relationship that other residents have with their environment. So far, people have used the map to investigate the city's nature and to support their own research on the city's trees.

For our organization, this has been one of the most challenging projects we have ever developed. But it is also one of the most valuable, because it shows how data journalism can be about more than just numbers: It can also play a role in creating, collecting and sharing culture and memories, help people notice things about the places they live (beyond graphs and charts), and multiply and change the relations between people, plants and stories in urban spaces.

About the Author

María Isabel Magaña is a Colombian data journalist and Professor at the Journalism School at the University of La Sabana. She created the first FOI platform in Colombia: QueremosDatos.co.

4. Behind the Numbers: Home Demolitions in Occupied East Jerusalem

Mohammed Haddad

Abstract

If you have patience and can count, then you can do data journalism.

Keywords: human stories, data journalism, Middle East, mapping, home demolitions

When you look at the chart below (Figure 4.1), you will see a series of steady orange and black bars followed by a large spike in 2016. Once you take a closer look at the caption you will understand that this chart shows the number of structures destroyed and people affected by Israel's policy of home demolitions.

As Nathan Yau, author of *Flowing Data*, put it, "data is an abstraction of real life" (2013). Each number represents a family, and each number tells a story.

"Broken Homes" is the most comprehensive project to date tracking home demolitions in East Jerusalem, a Palestinian neighbourhood that has been occupied by Israel for 50 years.[1]

Working closely with the United Nations, *Al Jazeera* tracked every single home demolition in East Jerusalem in 2016. It turned out to be a record year, with 190 structures destroyed and more than 1,200 Palestinians displaced or affected.

We decided to tackle this project after witnessing an escalation in violence between Israelis and Palestinians in late 2015. The goal was twofold: To

---

1   https://interactive.aljazeera.com/aje/2017/jerusalem-2016-home-demolitions/index.html

Bounegru, L. and J. Gray (eds.), *The Data Journalism Handbook: Towards a Critical Data Practice*. Amsterdam: Amsterdam University Press, 2021

DOI 10.5117/9789462989511_CH04

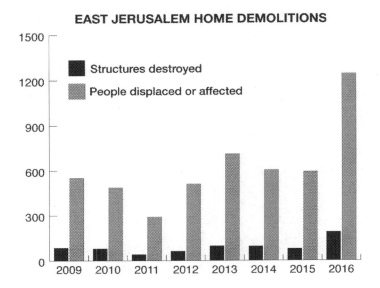

Figure 4.1. Graph showing East Jerusalem home demolitions, 2009–2016.
Source: *Al Jazeera*.

understand how Israel's home demolitions policy would be affected by the
increased tensions, and to tell readers the human stories behind the data.

The project reveals the impact on Palestinian families through video
testimony, 360-degree photos and an interactive map that highlights the
location, frequency and impact of each demolition.

Our producer in Doha began coordinating with the UN in late 2015 to
develop a framework for the project. The UN routinely gathers data on home
demolitions, and while some of it is available online, other aspects—including GPS coordinates—are only recorded internally. We wanted to be able
to show every demolition site on a map, so we began obtaining monthly
data sets from the UN. For each incident, we included the demolition date,
number of people and structures affected, a brief description of what happened, and a point on our East Jerusalem map showing the location. We
cross-checked these with news reports and other local information about
home demolitions. We then selected a case to highlight each month, as
a way of showing different facets of the Israeli policy—from punitive to
administrative demolitions, affecting everyone from young children to
elderly residents.

Our reporter on the ground travelled throughout East Jerusalem over
the course of the year to speak with many of the affected families, in order

Figure 4.2. Panoramic photograph of home demolished in May 2016.
Source: *Al Jazeera*.

to explore their losses in greater depth and to photograph and record the demolition sites.

There was a broad range of responses from the affected families. The interviews had to take place in the physical location of the demolition, which could be a difficult experience for those affected, so sensitivity and patience were required at all stages, from setting up the meetings to recording the material.

On the whole, the families responded well to the project. They were very generous with their time and in sharing their experiences. In one instance, a man had written down a list of things he wanted to say to us. In another case, it took a few attempts to convince the family to take part. One family declined to meet with us and so we had to liaise with the UN and find another family willing to speak about their home demolition.

Many news organizations, including *Al Jazeera*, have reported on individual home demolitions over the years. One of the main reasons for taking a data-driven approach this time was to clearly contextualize the scale of the story by counting each and every demolition. This context and fresh perspective are especially important when reporting on an ongoing topic to keep readers engaged.

A word of advice for aspiring data journalists: Taking a data-driven approach to a story doesn't need to be technical or expensive. Sometimes simply following and counting occurrences of an event over time tells you a lot about the scale of a problem. As long as your data-gathering methodology remains consistent, there are many stories that you can tell using data that you might not otherwise report on. Also, be patient. We gathered data for an entire year to tell this story. The most important thing is to thoroughly storyboard exactly what data you need before sending any reporters out into the field. Most of the time you won't need any special equipment either. We used an iPhone to take all the 360-degree images and capture the specific GPS coordinates.

The project—released in January 2017 in English, Arabic and Bosnian—presents a grim warning about what lies ahead as Israel continues to deny building permits to 98% of Palestinian applicants, ramping up the pressure on a large and growing population.

Works Cited

Yau, N. (2013, June 28). Understanding data—Context. *Big Think*. https://bigthink.com/experts-corner/understanding-data-context

About the Author

Mohammed Haddad is a data journalist and interactive editor at the Al Jazeera Media Network based in the Middle East.

5. Mapping Crash Incidents to Advocate for Road Safety in the Philippines

Aika Rey

Abstract

How a data story on road crash incidents in the Cagayan province in the Philippines led to positive policy and social change.

Keywords: data journalism, road safety, community engagement, mapping, Philippines, policy and social change

Data shows that fatalities from vehicular crash incidents in the Philippines have been increasing steadily over the years. Injuries from road crash incidents are now a top cause of death among Filipino youth.

Because of this, we built a microsite that compiled relevant information on road safety. We gathered and analyzed data, derived insights, published stories, and designed civic engagement opportunities—both on the ground and on digital—in order to educate the public about road safety.[1]

We also started running a video series entitled "Right of Way" which tackles motorist and commuter issues in Metro Manila. That is how *Rappler's* #SaferRoadsPH campaign was born.

Compiling relevant data about road traffic deaths and injuries was a challenge. With no comprehensive national database on road crash numbers, we knocked on doors and gathered data from over a dozen national and local government units, including police offices in various cities and provinces.

Data acquired from these repositories are not standardized. A significant part of the work involved cleaning the data for analysis. One big challenge

---

1   http://www.rappler.com/saferroadsph

Bounegru, L. and J. Gray (eds.), *The Data Journalism Handbook: Towards a Critical Data Practice.* Amsterdam: Amsterdam University Press, 2021
DOI 10.5117/9789462989511_CH05

was how to map data when location information is either incomplete or not consistently recorded.[2]

Using the open-source data-cleaning application OpenRefine, we were able to come up with a normalized database of information acquired from the different government agencies. This allowed us to determine locations, dates and the number of people affected by crash incidents. Although still incomplete, our collection is probably the biggest single compilation of data on road crash incidents in the Philippines at the moment.

But what made our approach distinctive is that on top of stories, analysis and visualizations based on our collection of data, we made the effort to present them directly to communities concerned not just online but in on-the-ground activities. In the process, data analytics led to civic engagement activities.

One particular story that stood out in our coverage was the in-depth story on the Cagayan province, located roughly 600 km north of Manila, which is the area most affected by vehicular crash fatalities. We visited key offices in the province to get road crash incident data, as well as to conduct interviews with victims, local police and public service officials.

Following this exercise, in June 2017, *Rappler* conducted a road safety awareness forum in the province's capital city Tuguegarao to present our findings. The forum sought to educate the public about road safety concerns in the province, as well as influence key officials to address the policy gap.[3]

Apart from graphs showing the times of day when critical incidents occur the most, at the forum we presented a heat map, created using Google Fusion Tables, which shows the locations with the greatest number of incidents in the Cagayan province (Figure 5.1).

Officials present attributed these numbers, among others, to the absence of pedestrian lanes. A check of schools in the city showed no pedestrian lanes in front of schools. After the forum, a social experiment was conducted where locals sketched pedestrian lanes using chalk in front of a school. Law enforcement officials wanted to see if motorists would stop at pedestrian lanes as students cross. *Rappler* later posted a video story on Facebook about this experiment.[4]

---

2   We published a full explanation of our data sources here: https://www.rappler.com/move-ph/issues/ road-safety/171657-road-crash-numbers-data-sources

3   https://www.rappler.com/move-ph/issues/road-safety/171778-road-crash-incidents-cagayan-valley

4   https://www.rappler.com/move-ph/issues/road-safety/172432-cagayan-police-pedestrian-lane-chalk

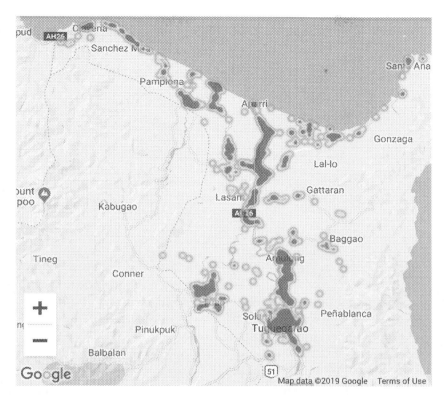

Figure 5.1. Areas in the Cagayan province marked in dark-grey have more occurrences of road crash incidents.
Source: *Rappler*.

The video generated a lot of interest. A *Rappler* reader who saw the video reached out to us and volunteered to provide paint for pedestrian lanes within the city. Months later, through the combined efforts of local government and volunteers, schools within the city finally got pedestrian lanes. The painting project was completed on 30 September 2017. Two years later, the city government approved a local ordinance on road safety.

This project showed that data-driven reporting need not end when the editor clicks publish. It is proof that combining data journalism with online and offline community engagement can lead to positive policy and social change.

About the Author

Aika Rey is a Filipino journalist at *Rappler*, where she worked on data-driven investigations on the national budget, the environment and transportation.

6.   Tracking Worker Deaths in Turkey

Pınar Dağ

Abstract
Documenting worker deaths in Turkey to advocate for improved working conditions.

Keywords: Turkey, Soma, labour conditions, data journalism, open data, freedom of information (FOI)

In the wake of the Soma mine disaster in Turkey in 2014, it transpired that it was extremely difficult to document the conditions of workers. There were discrepancies with figures on worker unionization and a scarcity of data on worker deaths over previous decades. What was available was often disorganized and lacking in detail. We wanted to make this data widely accessible and shed light on the deaths of workers in other sectors.

With this in mind, a programmer, an editor and myself developed the "Open Database of Deceased Workers in Turkey," a project hosted by the data journalism portal *Dağ Medya*, that gathered data from multiple sources, verified it, and made it available for everyone to access and use.[1]

In Turkey at least 130 workers die per month from a variety of causes. The most important goal of the project was to raise awareness of these deaths and their frequency, as well as to publicly recognize victims and the poor working conditions that they endured. The project comprised embeddable maps, graphs and data in different formats.[2] It covered the deaths of workers in over 20 sectors from 2011 to 2014. After the project was completed, we continued to report the death of workers through regular media monitoring

---

1   http://community.globaleditorsnetwork.org/content/open-database-deceased-workers-turkey-0

2   http://platform24.org/veri-gazeteciligi/451/turkiyede-isci-olumleri-veritabani-hazirlandi (Turkish language)

Bounegru, L. and J. Gray (eds.), *The Data Journalism Handbook: Towards a Critical Data Practice*. Amsterdam: Amsterdam University Press, 2021

DOI 10.5117/9789462989511_CH06

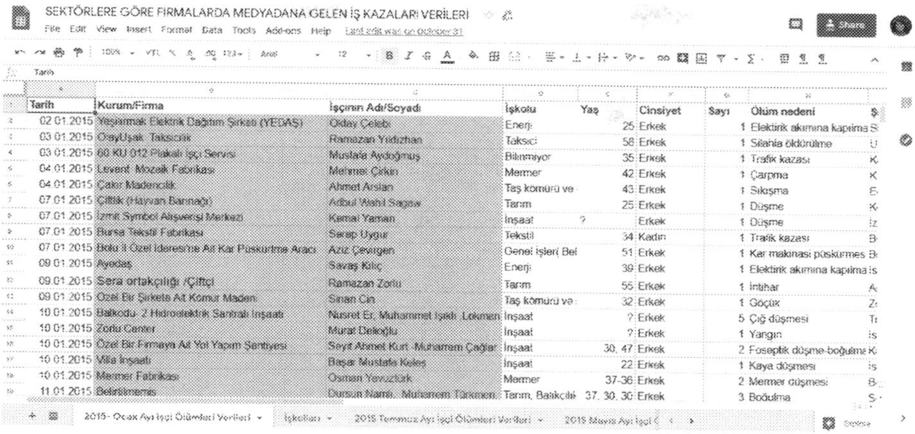

Figure 6.1. Collaborative spreadsheet with company names, based on media monitoring with Google Alerts. Source: Pınar Dağ.

each month. Crucially, the database includes the names of the companies that employed them (Figure 6.1).

The project began in 2015. We started by submitting freedom of information (FOI) requests and collecting data from trusted NGOs that were extracting data from various sources and were making it publicly accessible.

The first challenge we encountered was that it was not easy to get open data through FOI requests. Sometimes it took two weeks, sometimes four months, to obtain data through our requests. Next, a more unexpected challenge arose, which I am recounting because it surfaces conflicting perspectives on this type of work. When we announced the project, one of the projects whose data we were using—İSİG Meclisi (Health and Safety Labour Watch)—became unhappy about us using it.[3] The reason was, they claimed, that our project simply republished data that they had gathered. They understood our using of their data in this way as taking advantage of their labour. The opposition to the project persisted, in spite of our asking for permission and the fact that their data is publicly available. While they accused us of "pornifying" workers' deaths with our visualizations and tables, we saw our project as creating public value by increasing the outreach of the data they had collected, through visually accessible and readily downloadable formats.

While human stories are vital, we believed that unstructured, raw data was important in order to provide a more systematic view of these injustices. We found it difficult to reach consensus around this logic and struggled to

3   http://www.isigmeclisi.org/ (Turkish language)

make the case for the value of collaborative open data-sharing practices. We ended up publishing monthly worker deaths by comparing official data gathered through FOI requests with the data that we collected through our own monitoring of these cases.

Following this project, the institutions that we petitioned with FOI requests began to share their data in a more structured way and visualize it. We took this as evidence that we had accomplished one of our goals: To make this information more widely accessible. Ultimately, the project was recognized as a finalist in the 2015 Data Journalism Awards.

About the Author

Pınar Dağ is a Lecturer in the New Media Department of Kadir Has University and the co-founder of the Data Literacy Association (DLA).

Assembling Data

7. Building Your Own Data Set: Documenting Knife Crime in the United Kingdom

Caelainn Barr

Abstract
Building data sets for investigations and powerful storytelling.

Keywords: data journalism, crime, accountability, race, United Kingdom, databases

In early 2017 two colleagues, Gary Younge and Damien Gayle, approached me in *The Guardian* newsroom. They wanted to examine knife crime in the United Kingdom. While there was no shortage of write-ups detailing the deaths of victims of knife crime, follow-ups on the pursuit of suspects, and reports on the trials and convictions of the perpetrators, no one had looked at all the homicides as a whole.

My first question was, how many children and teenagers had been killed by knives in recent years? It seemed a straightforward query but once I set out to find the data it soon became apparent—no one could tell me. The data existed, somewhere, but it wasn't in the public domain. At this stage I had two options, give up or make a data set from scratch based on what I could access, build and verify myself. I decided to build my own data set.

Why Build Your Own Data Set?

Data journalism needn't be solely based on existing data sets. In fact there is a great case for making your own data. There is a wealth of information in data that is not routinely published or in some cases not even collected.

Bounegru, L. and J. Gray (eds.), *The Data Journalism Handbook: Towards a Critical Data Practice*. Amsterdam: Amsterdam University Press, 2021

DOI 10.5117/9789462989511_CH07

In building your own data set you create a unique set of information, a one-off source, with which to explore your story. The data and subsequent stories are likely to be exclusive and it can give you a competitive edge to find stories other reporters simply can't. Unique data sets can also help you identify what trends experts and policy makers haven't been able to spot.

Data is a source of information in journalism. The basis for using data in journalism is structured thinking. In order to use data to its full potential, at the outset of a project the journalist needs to think structurally: What is the story I want to be able to tell and what do I need to be able to tell it?

The key to successfully building a data set for your story is to have a structured approach to your story and query every source of data with a journalistic sense of curiosity. Building your own data set encompasses a lot of the vital skills of data journalism—thinking structurally, planned storytelling and finding data in creative ways. It also has a relatively low barrier to entry, as it can be done with or without programming skills. If you can type into a spreadsheet and sort a table, you're on your way to building the basic skills of data journalism.

That's not to say data journalism is straightforward. Solid and thorough data projects can be very complex and time-consuming work, but armed with a few key skills you can develop a strong foundation in using data for storytelling.

Building Your Own Data Set Step by Step

Plan what is required. The first step to making or gathering data for your analysis is assessing what is required and if it can be obtained. At the outset of any project it's worth making a story memo which sketches out what you expect the story will attempt to tell, where you think the data is, how long it will take to find it and where the potential pitfalls are. The memo will help you assess how long the work will take and if the outcome is worth the effort. It can also serve as a something to come back to when you're in the midst of the work at a later stage.

Think of the top line. At the outset of a data-driven story where the data does not exist you should ask what the top line of the story is. It's essential to know what the data should contain as this sets the parameters for what questions you can ask of the data. This is essential as the data will only ever answer questions based on what it contains. Therefore, to make a data set that will fulfil your needs, be very clear about what you want to be able to explore and what information you need to explore it.

Where might the data be held? The next step is to think through where the data may be held in any shape or form. One way to do this is to retrace your steps. How do you know there is a potential story here? Where did the idea come from and is there a potential data source behind it?

Research will also help you clarify what exists, so comb through all of the sources of information that refer to the issue of interest and talk to academics, researchers and statisticians who gather or work with the data. This will help you identify shortcomings and possible pitfalls in using the data. It should also spark ideas about other sources and ways of getting the data. All of this preparation before you start to build your data set will be invaluable if you need to work with difficult government agencies or decide to take another approach to gathering the data.

Ethical concerns. In planning and sourcing any story we need to weigh up the ethical concerns and working with data is no different. When building a data set we need to consider if the source and method we're using to collect the information is the most accurate and complete possible.

This is also the case with analysis—examine the information from multiple angles and don't torture the data to get it to say something that is not a fair reflection of the reality. In presenting the story be prepared to be transparent about the sourcing, analysis and limitations of the data. All of these considerations will help build a stronger story and develop trust with the reader.

Get the data. Once a potential source has been identified, the next step is to get the data. This may be done manually through data entry into a spreadsheet, transforming information locked in PDFs into structured data you can analyze, procuring documents through a human source or the Freedom of Information Act (FOIA), programming to scrape data from documents or web pages or automating data capture through an application programming interface (API).

Be kind to yourself! Don't sacrifice simplicity for the sake of it. Seek to find the most straightforward way of getting the information into a data set you can analyze. If possible, make your work process replicable, as this will help you check your work and add to the data set at a later stage, if needed.

In obtaining the data refer back to your story outline and ask, will the data allow me to fully explore this topic? Does it contain the information that might lead to the top lines I'm interested in?

Structure. The key difference between information contained in a stack of text-based paper documents and a data set is structure. Structure and repetition are essential to building a clean data set ready for analysis.

The first step is to familiarize yourself with the information. Ask yourself what the material contains—what will it allow you to say? What won't you be able to say with the data? Is there another data set you might want to combine the information with? Can you take steps in building this data set which will allow you to combine it with others?

Think of what the data set should look like at the end of the process. Consider the columns or variables you would want to be able to analyze. Look for inspiration in the methodology and structure underlying other similar data sets.

Cast the net wide to begin with, taking account of all the data you could gather and then pare it back by assessing what you need for the story and how long it will take to get it. Make sure the data you collect will compare like with like. Choose a format and stick to it—this will save you time in the end! Also consider the dimensions of the data set you're creating. Times and dates will allow you to analyze the information over time; geographic information will allow you to possibly plot the data to look for spatial trends.

Keep track of your work and check as you go. Keep notes of the sources you have used to create your data set and always keep a copy of the original documents and data sets. Write up a methodology and a data dictionary to keep track of your sources, how the data has been processed and what each column contains. This will help flag questions and shake out any potential errors as you gather and start to analyze the data.

Assume nothing and check all your findings with further reporting. Don't hold off talking to experts and statisticians to sense–check your approach and findings. The onus to bulletproof your work is even greater when you have collated the data, so take every step to ensure the data, analysis and write-up are correct.

Case Study: Beyond the Blade

At the beginning of 2017 the data projects team alongside Gary Younge, Damian Gayle and *The Guardian*'s community journalism team set out to document the death of every child and teenager killed by a knife in the United Kingdom.

In order to truly understand the issue and explore the key themes around knife crime the team needed data. We wanted to know—who are the young people dying in the United Kingdom as a result of stabbings? Are they young children or teenagers? What about sex and ethnicity? Where and when are these young people being killed?

After talking to statisticians, police officers and criminologists it became clear that the data existed but it was not public. Trying to piece together an answer to the question would consume much of my work over the next year.

The data I needed was held by the Home Office in a data set called the Homicide Index. The figures were reported to the Home Office by police forces in England and Wales. I had two potential routes to get the information—send a freedom of information request to the Home Office or send requests to every police force. To cover all eventualities, I did both. This would provide us with the historical figures back to 1977.

In order to track deaths in the current year we needed to begin counting the deaths as they happened. As there was no public or centrally collated data we decided to keep track of the information ourselves, through police reports, news clippings, Google Alerts, Facebook and Twitter.

We brainstormed what we wanted to know—name, age and date of the incident were all things we definitely wanted to record. But other aspects of the circumstances of the deaths were not so obvious. We discussed what we thought we already knew about knife crime—it was mostly male with a disproportionate number of Black male victims. To check our assumptions we added columns for sex and ethnicity. We verified all the figures by checking the details with police forces across the United Kingdom. In some instances this revealed cases we hadn't picked up and allowed us to cross-check our findings before reporting.

After a number of rejected FOI requests and lengthy delays the data was eventually released by the Home Office. It gave the age, ethnicity and sex of all people killed by knives by police force area for almost 40 years. This, combined with our current data set, allowed us to look at who was being killed and the trend over time.

The data revealed knife crime had killed 39 children and teenagers in England and Wales in 2017, making it one of the worst years for deaths of young people in nearly a decade. The figures raised concerns about a hidden public health crisis amid years of police cuts.

The figures also challenged commonly held assumptions about who knife crime affects. The data showed in England and Wales in the 10 years to 2015, one third of the victims were Black. However, outside the capital, stabbing deaths among young people were not mostly among Black boys, as in the same period less than one in five victims outside London were Black.

Although knife crime was a much-debated topic, the figures were not readily available to politicians and policy makers, prompting questions about how effective policy could be created when the basic details of who knife crime affects were not accessible.

The data provided the basis of our award-winning project which reframed the debate on knife crime. The project would not have been possible without building our own data set.

About the Author

Caelainn Barr is data projects editor at Guardian News & Media.

8. Narrating a Number and Staying With the Trouble of Value

Helen Verran

Abstract

Numbers are seemingly uncomplicated and straightforward measures of value, but beware—numbers hide moral and political trouble.

Keywords: ecosystems value, Australian environmental governance, sociology of quantification, data journalism, science and technology studies

At the turn of the century the Australian state developed an environmental policy that saw it fully subsidizing labour costs incurred by landowners if they undertook specifically agreed upon landscape work that was designed to reverse environmental degradation. However, given the almost total domination by neoliberal ideologues in this policy area at that time, the policy was described in the dizzying double-talk of value of ecosystems services. In policy documents it was described as "purchasing environmental interventions to enhance the state's environmental value." Thus in 2009 a state government department would make this almost incomprehensible claim about the success of this policy: In 2009 the contribution to Australia's GDP from transactions in which the state purchased environmental interventions to enhance ecosystems value from rural landholders in the Corangamite Natural Resource Management Region (NRMR) was calculated as AUD4.94 million.

The number that I narrate here emerged in a press statement issued by the government of the Australian state of Victoria in 2009. The media release announced the success of investment by the state government in environmental conservation in one of Australia's 57 NRMRs. The environmental administrative region of grassy basalt plains that spreads

Bounegru, L. and J. Gray (eds.), *The Data Journalism Handbook: Towards a Critical Data Practice*. Amsterdam: Amsterdam University Press, 2021
DOI 10.5117/9789462989511_CH08

east–west in south-central Victoria is named Corangamite, an Aboriginal term that replaced a name bestowed by the first British pastoralists who in the mid-19th century invaded this country from Tasmania. They called the region "Australia Felix" and set about cutting down all the trees. The squatters, who subsequently became landowners here, would in less than a century become a sort of colonial landed gentry. In 2008, in operating the EcoTender Programme in the Corangamite NRMR, the Victorian government purchased ecosystems services value from the descendants of those squatters in pay-as-bid auctions. In 2009 the contribution to Australia's GDP from these transactions was calculated as AUD4.94 million. The announcement of this value was the occasion of the media release where I first met the number.

I doubt that any journalists picked up on the news promulgated in this brief, including its numbered value; this number is hardly hot news. In the context of a press release the naming of a specific number value reassures. The national accounts are important and real, and if this regional government intervention features as a specified value contributing to the national economy, then clearly the government intervention is a good thing. The specification of value here claims a realness for the improvements that the government interventions are having. The implication is that this policy leads to good environmental governance. Of course, the actual value the number name (AUD4.94 million) points to, what it implicitly claims to index, is not of much interest to anyone. That a number appears to correspond to something "out there" that can be valued, is good enough for purposes of reassuring.

My narration of this number offers a mind-numbingly detailed account of the sociotechnical means by which the number came to life. The story has the disturbing effect of revealing that this banal number in its workaday media release is a paper-thin cover-up. Profound troubles lurk. Before I begin to tell my story and articulate the nature of these profound troubles that seem to shadow any doing of valuation, even such a banal doing, let me pre-emptively respond to some questions that I imagine might be beginning to emerge for readers of *The Data Journalism Handbook*.

First, I acknowledge that telling a story of how a number has come to life rather than finding some means to promote visualization of what that number means in a particular context, is rather an unusual approach in contemporary data journalism. I can imagine a data journalist doubting that such storytelling would work. Perhaps a first response is to remind you that it is not an either/or choice and that working by intertwining narrative and visualizing resources in decoding and interpreting is an effective way to get ideas across. In presenting such an intertwining, journalists should always remember that there are two basic speaking positions in mixing narratives and visuals. One might proceed as if the visual is embedded within the narrative, in which case you are speaking *to* the visual, which seems to represent or illustrate something in the story. Or, you can proceed as if the narrative is embedded in the visual, in which case you are speaking *from within*, diagram. This is a less common strategy in data journalism, yet I can imagine that the story I tell here could well be used in that way. Of course, switching between these speaking positions within a single piece is perhaps the most effective strategy (for an account of such switching, see Verran & Winthereik, 2016).

Second, you might see it as odd to tell a story of a very particular number when what clearly has agency when it comes to decision–making and policy design, and what data journalists are interested in, is what can be made of data sets in mobilizing this algorithm or that. This worry might prompt you to ask about relations between numbers and data sets. The answer to such a query is fairly straightforward and not very interesting. There are many numbers in a data set; the relation is a one–many relation albeit that numbers are assembled in very precise arrays. The more interesting question enquires about the relation between numbers and algorithms. My answer would be that while algorithms mobilize a protocol that elaborates how to work relations embedded in a database, numbers express a protocol that lays out how to work relations of collective being. Numbering is a form of algorithming and vice versa.[1] We could say that numbers are to algorithms as a seed is to the plant that might germinate from it; to mix metaphors, they have a chicken-and-egg relation. While there are certain interestingly different sociotechnical characteristics of generating enumerated value by analogue means (mixing cognitive, linguistic and graphic resources), of conventional enumeration as taught to primary school children, and of contriving enumerated value by digital computation, it is the sameness that matters here: AUD4.94 million has been generated algorithmically and expresses a particular set of relations embedded in a particular data set, but it still presents as just a number.[2]

---

1   The idea that numbers and algorithms have a sameness is possibly new for many readers, so used are they to thinking of numbers as "abstractions." My (unusual) account of numbers has them as very ordinary material semiotic entities that inhabit the here and now. For an account of differing protocols mobilizing relations within a single moment of collective being, see Watson, H. (1990). Investigating the social foundations of mathematics: Natural number in culturally diverse forms of life. *Social Studies of Science*, 20(2), 283–312. https://doi.org/10.1177/030631290020002004, or Verran, H. (2001). Two consistent logics of numbering. In *Science and an African logic* (pp. 177–205). University of Chicago Press.

2   For an account of differing sociotechnical characteristics of three numbers that variously emerge in analogue or digital environments, see Verran, H. (2015). Enumerated entities in public policy and governance. In E. Davis & P. J. Davis (Eds.), *Mathematics, substance and surmise: Views*

So now, to turn to my story. The intimate account of number making I tell here as a story would enable a journalist to recognize that the good news story that the government is slyly soliciting with its media release is not a straightforward matter. We see that perhaps a political exposé would be more appropriate. The details of how the number is made reveal that this public–private partnership environmental intervention programme involves the state paying very rich landowners to do work that will increase the value of their own property. The question my story might precipitate is, how could a journalist either celebrate or expose this number in good faith? When I finish the story, I will suggest that that is not the right question.

Narrating a Number

What is the series of sociotechnical processes by which ecosystems services value comes into existence in this public-private partnership programme in order that this value might be traded between government as buyer and landowner as vendor? And exactly how does the economic value of the trade come to contribute to the total marginal gains achieved in the totality of Australian economic activity, Australia's gross domestic product (GDP)? I attend to this double-barrelled question with a step-by-step laying out of what is required for a landholder to create a product—"ecosystems services value"—that can compete in a government-organized auction for a contract to supply the government with ecosystem services value. The messy work in which this product comes to life involves mucking around in the dirt, planting tree seedlings, fixing fences, and generally attempting to repair the damage done to the land perhaps by the landowner's grandparents, who heedlessly and greedily denuded the country of trees and seeded it with water-hungry plants, in hopes of more grain or more wool and family fortune. Ecosystems services value is generated by intervening in environmental processes.

The value, which is the product to be traded, begins in the work of public servants employed by a Victorian state government department (at that time the Department of Sustainability and Environment, DSE). Collectively these officials decide the areas of the state within which the administration will "run" tenders. In doing this, EnSym, an environmental systems modelling platform, is a crucial tool. This computing capacity is a marvel; it knows

on the meaning and ontology of mathematics (pp. 365–379). Springer International Publishing. https://doi.org/10.1007/978-3-319-21473-3_18

"nature out there" as no scientist has ever known nature. Precise and focused representations can be produced—probably overnight.

> This software has been developed by the ecoMarkets team and incorporates science, standards, metrics and information developed within DSE, as well as many leading international and national scientific models. EnSym contains three main tools—the "Site Assessment Tool" for field work, the "Landscape Preference Tool" for asset prioritisation and metric building, and "BioSim" for catchment planning. (DSE, 2018)

Prioritizing and mapping the areas of the state where auctions will be established, specifying and quantifying the environmental benefits, the ecological values, that might be enhanced through on-ground conservation and revegetation works, are recorded in numerical form. They represent ecosystem properties in the "out there" land. And the computer program can do more than that, it can also produce a script for intervention by humans. Just as the script of a play calls for production, so too does this script. And, as that script comes to life, "nature out there" seems to draw closer. It ceases to be an entirely removed "nature out there" and becomes nature as an infrastructure of human lives, an infrastructure that we might poke around in so as to fix the "plumbing."

When the script for a choreographed production of collective human effort is ready, the government calls for expressions of interest from landholders in the project area as the next step. In response to submitted expressions of interest, a government officer visits all properties. We can imagine this officer as taking the general script generated by EnSym along to an actual place at a given time. He or she has a formidable translation task ahead.

The field officer assesses possible sites for works that might become a stage for the production of the script. The aim is to enhance the generation of the specified ecosystems services, so the officer needs to assess the likelihood that specified actions in a particular place will produce an increase in services provision from the ecosystem, thus increasing the value of that particular ecosystems service generated by that property, and through adding together the many such increases generated in this intervention programme, by the state as a whole. Together the landowner and the government officer hatch a plan. In ongoing negotiation, a formalized management plan for specified plots is devised. The field officer develops this plan in contractable terms. Landholders specify in detail the actual work they will do to carry out the plan. Thus, a product that takes the form of a particular "ecosystems services value" is designed and specified as a series of specified tasks to be completed in a specified time period: So many seedlings of this set of species, planted in this array, in this particular corner of this particular paddock, and fenced off to effect a conservation plot of such and such dimensions, using these materials.

Landholders calculate the cost of the works specified by the state, no doubt including a generous labour payment. They come up with a price the government must pay if it is to buy this product, a particular "ecosystems services value." Here they are specifying the amount of money they are willing accept to undertake the specified works and hence deliver the ecosystems services value by the specified date. They submit relevant documents to the government in a sealed envelope.

So how does the subsequent auction work? Here EnSym becomes significant again in assessing the bids. Not only a knower of "nature out there," and a writer of scripts for intervention in that "out there" imagined as infrastructure, EnSym is also a removed judging observer that can evaluate the bids that have been made to produce that script, much like a Warner Bros. might evaluate competing bids to produce a movie. Bids are ranked according to a calculated "environmental benefits index" and the price proposed by the landowner. We must suppose that the government buys the product which offers the highest "environmental benefits index" per unit cost.

> Bid assessment. All bids are assessed objectively on the basis of the estimated change in environmental outcomes; the value of the change in environmental outcomes; the value of the assets affected by these changes (significance); dollar cost (price determined by the landholder). (DSE, 2018)

When the results of the auction are announced, selected bidders sign a final agreement based on the management plan and submitted schedule of works, as defined spatial and temporal organization. When all documents are signed, reporting arrangements are implemented and payment can begin: "DSE forwards payment to signed-up landholders on receipt of an invoice. Payments occur subject to satisfactory progress against actions as specified in the Management Agreement" (DSE, 2018).

This Is a Good Thing, Right?

What I have laid out is a precise description of how to buy and sell ecosystems services value. This takes me back to the press release. A quick reading of the media statement might leave a reader with the impression that AUD4.94 million is the value of the additional natural capital value that this government programme has generated. At first glance AUD4.94 million appears to be the marginal gain in Australia's natural capital value that was achieved in the programme. But that is a mistake. AUD4.94 million is *not* the name of a natural capital value. I explain what this number name references below. At this point I want to stay with the product that has been bought and sold in this auction. This product is the trouble I want to stay with.

I want to ask about the value of the increase in "ecosystems services value" that this elaborate and rather costly government programme has achieved. A careful reading of the details of the work by which this increase in value comes into being reveals that nowhere and at no time in the process has that value ever been named or specified. The product that is so rigorously bought and sold is an *absence*. And worse, there is literally no way that it could ever be otherwise. The programme is a very elaborate accounting exercise for a means of giving away money. When this becomes clear to an outsider, it also becomes obvious that this actuality of what the exercise *is* has never been hidden. When it comes down to it, this programme is a legitimate means for shifting money from the state coffers into the hands of private landowners.

Recognizing that this is a programme of environmental governance in a liberal parliamentary democracy in which the social technology of the political party is crucial, let me as your narrator temporarily put on a party-political hat. Corangamite is an electorate that has a history of swinging between choosing a member of the left-of-centre party (Labour Party) or a member of the right-of-centre party (Liberal Party) to represent the people of the area in the Victorian Parliament. It is clearly in the interests of any government—left-leaning or right-leaning—to appeal to the voters of the electorate. And there is no better way to do that than by finding ways to legitimately transfer resources from the state to the bank accounts of constituents. That there is no possibility of putting a number on the value of the product the state buys and the landowners sell here, is, on this reading, of no concern.

So, let me sum up. Economically this programme is justified as generating environmental services value. Described in this way this is a good news story. Taxpayer money used well to improve the environment and get trees planted to ameliorate Victoria's excessive carbon dioxide generation. Problematically the increase in the value of Victoria's natural capital cannot be named, articulated as a number, despite it being a product that is bought and sold. It seems that while there are still technical hitches, clearly, *this is a good thing.*

But equally, using a different economics this programme can just as legitimately be described as funding the labour of tree planting to enhance property values of private landowners. It is a means of intervening to put right damage caused by previous government programmes subsidizing the misallocated labour of land clearing that in all likelihood the landowner's grandparents profited by, creating a benefit which the landowner continues to enjoy. On this reading the government policy effected in EcoTender is an expensive programme to legitimately give away taxpayer money. Clearly, *this is a bad thing.*

On Not Disrespecting Numbers and Algorithms: Staying With the Troubles of Value

So, what is a journalist to do? Writing as a scholar and not as a journalist, I can respond to that obvious question only vaguely. In the beginning I return to my claim that the number name used in the press release is a paper-thin cover-up to divert attention from lurking trouble. As I see it, valuation always brings moral trouble that can never be contained for long. The right question to ask I think is, "How might a data journalist respond to that moral trouble?"

First, I clear up the matter of the AUD4.94 million. What is this figure? Where does this neatly named monetary value come from? This is how it is described in an academic paper offering critical commentary on the EcoTender programme:

> Under this market-based model economic value from ecosystems services is created when the per-unit costs of complying with the conservation contract are less than the per-unit price awarded to the successful partici-pants in the auction. While [for these sellers] some economic value is lost through the possibility of foregone production of marketed commodities, the participation constraint of rational landowners ensures that there will be a net increase in [economic] value created in the conduct of the auction. (G. Stoneham et al., 2012)

Under the economic modelling of this policy, the assumption is that land-owners will efficiently calculate the costs they will incur in producing the government's script for intervening in nature as infrastructure—in generat-ing a more efficient performance of the workings of natural infrastructure. Everyone assumes that a profit will be made by the landowner, although, of course, it is always possible that instead of a profit the landowner will have miscalculated and made a loss, but that is of no interest to the government as the buyer of the value generated by the landowners' labour.

What is of interest to the government is the issue of how this economic transaction can be articulated in a seemly manner. This is quite a problem when the product bought and sold has an existence solely within the circuit of an auction. The solution to this problematic form of being of the product is the elaborate, complex and complicated technology of the national accounts system. Establishing a market for ecosystems services value, the government wants to show itself as making a difference in nature. And the national accounts are the very convenient place where this can be shown in monetary terms. The "environmental benefits index," the particular value on the basis of which the government has purchased a particular product—an environmental services value—is ephemeral. It exists solely as a flash, a moment in the auction (Roffe, 2015). Despite this difficulty in the form of its existence, by ingenious contrivance, both the means of buying and selling something that has a single ephemeral moment of existence is achieved, and evidence of the specific instance of economic activity can be incorporated into the national accounts, albeit that some economists have serious reservations about accuracy (G. Stoneham et al., 2012).

AUD4.94 million is remote from the action of the EcoTender programme and from the nature it is designed to improve. But clearly, if the government makes a statement that its programmes have successfully improved a degraded and damaged nature it is best to find a way to indicate the extent of that improvement. It seems any number is better than none in this situation. And certainly, this is a happy, positive number. An unhappy, negative number that no doubt is available to the government accountants—the value of the cost of running the government programme—would never do here. Why go on about this oddly out of place number name? Surely this is going a bit far? What is the harm of a little sleight of hand that is relatively easily picked up? My worry here is that this is a misuse of a number that seems to be deliberate. It fails to respect numbers, and refuses to acknowledge the trouble that numbering, or in this case algorithming, always precipitates. It trashes a protocol.

My narrating of a number I found on a visit to a government website has unambiguously revealed a government programme that generates social goods and bads simultaneously. The sleight of hand number naming (using the precise value AUD4.94 million in the media release) that I also found in my narration, points off to the side, at something that is always threatening to overwhelm us: Valuation as a site of moral tension and trouble.

Is the big claim here that value is moral trouble that can never be contained for long? Value theory is a vast topic that has ancient roots in all philosophical traditions, and this is a rabbit warren of vast proportions that I decline to enter. I merely note that claims, often heard over the past 30 years, that the invisible hand of the market tames the moral trouble that tracks with value, are a dangerous exaggeration. Markets might find ways to momentarily and ephemerally tame value—as my story reveals. But the trouble with value always returns. Attending to *that* is the calling of the data journalist.

Here are a few suggestions on how a data journalist might respect numbers and algorithms—as protocols. When you are faced with an untroubled surface, where no hint of moral tension is to be found, but still something lurks, then "prick up" your ears and eyes. Attune yourself to numbers and algorithms in situ; work out how to think with a number that catches at you. Find ways to dilate the peepholes that number names cover. Cultivate respectful forms of address for numbers and algorithms in practicing curiosity in disciplined ways. Recognize that numbers have pre-established natures and special abilities that emerge in encounter; that the actualities of series of practices by which they come to be, matter. Be sure that when you can do these well enough, surprises lie in store. Interesting things happen inside numbers as they come to be.

Works Cited

DSE. (2018). Innovative market approaches: EcoMarkets. EcoTender and BushTender. Department of Sustainability and Environment [now Department of Environment, Land, Water and Planning (DELWP)], Victoria State Government, Australia. https://www.environment.vic.gov.au/innovative-market-approaches/

Roffe, J. (2015). *Abstract market theory*. Palgrave Macmillan UK.

Stoneham, G., O'Keefe, A., Eigenraam, M., & Bain, D. (2012). Creating physical environmental asset accounts from markets for ecosystem conservation. *Ecological Economics*, *82*, 114–122. https://doi.org/10.1016/j.ecolecon.2012.06.017

Verran, H., & Winthereik, B. R. (2016). Innovation with words and visuals. A baroque sensibility. In J. Law & E. Ruppert (Eds.), *Modes of knowing* (pp. 197–223). Mattering Press.

About the Author

Helen Verran is a Professor at Charles Darwin University and has been puzzling about how numbers come to be since meeting some quite amazing numbers in Yorubaland in Nigeria many years ago.

9. Indigenous Data Sovereignty: Implications for Data Journalism

Tahu Kukutai and Maggie Walter

Abstract

This chapter discusses some of the potential harms of digitalization and considers how Indigenous data sovereignty (ID-SOV), as an emerging site of science and activism, can mediate risks while providing pathways to benefit.

Keywords: Indigenous data sovereignty, activism, data journalism, statistical surveillance, Indigenous peoples

Digital technologies, including monitoring and information technologies and artificial intelligence (AI), are increasingly becoming a feature of Indigenous peoples' lives, especially for peoples in developed and transition economies. Yet, while data-driven technologies can drive innovation and improve human well-being, Indigenous peoples are unlikely to share equitably in these benefits given their nearly universal position of socio-economic, cultural and political marginalization. The growing use of linked and integrated big data by governments and businesses also brings significant risks for Indigenous peoples. These include the appropriation of cultural knowledge and intellectual property; the exploitation of land and other natural resources; and the perpetuation of discrimination, stigma and ongoing marginalization. These risks are amplified by journalistic storytelling practices that recycle well-rehearsed tropes about Indigenous dysfunction. In this chapter we discuss some of the potential harms of digitalization and consider how Indigenous data sovereignty (ID-SOV), as an emerging site of science and activism, can mediate risks while providing pathways to benefit. We conclude by suggesting that ID-SOV research and networks also represent valuable sources of data and data expertise that can inform more

Bounegru, L. and J. Gray (eds.), *The Data Journalism Handbook: Towards a Critical Data Practice.* Amsterdam: Amsterdam University Press, 2021
DOI 10.5117/9789462989511_CH09

equitable, critical and just approaches to journalism involving Indigenous peoples and issues.

Indigenous Peoples and Data

There are an estimated 370 million Indigenous peoples globally, covering every continent and speaking thousands of distinct languages (United Nations, 2009). The actual global count is impossible to know as the majority of countries that encapsulate Indigenous peoples do not identify them in their national data collections (Mullane-Ronaki, 2017). Notwithstanding these Indigenous "data deserts" and the significant global variation in Indigenous political autonomy and living standards, there is ample evidence that Indigenous people are often among the poorest population groups in their homelands, carrying the heaviest burden of disease, over-incarceration and broad spectrum inequality (Anderson et al., 2016; Stephens et al., 2006). This shared positioning of marginalization is not coincidental; it is directly related to their history as colonized and dispossessed peoples. However, the devastating consequences of colonialism and its bedfellows, White supremacy and racism, are rarely acknowledged, let alone critiqued, in mainstream journalistic portrayals of Indigenous peoples and communities.

Indigenous peoples have always been active in what is now known as data, with ancient traditions of recording and protecting information and knowledge through, for example, art, carving, totem poles, song, chants, dance and prayers. Deliberate efforts to expunge these practices and knowledge systems were part and parcel of colonizing processes. At the same time Indigenous peoples were made legible through the writings of European travellers, explorers and scientists who were presented as more objective, scientific and credible "knowers" of Indigenous peoples and their cultures. Over time the racial hierarchies that justified and sustained colonialism became naturalized and embedded through ideological structures, institutional arrangements (e.g., slavery, segregation) and state classifying practices. For example, Aboriginal and Torres Strait Islander people in Australia were specifically excluded from the national census until 1971 and this exclusion was linked to similar exclusions from basic citizenship rights such as the Age Pension (Chesterman & Galligan, 1997). In modern times, the power to decide whether and how Indigenous peoples are counted, classified, analyzed and acted upon continues to lie with governments rather than Indigenous peoples themselves. Transforming the locus of power over Indigenous data from the nation state back to Indigenous peoples lies at the heart of ID-SOV.

Defining ID-SOV

The terminology of ID-SOV is relatively recent, with the first major publication on the topic only surfacing in 2015 (Kukutai & Taylor, 2016). ID-SOV is concerned with the rights of Indigenous peoples to own, control, access and possess data that derive from them, and which pertain to their members, knowledge systems, customs or territories (First Nations Information Governance Centre, 2016; Snipp, 2016).[1] ID-SOV is supported by Indigenous peoples' inherent rights of self-determination and governance over their peoples, country (including lands, waters and sky) and resources as described in the United Nations Declaration on the Rights of Indigenous Peoples (UNDRIP).[2] Implicit in ID-SOV is the desire for data to be used in ways that support and enhance the collective well-being and self-determination of Indigenous peoples—a sentiment emphasized by Indigenous NGOs, communities and tribes (First Nations Information Governance Centre, 2016; Hudson et al., 2016). In practice ID-SOV means that Indigenous peoples need to be the decision-makers around how data about them are used or deployed. ID-SOV thus begets questions such as: Who owns the data? Who has the power to make decisions about how data is accessed and under what circumstances? Who are the intended beneficiaries of the data and its application?

ID-SOV is also concerned with thorny questions about how to balance individuals' rights (including privacy rights), risks and benefits with those of the groups of which they are a part. The focus on collective rights and interests is an important one because it transcends the narrow focus on personal data protection and control that permeates policy and regulatory approaches such as the European Union's General Data Protection Regulation (GDPR). Anglo-European legal concepts of individual privacy and ownership translate poorly in Indigenous contexts where individuals are part of a broader group defined, for example, by shared genealogies or genes. In such contexts the sharing of data that encodes information about other group members cannot rest solely on personal consent but must also take account of collective rights and interests (Hudson et al., 2020). Closely linked to ID-SOV is the concept of Indigenous data governance, which can be broadly defined as the principles, structures, accountability mechanisms

---

1   In Aotearoa New Zealand, the ID-SOV network Te Mana Raraunga defines Māori data as "digital or digitisable information of knowledge that is about or from Maori people, our language, cultures, resources or environments" (Te Mana Raraunga, 2018a).

2   https://www.un.org/esa/socdev/unpfii/documents/DRIPS_en.pdf

legal instruments and policies through which Indigenous peoples exercise control over Indigenous data (Te Mana Raraunga, 2018a). Indigenous data governance, at its essence, is a way of operationalizing ID-SOV (Carroll et al., 2017). It is through Indigenous data governance that Indigenous rights and interests in relation to data can be asserted (Walter, 2018).

Statistical Surveillance and Indigenous Peoples

The profiling of Indigenous populations and the targeting of services is not new; surveillance by the state, its institutions and agents have long been enduring characteristics of colonialism (Berda, 2013). Even through the official exclusion of Aboriginal and Torres Strait Islander peoples from the national census in Australia, surveillance of Aboriginal populations was a constant process (Briscoe, 2003). What is new in the social policy arena are the opaque, complex and increasingly automated processes that shape targeting and profiling (Henman, 2018). As "data subjects" (Van Alsenoy et al., 2009), Indigenous peoples are included in a diverse range of data aggregations, from self-identified political and social groupings (e.g., tribes, ethnic/racial groups), to clusters of interest defined by data analysts on the basis of characteristics, behaviour and/or circumstances.

The position of Indigenous peoples within these data processes is not benign. Rather, while the sources of data about Indigenous peoples are rapidly evolving, the characteristics of those data as a relentless descriptive count of the various dire socio-economic and health inequalities borne by Indigenous peoples remains the same. Walter (2016) has termed these data 5D data: Data that focus on Difference, Disparity, Disadvantage, Dysfunction and Deprivation. Evidence to support this claim is easily found through a Google search of the term "Indigenous statistics" or by inserting the name of an Indigenous people into the search (i.e., Native American, Aboriginal and Torres Strait Islander, Maori, Native Hawaiian, First Nations, Alaskan Native). What comes up, invariably, is a sad list detailing Indigenous over-representation in negative health, education, poverty and incarceration rate data.

The impact of 5D data on Indigenous lives is also not benign. As the primary way that Indigenous peoples are positioned in the national narrative, such data shape the way the dominant non-Indigenous population understand Indigenous peoples. These data stories that influence these narratives are frequently promulgated through media reporting. For example, Stoneham (2014) reports on a study of all articles relating to Aboriginal

Health from four prominent Australian online and print media sources. Three quarters of these articles were negative, focusing on topics such as alcohol, child abuse, drugs, violence, suicide and crime, compared to just 15% of articles deemed positive (11% were rated as neutral); a ratio of seven negative articles to one positive. Such narratives are also mostly decontextualized from their social and cultural context and simplistically analyzed, with the Indigenous population systematically compared to the (unstated) non-Indigenous norm (Walter & Andersen, 2013). The result is that in the national imagination Indigenous peoples are pejoratively portrayed as the problem rather than as peoples bearing an inordinate burden of historic and contemporary inequality.

There is growing evidence that the racial biases embedded in big data, and the algorithms developed to analyze them, will amplify, rather than reduce the impact of 5D data on Indigenous peoples (Henman, 2018). So, while in highly developed settler states such as Aotearoa NZ and Australia the prejudicial outcomes of discriminatory policies have been unwound, to some extent, by Indigenous activism and social justice movements over many years, these emerging data practices may unintentionally entrench existing inequalities and reactivate older patterns. With the detection (and amelioration) of social problems now increasingly deferred to algorithms, the likelihood of injustice reworking its way back into the system in ways that disadvantage Indigenous peoples rises exponentially. Reworking the old adage around data: If the algorithm data "rules" target problems where Indigenous peoples are over-represented; then the problematic Indigene will be the target.

ID-SOV in Practice

ID-SOV movements are active in the so-called CANZUS (Canada, Australia, New Zealand and the United States) states and have growing influence. The ID-SOV pioneers are First Nations in Canada. Tired of non-Indigenous data users assuming the mantle of unbiased "experts" on First Nations peoples, community activists developed a new model which provided for First Nations collective control over their own data. The trademarked OCAP® principles assert their right to retain collective ownership of, control over, access to and possession of First Nations data and, 20 years on, have become the de facto standard for how to conduct research with First Nations (First Nations Information Governance Centre, 2016). In Aotearoa NZ the Māori data sovereignty network Te Mana Raraunga (TMR) was established in 2015, drawing together more than a hundred Māori researchers, practitioners and entrepreneurs across the research, IT, community and NGO sectors.[3] TMR has been very active in promoting the need for Māori data sovereignty and data governance across the public sector, and in 2018 took the national statistics agency to task over its handling of the New Zealand Census (Te Mana Raraunga, 2018b) which was widely reported by mainstream and Indigenous media. TMR has also raised concerns relating to "social licence" for data use in the context of Māori data (Te Mana Raraunga, 2017) and developed its own set of Māori data sovereignty principles to guide the ethical use of Māori data (Te Mana Raraunga, 2018a). For advocates of Māori data sovereignty, including TMR, the goal is not only to protect Māori individuals and communities from future harm and stigma, but also to safeguard Māori knowledge and intellectual property rights, and to ensure that public data investments create benefits and value in a fair and equitable manner that Māori can fully share in.

In Australia, the Maiam nayri Wingara Indigenous Data Sovereignty Collective was formed in 2016, and in 2018, in partnership with the Australian Institute of Indigenous Governance, issued a communique from a national meeting of Aboriginal and Torres Strait Islander leaders. The communique stated the demand for Indigenous decision and control of the data ecosystem, including creation, development, stewardship, analysis, dissemination and infrastructure (Maiam nayri Wingara Indigenous Data Sovereignty Collective & Australian Indigenous Governance Institute, 2018). Maiam nayri Wingara, alongside other Indigenous bodies, is actively advocating for changes in the way Indigenous data in Australia is conceptualized, purposed, deployed, constructed, analyzed and interpreted. The aspiration is to activate the contribution data can make to Aboriginal and Torres Strait Islander well-being. What is required for this to happen is a reinvention of the relationship between Indigenous data holders/generators and the Indigenous peoples to whom those data relate to one built around Indigenous data governance.

Towards a Greater Role for ID-SOV Initiatives in Data Journalism

Data journalism is well positioned to challenge rather than reinscribe the five Ds of Indigenous data. Data journalists have ample opportunities to rethink how they use data to represent Indigenous peoples and stories, and to expose the complex ways in which Indigenous data is produced, controlled, disseminated and "put to work" by government and industry. In so doing data

3   https://www.temanararaunga.maori.nz/tutohinga/

journalists ought not to rely on non-Indigenous data producers and users; the rise of ID-SOV networks means there are a growing number of Indigenous data experts to call on. Many of those involved in ID-SOV work have close ties to their communities and are driven by a strong commitment to data justice and to finding ways for "good data" to empower "good outcomes." The questions raised by ID-SOV, particularly around data ownership, control, harm and collective benefit, have wider application beyond Indigenous communities. By engaging with ID-SOV approaches and principles, data journalists can open up meaningful spaces for Indigenous perspectives and concerns to frame their narratives, while also sharpening their lenses to hold those in power to account.

Works Cited

Anderson, I., et al. (2016). Indigenous and tribal peoples' health (The Lancet–Lowitja Institute Global Collaboration): A population study. *The Lancet, 388*(10040), 131–157. https://doi.org/10.1016/S0140-6736(16)00345-7

Berda, Y. (2013). Managing dangerous populations: Colonial legacies of security and surveillance. *Sociological Forum, 28*(3), 627–630. https://doi.org/10.1111/socf.12042

Briscoe, G. (2003). *Counting, health and identity: A history of aboriginal health and demography in Western Australia and Queensland 1900–1940*. Aboriginal Studies Press.

Carroll, R. S., Rodriguez-Lonebear, D., & Martinez, A. (2017). *Policy brief (Version 2): Data governance for native nation rebuilding*. Native Nations Institute. usindigenousdata.arizona.edu

Chesterman, J., & Galligan, B. (1997). *Citizens without rights: Aborigines and Australian citizenship*. Cambridge University Press.

First Nations Information Governance Centre. (2016). Pathways to First Nations' data and information sovereignty. In T. Kukutai & J. Taylor (Eds.), *Indigenous data sovereignty: Toward an agenda* (pp. 139–155). Australian National University Press. https://doi.org/10.22459/CAEPR38.11.2016.08

Henman, P. (2018). Of algorithms, apps and advice: Digital social policy and service delivery. *Journal of Asian Public Policy, 12*(2), 1–19. https://doi.org/10.1080/17516 234.2018.1495885

Hudson, M., et al. (2020). Rights, interests and expectations: Indigenous perspectives on unrestricted access to genomic data. *Nature Reviews Genetics, 21*(6), 377–384. https://doi.org/10.1038/s41576-020-0228-x

Hudson, M., Farrar, D., & McLean, L. (2016). Tribal data sovereignty: Whakatōhea rights and interests. In T. Kukutai & J. Taylor (Eds.), *Indigenous data sovereignty:*

Toward an agenda (pp. 157–178). Australian National University Press. https://doi.org/10.22459/CAEPR38.11.2016.09

Kukutai, T., & Taylor, J. (Eds.). (2016). *Indigenous data sovereignty: Toward an agenda.* Australian National University Press.

Maiam nayri Wingara Indigenous Data Sovereignty Collective & Australian Indigenous Governance Institute. (2018). Indigenous data sovereignty summit communique. https://web.archive.org/web/20190305225218/http://www.aigi.com.au/wp-content/uploads/2018/07/Communique-Indigenous-Data-Sovereignty-Summit.pdf

Mullane-Ronaki, M.-T. T. K. K. (2017). *Indigenising the national census? A global study of the enumeration of indigenous peoples, 1985-2014* [Thesis]. University of Waikato.

Snipp, M. (2016). What does data sovereignty imply: What does it look like? In T. Kukutai & J. Taylor (Eds.), *Indigenous data sovereignty: Toward an agenda* (pp. 39–56). Australian National University Press.

Stephens, C., Porter, J., Nettleton, C., & Willis, R. (2006). Disappearing, displaced, and undervalued: A call to action for Indigenous health worldwide. *The Lancet, 367*(9527), 2019–2028. https://doi.org/10.1016/S0140-6736(06)68892-2

Stoneham, M. (2014, April 1). Bad news: Negative Indigenous health coverage reinforces stigma. *The Conversation.* http://theconversation.com/bad-news-negative-indigenous-health-coverage-reinforces-stigma-24851

Te Mana Raraunga. (2017). Statement on social licence. https://www.temanararaunga.maori.nz/panui/

Te Mana Raraunga. (2018a). Principles of Māori data sovereignty. https://www.temanararaunga.maori.nz/new-page-2/

Te Mana Raraunga. (2018b). Te Mana Raraunga statement on 2018 New Zealand Census of Population and Dwellings: A call for action on Māori census data. https://www.temanararaunga.maori.nz/panui/

United Nations. (2009). State of the world's indigenous peoples. https://www.un.org/esa/socdev/unpfii/documents/SOWIP/en/SOWIP_web.pdf

Van Alsenoy, B., Ballet, J., Kuczerawy, A., & Dumortier, J. (2009). Social networks and web 2.0: Are users also bound by data protection regulations? *Identity in the Information Society, 2*(1), 65–79. https://doi.org/10.1007/s12394-009-0017-3

Walter, M. (2016). Data politics and Indigenous representation in Australian statistics. In T. Kukutai & J. Taylor (Eds.), *Indigenous data sovereignty: Toward an agenda* (pp. 79–98). Australian National University Press.

Walter, M. (2018). The voice of indigenous data: Beyond the markers of disadvantage. *Griffith Review, 60*, 256.

Walter, M., & Andersen, C. (2013). *Indigenous statistics: A quantitative research methodology.* Left Coast Press.

About the Authors

Tahu Kukutai (Ngāti Tiipa tribe) is Professor at the National Institute of Demographic and Economic Analysis, the University of Waikato, and a founding member of the Māori data sovereignty network Te Mana Raraunga.

Maggie Walter (PhD) is a palawa (Tasmanian Aboriginal) sociologist and a founding member of the Maiam nayri Wingara Australian Data Sovereignty Data Collective.

10. Alternative Data Practices in China

Yolanda Jinxin Ma

Abstract
This chapter gives an insider view of the landscape of data journalism in China, its key players and data culture, as well as some practical tips.

Keywords: China, data culture, citizen participation, open data, data journalism, data visualization

A couple of years ago, I delivered a presentation introducing data journalism in China at the Google News Summit, organized by Google News Lab. It was a beautiful winter day in the heart of Silicon Valley, and the audience comprised a packed room of a hundred or so senior media professionals, mainly from Western countries. I started by asking them to raise their hands if they think, firstly, that there is no good data in China, and secondly, that there is no real journalism in China. Both questions got quite some hands up, along with some laughter.

These are two common beliefs, if not biases, that I encounter often when I attend or speak at international journalism conferences. From my observations over the past six years, far from there being no data, in fact a vast quantity of data is generated every day in China, and of rapidly improving quality and broader societal relevance. Instead of no "real" journalism being done, there are many journalists producing important stories every day, although not all of them are ultimately published.

Issue-Driven Data Creation

Data stories were being produced even before the term "data journalism" was introduced in China. While nowadays we normally use the term "data-driven stories" in China, there was a period when we saw the contrary: Instead of

Bounegru, L. and J. Gray (eds.), *The Data Journalism Handbook: Towards a Critical Data Practice.* Amsterdam: Amsterdam University Press, 2021
DOI 10.5117/9789462989511_CH10

data being the driver of stories, we witnessed stories, or particular issues, driving the production of data. This typically occurred in relation to issues that resonate with regular citizens, such as air pollution.

Since 2010, the Ministry of the Environment has published a real-time air pollution index, but one important figure was missing.[1] The data on particulate matter (PM), or pollutants that measure less than 2.5 micrometres in diameter, which can cause irreversible harm to human bodies, was not published.

Given the severity of air pollution and the lack of official data on $PM_{2.5}$, a nationwide campaign started in November 2011 called "I test the air for the motherland." The campaign advocated for every citizen to contribute to monitoring air quality and to publish the results on social media platforms.[2] The campaign was initiated by an environmental non-profit. The testing equipment was crowd-funded by citizens, and the non-profit organization provided training to interested volunteers. This mobilization gained broader momentum after a few online influencers joined forces, including Pan Shiyi, a well-known business leader, who then had more than 7 million followers on Sina Weibo, one of China's most widely used social media platforms (Page, 2011).

After two years of public campaigning, the data on $PM_{2.5}$ was finally included in the government data release. It was a good start, but challenges remained. Doubts about the accuracy of the data were prompted by discrepancies between the data released by the government and that released by the U.S. embassy in China (Spegele, 2012).

The data was also not journalist-friendly. Despite hourly updates from more than a hundred cities, the information was only provided on a rolling basis on the web page, with no option to download a data set in any format. Although data has been centralized, historical data is not publicly accessible. In other words, without being able to write a script to scrape the data every hour and save it locally, it is impossible to do any analysis of trends over time or undertake comparisons between cities.

That is not the end of the story. Issue-driven data generation continues. When the data is not well structured and when data journalists struggle due to limited technical skills, civil society and "tech geeks" step in to provide support.

One early example back in 2011 was PM25.in, which scrapes air pollution data and releases it in a clean format. The site claims more than 1 billion search queries since they started operating.[3] Another example is Qing Yue, a non-governmental organization which collects and cleans environmental data from government websites at all levels, and then releases it to the public in user-friendly formats. Their processed data is widely used not only by data teams in established media outlets but also by government agencies themselves for better policymaking.

The generation of data and the rising awareness around certain issues have gone hand in hand. In 2015, a documentary investigating the severity of air pollution took the country by storm. The self-funded film, entitled *Under the Dome*, exposed the environmental crisis of noxious smog across the country and traced the roots of the problem and the various parties responsible (Jing, 2015). The film has been compared with Al Gore's *An Inconvenient Truth* in both style and impact. The storytelling featured a lot of scientific data, charts explaining yearly trends, and social network visualizations of corruption within environment and energy industries. As soon as it was released online, the film went viral and reached 200 million hits within three days, before it was censored and taken down within a week. But it had successfully raised public awareness and ignited a national debate on the issue, including around the accessibility and quality of air pollution data. It has also successfully made the country's leadership aware of the significance of the issue.

Two weeks after the release of the documentary, at a press conference held by the National People's Congress, Premier Li Keqiang addressed a question about air pollution which referred to the film, admitting that the government was failing to satisfy public demands to halt pollution. He acknowledged some of the problems raised by the documentary, including lax enforcement of pollution restrictions, and emphasized that the government would impose heavier punishments to cut the toxic smog (Wong & Buckley, 2015). At the end of August 2015, the new Air Pollution Prevention and Control Law was issued, and it was implemented January 2016 (Lijian et al., 2015).

Air pollution is only one example illustrating that even when data availability or accessibility pose a challenge, public concern with issues can lead to citizen contributions to data generation, as well as to changes in government attitudes and in the availability of public sector data on the issues at hand. In more established ecosystems, data may be more readily available and easy to use, and the journalist's job more straightforward: To find data and use it as a basis for stories. In China the process can be less

3   https://chrome.google.com/webstore/detail/pm25by-bestapp-labs/bgjclhmlafjipakmliln-loihemmlfndj

linear, and citizens, government, civil society and the media may interact at multiple stages in this process. Data, instead of just serving as the starting point for stories, can also come into the picture at a later stage to enable new kinds of relations between journalists and their publics.

Evolving Data Culture

The data environment in China has been changing rapidly in the past decade. This is partly driven by the dynamics described thus far in this chapter, and partly due to other factors, including the global open data movement, rapidly growing Internet companies and a surprisingly high mobile penetration rate. Data culture has been evolving around these trends as well.

Government legislation provides the policy backbone for data availability. To the surprise of many, China does have laws around freedom of information. The State Council Regulations on the Disclosure of Government Information was adopted in 2007 and came into force on May 1, 2008. The law has a disclosure mandate and affirms a commitment to government transparency. Following the regulation, government agencies at all levels set up dedicated web pages to disclose information they hold, including data sets.

However, although it gave journalists the right to request certain data or information from the authorities, in the first three years since the law was enforced, there are no publicly known cases of any media or journalists requesting data disclosure, according to a 2011 study published by Caixin, a media group based in Beijing and known for investigative journalism.[4] The study revealed that, in 2010, the *Southern Weekly*, a leading newspaper, only got a 44% response rate to a request sent to 29 environmental bureaus to test their degree of compliance with the law. Media organizations do not usually have a legal team or other systems to support journalists to advance their investigations and further their information requests. In another instance, one journalist who, in his personal capacity, took the government to the court for not disclosing information, ended up losing his job. The difficulties and risks that Chinese journalists encounter when leveraging legal tools can be much greater than those experienced by their Western peers.

China is also responding to the global open data movement and increasing interest in big data. In 2012, both Shanghai and Beijing launched their own

---

4   http://finance.ifeng.com/leadership/gdsp/20110901/4512444.shtml (Chinese language)

open data portals. Each of them holds hundreds of data sets on issues such as land usage, transportation, education and pollution monitoring. In the following years, more than a dozen open data portals have been set up, not only in the biggest cities, but also in local districts and less-developed provinces. The development was rather bottom-up, without a template or standard structure for data release at the local level, which did not contribute to the broader comparability or usability of this data.

By 2015, the State Council had released the Big Data Development Action Plan, where open data was officially recognized as one of the ten key national projects, and a concrete timeline for opening government data was presented.[5] However, official data is not always where journalists start, and also not always aligned with public interests and concerns.

On the other hand, the private sector, especially the technology giants such as Alibaba or Tencent, have over the years accumulated huge amounts of data. According to its latest official results, Alibaba's annual active consumers reached 601 million by September 30, 2018 ("Alibaba Group Announces," 2018). The e-commerce data from such a strong user base—equivalent to the entire Southeast Asian population—can reveal lots of trading trends, demographic shifts, urban migration directions, consumer habit changes and so on. There are also vertical review sites where more specific data is available, such as Dianping, the Chinese equivalent of Yelp. Despite concerns around privacy and security, if used properly, those platforms provide rich resources for data journalists to mine.

One outstanding example in leveraging big data is the Rising Lab, a team under the Shanghai Media Group, specializing in data stories about urban life.[6] The Lab was set up as an answer to the emerging trend of urbanization: China has more than 600 cities now, compared to 193 in 1978, with 56% of the population living in urban areas, according to a 2016 government report ("Gov't Report: China's Urbanization," 2016). Shifting together with the rapid urbanization is the rise of Internet and mobile use, as well as lifestyle changes, such as the rapid adoption of sharing economy models. These trends are having a big impact on data aggregation.

With partnership agreements and technical support from tech companies, the Lab collected data from websites and apps frequently used by city dwellers. This data reflected various aspects of urban life, including property prices, numbers of coffee shops and bars, numbers of co-working spaces, and quality of public transportation. Coupled with its original methodology,

5   http://www.gov.cn/zhengce/content/2015-09/05/content_10137.htm (Chinese language)
6   https://zhuanlan.zhihu.com/therisinglab (Chinese language)

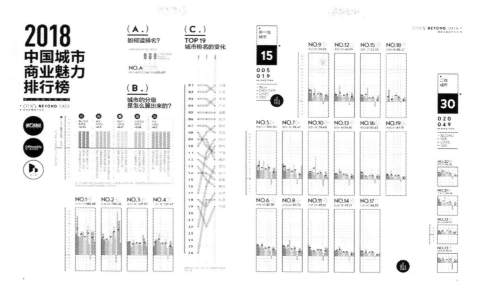

Figure 10.1. Cities Beyond Data 2018: Ranking of business attractiveness of cities in China. Source: *The Rising Lab.*

the Lab has produced a series of city rankings taking into account aspects such as commercial attractiveness, level of innovation and diversity of life (Figure 10.1). The rankings and the stories are updated every year based on new data, but follow the same methodology to ensure consistency. The concept and stories have been well received by the public and have begun to influence urban planning policies and companies' business decisions, according to Shen Congle, director of the Lab (Shen, 2018).

The Lab's success illustrates the new dynamics emerging between data providers, journalists, and citizens. It shows how softer topics have also become a playground for data journalism, alongside other pressing issues, such as the environmental crisis, corruption, judicial injustice, public health and money laundering. It also explores new potential business models for data journalism, as well as how data-based products can bring value to governments and businesses.

Readers' news consumption practices have also had an impact on the development of data journalism. Two aspects deserve attention here, one being visual news consumption and the other, mobile news consumption. Since 2011, infographics have become popular thanks to a few major news portals' efforts to build dedicated vertices with infographics stories, mostly driven by data. In 2014, the story of the downfall of the former security chief Zhou Yongkang, one of the nine most senior politicians in China, was the

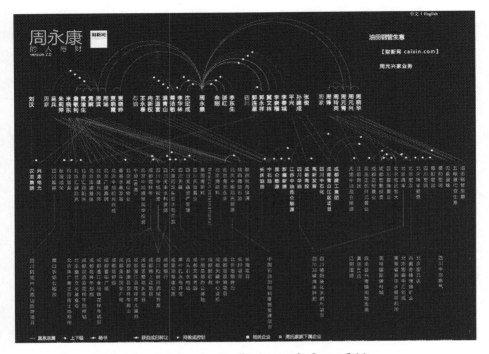

Figure 10.2. An interactive piece showing Zhou's networks. Source: *Caixin*.

biggest news of the year. Together with the news story, Caixin produced an interactive social network visualization (Figure 10.2) to illustrate the complex network around Zhou, including 37 people and 105 companies or projects connected to him, and the relationship between these entities, all based on the 60,000-word investigative piece produced by its reporting team. The interactive received 4 million hits within one week, and another 20 million views on social media, according to Caixin.[7] The wide circulation of this project brought new kinds of data storytelling to new publics, and created an appetite for visual stories which didn't exist before.

Almost at the same time, the media industry was welcoming the mobile era. More and more data stories, like any other online content in China, are now disseminated mostly on mobile. According to the China Internet Network Information Center (CNNIC), more than 95% of Internet users in the country used a mobile device to access the Internet in 2016 (Chung, 2017). WeChat, the domestic popular messaging app and social media platform, reached 1 billion users in March 2018 (Jao, 2018). The

7   http://bit.ly/storybench-caixin (Chinese language, Storybench, How a 4-million-hit data journalism product was produced, October 10, 2017)

dominance of mobile platforms means data stories in China are now not only mobile-first, but in many cases mobile-only. Such market demand led to a lot of lean, simple and sometime creative interactives that are mobile friendly.

In short, the data culture in China has been evolving, driven by various factors from global movements to government legislation, from public demand to media requests, from new generations of data providers, to new generations of news consumers. The interdependent relationships between players have created very complex dynamics, where constraints and opportunities coexist. Data journalism has bloomed and advanced along its own path in China.

Practical Tips

This final section is aimed at readers of this book who are looking to work on China-related stories and wondering where to get started. It will not be easy. If you are not a Chinese language speaker, you will be faced with language barriers, as most data sources are only available in Chinese. Next you will be faced with common issues pertaining to working with data: Data accuracy, data completeness, data inconsistency, etc., but we will assume that, as a reader of this book, you have the skills to deal with these issues, or at least a willingness to learn. A good way to start would be to identify the biggest players in data journalism in China. Quite a few of the leading media outlets have data teams, and it is good to follow their stories and talk to their reporters for tips. Here are a few you should know: The Data Visualisation Lab (Caixin), Beautiful Data Channel (The Paper), The Rising Lab (Shanghai Media Group), and DT Finance.[8]

The second question pertains to where to find data. A comprehensive list of data sources would be a separate book, so here are just a few suggestions to get started. Start with government websites, both central ministries and local agencies. You would need to know which department is the right one for the data you are looking for, and you should check both the thematic areas of ministries (for example, the Ministry of Environmental Protection) and the dedicated data website at the local level, if it exists.

---

8   http://datanews.caixin.com/ (Chinese language), https://www.thepaper.cn/list_25635 (Chinese language), https://www.cbnweek.com/topics/10 (Chinese language), https://www.dtcj.com/ (Chinese language)

There will be data that you don't even expect—for example, would you expect that the Chinese government published millions of court judgements after 2014 in full text? Legal documents are relatively transparent in the United States but not in China. But the Supreme People's Court (SPC) started a database called China Judgments Online doing just that.

Once you find some data that could be useful online, make sure to download a local copy. It is still common that data is not available online. Sometimes the data is published in the form of annual government reports which you can order online, or available only in paper archives. For example, certain government agencies have the records of private companies but not all of these are available online.

If the data is not released at all by the government, check if any user-generated content is available. For example, data on public health is very limited, but there are dedicated websites with information on hospital registrations or elderly centres, among others. Scraping and cleaning this data would help you gain a good overview of the topic.

It is also recommended to utilize databases in Hong Kong, anything from official ones like the Hong Kong Companies Registry, to independent ones such as Webb-site Reports. As mainland China and Hong Kong are becoming politically and financially closer, more information is available there, thanks to Hong Kong's transparent environment and legal enforcement, which may be valuable for tracing money.

There is also data about China not necessarily held in China. There are international organizations or academic institutions that have rich China-related data sets. For example, The Paper used data from NASA and Harvard University in one of its latest stories.

Last but not least, while some challenges and experience are unique to China, a lot of them could potentially provide useful lessons for journalists in other countries, where the social, cultural and political arrangements have a different shape but similar constraints.

Works Cited

Alibaba Group announces September quarter 2018 results. (2018, November 2). *Business Wire*. https://www.businesswire.com/news/home/20181102005230/en/Alibaba-Group-Announces-September-Quarter-2018-Results

Chung, M.-C. (2017, February 2). More than 95% of Internet users in China use mobile devices to go online. EMarketer. https://www.emarketer.com/Article/More-than-95-of-Internet-Users-China-Use-Mobile-Devices-Go-Online/1015155

Gov't report: China's urbanization level reached 56.1%. (2016, April 20). *CNTV.*
    http://english.www.gov.cn/news/video/2016/04/20/content_281475331447793.htm

Jao, N. (2018, March 5). WeChat now has over 1 billion active monthly users world-
    wide. *TechNode.* https://technode.com/2018/03/05/wechat-1-billion-users/

Jing, C. (2015, February 28). Chai Jing's review: Under the dome—investigating
    China's smog. https://www.youtube.com/watch?v=T6X2uwlQGQM

Lijian, Z., Xie, T., & Tang, J. (2015, December 30). How China's new air law aims to
    curb pollution. *China Dialogue.* https://www.chinadialogue.net/article/show/
    single/en/8512-How-China-s-new-air-law-aims-to-curb-pollution

Page, J. (2011, November 8). Microbloggers pressure Beijing to improve air pollution mon-
    itoring. *The Wall Street Journal.* https://blogs.wsj.com/chinarealtime/2011/11/08/
    internet-puts-pressure-on-beijing-to-improve-air-pollution-monitoring/

Shen, J. (2018, October). Data journalism in China panel. Uncovering Asia, Investiga-
    tive Journalism Conference, Seoul. https://2018.uncoveringasia.org/schedule/

Spegele, B. (2012, January 23). Comparing pollution data: Beijing vs. U.S. embassy on
    PM2.5. *The Wall Street Journal.* https://blogs.wsj.com/chinarealtime/2012/01/23/
    comparing-pollution-data-beijing-vs-u-s-embassy-on-pm2-5/

Wong, E., & Buckley, C. (2015, March 15). Chinese premier vows tougher regulation
    on air pollution. *The New York Times.* https://www.nytimes.com/2015/03/16/world/
    asia/chinese-premier-li-keqiang-vows-tougher-regulation-on-air-pollution.html

About the Author

Yolanda Jinxin Ma is a Digital Transformation Specialist with the United Nations, and before that she was a data journalism practitioner and evangelist
who introduced data journalism to China and across Asia.

11.   Making a Database to Document Land Conflicts Across India

Kumar Sambhav Shrivastava and Ankur Paliwal

Abstract
Documenting land conflicts to tell deeper, more nuanced and bigger stories of land and its relationship with India's diverse society.

Keywords: land conflict, India, data journalism, databases, collaboration

Land is a scarce resource in India. The country only has 2.4% of the world's land area but supports over 17% of the world's population. As one of the world's fastest-growing economies, it requires large swathes of lands to fuel its ambitious agenda of industrial and infrastructure growth. At least 11 million hectares of land are required for development projects in the next 15 years. But a huge section of India's population—mostly marginalized communities—depend on land for their sustenance and livelihood. Over 200 million people depend on forests while 118.9 million depend on farming land in India.

These competing demands cause conflicts. In many cases land is forcefully acquired or fraudulently grabbed by the state or private interests, dissenters are booked by the state agencies under false charges, compensation is paid partially, communities are displaced, houses are torched, and people get killed. Social disparities around caste, class and gender also fuel land struggles. Climate change-induced calamities are making land-dependent communities further vulnerable to displacements. All this is reflected in the many battles taking place over land across India.

As journalists writing about development issues in India, we come across many such conflicts. However, we realized it was not easy to sell those stories happening in remote corners of India to the editors in New Delhi. The mainstream media did not report on land conflicts except the ones that turned

Bounegru, L. and J. Gray (eds.), *The Data Journalism Handbook: Towards a Critical Data Practice.*
Amsterdam: Amsterdam University Press, 2021
DOI 10.5117/9789462989511_CH11

fatally violent or that were fought in the national courts. Sporadic reporting by a few journalists had little impact. Voices of the people affected by such conflicts remained unheard. Their concerns remained unaddressed.

The reason, we thought, was that the reporters and the editors looked at the conflicts as isolated incidents. We knew land conflicts were one of the most important stories about India's political economy. But the question was how to sell it to editors and readers. We thought that if journalists could scale up their reporting on individual cases of conflict to examine broader trends, their stories could not only have wider reach but might also show the intensity of various kind of conflicts and their impact on people, the economy and the environment. The biggest challenge to achieving this was the lack of a database which journalists could explore to see what trends are emerging around specific kinds of conflicts, such as those over roads, townships, mining or wildlife-protected areas. There was no such database of ongoing land conflicts in India. So we decided to build one.

In November 2016, we started Land Conflict Watch, a research-based data journalism project which aims to map and document all ongoing land conflicts in India. We developed a documentation methodology in consultation with academics working on land governance. We put together a network of researchers and journalists, who live across the country, to document the conflicts in their regions following this methodology.

For the purpose of this project, we defined land conflict as any situation that has conflicting demands or claims over the use or ownership of land, and where communities are one of the contesting parties. Ongoing conflicts where such demands or claims have already been recorded in a written or audio-visual format at any place, from the village level to the national level, are included. These records could be news reports, village assembly resolutions, records of public consultation for development projects, complaints submitted by people to government authorities, police records or court documents. Conflicts such as property disputes between two private parties or between a private party and the government are excluded unless they directly affect broader publics.

The researchers and journalists track national and local media coverage about their regions and interact with local activists, community organizations and lawyers to find cases of conflict. They then collect and verify information from publicly available government documents and independent studies, and by talking to affected parties. Data such as location of conflict, reasons behind the conflict, number of affected people, affected area, land type—whether private, common or forest—names of the government and corporate agencies involved, and a narrative summary of the conflict are documented.

Researchers file all the data into reporting-and-review software built into the Land Conflict Watch website. Data is examined and verified by dedicated reviewers. The software allows to-and-fro workflow between the researchers and the reviewers before the data is published. The dashboard, on the portal, not only presents the macro picture of the ongoing conflicts at the national level but zooms in to give details of each conflict, along with the supporting documents, at the micro level. It also provides the approximate location of the conflict on an interactive map.

About 35 journalists and researchers are currently contributing. As of September 2018, the project had documented over 640 cases. These conflicts affect close to 7.3 million people and span over 2.4 million hectares of land. Investments worth USD186 billion are attached to projects and schemes affected by these conflicts.

As a conflict is documented, it is profiled on the portal as well as on social media to give a heads-up to national journalists and researchers. The project team then collaborates with journalists to create in-depth, investigative stories at the intersection of land rights, land conflicts, politics, economy, class, gender and the environment using this data. We also collaborate with national and international media to get these stories published. Many of these stories have been republished by other mainstream media outlets. We have also conducted training to support journalists in using the database to find and scale up stories around land governance.

Land Conflict Watch is an ongoing project. Apart from designing stories, we also work with academics, researchers and students to initiate public debates. Land Conflict Watch's data has been cited by policy think tanks in their reports. Land-governance experts have written op-eds in national newspapers using the data. We regularly get requests from students at Indian and foreign universities to use our data in their research. Non-profit organizations use land conflict data, documents and cases to strengthen their campaigns to fight for the land rights of conflict affected communities. The stories inform people and help shape discourse around land rights and governance-related issues in India.

About the Authors

Kumar Sambhav Shrivastava is an Indian journalist who reports at the intersection of public policy, business and social justice.

Ankur Paliwal is a journalist who writes at the intersection of science and the human condition.

12. Reassembling Public Data in Cuba: Collaborations When Information Is Missing, Outdated or Scarce

Saimi Reyes Carmona, Yudivián Almeida Cruz and Ernesto Guerra

Abstract

How a small data journalism team in Cuba fights against the lack of data.

Keywords: Cuba, scarce data, data learning, artificial intelligence, data journalism, researcher–journalist collaborations

Postdata.club is a small team. We started as four journalists and a specialist in mathematics and computer science, who, in 2014, decided to venture together into data journalism in Cuba. Until that moment, there was no media outlet that was explicitly dedicated to data journalism in Cuba and we were interested in understanding what the practice entailed.

Today we are two journalists and a data scientist working in our free time on data stories for Postdata.club. Data journalism does not feature in our daily jobs. Saimi Reyes is editor of a cultural website, Yudivián Almeida is a professor of the School of Math and Computer Science at the University of Havana, and Ernesto Guerra is a journalist at a popular science and technology magazine. Our purpose is to be not just a media organization, but an experimental space where it is possible to explore and learn about the nation we live in with and through data.

Postdata.club lives on GitHub. This is because we want to share not just stories but also the way we do research and investigations. Depending on the requirements of the story we want to tell, we decide on the resources we will use, be they graphics, images, videos or audio. We focus on journalism with social impact, sometimes long-form, sometimes short-form. We are

Bounegru, L. and J. Gray (eds.), *The Data Journalism Handbook: Towards a Critical Data Practice.* Amsterdam: Amsterdam University Press, 2021

DOI 10.5117/9789462989511_CH12

interested in all the subjects that we can approach with data, but, above all, those related to Cuba or its people.

The way we approach our investigations depends on the data that we have access to. Sometimes we have access to public and open databases. With these, we undertake data analyses to see if there may be a story to tell. Sometimes we have questions and go to the data to find answers that could constitute a story. In other cases, we explore the data and, in the process, find interesting leads or questions which may be answered by data we do not yet hold.

Other times—and on more than a few occasions—to support our analysis and investigations, we have to create databases ourselves based on information that is public but not properly structured. For example, to report on the Cuban elections, we had to build databases by combining information from different sources. We started with data published on the site of the Cuban Parliament. This data, however, was not complete, so we complemented it with press reports and information from Communist Party of Cuba websites.

To report on the recently designated Council of Ministers, it was also necessary to build a database. In that case, the information provided by the National Assembly was not complete and we used press reports, the Official Gazette and other websites to get a more comprehensive picture. In both cases, we created databases in JSON format which were analyzed and used for most of the articles we wrote about the elections and the executive and legislative powers in Cuba.

In most cases we share such databases on our website with an explanation of our methods. However, our work is sometimes complicated by the lack of data that should be public and accessible. Much of the information we use is provided by government entities, but in our country many institutions do not have an online presence or do not publicly report all the information that they should. In some cases we went directly to these institutions to request access to certain information, a procedure which is often cumbersome, but important.

For us, one of the biggest issues with the data that we can obtain in Cuba is its outdatedness. When we finally get access to the information we are looking for, it is often incomplete or very outdated. Thus, the data may be available for consultation and download on a website, but the most recent date covered is from five years ago. In these cases we identify other reliable websites which provide up-to-date information or resort to documents in print, scans or human sources.

Collaborations with students and researchers are one of the ways we approach situations where information is missing, outdated or scarce. Since

2017, we have taught a data journalism course to journalism students at the University of Havana School of Communication. Through our exchanges with these future journalists and communication professionals we have learned new ways of working and discovered new ways to access information.

One of the things we do in these classes is to involve students in the construction of a database. For example, there was no single source in Cuba to obtain the names of the people who have received national awards, based on their life's work, in different areas. Together with students and teachers, we collected and structured a database of the recipients of more than 27 awards since they began to be granted until today. This information allowed us to reveal that there was a gender gap in awarding prizes. Women received these prizes only 25% of the time. With this discovery we were able, together, to write a story that encouraged reflection about gender issues in relation to the national recognition of different kinds of work.

In 2017 we had another revealing experience. This experience helped us to understand that, in many cases, we should not to settle for existing published databases and we should not make too many early assumptions about what is and is not possible. As part of their final coursework, we asked students to form small teams to carry out an investigation. These were composed, in each case, by one of the four members of the Postdata.club team, two journalism students and a student of computer science. One of the teams proposed tackling new initiatives of self-employment in Cuba. Here, these people are called *cuentapropistas*. What was a few years ago a very limited practice, is now rapidly growing due to the gradual acceptance of this form of employment in society.

We wanted to investigate the self-employment phenomenon in Cuba. Although the issue had been frequently addressed, there was almost nothing about the specificities of self-employment by province, the number of licenses granted per area of activity or trends over time. Together with the students, we discussed which questions to address and came to the conclusion that we lacked good data sources. In places where this information should have been posted publicly, there was no trace. Other than some interviews and isolated figures, not much information on this topic was available in the national press.

We thought that the data would be difficult to obtain. Nevertheless, journalism students from our programme approached the Ministry of Labour and Social Security and asked for information about self-employment in Cuba. In a few days the students had a database in their hands. Suddenly, we had information that would be of interest to many Cubans, and we could share it alongside our stories. We had wrongly assumed that the data was not intended for the public, whereas the ministry simply did not have an up-to-date Internet portal.

Coincidentally, the information came into our hands at a particularly convenient moment. At that time, the Ministry of Labour and Social Security decided to limit license issuing for 28 of the activities authorized for non-state employment. We were thus able to quickly use the data we had obtained to analyze how these new measures would affect the economy of the country and the lives of self-employed workers.

Most of our readers were surprised that we were able to obtain the data and that it was relatively easy to obtain. In the end it was possible to access this data because our students had asked the ministry and until today Postdata.club is the online place that makes this information publicly accessible.

Doing data journalism in Cuba continues to be a challenge. Amongst other things, the dynamics of creating and accessing data and the political and institutional cultures are different from other countries where data can be more readily available. Therefore, we must always be creative in looking for new ways of accessing information to tell stories that matter. It is only possible if we continue to try, and at Postdata.club we will always strive to be an example of how data journalism is possible even in regions where data can be harder to come by.

About the Authors

Saimi Reyes is a journalist, founder and editor-in-chief of Postdata.club.

Yudivián Almeida Cruz is a journalist, founder and data editor at Post-data.club and Computer Science and Data Journalism Professor at Havana University.

Ernesto Guerra is a journalist and one of the founders of the first data journalism websites in Cuba.

13. Making Data With Readers at *La Nación*

Flor Coelho

Abstract
Using civic marathons and the open-source platform Vozdata to collaborate with readers, universities and NGOs around large data-driven investigations.

Keywords: civic marathons, crowdsourcing, investigative journalism, open source, researcher–journalist collaborations, open data

At *La Nación* we have produced large data-driven investigations by teaming up with our readers. This chapter takes a look behind the scenes at how we have organized reader participation around some of these projects, including through setting goals, supporting investigative communities, and nurturing long-term collaborations with our readers and other external organizations and partners.

In such projects often our goal is to tackle the "impossible" by using technology to facilitate large-scale collaborations, enabling users to engage with investigative journalism and the process of making official data public.

For example, we spent around five years transcribing 10,000 PDFs of Senate expenses, two years listening to 40,000 intercepted phone calls and a couple of months digitizing more than 20,000 hand-written electoral forms.[1]

For these kinds of crowdsourcing initiatives, we relied on the online collaborative platform Vozdata. The platform was inspired by *The Guardian*'s MPs' expenses and *ProPublica*'s "Free the Files" crowdsourcing campaigns

[1] http://blogs.lanacion.com.ar/projects/data/argentina%C2%B4s-senate-expenses-2004-2013/, http://blogs.lanacion.com.ar/projects/data/prosecutor-nisman-phone-interceptions-mapped-in-playlists/, http://blogs.lanacion.com.ar/projects/data/vozdata-2015-unveiling-argentina%c2%b4s-elections-system-failures-with-impact/

Bounegru, L. and J. Gray (eds.), *The Data Journalism Handbook: Towards a Critical Data Practice.* Amsterdam: Amsterdam University Press, 2021
DOI 10.5117/9789462989511_CH13

and was developed with the support of Knight-Mozilla OpenNews and CIVICUS, a global alliance of civil society organizations and activists. The software behind Vozdata was open-sourced as Crowdata.[2]

Organizing Participation

For these projects our collaborators were mainly journalism students, civic volunteers, transparency NGOs and retired citizens. They have different motivations to participate depending on the project. These may include contributing to public interest projects, working with our data team and getting to know other people at our meetups.

Vozdata has teams and live ranking features. We have been exploring how these can enhance participation through "gamification." We had excellent results in fostering civic participation in this way around Argentina's national holidays. Participation in the construction of collaborative databases is mostly undertaken remotely (online). But we have also encouraged users to participate in "offline" civic events held at *La Nación* or during hackathons at various events. Sometimes we have built open (i.e., freely reusable) databases with journalism students at partner universities.

While hackathons are events that usually take one or two days, our online marathons can continue for months. The progress bar shows how many documents have been completed and the percentage that remain to be completed.

Setting Big Goals

The main role of collaborators in the Senate Expenses and Electoral Telegrams projects was to gather specific structured data from the documents provided. This involved over a thousand unique users. As well as extracting these details, readers also had the opportunity to flag data as suspicious or unacceptable and leave a comment with additional information. The latter feature was rarely used. When you have a deadline to finish a crowdsourcing project, you may not reach your target. That happened to us in the Electoral

---

2   http://blogs.lanacion.com.ar/projects/data/vozdata-ii-civic-participation-for-investigative-reporting-and-educational-platform/, http://www.theguardian.com/news/datablog/2009/jun/18/mps-expenses-houseofcommons, https://www.propublica.org/series/free-the-files, https://github.com/crowdata/crowdata

Figure 13.1. Opening of the Vozdata civic marathon on senate expenses at *La Nacion* in 2017. Source: *La Nacion*.

Telegrams project. The election day was approaching and we needed to publish some conclusions. While some provinces reached 100%, many had only completed 10% to 15% of the files, which we acknowledged when we published.

Supporting Investigative Communities

For Prosecutor Nisman's 40,000 files investigation, we worked with a trusted network of a hundred collaborators. Many audio files related to private conversations (e.g., family dialogues) held by the Iranian agent whose phone was tapped by a federal court. A group of six volunteers got really deep into the investigation. We created a WhatsApp group where anyone could suggest leads and curiosities.

One of our volunteers resolved a mystery that kept us busy for a couple of months. We had flagged several conversations where two people talked in code using nicknames and numbers (e.g., "Mr. Dragon, 2000"). Many volunteers had heard and transcribed such recordings. We thought about making a separate database to analyze the code behind them. One day, a volunteer discovered that the conversations were about betting on horse races! A quick Google search confirmed many names as racing horses.

You always have power users. But, depending on the scale of the project, many volunteers collaborating with a few documents each usually exceed the "superuser contribution."

Nurturing Collaborations

Our advice for journalists and organizations who want to involve their readers in data investigations is to appoint a dedicated community manager to organize and deliver communications through collaborative spreadsheets (e.g., Google Sheets), mailing lists and social media.

Large collections of documents can be a good place to start: The learning curve is fast and participants feel part of something bigger. It's also valuable to support collaborators with video tutorials or contextual introductions in-house at your organization or at dedicated events.

When we won an award related to these collaborative projects, we hosted a breakfast to share the prize with the volunteers. These are long-term relationships with your readers, so we made sure to dedicate time and energy to meeting up at events, visiting universities, giving interviews for student projects and so on.

Regarding partnerships with universities, professors usually act as nodes. Every year they have a new class of students who are usually eager to team, with us in collaborative projects (plan for this in advance!).

Transparency NGOs can also demonstrate the benefits of these projects. In our platform, every task can be registered, so they can easily showcase projects and media recognition for their donors.

When publishing outputs and stories, we recommend acknowledging the collaboration process and participant organizations in every platform (print, online and social media) and in mailouts. Emphasizing the collective character of such projects can send a stronger message to those who we want to hold accountable.

Conclusion

To make data with readers it is vital to allocate time and resources to engage with your community, deal with requests, analyze outputs, enjoy interactions and participate in events.

Volunteers classify documents because they think a project matters. For governments and those being reported on it is a sign that the project is not only a press concern, but also affects civil society. Through such projects, participants can become passionate advocates and online distributors of the content.

About the Author

Flor Coelho is a new media research and trainer manager at *La Nación* (Argentina).

14. Running Surveys for Investigations

Crina-Gabriela Boroş

Abstract

Read this first before running a survey for accountability journalism: dos, don'ts and how to handle imperfect circumstances.

Keywords: statistics, data journalism, surveys, accountability

Is an issue anecdotal or systematic? You're attempting to discover this when you realize there is not any tabular data—a fancy phrase that simply means information supplied in rows and columns. What should you do?

What is data, anyway? There are many nerdy definitions floating around, some of which are intimidating.[1] Let's trade them for the simple concept of "information." And as you gather it, in any shape or form, you need to be able to find patterns and outliers. This means that you have to have a considerable amount of systematically gathered raw material that documents an issue according to a specific method (think fill-in forms). Whether you use a spreadsheet, a coding environment, an app, or pen and paper, it does not matter.

Sometimes, thoughts, feelings or past intimate experiences trapped in people's hearts and minds can be articulated as data. One method of harvesting this precious information is to design a survey that would gather and order such feelings and experiences into a table, archive or a database that nobody else but you has access to.

For instance, the Thomson Reuters Foundation (TRF) undertook a project reporting on how women in the world's largest capitals perceived sexual violence on public transport affects them.[2] It was a survey-driven effort to

---

1   See 130 definitions of data, information and knowledge in Zins, C. (2007). Conceptual approaches for defining data, information, and knowledge. *Journal of the American Society for Information Science and Technology, 58,* 479–493.

2   http://news.trust.org/spotlight/most-dangerous-transport-systems-for-women/?tab=stories

Bounegru, L. and J. Gray (eds.), *The Data Journalism Handbook: Towards a Critical Data Practice.* Amsterdam: Amsterdam University Press, 2021

DOI 10.5117/9789462989511_CH14

raise awareness of the issue, but also to compare and contrast (the stuff stats do).

To deliver this spotlight, we went through several circles of Hell, as there are rigorous conventions that social scientific methods, like surveying, require, even when imported by journalists into their practice.

Here are a few main polling rules that journalists would benefit from knowing, but often don't receive training for.

Respondents cannot be handpicked. In order to be considered "representative" a pool of respondents would conventionally include people from all social categories, age groups, education levels and geographical areas that we have to report on. According to established methods, samples of the population under study need to be representative.

The selection of respondents needs to be randomised—meaning everyone has the same chance of having their name drawn from a hat. If you're conducting a poll and speaking to whomever is closest to hand without any criteria or method, there is considered to be a risk of producing misleading data, especially if you are aiming to make more general claims.

The number of people taking a survey must also reach a certain threshold for it to be representative. There are helpful online calculators, like those provided by Raosoft, Survey Monkey or Survey Systems.[3] As a rule of thumb: Keep the confidence level at 95% and the margin of error no bigger than 5%.

Answer options must allow respondents to not know or not be certain. When reporters follow these basic rules, their findings are close to unattackable. At the time of the TRF public transport safety research, our polling methodology stuck to the conservative rules of social sciences. Our subject addressed such a common human experience that speaks volumes about how societies function, that a UN agency offered to join in our effort. An honour, but one which, as journalists, we had to decline.

If you like the sound of this, it's time to take a stats course.

Sometimes rigorous polling is unrealistic. This doesn't always mean you shouldn't poll.

While there are established methods for surveying, these don't exhaust what is possible, legitimate or interesting. There may be other ways of doing polls, depending on your concerns, constraints and resources.

For example, when *openDemocracy* wanted to interview reporters across 47 European Council member states about commercial pressure inside newsrooms, there was little chance for statistical significance.

---

3   http://www.raosoft.com/samplesize.html, https://www.surveymonkey.com/mp/sample-size-calculator/, https://www.surveysystem.com/sscalc.htm

"Why?" you might ask.

All respondents became whistle-blowers. Whistle-blowers need protection, including not disclosing important real demographic data, such as age or sex. We were expecting some contributions from countries where exercising freedom of speech may lead to severe personal consequences. We decided that providing personal data should not be compulsory; nor, if provided, should these data sit on a server with a company that co-owns our information.

The EU had wildly different and incomplete counts of journalists in the region, meaning establishing a country-level representative sample was tricky.

We couldn't line up all press unions and associations and randomize respondents because membership lists are private. They also don't include everyone, although it would have been an acceptable base as long as we were honest about our limitations. Plus, in some countries, transparency projects lead to suppression and we received expert advice in which countries we could not solicit the support of unions without attracting either surveillance or punitive consequences.

In cases like this, you needn't throw the baby out with the bathwater. We didn't.

Instead, we identified what mattered for our reporting and how polling methods could be adjusted to deliver stories.

We decided that our main focus was examples of commercial pressure inside national newsrooms; whether there was a *pattern of how they happened; and whether patterns matched across the region.* We were also interested in the types of entities accused of image-laundering activities in the press.

We went ahead and built a survey, based on background interviews with journalists, media freedom reports and focus group feedback. We included sections for open answers.

We pushed the survey through all vetted journalism organization channels. In essence, we were not randomizing, but we also had no control over who in the press took it. We also had partners—including Reporters sans frontières, the National Union of Journalists and the European Federation of Journalists—who helped spread the questionnaire.

The feedback coming through the survey was added to a unique database, assigning scores to answers and counting respondents per country, drawing comparisons between anecdotal evidence (issues reported sporadically) and systemic issues (problems reported across the board).

The open text fields proved particularly useful: Respondents used them to tip us. We researched their feedback, with an eye for economic censorship patterns and types of alleged wrongdoers. This informed our subsequent reporting on press freedom.[4]

Although we did publish an overview of the findings, we never released a data breakdown for the simple reason that the selection could not be randomized and country-level sample sizes were not always reached.[5] But we built a pretty good understanding of how free the press is according to its own staff, how media corruption happens, how it evolves and sadly, how vulnerable reporters and the truth are.[6]

So, are there rules for breaking the rules?

Just a few. Always describe your efforts accurately. If you polled three top economic government advisers on a yes–no question, say so. If you interviewed ten bullying victims, describe how you chose them and why them in particular. Do not label interviews as surveys easily.

If you run a statistically significant study, have the courtesy to release its methodology.[7] That affords the necessary scrutiny for your audience and experts to trust your reporting. No methodology, no trust.

Don't be the next biggest "fake news" author. If an editor is pushing you to draw correlations based on inferences rather than precise data collection, use a language that does not suggest causality or scientific strength. Our job is to report the truth, not just facts. Do not use facts to cover up a lack of certainty over what the truth is.

Where does your story lie? In a pattern? In an outlier? Decide what data you need to collect based on this answer. Figure out where and how the data can be obtained before you decide on the most appropriate methods. The method is never the point, the story is.

If you run a survey, field-test your findings and protect your reporting against potentially problematic claims. For example, say a survey suggests that the part of the city you live in has the highest crime rate. Yet you feel safe and experienced almost weekly street violence in another neighbourhood you lived in for a year, so you may not yet trust the data. To check if you can trust your data, visit the places that you compare and contrast; talk to people on the streets, in shops, banks, pubs and schools; look at what data was collected; are residents in one area more likely to file complaints than residents in another area? What types of crime are we talking about?

4   https://www.opendemocracy.net/en/author/crina-boros-2/
5   https://www.opendemocracy.net/openmedia/mary-fitzgerald/welcome-to-openmedia
6   https://www.opendemocracy.net/en/welcome-to-openmedia/
7   http://news.trust.org/spotlight/most-dangerous-transport-systems-for-women/?tab=methodology

Have the types of crime considered in the analysis been weighted, or does a theft equal a murder? Such "ground truthing" efforts will allow you to evaluate your data and decide to what extent you can trust the results of further analysis.

About the Author

Crina-Gabriela Boroş is a UK-based award-winning investigative reporter who teaches data-driven journalism internationally and has established a strategic data journalism training programme at the annual conference Data Harvest.

Working With Data

15. Data Journalism: What's Feminism Got to Do With I.T.?

Catherine D'Ignazio

Abstract

Taking a feminist approach to data journalism means tuning in to the ways in which inequality enters databases and algorithms, as well as developing strategies to mitigate those biases.

Keywords: data journalism, feminism, gender, ethics, inequality, databases

Because of advances in technology over the last 70 years, people can store and process more information than ever before. The most successful technology companies in the world—Google, Facebook, Amazon, Microsoft, Apple—make their money by aggregating data. In business and government, it is increasingly valued to make "data-driven" decisions. Data are powerful—because they are financially lucrative and valued by the powerful—but they are not distributed equally, nor are the skills to work with them, nor are the technological resources required to store and process them. The people that work with data are not representative of the general population—they are disproportionately male, white, from the Global North and highly educated.

Precisely because of these basic inequalities in the data ecosystem, taking a feminist approach to data journalism can be helpful to uncover hidden biases in the information pipeline. Feminism can be simply defined as the belief in the social, political and economic equality of the sexes and organized activity on behalf of that belief. Feminist concepts and tools can be helpful for interrogating social power using gender as a central (but not the only) dimension of analysis. One of the defining features of contemporary feminism is its insistence on *intersectionality*—the idea that we must consider not only sexism, but also racism, classism, ableism and other structural forces in thinking about how power imbalances can obscure

Bounegru, L. and J. Gray (eds.), *The Data Journalism Handbook: Towards a Critical Data Practice.* Amsterdam: Amsterdam University Press, 2021
DOI 10.5117/9789462989511_CH15

the truth.[1] For journalists who identify with the profession's convention of "speaking truth to power," a feminist approach may feel quite familiar.

This essay looks across several stages in the data-processing pipeline—data collection, data context and data communication—and points out pitfalls for bias as well as opportunities for employing a feminist lens. Note that a feminist approach is not only useful for data pertaining to women or gender issues, but suitable for any project about human beings or human institutions (read: pretty much every project), because where you have humans you have social inequality.[2]

Data Collection

Examining power—how it works and who benefits—has always been a central part of feminist projects. Sociologist Patricia Hill Collins' concept of the *matrix of domination* helps us understand that power is complicated and that "there are few pure victims and oppressors" (Hill Collins, 2000, p. 332). While we tend to think of injustice in the interpersonal domain (e.g., a sexist comment), there are systemic forces that we need to understand and expose (e.g., sexism in institutions that collect data) in order to make change.

Structural inequality shows up in data collection in two ways. First, specific bodies are *overcounted* in a data collection process. Overcounting typically relates to the surveillance practiced by those in power on those with less power. For example, the Boston Police released data about their stop-and-frisk programme in 2015. The data show that police disproportionately patrol Black, immigrant and Latinx neighbourhoods and disproportionately stop young Black men. In cases like this of overcounting, it is important to be tuned into which groups hold power and which groups are likely to be targeted for surveillance. A data journalist's role is to recognize and quantify the disparity, as well as name the structural forces at work—in this case, racism.

The second way that structural inequality shows up in data collection is *undercounting* or not counting at all. For example, why is the most comprehensive database on feminicides (gender-based killings) in Mexico being collected by a woman who goes by the pseudonym of Princesa?[3] Despite the

---

1 Indeed, feminism that does not consider how other factors of identity intersect with gender should be qualified as "white feminism." Intersectionality was first named by legal scholar Kimberlé Crenshaw and comes out of an intellectual legacy of Black feminists who asserted that gender inequality cannot be considered in isolation from race- and class-based inequality.

2 For example, see Kukutai and Walter's chapter on Indigenous data sovereignty.

3 https://feminicidios.mx

fact that women's deaths in Ciudad Juárez and around the country continue to rise, despite the establishment of a special commission on femicide in 2006, despite a 2009 ruling against the Mexican state by the Inter-American Human Rights Court, the state does not comprehensively track femicides. Undercounting is the case with many issues that relate to women and people of colour in which counting institutions systematically neglect to account for harms that they themselves are responsible for. Which is to say—the collection environment is compromised. In cases of undercounting, data journalists can do exactly what Princesa has done: Count it yourself, to the best of your abilities. Typically, this involves a combination of crowdsourcing, story collection and statistical inference. In the US context, other examples of undercounting include police killings and maternal mortality, both of which have been taken up as data collection projects by journalists.

Data Context

While the open data movement and the proliferation of APIs would seem to be a good thing for data journalists, data acquired "in the wild" comes with its own set of concerns, particularly when it comes to human and social phenomena. The feminist philosopher Donna Haraway says that all knowledge is "situated," meaning that it is always situated in a social, cultural, historical and material context. Untangling and investigating how it is that data sets are products of those contexts can help us understand the ways in which power and privilege may be obscuring the truth.

For example, students in my data visualization class wanted to do their final project about sexual assault on college campuses.[4] Colleges and universities in the United States are required to report sexual assault and other campus crimes annually per the Clery Act, so there appeared to be a comprehensive national database on the matter. But the Clery data troubled the students—Williams College, for example, had extremely high numbers in comparison to other urban colleges. What the students found by investigating context and interrogating how the collection environment was structured is that the numbers told a story that was likely the *opposite* of the truth. Sexual assault is a stigmatized issue and survivors often fear victim-blaming and retaliation and do not come forward. So the colleges that were reporting high numbers were places that had devoted more resources

4   The final story by Patrick Torphy, Michaele Gagnon and Jillian Meehan is published here: https://cleryactfallsshort.atavist.com/reporting-sexual-assault-what-the-clery-act-doesnt-tell-us

to creating an environment in which survivors would feel safe to report. Conversely, those with low numbers of sexual assault had a hostile climate that did not support survivors to break their silence.

Here, there is a pitfall and an opportunity. The pitfall is that journalists take numbers downloaded from the web at face value without understanding the nuances of the collection environment, including power differentials, social stigma and cultural norms around being made visible to institutions (e.g., groups like women, immigrants and people of colour generally feel less confidence in counting institutions, with extremely good reason). The opportunity is that there are many more data context stories to be told. Rather than always using numbers to look forward to new analyses, data journalists can use the numbers to interrogate the collection environment, point out flawed practices and power imbalances, and shift counting practices so that institutions are accounting for what truly matters.

Data Communication

Contemporary Western thinking about data has evolved from a "master stereotype" where what is perceived as rational and objective is valued more than that which is perceived as emotional and subjective. (Think about which sex is identified as "rational" and which as "emotional.") The master stereotype would say that emotions cloud judgement and distance amplifies objectivity. But a feminist perspective challenges everything about that master stereotype. Emotions don't cloud judgement—they produce curiosity, engagement and incentive to learn more. Patricia Hill Collins (2000, p. 266), for example, describes an ideal knowledge situation as one in which "neither ethics nor emotions are subordinated to reason."

What does this mean for data communication? While prior practices in data visualization favoured minimalist charts and graphics as being more rational, both researchers and journalists are learning that leveraging visualization's unique properties as a form of creative rhetoric yields more memorable, shareable graphics. Take, for example, the "Monstrous Costs" chart created by Nigel Holmes in 1984 to depict the rising costs of political campaigns. Previously derided as an instance of "junk charts," researchers have now proven what most of us know intuitively: Some readers like monsters more than boring bar charts (Bateman et al., 2010).

As with every other communications medium, leveraging emotion in data comes with ethical responsibilities. Researchers have also recently demonstrated the importance of the title of a visualization in how people

Figure 15.1. Chart by Nigel Holmes from *Designer's Guide to Creating Charts and Diagrams* (1984).

interpret the chart (Borkin et al., 2016). Typical titling practices tend towards the "rational," which is to say that they depict the data as neutral and objective—something like "Reports of Sexual Assault on College Campuses 2012–2014." But there are many cases—again, usually having to do with women and other marginalized groups—in which a neutral title actually does harm to the group depicted by the data. In the case of sexual assault, for example, a neutral title implicitly communicates that the data that we have is true and complete, while we actually know that to be quite false. In other cases, a neutral title like "Mentally Ill Women Killed in Encounters with Police 2012–2014" opens the door to the perpetuation of harmful stereotypes, precisely because it is not naming the structural forces at work, including ableism and sexism, that make mentally ill women disproportionately victims of police violence in the United States.

Conclusion

Taking a feminist approach to data journalism means tuning in to the ways in which existing institutions and practices favour a status quo in which elite men are on top and others placed at various intersections in

Collins' matrix of domination. Patriarchy, white supremacy and settler colonialism are structural forces, thus they lend themselves particularly well to systemic data-driven investigation and visualization. We need to question enough of the received wisdom in data journalism to ensure that we are not inadvertently perpetuating that status quo and, at the same time, use our tools to expose and dismantle injustice. Those who wish to go further in this direction may look to my book *Data Feminism* (2020), co-authored with Lauren F. Klein, which introduces in more detail how feminist concepts may be applied to data science and data communication.

Works Cited

Bateman, S., Mandryk, R. L., Gutwin, C., Genest, A., McDine, D., & Brooks, C. (2010). Useful junk? The effects of visual embellishment on comprehension and memorability of charts. In *Proceedings of the 28th International Conference on Human Factors in Computing Systems—CHI '10* (pp. 2573–2582). https://doi.org/10.1145/1753326.1753716

Borkin, M. A., Bylinskii, Z., Kim, N. W., Bainbridge, C. M., Yeh, C. S., Borkin, D., Pfister, H., & Oliva, A. (2016). Beyond memorability: Visualization recognition and recall. *IEEE Transactions on Visualization and Computer Graphics, 22*(1), 519–528. https://doi.org/10.1109/TVCG.2015.2467732

D'Ignazio, C., & Klein, L. F. (2020). *Data feminism.* MIT Press.

Hill Collins, P. (2000). *Black feminist thought: Knowledge, consciousness and the politics of empowerment.* Routledge. http://www.hartford-hwp.com/archives/45a/252.html

About the Author

Catherine D'Ignazio is an Assistant Professor of Urban Science and Planning and the director of the Data + Feminism Lab at the Massachusetts Institute of Technology.

16. Infrastructuring Collaborations Around the Panama and Paradise Papers

Emilia Díaz-Struck, Cécile Schilis-Gallego and Pierre Romera

Abstract

How the International Consortium of Investigative Journalists (ICIJ) makes digging through gigantic amounts of documents and data more efficient.

Keywords: data leaks, text extraction, radical sharing, cross-border investigation, data journalism, International Consortium of Investigative Journalists

The International Consortium of Investigative Journalists (ICIJ) is an international network of journalists launched in 1997. Journalists who are part of ICIJ's large collaborations have diverse backgrounds and profiles. There is a wide range of reporters with different skills, some with strong data and coding skills, others with the best sources and shoe-leather reporting skills. All are united by an interest in journalism, collaboration and data.

When ICIJ's director Gerard Ryle received a hard drive in Australia with corporate data related to tax havens and people around the world as a result of his three-year investigation of Australia's Firepower scandal, he couldn't at that time imagine how it would transform the story of collaborations in journalism. He arrived at ICIJ in 2011 with more than 260 gigabytes of data about offshore entities, about 2.5 million files, which ended up turning in a collaboration of more than 86 journalists from 46 countries known as Offshore Leaks (published in 2013).[1]

---

1   https://www.icij.org/investigations/offshore/how-icijs-project-team-analyzed-offshore-files/

Bounegru, L. and J. Gray (eds.), *The Data Journalism Handbook: Towards a Critical Data Practice.* Amsterdam: Amsterdam University Press, 2021
DOI 10.5117/9789462989511_CH16

After Offshore Leaks came more investigative projects with large data sets and millions of files, more ad hoc developed technologies to explore them, and more networks of journalists to report on them. For instance, we recently shared with partners a new trove of 1.2 million leaked documents from the same law firm at the heart of the Panama Papers investigation, Mossack Fonseca.[2] This was on top of the 11.5 million Panama Papers files brought to us in 2015 by the German newspaper *Süddeutsche Zeitung* and 13.6 million documents that were the basis of the subsequent Paradise Papers probe.[3]

If a single journalist were to spend one minute reading each file in the Paradise Papers, it would take 26 years to go through all of them. Obviously, that's not realistic. So, we asked ourselves, how can we find a shortcut? How can we make research more efficient and less time consuming? How can technology help us find new leads in this gigantic trove of documents and support our collaborative model?

In this chapter we show how we deal with large collections of leaked documents not just through sophisticated "big data" technologies, but rather through an ad hoc analytical apparatus comprising of: (a) international collaborative networks, (b) secure communication practices and infrastructures, (c) processes and pipelines for creating structured data from unstructured documents, and (d) graph databases and exploratory visualizations to explore connections together.

Engaging With Partners

The ICIJ's model is to investigate the global tax system with a worldwide network of journalists. We rally leading reporters on five continents to improve research efforts and connect the data dots from one country to another.[4]

Tax stories are like puzzles with missing pieces: A reporter in Estonia might understand one part of the story; a Brazilian reporter might come across another part. Bring them together, and you get a fuller picture. ICIJ's job is both to connect those reporters and to ensure that they share everything they find in the data.

We call our philosophy "radical sharing": ICIJ's partners communicate their findings as they are working, not only with their immediate co-workers, but also with journalists halfway around the world.

---

2   https://www.icij.org/investigations/panama-papers/
3   https://www.icij.org/investigations/paradise-papers/
4   http://www.icij.org/journalists

In order to promote collaboration, ICIJ provides a communication platform called the Global I-Hub, building on open-source software components.[5] It has been described by its users as a "private Facebook" and allows the same kind of direct sharing of information that occurs in a physical newsroom. Reporters join groups that follow specific subjects—countries, sports, arts, litigation or any other topic of interest. Within those groups, they can post about even more specific topics, such as a politician they found in the data or a specific transaction they are looking into. This is where most of the discussion happens, where journalists cross-check information and share notes and interesting documents.

It took ICIJ several projects to get reporters comfortable with the I-Hub. To ease their way onto the platform and deal with technical issues, ICIJ's regional coordinators offer support. This is key to ensuring reporters meet the required security standard.

Encrypting Everything

When you conduct an investigation involving 396 journalists, you have to be realistic about security: Every individual is a potential target for attackers, and the risk of breach is high. To mitigate this risk, ICIJ uses multiple defences.

It is mandatory when joining an ICIJ investigation to setup a PGP key pair to encrypt emails. The principle of PGP is simple.[6] You own two keys: One is public and is communicated to any potential correspondent who can use it to send you encrypted emails. The second key is private and should never leave your computer. The private key serves only one purpose: To decrypt emails encrypted with your public key.

Think of PGP as a safe box where people can store messages for you. Only you have the key to open it and read the messages. Like every security measure, PGP has vulnerabilities. For instance, it could easily be compromised if spyware is running on your computer, recording words as you type or sniffing every file on your disk. This highlights the importance of accumulating several layers of security. If one of those layers breaks, we hope the other layers will narrow the impact of a breach.

---

5   See https://www.icij.org/blog/2014/07/icij-build-global-i-hub-new-secure-collaboration-tool/. For a different perspective on journalistic platforms such as the I-Hub, see Cândea's chapter in this book.

6   https://www.gnupg.org/

To ensure the identity of its partners, ICIJ implements two-factor authentication on all of its platforms. This technique is very popular with major websites, including Google, Twitter and Facebook. It provides the user with a second, temporary code required to log in, which is usually generated on a different device (e.g., your phone) and disappears quickly. On some sensitive platforms, we even add third-factor authentication: The client certificate. Basically, it is a small file reporters store and configure on their laptops. Our network system will deny access to any device that doesn't have this certificate. Another noteworthy mechanism ICIJ uses to improve its security is Ciphermail. This software runs between our platforms and users' mailboxes, to ensure that any email reporters receive from ICIJ is encrypted.

Dealing With Unstructured Data

The Paradise Papers was a cache of 13.6 million documents. One of the main challenges in exploring them came from the fact that the leak came from a variety of sources: Appleby, Asiaciti Trust and 19 national corporate registries.[7] When you have a closer look at the documents, you quickly notice their diverse content and character and the large presence of "non-machine readable" formats, such as emails, PDFs and Word documents, which cannot directly be parsed by software for analyzing structured data. These documents reflect the internal activities of the two offshore law firms ICIJ investigated.

ICIJ's engineers put together a complex and powerful framework to allow reporters to search these documents. Using the expandable capacity of cloud computing, the documents were stored on an encrypted disk that was submitted to a "data extraction pipeline," a series of software systems that takes text from documents and converts it into data that our search engine can use.

Most of the files were PDFs, images, emails, invoices and suchlike which were not easily searchable. Using technologies like Apache Tika (to extract metadata and text), Apache Solr (to build search engines) or Tesseract (to turn images into text), the team built an open-source software called

---

7   https://www.icij.org/investigations/paradise-papers/paradise-papers-exposes-donald-trump-russia-links-and-piggy-banks-of-the-wealthiest-1-percent/, https://www.icij.org/investigations/paradise-papers/appleby-offshore-magic-circle-law-firm-record-of-compliance-failures-icij/, https://www.icij.org/investigations/paradise-papers/roll-roll-asiacitis-u-s-marketing-tour/

Figure 16.1. Inside the leak.

Extract with the single mission of turning these documents into searchable, machine-readable content.[8] This tool was particularly helpful in distributing this now-accessible data on up to 30 servers.

ICIJ also built a user interface to allow journalists to explore the refined information extracted from "unstructured data": The hodgepodge of different types of documents from various sources. Once again the choice was to reuse an open-source tool named Blacklight which offers a user-friendly web portal where journalists can look into documents and use advanced search queries (like approximate string matching) to identify leads hidden in the leak.[9]

Using Graphs to Find Hidden Gems Together

ICIJ published its first edition of the Offshore Leaks database in 2013 using graph databases to allow readers to explore connections between officers and more than 100,000 offshore entities. This has grown to over 785,000 offshore entities at the time of writing, including from subsequent leaks such as the Panama and Paradise Papers.

ICIJ first attempted to use graph databases with Swiss Leaks, but it was with the Panama Papers that graph databases started playing a key role during the research and reporting phase. To explore 11.5 million complex financial and legal records amounting to 2.6 terabytes of data was not an easy task. By using network graph tools such as Neo4J and Linkurious, ICIJ

8   https://github.com/ICIJ/extract/
9   https://github.com/projectblacklight/blacklight, https://en.wikipedia.org/wiki/Approximate_string_matching

was able to allow partners to quickly explore connections between people and offshore entities.

Our data and research teams extracted information from the files, structured it and made data searchable through Linkurious. Suddenly partners were able to query for the names of people of public interest and discover, for instance, that the then Icelandic prime minister, Sigmundur Gunnlaugsson, was a shareholder of a company named Wintris. The visualization with this finding could be saved and shared with other colleagues working on the investigation in other parts of the world.

One could then jump back into the document platform Blacklight to do more advanced searches and explore records related to Wintris. Blacklight later evolved to the Knowledge Center in the Paradise Papers. Key findings that came through exploring data and documents were shared through the Global I-Hub, as well as findings that came from the shoe-leather reporting.

Graph databases and technologies powered ICIJ's radical sharing model. "Like magic!" several partners said. No coding skills were needed to explore the data. ICIJ did training on the use of our technologies for research and security, and suddenly more than 380 journalists were mining millions of documents, using graph databases, doing advanced searches (including batch searches), and sharing not only findings and results of the reporting, but also useful tips on query strategies.

For the Panama Papers project, graph databases and other ad hoc technologies like the Knowledge Center and the Global I-Hub connected journalists from nearly 80 countries working in 25 languages through a global virtual newsroom.

The fact that structured data connected to the large number of documents was shared with the audience through the Offshore Leaks database has allowed new journalists to explore new leads and work on new collaborations like the Alma Mater and West Africa Leaks projects. It has also allowed citizens and public institutions to use them independently for their own research and investigations. As of April 2019, governments around the world have recouped more than USD1.2 billion in fines and back taxes as a result of the Panama Papers investigation.

Since the first publication of the Panama Papers back in 2016, the groups of journalists using ICIJ technologies has grown and more than 500 have been able to explore financial leaked documents and continue to publish public interest stories linked to these millions of records.

About the Authors

Emilia Díaz-Struck is research editor and Latin American coordinator at the International Consortium of Investigative Journalists (ICIJ).

Cécile Schilis-Gallego is a journalist at Forbidden Stories and she previously worked as a data journalist at the ICIJ.

Pierre Romera is Chief Technology Officer at the ICIJ.

17. Text as Data: Finding Stories in Text Collections

Barbara Maseda

Abstract
How to find data stories in collections of documents and speeches.

Keywords: data journalism, unstructured data, text analysis, text mining, computational journalism

Looking at data journalism production over the past few years, you may notice that stories based on unstructured data (e.g., text) are much less common than their structured data counterparts.

For instance, an analysis of more than 200 nominations to the Data Journalism Awards from 2012 to 2016 revealed that the works competing relied predominantly on geographical and financial data, followed by other frequent types of sources, such as sensor, socio-demographic and personal data, metadata and polls (Loosen et al., 2020); in other words, mostly structured data.[1]

But as newsrooms have been having to deal with ever-increasing amounts of social media posts, speeches, emails and lengthy official reports, computational approaches to processing and analyzing these sources are becoming more relevant. You may have come across stories produced this way: Think of the statistical summaries of President Trump's tweets; or visualizations of the main topics addressed in public communications or during debates by the presidential candidates in the US elections.

Treating text as data is no mean feat. Documents tend to have the most varied formats, layouts and contents, which complicates one-size-fits-all solutions or attempts to replicate one investigation with a different set of

---

1   For more on the Data Journalism Awards, see Loosen's chapter in this volume.

Bounegru, L. and J. Gray (eds.), *The Data Journalism Handbook: Towards a Critical Data Practice.* Amsterdam: Amsterdam University Press, 2021
DOI 10.5117/9789462989511_CH17

documents. Data cleaning, preparation and analysis may vary considerably from one document collection to another, and some steps will require further human review before we can make newsworthy assertions or present findings in a way that reveals something meaningful not just for researchers but also for broader publics.[2]

In this chapter I examine five ways in which journalists can use text analysis to tell stories, illustrated with reference to a variety of exemplary data journalism projects.

Length: How Much They Wrote or Spoke

Counting sentences or words is the simplest quantitative approach to documents. Computationally speaking, this is a task that has been around for a long time, and can be easily performed by most word processors. If you are a student or a reporter who ever had to submit an assignment with a word limit, you will not need any special data training to understand this.

The problem with word counts lies in interpreting the results against a meaningful baseline. Such measures are not as widely known as temperature or speed, and therefore deriving meaning from the fact that a speech is 2,000 words long may not be as straightforward. In practice, many times the only option is to create those baselines or references for comparison ourselves, which may translate into further work.

In some cases, it is possible to find context in the history of the event or speaker you are examining. For instance, for its coverage of the US president's annual State of the Union address in 2016, *Vox* calculated the length of the whole collection of historic speeches to determine that "President Obama was among the wordiest State of the Union speakers ever" (Chang, 2016).

In events involving more than one speaker, it is possible to explore how much, and when, each person talks in relation to the total number of words spoken. For an example, see Figure 17.1.

---

2   Data cleaning and preparation may include one or more of the following steps: Breaking down the text into units or tokens (a process known as "tokenization"); "grouping" words that share a common family or root (stemming and lemmatization); eliminating superfluous elements, such as stopwords and punctuation; changing the case of the text; choosing to focus on the words and ignore their order (a model called "bag of words"); and transforming the text into a vector representation.

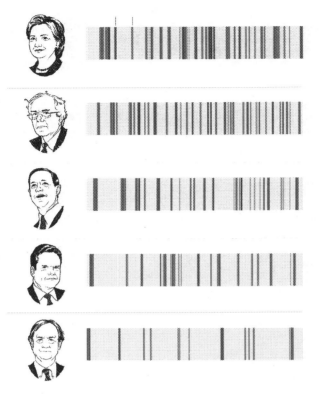

Figure 17.1. Visualisation of the Democratic Party debate (2015). Source: *The Washington Post*, https://www.washingtonpost.com/graphics/politics/2016-election/debates/oct-13-speakers/

Mentions: Who Said What, When and How Many Times

Counting the number of times a term or concept was used in speech or writing is another simple task that provides useful statistical overviews of our data. To do this, it is important to make sure that we choose to count the most appropriate elements.

Depending on the questions that you are looking to ask from the data, you may count the repetitions of each word, or of a series of words sharing a common root by using normalization operations such as "stemming" or "lemmatization."[3] Another approach is to focus on the most relevant terms

---

3   Stemming and lemmatization are operations to reduce derived words to their root form, so that occurrences of "reporter," "reporting" and "reported" can all be counted under the umbrella of "report." They differ in the way that the algorithm determines the root of the word. Unlike

in each document using a weighted measure called "term frequency/inverse document frequency" (TF-IDF).[4] The following are a few examples.

Frequent terms and topics. For its coverage of the London mayoral elections in 2016, *The Guardian* analyzed the number of times the two candidates had addressed various campaign issues (e.g., crime, pollution, housing and transport) in the UK Parliament in the six years preceding the race (Barr, 2016). Topics to be analyzed can be decided beforehand, as in this case, and explored through a number of relevant keywords (or groups of keywords linked to a topic) in comparable or analogous text collections. Search terms can also be analogous and not necessarily the same. Take, for instance, *FiveThirtyEight*'s analysis of how the same media outlets covered three different hurricanes in 2017 (Harvey, Irma and Maria) (Mehta, 2017). Another approach is to simply look at the most common words in a text as a topic detection strategy.

Speech over time. Looking at speech over time can also be a way to point to topics that have never been mentioned before, or that have not been addressed in a long time. This was, for instance, the approach chosen by *The Washington Post* for its coverage of the State of the Union address in 2018, in a piece that highlighted which president had used which words first in the history of this event (Fischer-Baum et al., 2018). The fact that readers can very quickly learn that Trump was the first president ever to mention *Walmart* (in 2017) or *freeloading* (in 2019), without having to read hundreds of pages of speeches, shows how effective text-data summaries and visualizations can be.

Omissions. A low number or absence of mentions may be newsworthy as well. These omissions can be analyzed over time, but also based on the expectation that a person or organization mentions something in a given context. During the 2016 presidential campaign in the United States, *FiveThirtyEight* reported that candidate Donald Trump had stopped tweeting about polls when they found a comparatively low number of mentions of keywords related to polling in his posts (Mehta & Enten, 2016). Such omissions can be detected by monitoring the same speaker over time, like in this case, in which, months before, *FiveThirtyEight* had discovered that Trump was tweeting a lot about polls that were making him look like

lemattizers, stemmers strip words of their suffixes without taking into consideration what part of speech they are.

4   TF-IDF is a measure used by algorithms to understand the weight of a word in a collection. TF-IDF Weight (w, d) = TermFreq$(w, d) \cdot \log (N / \text{DocFreq}(w))$, where TermFreq$(w, d)$ is the frequency of the word in the document (d), N is the number of all documents and DocFreq(w) is the number of documents containing the word w (Feldman and Sanger, 2007).

a winner (Bialik & Enten, 2015). This is also a good example of how news reports based on text analysis can later become the context for a follow-up piece, as a way to address the above-mentioned problem of contextualizing text statistics. The absence of a topic can be also measured based on the expectation that a person or organization mentions it in a given context.

People, places, nouns, verbs. Natural language processing (NLP) tools enable the extraction of proper names, names of places, companies and other elements (through a task called named entity recognition or NER), as well as the identification of nouns, adjectives and other types of words (through a task called part of speech tagging or POS). In *The Washington Post* piece mentioned earlier, the visualization includes filters to focus on companies, religious terms and verbs.

Comparisons

Determining how similar two or more documents are can be the starting point for different kinds of stories. We can use approximate sentence matching (also known as "fuzzy matching") to expose plagiarism, reveal like-mindedness of public figures or describe how a piece of legislation has changed. In 2012, *ProPublica* did this to track changes in emails sent to voters by campaigns, showing successive versions of the same messages side by side and visualizing deletions, insertions and unchanged text (Larson & Shaw, 2012).

Classification

Text can be classified into categories according to certain predefined features, using machine learning algorithms. In general, the process consists of training a model to classify entries based on a given feature, and then using it to categorize new data.

For instance, in 2015, the *Los Angeles Times* analyzed more than 400,000 police reports obtained through a public records request, and revealed that an estimated 14,000 serious assaults had been misclassified by the Los Angeles Police Department as minor offenses (Poston et al., 2015). Instead of using MySQL to search for keywords (e.g., *stab, knife*) that would point to violent offenses—as they had done in a previous investigation covering a smaller amount of data—the reporters used machine learning classifiers (SVM and MaxEnt) to re-classify and review eight years' worth of data in half the time needed for the first investigation, which covered one year only (Poston & Rubin, 2014). This example shows how machine learning approaches can also save time and multiply our investigative power.

Sentiment

Many journalists would recognize the value of classifying sentences or documents as positive, negative or neutral (other grading scales are possible), according to the attitude of the speaker towards the subject in question. Applications may include analyzing a topic, a hashtag or posts by a Twitter user to evaluate the sentiment around an issue, and doing similar computations on press releases or users' comments on a website. Take, for example, *The Economist*'s comparison of the tone of party convention speeches by Hillary Clinton and Donald Trump ("How Clinton's and Trump's Convention Speeches," 2016). Analyzing the polarity of the words used by these and previous candidates, they were able to show that Trump had "delivered the most negative speech in recent memory," and Clinton "one of the most level-headed speeches of the past four decades."

Becoming a "Text-Miner" Journalist

Using off-the-shelf text mining software is a good starting point to get familiar with basic text analysis operations and their outcomes (word counts, entity extraction, connections between documents, etc.). Platforms designed for journalists—such as DocumentCloud and Overview—include some of these features.[5] The Google Cloud Natural Language API can handle various tasks, including sentiment analysis, entity analysis, content classification and syntax analysis.[6]

For those interested in learning more about text mining, there are free and open-source tools that allow for more personalized analyses, including resources in Python (NLTK, spaCy, gensim, textblob, scikit-learn) and R (tm, tidytext and much more), which may be more convenient for journalists already familiar with these languages. A good command of regular expressions and the tools and techniques needed to collect texts (web scraping, API querying, FOIA requests) and process them (optical character recognition or

5   https://www.documentcloud.org/, https://www.overviewdocs.com/
6   https://cloud.google.com/natural-language/

OCR, file format conversion, etc.) are must-haves as well.[7] And, of course, it can be useful to obtain a grasp of the theory and principles behind text data work, including information retrieval, relevant models and algorithms, and text data visualization.[8]

Conclusions

The possibility of revealing new insights to audiences with and about documents, and of multiplying our capacities to analyze long texts that would take months or years to read, are good reasons to give serious consideration to the development of text analysis as a useful tool in journalism. There are still many challenges involved, from ambiguity issues—computers may have a harder time "understanding" the context of language than we humans do—to language-specific problems that can be easier to solve in English than in German, or that have simply been addressed more in some languages than in others. Our work as journalists can contribute to advancing this field. Many reporting projects could be thought of as ways of expanding the number of available annotated data sets and identifying challenges, and as new application ideas. Judging by the growing number of recent stories produced with this approach, text mining appears to be a promising and exciting area of growth in data journalism.

Works Cited

Barr, C. (2016, May 3). London mayor: Commons speeches reveal candidates' differing issue focus. *The Guardian*. https://www.theguardian.com/politics/datablog/2016/may/03/london-mayor-data-indicates-candidates-differing-focus-on-issues

Bialik, C., & Enten, H. (2015, December 15). Shocker: Trump tweets the polls that make him look most like a winner. *FiveThirtyEight*. https://fivethirtyeight.com/features/shocker-trump-tweets-the-polls-that-make-him-look-most-like-a-winner/

Chang, A. (2016, January 11). President Obama is among the wordiest State of the Union speakers ever. *Vox*. https://www.vox.com/2016/1/11/10736570/obama-wordy-state-of-the-union

---

7   http://regex.bastardsbook.com/
8   For further reading, see *Speech and Language Processing* by Daniel Jurafsky and James H. Martin; *The Text Mining Handbook* by Ronen Feldman and James Sanger. There are also numerous free online courses on these and associated topics.

Feldman, R., & Sanger, J. (2007). *The text mining handbook: Advanced approaches in analyzing unstructured data*. Cambridge University Press.

Fischer-Baum, R., Mellnik, T., & Schaul, K. (2018, January 30). The words Trump used in his State of the Union that had never been used before. *The Washington Post*. https://www.washingtonpost.com/graphics/politics/presidential-lexicon-state-of-the-union/

How Clinton's and Trump's convention speeches compared to those of their predecessors. (2016, July 29). *The Economist*. https://www.economist.com/graphic-detail/2016/07/29/how-clintons-and-trumps-convention-speeches-compared-to-those-of-their-predecessors

Jurafsky, D., & Martin, J. H. (2008). *Speech and Language Processing*. Pearson.

Larson, J., & Shaw, A. (2012, July 17). Message machine: Reverse engineering the 2012 campaign. *ProPublica*. http://projects.propublica.org/emails/

Loosen, W., Reimer, J., & De Silva-Schmidt, F. (2020). Data-driven reporting: An on-going (r)evolution? An analysis of projects nominated for the Data Journalism Awards 2013–2016. *Journalism*, *21*(9), 1246–1263. https://doi.org/10.1177/1464884917735691

Mehta, D. (2017, September 28). The media really has neglected Puerto Rico. *FiveThirtyEight*. https://fivethirtyeight.com/features/the-media-really-has-neglected-puerto-rico/

Mehta, D., & Enten, Ha. (2016, August 19). Trump isn't tweeting about the polls anymore. *FiveThirtyEight*. https://fivethirtyeight.com/features/trump-isnt-tweeting-about-the-polls-anymore/

Poston, B., & Rubin, J. (2014, August 10). Times Investigation: LAPD misclassified nearly 1,200 violent crimes as minor offenses. *Los Angeles Times*. https://www.latimes.com/local/la-me-crimestats-lapd-20140810-story.html

Poston, B., Rubin, J., & Pesce, A. (2015, October 15). LAPD underreported serious assaults, skewing crime stats for 8 years. *Los Angeles Times*. https://www.latimes.com/local/cityhall/la-me-crime-stats-20151015-story.html

About the Author

Barbara Maseda is the founder and data editor of Proyecto Inventario (Cuba).

18. Coding With Data in the Newsroom

Basile Simon

Abstract

Newsrooms present unique challenges to coders and technically minded journalists.

Keywords: computational journalism, programming, data cleaning, databases, data visualization

Inevitably, there is a point where data and code become companions. Perhaps when Google Sheets slows down because of the size of a data set; when Excel formulas become too arcane; or when it becomes impossible to make sense of data spanning hundreds of rows. Coding can make working with data simpler, more elegant, less repetitive and more repeatable. This does not mean that spreadsheets will be abandoned, but rather that they will become one of a number of different tools available. Data journalists often jump between techniques as they need: Scraping data with Python notebooks, throwing the result into a spreadsheet, copying it for cleaning in Refine before pasting it back again.

Different people learn different programming languages and techniques; different newsrooms produce their work in different languages, too. This partly comes from an organization's choice of "stack," the set of technologies used internally (for example, most of the data, visual and development work at *The Times* (of London) is done in R, JavaScript and React; across the pond *ProPublica* uses Ruby for many of their web apps). While it is often individuals who choose their tools, the practices and cultures of news organizations can heavily influence these choices. For example, the BBC is progressively moving its data visualization workflow to R (BBC Data Journalism team, n.d.); *The Economist* shifted their world-famous Big Mac Index from Excel-based calculations to R and a React/d3.js dashboard (González et al., 2018). There are many options and no single right answer.

Bounegru, L. and J. Gray (eds.), *The Data Journalism Handbook: Towards a Critical Data Practice.*
Amsterdam: Amsterdam University Press, 2021
DOI 10.5117/9789462989511_CH18

The good news for those getting started is that many core concepts apply to all programming languages. Once you understand how to store data points in a list (as you would in a spreadsheet row or column) and how to do various operations in Python, doing the same thing in JavaScript, R or Ruby is a matter of learning the syntax.

For the purpose of this chapter, we can think of data journalism's coding as being subdivided into three core areas: Data work—including scraping, cleaning, statistics (work you could do in a spreadsheet); back-end work—the esoteric world of databases, servers and APIs; and front-end work—most of what happens in a web browser, including interactive data visualizations. This chapter explores how these different areas of work are shaped by several constraints that data journalists routinely face in working with code in newsrooms, including (a) time to learn, (b) working with deadlines and (c) reviewing code.

Time to Learn

One of the wonderful traits uniting the data journalism community is the appetite to learn. Whether you are a reporter keen on learning the ropes, a student looking to get a job in this field or an accomplished practitioner, there is plenty to learn. As technology evolves very quickly, and as some tools fall out of fashion while others are created by talented and generous people, there are always new things that can be done and learned. There are often successive iterations and versions of tools for a given task (e.g., libraries for obtaining data from Twitter's API). Tools often build and expand on previous ones (e.g., extensions and add-ons for the D3 data visualization library). Coding in data journalism is thus an ongoing learning process which takes time and energy, on top of an initial investment of time to learn.

One issue that comes with learning programming is the initial reduction of speed and efficiency that comes with grappling with unfamiliar concepts. Programming boot camps can get you up to speed in a matter of weeks, although they can be expensive. Workshops at conferences are shorter and cheaper, and for beginners as well as advanced users. Having time to learn on the clock, as part of your job, is a necessity. There you will face real, practical problems, and if you are lucky you will have colleagues to help you. There's a knack to finding solutions to your problems: Querying for issues over and over again and developing a certain "nose" for what is causing an issue.

This investment in time and resources can pay off: Coding opens many new possibilities and provides many rewards. One issue that remains at all stages of experience is that it is hard to estimate how long a task will take. This is challenging, because newsroom work is made of deadlines.

Working With Deadlines

Delivering on time is an essential part of the job in journalism. Coding, as reporting, can be unpredictable. Regardless of your level of experience, delays can—and invariably will—happen.

One challenge for beginners is slowdown caused by learning a new way to work. When setting off to do something new, particularly in the beginning of your learning, make sure you leave yourself enough time to be able to complete your task with a tool you know (e.g., spreadsheet). If you are just starting to learn and strapped for time, you may want to use a familiar tool and wait until you have more time to experiment.

When working on larger projects, tech companies use various methods to break projects down into tasks and sub-tasks (until the tasks are small and self-contained enough to estimate how long they will take) as well as to list and prioritize tasks by importance.

Data journalists can draw on such methods. For example, in one *The Sunday Times* project on the proportion of reported crimes that UK police forces are able to solve, we prioritized displaying numbers for the reader's local area. Once this was done and there was a bit of extra time, we did the next item on the list: A visualization comparing the reader's local area to other areas, and the national average. The project could have gone to publication at any point thanks to how we worked. This iterative workflow helps you focus and manage expectations at the same time.

Reviewing Code

Newsrooms often have systems in place to maintain standards for many of their products. A reporter doesn't simply file their story and it gets printed: It is scrutinized by both editors and sub-editors.

Software developers have their own systems to ensure quality and to avoid introducing bugs to collaborative projects. This includes "code reviews," where one programmer submits their work and others test and review it, as well as automated code tests.

According to the 2017 Global Data Journalism Survey, 40% of responding data teams were three to five members and 30% of them counted only one or two members (Heravi, 2017). These small numbers pose a challenge to internal code reviewing practices. Data journalists thus often work on their own, either because they don't have colleagues, because there are no peer-review systems in place or because there is no one with the right skills to review their code.

Internal quality control mechanisms can therefore become a luxury that only a few data journalism teams can afford (there are no sub-editors for coding!). The cost of not having such control is potential bugs left unattended, sub-optimal performance or, worst of all, errors left unseen. These resource constraints are perhaps partly why it is important for many journalists to look for input on and collaboration around their work outside their organizations, for example from online coding communities.[1]

Works Cited

BBC Data Journalism team. (n.d.). What software do the BBC use? [Interview]. https://warwick.ac.uk/fac/cross_fac/cim/news/bbc-r-interview/

González, M., Hensleigh, E., McLean, M., Segger, M., & Selby-Boothroyd, A. (2018, August 6). How we made the new Big Mac Index interactive. *Source.* https://source.opennews.org/articles/how-we-made-new-big-mac-index-interactive/

Heravi, B. (2017, August 1). State of data journalism globally: First insights into the global data journalism survey. *Medium.* https://medium.com/ucd-ischool/state-of-data-journalism-globally-cb2f4696ad3d

About the Author

Basile Simon is graphics editor at Reuters Graphics and a Visiting Lecturer in Interactive Journalism at City, University of London.

---

1   More on data journalism code transparency and reviewing practices can be found in chapters in this volume by Leon and Mazotte.

19. Accounting for Methods: Spreadsheets, Scripts and Programming Notebooks

Sam Leon

Abstract

This chapter explores the ways in which literate programming environments such as Jupyter Notebooks can help make data journalism reproducible, less error prone and more collaborative.

Keywords: Jupyter Notebooks, reproducibility, programming, Python, literate programming environments, data journalism

With the rise of data journalism, ideas around what can be considered a journalistic source are changing. Sources come in many forms now: Public data sets, leaked troves of emails, scanned documents, satellite imagery and sensor data. In tandem with this, new methods for finding stories in these sources are emerging. Machine learning, text analysis and some of the other techniques explored elsewhere in this book are increasingly being deployed in the service of the scoop.

But data, despite its aura of hard objective truth, can be distorted and misrepresented. There are many ways in which data journalists can introduce error into their interpretation of a data set and publish a misleading story. There could be issues at the point of data collection which prevent general inferences being made to a broader population. This could, for instance, be a result of a self-selection bias in the way a sample was chosen, something that has become a common problem in the age of Internet polls and surveys. Errors can also be introduced at the data-processing stage. Data processing or cleaning can involve geocoding, correcting misspelled names, harmonizing categories or excluding certain data points altogether if, for instance, they are considered statistical outliers. A good example of this kind of error at work is the inaccurate geocoding of IP addresses in a

Bounegru, L. and J. Gray (eds.), *The Data Journalism Handbook: Towards a Critical Data Practice.* Amsterdam: Amsterdam University Press, 2021

DOI 10.5117/9789462989511_CH19

widely reported study that purported to show a correlation between political persuasion and consumption of porn (Harris, 2014). Then, of course, we have the meat of the data journalist's work, analysis. Any number of statistical fallacies may affect this portion of the work, such as mistaking correlation with causation or choosing an inappropriate statistic to summarize the data set in question.

Given the ways in which collection, treatment and analysis of data can change a narrative—how does the data journalist reassure the reader that the sources they have used are reliable and that the work done to derive their conclusions is sound?

In the case that the data journalist is simply reporting the data or research findings of a third party, they need not deviate from traditional editorial standards adopted by many major news outlets. A reference to the institution that collected and analyzed the data is generally sufficient. For example, a recent *Financial Times* chart on life expectancy in the United Kingdom is accompanied by a note which says: "Source: Club Vita calculations based on Eurostat data." In principle, the reader can then make an assessment of the credibility of the institution quoted. While a responsible journalist will only report studies they believe to be reliable, the third-party institution is largely responsible for accounting for the methods through which it arrived at its conclusions. In an academic context, this will likely include processes of peer review and in the case of scientific publishing it will invariably include some level of methodological transparency.

In the increasingly common case where the journalistic organization produces the data-driven research, then they themselves are accountable to the reader for the reliability of the results they are reporting. Journalists have responded to the challenge of accounting for their methods in different ways. One common approach is to give a description of the general methodology used to arrive at the conclusions within a story. These descriptions should be framed as far as possible in plain, non-technical language so as to be comprehensible to the widest possible audience. A good example of this approach was taken by *The Guardian* and Global Witness in explaining how they counted deaths of environmental activists for their "Environmental Defenders" series (Leather, 2017; Leather & Kyte, 2017).

But—as with all ways of accounting for social life—written accounts have their limits. The most significant issue with them is that they generally do not specify the exact procedures used to produce the analysis or prepare the data. This makes it difficult, or in some cases impossible, to exactly reproduce steps taken by the reporters to reach their conclusions. In other words, a written account is generally not a reproducible one. In the example above, where the data acquisition, processing and analysis steps are relatively straightforward, there may be no additional value in going beyond a general written description. However, when more complicated techniques are employed there may be a strong case for employing reproducible approaches.

Reproducible Data Journalism

Reproducibility is widely regarded as a pillar of the modern scientific method. It aids in the process of corroborating results and identifying and addressing problematic findings or questionable theories. In principle, the same mechanisms can help to weed out erroneous or misleading uses of data in the journalistic context.

A look at one of the most well-publicized methodological errors in recent academic history can be instructive. In a 2010 paper, Harvard's Carmen Reinhart and Kenneth Rogoff purposed to have shown that average real economic growth slows to -0.1% when a country's public debt rises to more than 90% of gross domestic product (Reinhart & Rogoff, 2010). This figure was then used as ammunition by politicians endorsing austerity measures.

As it turned out, the analysis was based on an Excel error. Rather than taking the mean of a whole row of countries, Reinhart and Rogoff had made an error in their formula which meant only 15 out of the 20 countries they looked at were incorporated. Once the all the countries were considered the 0.1% "decline" became a 2.2% average increase in economic growth. The mistake was only picked up when PhD candidate Thomas Herndon and professors Michael Ash and Robert Pollin looked at the original spreadsheet that Reinhard and Rogoff had worked off. This demonstrates the importance of having not just the method written out in plain language—but also having the data and technology used for the analysis itself. But the Reinhart–Rogoff error perhaps points to something else as well—Microsoft Excel, and spreadsheet software in general, may not be the best technology for creating reproducible analysis.

Excel hides much of the process of working with data by design. Formulas—which do most of the analytical work in a spreadsheet—are only visible when clicking on a cell. This means that it is harder to review the actual steps taken to reaching a given conclusion. While we will never know for sure, one may imagine that had Reinhart and Rogoff's analytical work been done in a language in which the steps had to be declared explicitly (e.g., a programming language) the error could have been spotted prior to publication.

Excel-based workflows generally encourage the removal of the steps taken to arrive at a conclusion. Values rather than formulas are often copied across to other sheets or columns, leaving the "undo" key as the only route back to how a given number was actually generated. "Undo" histories, of course, are generally erased when an application is closed, and are therefore not a good place for storing important methodological information.

The Rise of the Literate Programming Environment: Jupyter Notebooks in the Newsroom

An emerging approach to methodological transparency is to use so-called "literate programming" environments. Organizations like *Buzzfeed, The New York Times* and Correctiv are using them to provide human-readable documents that can also be executed by a machine in order to reproduce exactly the steps taken in a given analysis.[1]

First articulated by Donald Knuth in the 1980s, literate programming is an approach to writing computer code where the author intersperses code with ordinary human language explaining the steps taken (Knuth, 1992). The two main literate programming environments in use today are Jupyter Notebooks and R Markdown.[2] Both produce human-readable documents that mix plain English, visualizations and code in a single document that can be rendered in HTML and published on the web. Original data can be linked to explicitly, and any other technical dependencies such as third-party libraries will be clearly identified.

Not only is there an emphasis on human-readable explanation, the code is ordered so as to reflect human logic. Documents written in this paradigm can therefore read like a set of steps in an argument or a series of answers to a set of research questions.

> The practitioner of literate programming can be regarded as an essayist, whose main concern is with exposition and excellence of style. Such an author, with thesaurus in hand, chooses the names of variables carefully and explains what each variable means. He or she strives for a program that is comprehensible because its concepts have been introduced in an order that is best for human understanding, using a mixture of formal and informal methods that reinforce each other. (Knuth, 1984)

1   https://github.com/TheUpshot
2   http://jupyter.org/, https://rmarkdown.rstudio.com/

A good example of the form is found in *Buzzfeed News'* Jupyter Notebook detailing how they analyzed trends in California's wildfires.[3] Whilst the notebook contains all the code and links to source data required to reproduce the analysis, the thrust of the document is a narrative or conversation with the source data. Explanations are set out under headings that follow a logical line of enquiry. Visualizations and charts are used to bring out key themes.

One aspect of the "literate" approach to programming is that the documents produced (as Jupyter Notebook or R Markdown files) may be capable of reassuring even those readers who cannot read the code itself that the steps taken to produce the conclusions are sound. The idea is similar to Steven Shapin and Simon Schaffer's account of "virtual witnessing" as a means of establishing matters of fact in early modern science. Using Robert Boyle's experimental program as an example, Shapin and Schaffer set out the role that "virtual witnessing" had:

> The technology of virtual witnessing involves the production in a reader's mind of such an image of an experimental scene as obviates the necessity for either direct witness or replication. Through virtual witnessing the multiplication of witnesses could be, in principle, unlimited. It was therefore the most powerful technology for constituting matters of fact. The validation of experiments, and the crediting of their outcomes as matters of fact, necessarily entailed their realization in the laboratory of the mind and the mind's eye. What was required was a technology of trust and assurance that the things had been done and done in the way claimed. (Shapin & Schaffer, 1985)

Documents produced by literate programming environments such as Jupyter Notebooks—when published alongside articles—may have a similar effect in that they enable the non-programming reader to visualize the steps taken to produce the findings in a particular story. While the non-programming reader may not be able to understand or run the code itself, comments and explanations in the document may be capable of reassuring them that appropriate steps were taken to mitigate error.

Take, for instance, a recent *Buzzfeed News* story on children's home inspections in the United Kingdom.[4] The Jupyter Notebook has specific steps to check that data has been correctly filtered (Figure 19.1), providing a backstop against the types of simple but serious mistakes that caught Reinhart and

3   https://buzzfeednews.github.io/2018-07-wildfire-trends/
4   https://www.buzzfeed.com/richholmes/care-price

```
In [11]:   # Make sure that we've identified all private-sector owners
           assert (
               as_at_data_filtered
               .loc[lambda df: df["Sector"] == "Private"]
               ["Owner"].isnull()
               .sum()
           ) == 0
```

Figure 19.1. A cell from the *Buzzfeed* Jupyter notebook with a human readable explanation or comment explaining that its purpose is to check that the filtering of the raw data was performed correctly. Source: Jeremy Singer-Vine, *Buzzfeed*.

Rogoff out.[5] While the exact content of the code may not be comprehensible to the non-technical reader, the presence of these tests and backstops against error with appropriately plain English explanations may go some way to showing that the steps taken to produce the journalist's findings were sound.

More Than Just Reproducibility

Using literate programming environments for data stories does not just help make them more reproducible.

Publishing code can aid collaboration between organizations. In 2016, Global Witness published a web scraper that extracted details on companies and their shareholders from the Papua New Guinea company register.[6] The initial piece of research aimed to identify the key beneficiaries of the corruption-prone trade in tropical timber, which is having a devastating impact on local communities. While Global Witness had no immediate plans to reuse the scraper it developed, the underlying code was published on GitHub—the popular code-sharing website.

Not long after, a community advocacy organization, ACT NOW!, downloaded the code from the scraper, improved it and incorporated it into their iPNG project that lets members of the public cross-check names of company shareholders and directors against other public interest sources.[7] The scraper is now part of the core data infrastructure of the site, retrieving data from the Papua New Guinea company registry twice a year.

Writing code within a literate programming environment can also help to streamline certain internal processes where others within an organization

---

5   https://github.com/BuzzFeedNews/2018-07-ofsted-inspections/blob/master/notebooks/00-analyze-ofsted-data.ipynb

6   https://github.com/Global-Witness/papua-new-guinea-ipa

7   https://pngiportal.org/

need to understand and check an analysis prior to publication. At Global Witness, Jupyter Notebooks have been used to streamline the legal review process. As notebooks set out the steps taken to get a certain finding in a logical order, lawyers can then make a more accurate assessment of the legal risks associated with a particular allegation.

In the context of investigative journalism, one area where this can be particularly important is where assumptions are made around the identity of specific individuals referenced in a data set. As part of our recent work on the state of corporate transparency in the United Kingdom, we wanted to establish which individuals controlled a very large number of companies. This is indicative (although not proof) of them being a so-called "nominee" which in certain contexts—such as when the individual is listed as a Person of Significant Control (PSC)—is illegal. When publishing the list of names of those individuals who controlled the most companies, the legal team wanted to know how we knew a specific individual, let's say John Barry Smith, was the same as another individual named John B. Smith.[8] A Jupyter Notebook was able to clearly capture how we had performed this type of deduplication by presenting a table at the relevant step that set out the fields that were used to assert the identity of individuals.[9] These same processes have been used at Global Witness for fact-checking purposes as well.

Jupyter Notebooks have also proven particularly useful at Global Witness when there is need to monitor a specific data set over time. For instance, in 2018 Global Witness wanted to establish how the corruption risk in the London property market had changed over a two-year period.[10] We acquired a new snapshot from the land registry of properties owned by foreign companies and reused and published a notebook we had developed for the same purpose two years previously.[11] This yielded comparable results with minimal overheads. The notebook has an additional advantage in this context, too: It allowed Global Witness to show its methodology in the absence of being able to republish the underlying source data which, at the time of analysis, had certain licensing restrictions. This is something very difficult to do in a spreadsheet-based workflow. Of course, the most effective

8   https://www.globalwitness.org/en/campaigns/corruption-and-money-laundering/anonymous-company-owners/companies-we-keep/

9   https://github.com/Global-Witness/the-companies-we-keep/blob/master/companies_we_keep_analysis.ipynb

10   https://www.globalwitness.org/en/blog/two-years-still-dark-about-86000-anonymously-owned-uk-homes/

11   https://github.com/Global-Witness/overseas-companies-land-ownership/blob/master/overseas_companies_land_ownership_analysis.ipynb

way of accounting for your method will always be to publish the raw data used. However, journalists often use data that cannot be republished for reasons of copyright, privacy or source protection.

While literate programming environments can clearly enhance the accountability and reproducibility of a journalist's data work, alongside other benefits, there are some important limitations.

One such limitation is that to reproduce (rather than just follow or "virtually witness") an approach set out in a Jupyter Notebook or R Markdown document you need to know how to write, or at least run, code. The relatively nascent state of data journalism means that there is still a fairly small group of journalists, let alone general consumers of journalism, who can code. This means that it is unlikely that the GitHub repositories of newspapers will receive the same level of scrutiny as, say, peer-reviewed code referenced in an academic journal where larger portions of the community can actually interrogate the code itself. Data journalism may, therefore, be more prone to hidden errors in code itself when compared to research with a more technically literate audience. As Jeff Harris (2013) points out, it might not be long before we see programming corrections published alongside traditional reporting corrections. It is worth noting in this context that tools like Workbench (which is also mentioned in Stray's chapter in this book) are starting to be developed for journalists, which promise to deliver some of the functionality of literate programming environments without the need to write or understand any code.[12]

At this point it is also worth considering whether the new mechanisms for accountability in journalism may not just be new means through which a pre-existing "public" can scrutinize methods, but indeed play a role in the formation of new types of "publics." This is a point made by Andrew Barry in his essay "Transparency as a Political Device":

> Transparency implies not just the publication of specific information; it also implies the formation of a society that is in a position to recognize and assess the value of—and if necessary to modify—the information that is made public. The operation of transparency is addressed to local witnesses, yet these witnesses are expected to be properly assembled, and their presence validated. There is thus a circular relation between the constitution of political assemblies and accounts of the oil economy—one brings the other into being. Transparency is not just intended to make information public, but to form a public which is interested in being informed. (Barry, 2010)

12 http://workbenchdata.com/

The methods elaborated on above for accounting for data journalistic work in themselves may play a role in the emergence of new groups of more technically aware publics that wish to scrutinize and hold reporters to account in ways not previously possible before the advent and use of technologies like literate programming environments.

This idea speaks to some of Global Witness' work on data literacy in order to enhance the accountability of the extractives sector. Landmark legislation in the European Union that forces extractives companies to publish project-level payments to governments for oil, gas and mining projects, an area highly vulnerable to corruption, has opened the possibility for far greater scrutiny of where these revenues actually accumulate. However, Global Witness and other advocacy groups within the Publish What You Pay coalition have long observed that there is no pre-existing "public" which could immediately play this role. As a result, Global Witness and others have developed resources and training programmes to assemble journalists and civil society groups in resource-rich countries who can be supported in developing the skills to use this data to more readily hold companies to account. One component of this effort has been the development and publication of specific methodologies for red-flagging suspicious payment reports that could be corrupt.[13]

Literate programming environments are currently a promising means through which data journalists are making their methodologies more transparent and accountable. While data will always remain open to multiple interpretations, technologies that make a reporter's assumptions explicit and their methods reproducible are valuable. They aid collaboration and open up an increasingly technical discipline to scrutiny from various publics. Given the current crisis of trust in journalism, a wider embrace of reproducible approaches may be one important way in which data teams can maintain their credibility.

Works Cited

Barry, A. (2010). Transparency as a political device. In M. Akrich, Y. Barthe, F. Muniesa, & P. Mustar (Eds.), *Débordements: Mélanges offerts à Michel Callon* (pp. 21–39). Presses des Mines. http://books.openedition.org/pressesmines/721

Harris, J. (2013, September 19). *The Times* regrets the programmer error. *Source*. https://source.opennews.org/articles/times-regrets-programmer-error/

13   https://www.globalwitness.org/en/campaigns/oil-gas-and-mining/finding-missing-millions/

Harris, J. (2014, May 22). Distrust your data. *Source*. https://source.opennews.org/articles/distrust-your-data/

Knuth, D. E. (1984). Literate programming. *The Computer Journal*, 27(2), pp. 97–111. https://doi.org/10.1093/comjnl/27.2.97

Knuth, D. E. (1992). *Literate programming*. Center for the Study of Language and Information.

Leather, B. (2017, July 13). Environmental defenders: Who are they and how do we decide if they have died in defence of their environment? *The Guardian*. https://www.theguardian.com/environment/2017/jul/13/environmental-defenders-who-are-they-and-how-do-we-decide-if-they-have-died-in-defence-of-their-environment

Leather, B., & Kyte, B. (2017, July 13). Defenders: Methodology. Global Witness. https://www.globalwitness.org/en/campaigns/environmental-activists/defendersmethodology/

Reinhart, C. M., & Rogoff, K. S. (2010). *Growth in a time of debt* (Working Paper No. 15639). National Bureau of Economic Research. https://doi.org/10.3386/w15639

Shapin, S., & Schaffer, S. (1985). *Leviathan and the air-pump: Hobbes, Boyle, and the experimental life*. Princeton University Press.

About the Author

Sam Leon is Data Investigations Lead at Global Witness, where he researches and campaigns against corruption and environmental destruction.

20. Working Openly in Data Journalism

Natalia Mazotte

Abstract

This chapter examines some examples and benefits of data journalists working more openly, as well as some ways to get started.

Keywords: data journalism, open source, free software, transparency, trust, programming

Many prominent software and web projects—such as Linux, Android, Wikipedia, WordPress and TensorFlow—have been developed collaboratively based on a free flow of knowledge.[1] Stallman (2002), a noted hacker who founded the GNU Project and the Free Software Foundation, says that when he started working at MIT in 1971, sharing software source code was as common as exchanging recipes.

For years such an open approach was unthinkable in journalism. Early in my career as a journalist, I worked with open-source communities in Brazil and began to see openness as the only viable path for journalism. But transparency hasn't been a priority or core value for journalists and media organizations. For much of its modern history, journalism has been undertaken in a paradigm of competition over scarce information.

When access to information is the privilege of a few and when an important finding is only available to eyewitnesses or insiders, ways of ensuring accountability are limited. Citing a document or mentioning an interview source may not require such elaborate transparency mechanisms. In some cases, preserving the secrecy means ensuring the security of the source, and is even desirable. But when information is abundant, not sharing the *how-we-got-there* may deprive the reader of the means to understand and make sense of a story.

---

[1]	This chapter was written by Natalia Mazotte with contributions from Marco Túlio Pires.

Bounegru, L. and J. Gray (eds.), *The Data Journalism Handbook: Towards a Critical Data Practice.*
Amsterdam: Amsterdam University Press, 2021
DOI 10.5117/9789462989511_CH20

As journalists both report on and rely on data and algorithms, might they adopt an ethos which is similar to that of open-source communities? What are the advantages of journalists who adopt emerging digital practices and values associated with these communities? This chapter examines some examples and benefits of data journalists working more openly, as well as some ways to get started.[2]

Examples and Benefits of Openness

The Washington Post provided an unprecedented look at the prescription opioid epidemic in the United States by digging into a database on the sales of millions of painkillers.[3] They also made the data set and its methodology publicly accessible. This enabled local reporters from over 30 states to publish more than 90 articles about the impact of this crisis in their communities (Sánchez Díez, 2019).[4]

Two computational journalists analyzed Uber's surge pricing algorithm and revealed that the company seems to offer better service in areas with more White people (Stark & Diakopoulos, 2016). The story was published by *The Washington Post*, and the data collection and analysis code used were made freely available on GitHub, an online platform that helps developers store and manage their code.[5] This meant that a reader who was looking at the database and encountered an error was able to report this to the authors of the article, who were in turn able to fix the bug and correct the story.

Gênero e Número (Gender and number), a Brazilian digital magazine I co-founded, ran a project to classify more than 800,000 street names to understand the lack of female representation in Brazilian public spaces. We did this by running a Python script to cross-reference street names with a database of names from the Brazilian National Statistical office (Mazotte & Justen, 2017). The same script was subsequently used by other initiatives to classify data sets that did not contain gender information—such as lists of electoral candidates and magistrates (Justen, 2019).

Working openly and making various data sets, tools, code, methods and processes transparent and available can potentially help data journalists in a

---

2   For more on data journalism and open-source, see also chapters by Leon, Baack, and Pitts and Muscato in this book.

3   https://www.washingtonpost.com/national/2019/07/20/opioid-files/

4   https://www.washingtonpost.com/national/2019/08/12/post-released-deas-data-pain-pills-heres-what-local-journalists-are-using-it/

5   https://github.com/comp-journalism/2016-03-wapo-uber

number of ways. Firstly, it can help them to improve the quality of their work. Documenting processes can encourage journalists to be more organized, more accurate and less likely to miss errors. It can also lighten the burden of editing and reviewing complex stories, enabling readers to report issues. Secondly, it can broaden reach and impact. A story that can be built upon can gain different perspectives and serve different communities. Projects can take on a life of their own, no longer limited by the initial scope and constraints of their creators. And thirdly, it can foster data literacy amongst journalists and broader publics. Step-by-step accounts of your work mean that others can follow and learn—which can enrich and diversify data ecosystems, practices and communities.

In the so-called "post-truth" era there is also potential to increase public trust in the media, which has reached a new low according to the 2018 Edelman Trust Barometer.[6] Working openly could help decelerate or even reverse this trend. This can include journalists talking more openly about how they reach their conclusions and providing more detailed "how tos," in order to be honest about their biases and uncertainties, as well as to enable conversations with their audiences.[7]

As a caveat, practices and cultures of working openly and transparently in data journalism are an ongoing process of exploration and experimentation. Even as we advance our understanding of potential benefits, consideration is needed to understand when transparency is valuable, or might be less of a priority, or might even be harmful. For example, sometimes it's important to keep data and techniques confidential in order to protect the integrity of the investigation itself, as happened in the case of the Panama Papers.

Ways of Working Openly

If there are no impediments (and this should be analyzed on a case-by-case basis) then one common approach to transparency is through the methodology section, also known as the "nerd box." This can come in a variety of formats and lengths, depending on the complexity of the process and the intended audience.

---

6   https://www.edelman.com/research/2018-edelman-trust-barometer; https://www.edelman.com/sites/g/files/aatuss191/files/2018-10/2018_Edelman_Trust_Barometer_Global_Report_FEB.pdf

7   For more on issues around uncertainty in data journalism, see Anderson's chapter in this volume.

If your intention is to reach a wider audience, a box inside the article or even a footnote with a succinct explanation of your methods may be sufficient. Some publications opt to publish stand-alone articles explaining how they reported the story. In either case, it is important to avoid jargon, explain how data was obtained and used, ensure readers don't miss important caveats, and explain in the most clear and direct way how you reached your conclusion.

Many media outlets renowned for their work on data journalism—such as *FiveThirtyEight, ProPublica, The New York Times* and the *Los Angeles Times*—have repositories on code-sharing platforms such as GitHub. The *Buzzfeed News* team even has an index of all its open-source data, analysis, libraries, tools and guides.[8] They release not only the methodology behind their reporting, but also the scripts used to extract, clean, analyze and present data. This practice makes their work reproducible (as discussed further in Leon's chapter in this volume) as well as enabling interested readers to explore the data for themselves. As scientists have done for centuries, these journalists are inviting their peers to check their work and see if they can arrive at the same conclusions by following the documented steps.

It is not simple for many newsrooms to incorporate these levels of documentation and collaboration into their work. In the face of dwindling resources and shrinking teams, journalists who are keen to document their investigations can be discouraged by their organizations. This brings us to the constraints that journalists face: Many news organizations are fighting for their lives, as their role in the world and their business models are changing. In spite of these challenges, embracing some of the practices of free and open-source communities can be a way to stand out, as a marker of innovation and as a way of building trust and relationships with audiences in an increasingly complex and fast-changing world.

Works Cited

Justen, A. (2019, May 31). Classificando nomes por gênero usando dados públicos | Brasil.IO—Blog. *Brasil.IO*. https://blog.brasil.io/2019/05/31/classificando-nomes-por-genero-usando-dados-publicos/

Mazotte, N., & Justen, A. (2017, April 5). Como classificamos mais de 800 mil logradouros brasileiros por gênero. *Gênero e Número*. http://www.generonumero.media/como-classificamos-mais-de-800-mil-logradouros-brasileiros-por-genero/

8   https://github.com/BuzzFeedNews/everything#guides

Sánchez Díez, M. (2019, November 26). *The Post* released the DEA's data on pain pills. Here's what local journalists are using it for. *The Washington Post*. https://www.washingtonpost.com/national/2019/08/12/post-released-deas-data-pain-pills-heres-what-local-journalists-are-using-it/

Stallman, R. M. (2002). *Free software, free society: Selected essays of Richard M. Stallman* (J. Gay, Ed.). GNU Press.

Stark, J., & Diakopoulos, N. (2016, March 10). Uber seems to offer better service in areas with more White people. That raises some tough questions. *The Washington Post*. https://www.washingtonpost.com/news/wonk/wp/2016/03/10/uber-seems-to-offer-better-service-in-areas-with-more-white-people-that-raises-some-tough-questions/

About the Author

Natalia Mazotte is a Brazilian data journalist and entrepreneur. She co-founded the news start-up *Gênero e Número* and the School of Data Brazil.

21. Making Algorithms Work for Reporting

Jonathan Stray

Abstract

Sophisticated data analysis algorithms can greatly benefit investigative reporting, but most of the work is getting and cleaning data.

Keywords: algorithms, machine learning, computational journalism, data journalism, investigative journalism, data cleaning

The dirty secret of computational journalism is that the "algorithmic" part of a story is not the part that takes all of the time and effort.

Don't misunderstand me: Sophisticated algorithms can be extraordinarily useful in reporting, especially investigative reporting. Machine learning (training computers to find patterns) has been used to find key documents in huge volumes of data. Natural language processing (training computers to understand language) can extract the names of people and companies from documents, giving reporters a shortcut to understanding who's involved in a story. And journalists have used a variety of statistical analyses to detect wrongdoing or bias.

But actually running an algorithm is the easy part. Getting the data, cleaning it and following up algorithmic leads is the hard part.

To illustrate this, let's take a success for machine learning in investigative journalism, *The Atlanta Journal-Constitution*'s remarkable story on sex abuse by doctors, "License to Betray" (Teegardin et al., 2016). Reporters analyzed over 100,000 doctor disciplinary records from every US state, and found 2,400 cases where doctors who had sexually abused patients were allowed to continue to practice. Rather than reading every report, they first drastically reduced this pile by applying machine learning to find reports that were likely to concern sexual abuse. They were able to cut down their

Bounegru, L. and J. Gray (eds.), *The Data Journalism Handbook: Towards a Critical Data Practice.* Amsterdam: Amsterdam University Press, 2021

DOI 10.5117/9789462989511_CH21

pile more than 10 times, to just 6,000 documents, which they then read and reviewed manually.

This could not have been a national story without machine learning, according to reporter Jeff Ernsthausen. "Maybe there's a chance we would have made it a regional story," he said later (Diakopoulos, 2019).

This is as good a win for algorithms in journalism as we've yet seen, and this technique could be used far more widely. But the machine learning itself is not the hard part. The method that Ernsthausen used, "logistic regression," is a standard statistical approach to classifying documents based on which words they contain. It can be implemented in scarcely a dozen lines of Python, and there are many good tutorials online.

For most stories, most of the work is in setting things up and then exploiting the results. Data must be scraped, cleaned, formatted, loaded, checked, and corrected—endlessly prepared. And the results of algorithmic analysis are often only leads or hints, which only become a story after large amounts of very manual reporting, often by teams of reporters who need collaboration tools rather than analysis tools. This is the unglamorous part of data work, so we don't teach it very well or talk about it much. Yet it's this preparation and follow-up that takes most of the time and effort on a data-driven story.

For "License to Betray," just getting the data was a huge challenge. There is no national database of doctor disciplinary reports, just a series of state-level databases. Many of these databases do not contain a field indicating why a doctor was disciplined. Where there is a field, it often doesn't reliably code for sexual abuse. At first, the team tried to get the reports through freedom of information requests. This proved to be prohibitively expensive, with some states asking for thousands of dollars to provide the data. So, the team turned to scraping documents from state medical board websites (Ernsthausen, 2017). These documents had to be OCR'd (turned into text) and loaded into a custom web-based application for collaborative tagging and review.

Then the reporters had to manually tag several hundred documents to produce training data. After machine learning ranked the remaining 100,000, it took several more months to manually read the 6,000 documents that were predicted to be about sex abuse, plus thousands of other documents containing manually picked key words. And then, of course, there was the rest of the reporting, such as the investigation of hundreds of specific cases to flesh out the story. This relied on other sources, such as previous news stories and, of course, personal interviews with the people involved.

The use of an algorithm—machine learning—was a key, critical part of the investigation. But it was only a tiny amount of the time and effort spent. Surveys of data scientists consistently show that most of their work is data "wrangling" and cleaning—often up to 80%—and journalism is no different (Lohr, 2014).

Algorithms are often seen as a sort of magic ingredient. They may seem complex or opaque, yet they are unarguably powerful. This magic is a lot more fun to talk about than the mundane work of preparing data or following up a long list of leads. Technologists like to hype their technology, not the equally essential work that happens around it, and this bias for new and sophisticated tools sometimes carries over into journalism. We should teach and exploit technological advances, certainly, but our primary responsibility is to get journalism done, and that means grappling with the rest of the data pipeline, too.

In general, we underappreciate the tools used for data preparation. OpenRefine is a long-standing hero for all sorts of cleaning tasks. Dedupe. io is machine learning applied to the problem of merging near-duplicate names in a database. Classic text-wrangling methods like regular expressions should be a part of every data journalist's education. In this vein, my current project, Workbench, is focused on the time-consuming but mostly invisible work of preparing data for reporting—everything that happens before the "algorithm." It thus aims to make the whole process more collaborative, so reporters can work together on large data projects and learn from each other's work, including with machines.

Algorithms are important to reporting, but to make them work, we have to talk about all of the other parts of data-driven journalism. We need to enable the whole workflow, not just the especially glamorous, high-tech parts.

Works Cited

Diakopoulos, N. (2019). *Automating the news: How algorithms are rewriting the media*. Harvard University Press.

Ernsthausen, J. (2017). Doctors and sex abuse. NICAR 2017, Jacksonville. https://docs.google.com/presentation/d/1keGeDk_wpBPQgUOOhbRarPPFbyCculTOb-GLeAhOMmEM/edit?usp=embed_facebook

Lohr, S. (2014, August 17). For big-data scientists, "janitor work" is key hurdle to insights. *The New York Times*. https://www.nytimes.com/2014/08/18/technology/for-big-data-scientists-hurdle-to-insights-is-janitor-work.html

Teegardin, C., Robbins, D., Ernsthausen, J., & Hart, A. (2016, July 5). License to betray. *The Atlanta Journal-Constitution*, Doctors & Sex Abuse. http://doctors.ajc.com/doctors_sex_abuse/?ecmp=doctorssexabuse_microsite_nav

About the Author

Jonathan Stray, a Research Fellow at Partnership on AI, previously taught the dual masters degree in Computer Science and Journalism at Columbia University and built software for investigative journalism.

22. Journalism With Machines? From Computational Thinking to Distributed Cognition

Eddy Borges-Rey

Abstract

This chapter reflects on the ways news automation increasingly distributes journalistic knowledge and thought processes.

Keywords: automated journalism, distributed cognition, computational thinking, extended mind, databases, machine learning

Imagine you are a journalist in the not so distant future. You are working on a story, and in order to get the insight you are looking for, you ask your conversational agent (who you affectionately call Twiki) to stitch together over 15 anonymized databases. Given the magnitude and complexity of the fused data sets, visualization software is too rudimentary to isolate the anomalies you are searching for. So, using your brain implant, you plug into the system and easily navigate the abstraction of the data sets. Although, individually, each redacted data set is effective in protecting the identity and the personal data of the people listed, when combined, you are able to infer the identity of some top-profile individuals and put into context their personal data. Realizing the potential legal implications of revealing the names and the data attached to them, you ask Twiki to run a neural network to determine whether disclosing this information has ethical or legal implications. The network runs a "n+" number of simulations of virtual journalists making decisions based on a number of codes of ethics and regulatory frameworks. Whilst this runs in the background, you manage to isolate a few outliers and identify a couple of interesting trends. Since you want to make sure the anomalies have something to add to the story, and are

Bounegru, L. and J. Gray (eds.), *The Data Journalism Handbook: Towards a Critical Data Practice.* Amsterdam: Amsterdam University Press, 2021
DOI 10.5117/9789462989511_CH22

not simply errors, you ask Twiki to check through archival historic records to see if the outliers coincide with any major historical event. In addition, you ask Twiki to run a predictive model to calculate the likelihood that the identified trends will persist for the foreseeable future, thus triggering worrying implications.

This brief, fictional introduction is based on a fascinating conversation I had with former *Times* data journalist Nicola Hughes a few years ago. Although the scene it describes could well have come out of Philip K. Dick's "The Minority Report," it actually refers to a range of tools and techniques that are either already available and widely used, or in rapid development. More importantly, it also refers to a kind of journalistic workflow and professional mindset emerging in newsrooms, in a world where journalists are increasingly engaging with data and computation is becoming indispensable.

These recent changes reflect how historically, every time a major technological innovation has been introduced into the news production workflow, news reporting itself has not only been disrupted and consequently transformed, but journalists' thought processes and working professional ideals have invariably been modified.

Today, as we move beyond the era of big data to the era of artificial intelligence (AI) and automation, principles and working practices that hail from computing and data science become ever more pervasive in journalism. As Emily Bell, Founding Director of the Tow Center for Digital Journalism at Columbia University, puts it:

> Every company in every field, and every organization, whether they are corporate or public sector, will have to think about how they reorient themselves around AI in exactly the same way that 20 years ago they had to think about the way they reoriented themselves around web technologies. (Bell, personal communication, September 7, 2017)

In this context, this chapter reflects on the ways journalists who work closely with data and automated processes internalize a range of computing principles, that on the one hand augment their journalistic abilities, and on the other have begun to modify the very cornerstone of their journalistic approaches and ideals.

The chapter, thus, explores a range of theoretical concepts that could serve as a framework to envision journalistic cognition in an environment of pervasive computation. I adopt the notion of extended cognition to stimulate further discussion on the ways in which journalistic cognition is nowadays dependent on (and therefore distributed across) the machines used to report the news. Through this discussion I hope to encourage future work to investigate the role of computation in journalistic situations, including empirical work to test and further specify the concept of distributed journalistic cognition. This line of inquiry could be particularly useful for professional journalists who want to be aware of, and engage with, the changes journalism is likely to experience if datafication and automation become ubiquitous in news production.

Computational Thinking

In an attempt to trace the historical meaning of the concept of computation, Denning and Martell (2015) suggest that "[c]omputation was taken to be the mechanical steps followed to evaluate mathematical functions [and] computers were people who did computations." In the 1980s, however, the concept was more frequently associated with a new way of doing science, thus shifting its emphasis from machines to information processes (Denning & Martell, 2015).

This shift in emphasis is critical for my argument, as it aligns the ultimate goals of news reporting and computation: Journalism is also about managing information processes—in very general terms, the journalist's job consists of streamlining the flow of information, curating it and packaging it in a format that is palatable to an audience. Here, I would argue that the pervasiveness of a computational mindset in news reporting is partially due to the similarities that exist between both professional practices.

Both computing and journalism are formulaic, about solving problems and require syntactical mastery. Wing (2008) remarks that "[o]perationally, computing is concerned with answering 'How would I get a computer to solve this problem?'" (p. 3719), and this requires a relatively high level of computational thinking. As computation becomes a norm in newsrooms, computational thinking is employed by an increasing number of journalists to approach data stories. Bradshaw, for instance, argues that computational thinking "is at the heart of a data journalist's work," enabling them "to solve the problems that make up so much of modern journalism, and to be able to do so with the speed and accuracy that news processes demand" (Bradshaw, 2017).

Computational thinking is the reflexive process through which a set of programmatic steps are taken to solve a problem (Bradshaw, 2017; Wing, 2006, 2008). Wing contends that "the essence of computational thinking is abstraction" and that "in computing, we abstract notions beyond the physical dimensions of time and space" (Wing, 2008, p. 3717) to solve problems, design systems and understand human behaviour (Wing, 2006). The author argues that in order to answer the question "How would I get a computer to solve this problem?" computing professionals have to identify appropriate abstractions (Wing, 2008, p. 3717) which are suitable for designing and implementing a programmatic plan to solve the problem at hand.

Since the introduction of automation technologies in newsrooms, journalists working with computing professionals have faced a similar question: "How would I get a computer to investigate or write a news story to human standards?" Gynnild proposes that the infusion of computational thinking into professional journalism challenges the "fundamental thought system in journalism from descriptive storytelling to abstract reasoning, autonomous research and visualization of quantitative facts" that equips journalists with "complementary, logical and algorithmic skills, attitudes, and values" (Gynnild, 2014).

Of course, this is not to say that the idea of "computational" abstraction is a new one to journalists. In fact, journalists working on beats like finance, business, real estate or education exert abstraction on a daily basis to understand complex dynamics such as market performance, stock returns, household net worth, etc. And interestingly, as Myles (2019) remarks, contrary to expectations that automation would free up journalists from onerous tasks, it has introduced a range of new editorial activities not previously performed by journalists. For instance, he explains that the introduction of image recognition into the workflow of the Associated Press has seen journalists and photographers having to engage with tasks traditionally associated with machine learning, like labelling of training data, evaluation of test results, correcting metadata or generating definitions for concepts (Myles, 2019).

Cognitive Projection and Extended Creativity

So far, I have argued that journalists who, as part of their job, have to engage with the computational problems introduced by news automation, see their workflows and editorial responsibilities transformed. *The Wall Street Journal*, for instance, recently advertised for positions such as Machine Learning Journalist, Automation Editor and Emerging Processes Editor, all associated with the expansion of AI and automation. As a result of these kinds of infrastructural expansions, and the subsequent diversification of editorial responsibilities prompted by them, journalists often find themselves asking questions that project them into the shoes of a machine that has to think and perform like a journalist. An interesting paradox, which brings equally interesting challenges.

This idea of projection, I believe, is becoming prevalent in news automation. Take, for instance, the quintessential journalistic endeavour: Writing a news story. If we deconstruct the process, in general terms, journalists have to use their creativity to put together an account of events that engages and/ or informs the public. The question, then, is: How do I get a machine to write news that reads as if it were written by a human reporter? Journalists and technologists have collaborated over the last five years to project themselves, in an attempt to solve this question. A good example, on this front, is the implementation of natural language generation (NLG) technologies to automate the production of news stories. But counter to what we could expect, the process still involves human reporters writing templates of news stories, which contain blank spaces that are subsequently filled in by automation software using a database. This process, which has been quite successful in news organizations such as the Associated Press, and in RADAR, a collaboration between the Press Association and Urbs Media, seeks to augment the speed and scale of the news production operation in areas such as sports, company earnings and local news.

Creativity within this realm takes a new form, in which coder-journos have had to rethink storytelling as a machine that decodes and recodes the news-writing process. Instead of discerning which interview would better substantiate an argument or what words would make for a stronger headline, the goal has shifted to choosing which configuration of conditional statements would be more efficient in making the automated system decide which headline would appeal more effectively to the audience of the news organization where it functions. Following the principles of human–computer interaction (HCI) and user experience (UX) design, coder-journos have to anticipate the ways users want to engage with automated informational experiences, the potential ways in which they will navigate the different layers of information and the confines of the news piece. Wheeler (2018), conceptualizing the notion of extended creativity, explains that there are cases of intellectual creation in which "the material vehicles that realize the thinking and thoughts concerned are spatially distributed over brain, body and world." The concept of extended creativity then works well as a framework to explicate the idea that the mind of a journalist working with data and automation now functions in close connection with a series of automations, spanning into a series of Python libraries, Jupyter Notebooks, data sets, data analytics tools and online platforms. This dynamic consequently brings a series of additional challenges worthy of attention.

For example, Mevan Babakar, head of automated fact-checking at Full Fact, explains that one of the challenges they face with their automated fact-checker is context. She uses as an example the claim of former UK prime minister Theresa May that her government allocated more resources to the National Health Service (NHS) than the opposition Labour Party promised in their manifesto. And although the claim was fact-checked as accurate, for it to be meaningful and useful to the public, it needs to be understood within a wider context: The allocation was not enough for the NHS to perform efficiently (Babakar, personal communication, August 16, 2018). Therefore, as automated systems are not yet capable of making such contextual connections between sources of information, Babakar and her team have to resort to questions like "How do I get an automated fact-checker to understand the nuances of context?"

Journalistic Distributed Cognition

To conclude, I would like to further explore the idea of a journalistic distributed cognition and the questions it raises. Anderson, Wheeler and Sprevak (2018) argue that as computers become pervasive in human activity, cognition "spread[s] out over the brain, the non-neural body and . . . an environment consisting of objects, tools, other artefacts, texts, individuals, groups and/or social/institutional structures." In journalism, this means that, at present, as journalists use networked software and hardware to augment their capacity to produce news at scale and speed, their cognition becomes distributed across the range of platforms and tools they use. This of course, provides them with unlimited access to most of human knowledge online.

However, this idea of portable knowledge and distributed cognition begs the question of who owns and manages journalists' access to that wealth of knowledge and "free" analytical power. Who enables journalistic distributed cognition? This issue, worthy of deeper discussion, is a thorny one, as we experienced when Google shut down its online data visualization tool Google Fusion Tables. After the closure of the platform, dozens of data journalism projects that had been developed with the tool became unavailable as they were no longer supported by the company.

In this context, as journalists engage with computational dynamics on a daily basis, their computational thinking becomes normalized and facilitates the projection of their cognition into the machines they employ for their daily journalistic routines. As journalistic knowledge becomes distributed, does the same happen to journalistic authority and control? Inexorably, distribution shifts the boundaries that provide journalists with control over their routines and professional cultures, thus impacting on their epistemological authority. Looking ahead, as we did in this chapter's fictional introduction, distribution could also create an array of associated risks, once journalists begin to delegate important ethical considerations and decisions to machines. It is important then, that the infrastructure they use to distribute their cognition is open, and available for public scrutiny, if the cornerstone ideals of journalism are to be preserved in the age of data and automation.

Works Cited

Anderson, M., Wheeler, M., & Sprevak, M. (2018). Distributed cognition and the humanities. In M. Anderson, D. Cairns, & M. Sprevak (Eds.), *Distributed cognition in classical antiquity* (pp. 1–17). Edinburgh University Press.

Bradshaw, P. (2017). Computational thinking and the next wave of data journalism. *Online Journalism Blog.* https://onlinejournalismblog.com/2017/08/03/computational-thinking-data-journalism/

Denning, P. J., & Martell, C. H. (2015). *Great principles of computing.* The MIT Press.

Gynnild, A. (2014). Journalism innovation leads to innovation journalism: The impact of computational exploration on changing mindsets. *Journalism, 15*(6), 713–730. https://doi.org/10.1177/1464884913486393

Myles, S. (2019, February 1). *Photomation or fauxtomation? Automation in the newsroom and the impact on editorial labour: A case study.* [Technology]. Computation + Journalism Symposium 2019, University of Miami.

Wheeler, M. (2018). Talking about more than heads: The embodied, embedded and extended creative mind. In B. Gaut & M. Kieran (Eds.), *Creativity and philosophy* (pp. 230–250). Routledge. http://dspace.stir.ac.uk/handle/1893/26296

Wing, J. M. (2006). Computational thinking. *Communications of the ACM, 49,* 33–35. https://doi.org/10.1145/1118178.1118215

Wing, J. M. (2008). Computational thinking and thinking about computing. *Philosophical Transactions of the Royal Society A: Mathematical, Physical and Engineering Sciences, 366*(1881), 3717–3725. https://doi.org/10.1098/rsta.2008.0118

About the Author

Eddy Borges-Rey is an Associate Professor in Digital Journalism and Emerging Media at Northwestern University in Qatar, and a former broadcast journalist.

Experiencing Data

23. Ways of Doing Data Journalism

Sarah Cohen

Abstract
This chapter explores the various ways that data journalism has evolved and the different forms it takes, from traditional investigative reporting to news apps and visualizations.

Keywords: investigative journalism, news applications, data visualization, explanatory journalism, precision journalism

data (*dey-tah*)**:** a body of facts or information; individual facts, statistics or items of information ("Data," n.d.)
journalism: the occupation of reporting, writing, editing, photographing, or broadcasting news or of conducting any news organization as a business ("Journalism," n.d.)

If you're reading this handbook, you've decided that you want to learn a little about the trade that's become known as data journalism. But what, exactly, does that mean in an age of open data portals, dazzling visualizations and freedom of information battles around the world?

A dictionary definition of the two words doesn't help much—put together, it suggests that data journalism is an occupation of producing news made up of facts or information. Data journalism has come to mean virtually any act of journalism that touches electronically held records and statistics—in other words, virtually all of journalism.

That's why a lot of the people in the field don't think of themselves as data journalists—they're more likely to consider themselves explanatory writers, graphic or visual journalists, reporters, audience analysts, or news application developers—all more precise names for the many tribes of this growing field. That's not enough, so add in anything in a newsroom that requires the use

Bounegru, L. and J. Gray (eds.), *The Data Journalism Handbook: Towards a Critical Data Practice*. Amsterdam: Amsterdam University Press, 2021
DOI 10.5117/9789462989511_CH23

of numbers, or anything that requires computer programming. What was once a garage band has now grown big enough to make up an orchestra.

Data journalism is not very new. In fact, if you think of "data" as some sort of systematic collection, then some of the earliest data journalism in the United States dates back to the mid-1800s, when Frank Leslie, publisher of *Frank Leslie's Illustrated Newspaper*, hired detectives to follow dairy carts around New York City to document mislabelled and contaminated milk. Scott Klein (2016), a managing editor for the non-profit investigative site *ProPublica*, has documented a fascinating history of data journalism also dating to the 1800s, in which newspapers taught readers how to understand a bar chart. Chris Anderson also explores different genealogies of data journalism in the 1910s, 1960s and 2010s in his chapter in this volume.

With these histories, taxonomies of different branches of data journalism can help students and practitioners clarify their career preferences and the skills needed to make them successful. These different ways of doing data journalism are presented here in an approximate chronology of the development of the field.

Empirical Journalism, or Data in Service of Stories

Maurice Tamman of Reuters coined the term "empirical journalism" as a way to combine two data journalism traditions. Precision journalism, developed in the 1960s by Philip Meyer, sought to use social science methods in stories. His work ranged from conducting a survey of rioters in Detroit to directing the data collection and analysis of an investigation into racial bias in Philadelphia courts. He laid the groundwork for investigations for a generation. Empirical journalism can also encompass what became known as computer-assisted reporting in the 1990s, a genre led by Eliot Jaspin in Providence, Rhode Island. In this branch, reporters seek out documentary evidence in electronic form—or create it when they must—to investigate a tip or a story idea.

More recently, these reporters have begun using artificial intelligence and machine learning to assist in finding or simplifying story development. They can be used to help answer simple questions, such as the sex of a patient harmed by medical devices when the government tried to hide that detail. Or they can be used to identify difficult patterns, such Peter Aldhous' analysis of spy planes for *Buzzfeed* (Aldhous, 2017; Woodman, 2019).

These reporters are almost pure newsgatherers—their goal is not to produce a visualization nor to tell stories with data. Instead, they use records to explore a potential story. Their work is integral to the reporting project, often driving the development of an investigation. They are usually less involved in the presentation aspects of a story.

Arguably the newest entry into this world of "data journalism" could be the growing impact of visual and open-source investigations worldwide. This genre, which derives from intelligence and human rights research, expands our notion of "data" into videos, crowdsourced social media and other digital artefacts. While it's less dependent on coding, it fits solidly in the tradition of data journalism by uncovering—through original research—what others would like to hold secret.

One of the most famous examples, *Anatomy of a Killing* from BBC's Africa Eye documentary strand, uncovers where, precisely, the assassination of a family occurred in Cameroon, when it happened, and helps identify who was involved—after the Cameroonian government denied it as "fake news" (BBC News, 2018). The team used tools ranging from Google Earth to identify the outline of a mountain ridge to Facebook for documenting the clothing worn by the killers.

Data Visualization

Looking at the winners of the international Data Journalism Awards would lead a reader to think that visualization is the key to any data journalism.[1] If statistics are currency, visualization is the price of admission to the club.

Visualizations can be an important part of a data journalist's toolbox. But they require a toolkit that comes from the design and art world as much as the data, statistics and reporting worlds. Alberto Cairo, one of the most famous visual journalists working in academia today, came from the infographics world of magazines and newspapers. His work focuses on telling stories through visualization—a storytelling role as much as a newsgathering one.

News Applications

At *ProPublica*, most major investigations start or end with a news application—a site or feature that provides access to local or individual data through an engaging and insightful interface. *ProPublica* has become known for its news apps, and engineers who began their careers in coding have evolved into journalists who use code, rather than words, to tell stories.

---

[1]   See Loosen's chapter in this volume.

ProPublica's Ken Schwenke, a developer by training who has worked in newsrooms including the *Los Angeles Times* and *The New York Times*, became one of the nation's leading journalists covering hate crimes in the United States as part of the site's Documenting Hate project, which revolved around stories crowdsourced through *ProPublica*'s news application.

Data Stories

The term "data journalism" came of age as reporters, statisticians and other experts began writing about data as a form of journalism in itself. Simon Rogers, the creator of *The Guardian*'s Datablog, popularized the genre. *FiveThirtyEight*, *Vox* and, later, *The New York Times*' Upshot became this branch's standard bearers. Each viewed their role a little differently, but they converged on the idea that statistics and analysis are newsworthy on their own.

Some became best known for their political forecasts, placing odds on US presidential races. Others became known for finding quirky data sets that provide a glimpse into the public's psyche. One example of this is the 2014 map of baseball preferences derived from Facebook preferences in the US Table stakes. The entry point for this genre is a data set, and expertise in a subject matter is the way these practitioners distinguish themselves from the rest of the field. In fact, Nate Silver and others who defined this genre came not from a journalism background, but from the worlds of statistics and political science.

Amanda Cox, the editor of *The New York Times*' Upshot, has said she sees the site's role as occupying the space between known hard facts and the unknowable—journalism that provides insight from expert analysis of available data that rides the border between pure fact and pure opinion (Cox, personal communication, n.d.).

Investigating Algorithms

An emerging field of data journalism is really journalism about technology—the "algorithmic accountability" field, a term coined by Nicholas Diakopoulos at Northwestern University.[2] Reporters Julia Angwin and Jeff Larson left *ProPublica* to pursue this specialty by founding The Markup, a

2   For more on this field, see Diakopoulos' and Elmer's chapters in this book.

site that Angwin says will hold technology companies accountable for the results that their machine learning and artificial intelligence algorithms create in our society, from decisions on jail sentences to the prices charged based on a consumer's zip code.

This reporting has already prompted YouTube to review its recommendation engines to reduce its tendency to move viewers into increasingly violent videos. It has held Facebook to account for its potentially discriminatory housing ads, and has identified price discrimination in online stores based on a user's location (Dwoskin, 2019).

Works Cited

Aldhous, P. (2017, August 8). We trained a computer to search for hidden spy planes. This is what it found. *BuzzFeed News*. https://www.buzzfeednews.com/article/peteraldhous/hidden-spy-planes

BBC News. (2018, September 23). *Anatomy of a killing*. BBC Africa Eye. https://www.youtube.com/watch?v=4G9S-eoLgX4

Data. (n.d.). In *Dictionary.com*. Retrieved May 20, 2020, from https://www.dictionary.com/browse/data

Dwoskin, E. (2019, January 25). YouTube is changing its algorithms to stop recommending conspiracies. *The Washington Post*. https://www.washingtonpost.com/technology/2019/01/25/youtube-is-changing-its-algorithms-stop-recommending-conspiracies/

Journalism. (n.d.). In *Dictionary.com*. Retrieved May 20, 2020, from https://www.dictionary.com/browse/journalism

Klein, S. (2016, March 16). Infographics in the time of cholera. *ProPublica*. https://www.propublica.org/nerds/infographics-in-the-time-of-cholera

Woodman, S. (2019, October 22). Using the power of machines to complete impossible reporting tasks. ICIJ. https://www.icij.org/blog/2019/10/using-the-power-of-machines-to-complete-impossible-reporting-tasks/

About the Author

Sarah Cohen is the Knight Chair in Journalism at the Walter Cronkite School of Journalism and previously worked as the editor of a data journalism team at *The New York Times*.

24. Data Visualizations: Newsroom Trends and Everyday Engagements

Helen Kennedy, William Allen, Martin Engebretsen,
Rosemary Lucy Hill, Andy Kirk and Wibke Weber

Abstract
This chapter looks at the production of data visualizations (dataviz) in newsrooms and audiences' everyday engagements with them.

Keywords: data visualization, audience engagement, newsrooms, dataviz, storytelling, data publics

This chapter looks at both the production of data visualizations (henceforth "dataviz") in newsrooms and audiences' everyday engagements with dataviz, drawing on two separate research projects. The first is Seeing Data, which explored how people make sense of data visualizations, and the second is INDVIL, which explored dataviz as a semiotic, aesthetic and discursive resource in society.[1] The chapter starts by summarizing the main findings of an INDVIL sub-project focusing on dataviz in the news, in which we found that dataviz are perceived in diverse ways and deployed for diverse purposes. It then summarizes our main findings from Seeing Data,[2] where we also found great diversity, this time in how audiences make sense of dataviz. This diversity is important for the future work of both dataviz researchers and practitioners.

---

1   http://seeingdata.org/, https://indvil.org/
2   The second half of the chapter summarizes a longer article available online: Kennedy, H., Hill, R. L., Allen, W., & Kirk, A. (2016). Engaging with (big) data visualizations: Factors that affect engagement and resulting new definitions of effectiveness. *First Monday, 21*(11). https://doi.org/10.5210/fm.v21i11.6389

Bounegru, L. and J. Gray (eds.), *The Data Journalism Handbook: Towards a Critical Data Practice.* Amsterdam: Amsterdam University Press, 2021
DOI 10.5117/9789462989511_CH24

Data Visualization in Newsrooms: Trends and Challenges

How is data visualization being embedded into newsroom practice? What trends are emerging, and what challenges are arising? To answer these questions, in 2016 and 2017 we undertook 60 interviews in 26 newsrooms across six European countries: Norway (NO), Sweden (SE), Denmark (DK), Germany (DE), Switzerland (CH) and the United Kingdom (UK). Interviewees in mainstream, online news media organizations included editorial leaders, leaders of specialist data visualization teams, data journalists, visual journalists, graphic/data visualization designers and developers (although some didn't have job titles, a sign in itself that this is a rapidly emerging field). We present some highlights from our research here.

Changing Journalistic Storytelling

The growing use of data visualization within journalism means that there is a shift from writing as the main semiotic mode to data and visualization as central elements in journalistic storytelling. Many interviewees stated that data visualization is the driving force of a story, even when it is a simple graphic or diagram.

> The reader stats tell us that when we insert a simple data visualization in a story, readers stay on the page a little longer. (SE)

Dataviz are used with a broad range of communicative intentions, including: "to offer insight" (UK), "to explain more easily" (SE), "to communicate clearly, more clearly than words can" (UK), "to tell several facets in detail, which in text is only possible in an aggregated form" (DE), to make stories "more accessible" (DK), "to reveal deplorable states of affairs" (CH), "to help people understand the world" (UK). Data visualization is used to emphasize a point, to add empirical evidence, to enable users to explore data sets, as aesthetic attraction to stimulate interest and to offer entry into unseen stories.

These changes are accompanied by the emergence of multiskilled specialist groups within newsrooms, with data and dataviz skills prioritized in new recruits. But there are no patterns in the organization of dataviz production within newsrooms—in some, it happens in data teams, in others, in visual teams (one of our dataviz designer interviewees was also working on a virtual reality project at the time of the interview) and elsewhere, in different teams still. And just as new structures are emerging to accommodate this newly proliferating visual form, so too newsroom staff need to adapt to learn new tools, in-house and commercial, develop new skills, and understand how to communicate across teams and areas of expertise in order to produce effective data stories.

The "Mobile First" Mantra and Its Consequences

Widespread recognition that audiences increasingly consume news on small, mobile screens has led to equally widespread adoption of a "mobile first" mantra when it comes to producing dataviz in newsrooms. This means a turn away from the elaborate and interactive visualizations that characterized the early days of dataviz in the news, to greater simplicity and linearity, or simple visual forms with low levels of interactivity. This has led to a predominance of certain chart types, such as bar charts and line charts, and to the advent of *scrollytelling*, or stories that unfold as users scroll down the page, with the visualizations that are embedded in the article appearing at the appropriate time. Scrolling also triggers changes in visualizations themselves, such as zooming out.

> Often in our stories we use the scrolling technique. It is not necessary to click but to scroll, if you scroll down, something will happen in the story. (DE)

Tools to automate dataviz production and make it possible for journalists who are not dataviz experts to produce them also result in the spread of simplified chart forms. Nonetheless, some interviewees are keen to educate readers by presenting less common chart types (a scatterplot, for example) accompanied with information about how to make sense of them. Some believe that pictures can also present data effectively—a Scandinavian national tabloid represented the size of a freight plane by filling it with 427,000 pizzas. Others recognize the value of animation, for example, to show change over time, or of experimenting with zoomability in visualizations.

The Social Role of Journalism

Linking a dataviz to a data source, providing access to the raw data and explaining methodologies are seen by some participants as ethical practices which create transparency and counterbalance the subjectivity of selection and interpretation which, for some, is an inevitable aspect of visualizing data. Yet for others, linking to data sources means giving audiences "all of the data" and conflicts with the journalistic norm of identifying and then telling a story. For some, this conflict is addressed by complex processes of sharing different elements of data and process on different platforms (Twitter, Pinterest, GitHub).

This leads data journalists and visualization designers to reflect on how much data to share, their roles as fact providers and their social role more generally. Data journalist Paul Bradshaw sums this up on his blog:

> How much responsibility do we have for the stories that people tell with our information? And how much responsibility do we have for delivering as much information as someone needs? (Bradshaw, 2017)

Former *Guardian* editor Alan Rusbridger (2010) raised a similar question about the social role of journalism when he pointed to the range of actors who do what journalism has historically done—that is, act as a gatekeeper of data and official information (e.g., FixMyStreet and TheyWorkForYou in the United Kingdom). He concluded: "I don't know if that is journalism or not. I don't know if that matters" (Baack, 2018). Some of our interviewees work on large-scale projects similar to those discussed by Rusbridger—for example, one project collated all available data relating to schools in the United Kingdom and made this explorable by postcode to inform decision making about school preference. So the question of what counts as journalism in the context of widespread data and dataviz is not easy to answer.

What's more, sharing data sets assumes that audiences will interact with them, yet studies indicate that online interactivity is as much a myth as a reality, with the idealized image of an active and motivated explorer of a visualized data set contrasting with the more common quick and scrolling reader of news (e.g., Burmester et al., 2010). Similarly, a study of data journalism projects submitted to the Nordic Data Journalism Awards concludes that interactive elements often offer merely an *illusion* of interactivity, as most choices already are made or predefined by the journalists (Appelgren, 2017). This again calls into question the practice of sharing "all of the data" and raises questions about the changing social role of journalism.

Trust, Truth and Visualizations "in the Wild"

Other elements of the process of visualizing data raise issues of trust and truth and also relate to how journalists think about the social role of journalism. One aspect of dataviz work that points to these issues is how journalists working with data visualization think about data and their visual representation. Some see it as a form of truth-telling, others as a process of selection and interpretation, and others still believe that shaping data visualizations through choices is a way of revealing a story and so is precisely what journalists should do. These reflections highlight the relationship between (dis)trust and presentation, and between perspective and (un)truthfulness.

In our current, so-called "post-truth" context, in which audiences are said to have had enough of facts, data and experts and in which "fake news" circulates quickly and widely, our participants were alert to the potential ways in which audiences might respond to their data visualizations, which might include accepting naively, refuting sceptically, decontextualizing through social sharing, or even changing and falsifying. They felt that journalists increasingly need "soft knowledge of Internet culture" (UK), as one participant put it. This includes an understanding of how online content might be more open to interrogation than its offline equivalent, and of how data visualizations may be more likely to circulate online than text, floating free of their original contexts as combinations of numbers and pictures "in the wild" (Espeland & Sauder, 2007). This in turn requires understanding of strategies that might address these dangers, such as embedding explanatory text into a visualization file so that the image cannot be circulated without the explanation. These issues, alongside concern about audiences' data and visualization literacy, inform and reshape journalists' thinking about their audiences.

How Do People Engage With Data Visualizations?

In this section, we look at dataviz in the news from the perspective of the audience. How do audiences engage with and make sense of the visualizations that they encounter in media? Data journalists are often too busy to attend to this question. Data visualization researchers don't have this excuse, but nevertheless rarely focus their attention on what end users think of the visualizations that they see.

Enter Seeing Data, a research project which explored how people engage with the data visualizations that they encounter in their everyday lives, often in the media. It explored the factors that affect engagement and what this means for how we think about what makes a visualization effective. On Seeing Data we used focus groups and interviews to explore these questions, to enable us to get at the attitudes, feelings and beliefs that underlie people's engagements with dataviz. Forty-six people participated in the research, including a mix of participants who might be assumed to be interested in data, the visual or migration (which was the subject of a number of the visualizations that we showed them) and so "already engaged" in one of the issues at the heart of our project, and participants about whom we could not make these assumptions.

In the focus groups, we asked participants to evaluate eight visualizations, which we chose (after much discussion) because they represented a diversity of subject matters, chart types, original media sources and formats, and aimed either to explain or to invite exploration. Half of the visualizations were taken from journalism (BBC; *The New York Times*; *The Metro*, a freely distributed UK newspaper; and *Scientific American* magazine). Others came from organizations which visualize and share data as part of their work: The Migration Observatory at the University of Oxford; the UK Office for National Statistics (ONS); and the Organisation for Economic Co-operation and Development (OECD).

After the focus groups, seven participants kept diaries for a month, to provide us with further information about encounters with visualizations "in the wild" and not chosen by us.

Factors Which Affect Dataviz Engagement

Subject matter. Visualizations don't exist in isolation from the subject matter that they represent. When subject matter spoke to participants' interest, they were engaged—for example, civil society professionals who were interested in issues relating to migration and therefore in migration visualizations. In contrast, one participant (who was male, 38, White, British, an agricultural worker) was not interested in any of the visualizations we showed him in the focus group or confident to spend time looking. However, his lack of interest and confidence and his mistrust of the media (he said he felt they try "to confuse you") did not stop him from looking at visualizations completely: He told us that when he came across visualizations in *The Farmer's Guide*, a publication he read regularly because it speaks to his interests, he would take the time to look at them.

Source or media location. The source of visualizations is important: It has implications for whether users trust them. Concerns about the media setting out to confuse were shared by many participants and led some to view visualizations encountered within certain media as suspect. In contrast,

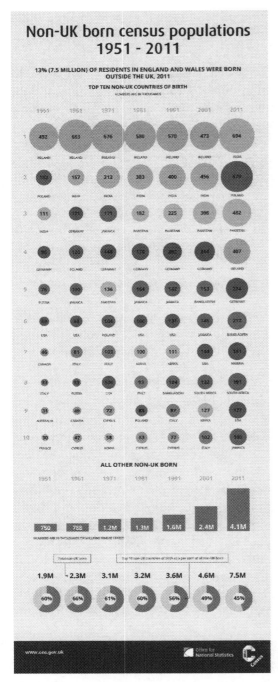

Figure 24.1. Non-UK born census populations 1951–2011.
Source: Office for National Statistics.

Figure 24.2: Migration in the census. Source: The Migration Observatory, University of Oxford. http://www.compas.ox.ac.uk/migrationinthecensus/, http://migrationobservatory.ox.ac.uk/

some participants trusted migration visualizations which carried the logo of the University of Oxford, because they felt that the "brand" of this university invokes quality and authority. But during the diary-keeping period, a different picture emerged. Participants tended to see visualizations in their favoured media, which they trusted, so they were likely to trust the visualizations they saw there, too. One participant (male, 24, White, British, agricultural worker), who reads *The Daily Mail*, demonstrated this when he remarked in his interview that "you see more things wrong or printed wrong in *The Sun*, I think." Given the ideological similarities between these two publications, this comment points to the importance of media location in dataviz engagement.

Beliefs and opinions. Participants trusted the newspapers they regularly read and therefore trusted the visualizations in these newspapers, because both the newspapers and the visualizations often fitted with their views of the world. This points to the importance of beliefs and opinions in influencing how and whether people take time to engage with particular visualizations. Some participants said they liked visualizations that confirmed their beliefs and opinions. But it is not just when visualizations confirm existing beliefs that beliefs matter. One participant (male, 34, White, British, IT worker) was surprised by the migration data in an ONS visualization in Figure 24.1. He said that he had not realized how many people in the United Kingdom were born in Ireland. This data questioned what he believed and he enjoyed that experience. Some people like, or are interested in, data in visualizations that call into question existing beliefs, because they provoke and challenge horizons. So beliefs and opinions matter in this way, too.

Time. Engaging with visualizations is seen as work by people for whom doing so does not come easily. Having time available is crucial in determining whether people are willing to do this "work." Most participants who said they lacked time to look at visualizations were women, and they put their lack of time down to work, family and home commitments. One working mother talked about how her combined paid and domestic labour were so tiring that when she finished her day, she didn't want to look at news, and that included looking at visualizations. Such activities felt like "work" to her, and she was too tired to undertake them at the end of her busy day. An agricultural worker told us in an email that his working hours were very long and this impacted on his ability to keep his month-long diary of engagement with visualizations after the focus group research.

Confidence and skills. Audiences need to feel that they have the necessary skills to decode visualizations, and many participants indicated a lack of confidence in this regard. A part-time careers advisor said of one visualization: "It was all these circles and colours and I thought, that looks like a bit of hard work; don't know if I understand." Many of our participants expressed concern about their lack of skills, or they demonstrated that they did not have the required skills, whether these were visual literacy skills, language skills, mathematical and statistical skills (like knowing how to read particular chart types), or critical thinking skills.

Emotions. Although last in our list, a major finding from our research was the important role that emotions play in people's engagements with data visualizations.[3] A broad range of emotions emerged in relation to engagements with dataviz, including pleasure, anger, sadness, guilt, shame, relief, worry, love, empathy, excitement, offence. Participants reported emotional responses to visualizations in general; represented data; visual style; the subject matter of data visualizations; the source or original location of visualizations; their own skill levels for making sense of visualizations.

For example, two civil society professionals used strong language to describe their feelings when they looked at the visualizations of migration in the United Kingdom shown in Figure 24.2. The data caused them to reflect on how it must feel to be a migrant who comes to the United Kingdom and

---

3   For more on the role of emotions in engagements with data visualization, see Kennedy, H., & Hill, R. L. (2018). The feeling of numbers: Emotions in everyday engagements with data and their visualisation. *Sociology*, 52(4), 830–848. https://doi.org/10.1177/0038038516674675

encounters the anti-immigration headlines of the media. They described themselves as feeling "guilty" and "ashamed" to be British.

Other participants had strong emotional responses to the visual style of some visualizations. A visualization of film box office receipts by *The New York Times* divided participants, with some drawn to its aesthetic and some put off by it (Bloch et al., 2008):

> It was a pleasure to look at this visual presentation because of the coordination between the image and the message it carries.
>
> Frustrated. It was an ugly representation to start with, difficult to see clearly, no information, just a mess.

What This Means for Making Effective Visualizations

A broad range of understandings of what makes a visualization effective emerged from our research. Visualizations in the media that are targeted at non-specialists might aim to persuade, for example. They all need to attract in order to draw people in, if they are to commit time to finding out about the data on which the visualization is based. Visualizations might stimulate particular emotions, which inspire people to look longer, deeper or further. They might provoke interest, or the opposite. An effective visualization could: Provoke questions/desire to engage in discussions with others; create empathy for other humans in the data; generate enough curiosity to draw the user in; reinforce or back up existing knowledge; provoke surprise; persuade or change minds; present something new; lead to new confidence in making sense of dataviz; present data useful for one's own purposes; enable an informed or critical engagement with a topic; be a pleasurable experience; provoke a strong emotional response.

What makes a visualization effective is fluid—no single definition applies across all dataviz. For example, being entertained by a visualization is relevant in some contexts, but not others. Visualizations have various objectives: to communicate new data; to inform a general audience; to influence decision making; to enable exploration and analysis of data; to surprise and affect behaviour. The factors that affect engagement which we identified in our research should be seen as *dimensions* of effectiveness, which carry different weight in relation to different visualizations, contexts and purposes. Many of these factors lie outside of the control of data visualizers, as they relate to consuming, not producing, visualizations. In other words, whether a visualization is effective depends in large part on how, by whom, when and where it is accessed. Sadly, our research doesn't suggest a simple checklist which guarantees the production of universally effective visualizations. However, if we want accessible and effective data visualizations, it's important that journalists working with data visualization engage with these findings.

Works Cited

Appelgren, E. (2017). An illusion of interactivity: The paternalistic side of data journalism. *Journalism Practice, 12*(3). https://doi.org/10.1080/17512786.2017.12 99032

Baack, S. (2018). *Knowing what counts: How journalists and civic technologists use and imagine data* [Doctoral dissertation], University of Groningen. https://www.rug.nl/research/portal/files/56718534/Complete_thesis.pdf

Bloch, M., Byron, L., Carter, S., & Cox, A. (2008, February 23). Ebb and flow of movies: Box office receipts 1986–2008. *The New York Times.* http://archive.nytimes.com/www.nytimes.com/interactive/2008/02/23/movies/20080223_REVENUE _GRAPHIC.html?_r=1

Bradshaw, P. (2017, September 14). No, I'm not abandoning the term "storytelling," Alberto—Just the opposite (and here's why). *Online Journalism Blog.* https://onlinejournalismblog.com/2017/09/14/narrative-storytelling-data-journalism-alberto-cairo/

Burmester, M., Mast, M., Tille, R., & Weber, W. (2010). How users perceive and use interactive information graphics: An exploratory study. In E. Banissi (Ed.), *Proceedings of the 14th International Conference Information Visualisation* (pp. 361–368). https://doi.org/10.1109/IV.2010.57

Espeland, W. N., & Sauder, M. (2007). Rankings and reactivity: How public measures recreate social worlds. *American Journal of Sociology, 113*(1), 1–40. https://doi.org/10.1086/517897

Rusbridger, A. (2010, July). *Why journalism matters.* Media Standards Trust Series, British Academy.

About the Authors

Helen Kennedy's research has traversed digital media landscapes; her current focus is on lived and visualized experiences of datafication and related phenomena (algorithms, AI, machine learning), inequalities, and everyday perspectives on "fair" data practices.

William Allen is a researcher based at Oxford's Centre on Migration, Policy, and Society (COMPAS), where his research examines the intersections of political communication and public attitudes using the lenses of migration and mobility.

Martin Engebretsen is Professor of Language and Communication at the University of Agder, with special expertise in the fields of multimodal discourse analysis and journalism studies.

Rosemary Lucy Hill researches gender, popular music and the politics of data visualizations and is author of *Gender, Metal and the Media: Women Fans and the Gendered Experience of Music* (Palgrave, 2016).

Andy Kirk is a data visualization specialist.

Wibke Weber is Professor of Media Linguistics at ZHAW (Zurich University of Applied Sciences) studying data visualization, information graphics, visual semiotics, comics journalism, VR and multimodality.

25. Sketching With Data

Mona Chalabi and Jonathan Gray

Abstract

An interview with celebrated data journalist Mona Chalabi exploring the development and reception of her practice of sketching as a way of making data relatable, including discussion of data as a means of providing context, visual practices of making things comparable, the role of humour and analogy in her work, data journalism as social commentary, and the importance of communicating the uncertainty of data and the provisionality of analysis.

Keywords: data sketching, data visualization, uncertainty, data publics, data journalism, visual practices

Jonathan Gray (JG): How did you start sketching with data?

Mona Chalabi (MC): When I was working at *FiveThirtyEight* I felt that they weren't catering to readers like me. They were catering to a slightly different kind of reader with their complex interactives. During this time I began sketching with data, which I could do while sitting at my desk. As I started to do them I had this realization that they could be quite an effective way to communicate the uncertainty of data projects. They could remind people that a human was responsible for making all of these design decisions. They could be quite democratizing, communicating with data in a way that anyone can do. I used to write this DIY column at *The Guardian* which took people through every single step of my process. It was fun that as a journalist you could talk people through not only where you found your data, exactly how you processed it and what you did to it, but you could also enable them to replicate it, breaking down the wall between them and you, and hopefully creating new kinds of accessibility, participation and relationships with readers.

JG: In the book we explore how data journalists do not just have to mirror and reinforce established forms of expertise (e.g., data science and

---

Bounegru, L. and J. Gray (eds.), *The Data Journalism Handbook: Towards a Critical Data Practice.*
Amsterdam: Amsterdam University Press, 2021
DOI 10.5117/9789462989511_CH25

Figure 25.1. Mona Chalabi illustration "Average Sentences". Source: *The Guardian*. https://www.the-guardian.com/news/datablog/2019/jan/12/intimate-partner-violence-gender-gap-cyntoia-brown

advanced statistical methods), but how they can also promote other kinds of data practices and data cultures. Do you consider your work to be partly about finding other ways of working with and relating to data?

MC: I don't have really advanced statistical skills. The way that I often start analyzing data is through relatively simple calculations that other people can replicate. In a way this makes the data that I'm using much more reliable. At a certain point with other more advanced statistical approaches you present readers with an ultimatum: Either you trust the journalist's analysis or you don't. This is different to the proposition of trusting government statistics and basic multiplication or not trusting them. There is a certain benefit to doing things with simple calculations. This is a big part of what I do and my approach.

Data can be used as an opportunity to do two different things: To "zoom in" or "zoom out." On the one hand, my responsibility as a data journalist is to zoom out from that one specific incident and give readers context using

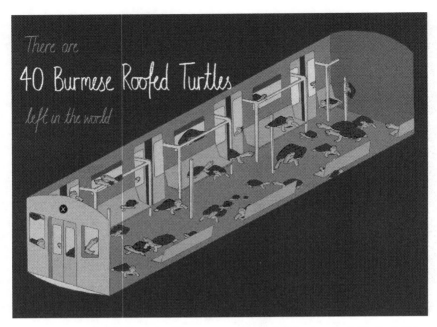

Figure 25.2. Mona Chalabi illustration "There are approximately 40 Burmese roofed turtles left in the world". Souce: *The Guardian*. https://www.theguardian.com/environment/gallery/2018/sep/17/endangered-species-on-a-train

data. For example, say there is an incident or an attack, we might show them how these attacks happen, where they happen, whether their prevalence increases over time and whether there are people who are more targeted than others. That is an opportunity for readers to understand broader trends, which can be really informative for them. Maybe it helps them to not freak out, or to duly freak out in response to the news.

On the other hand, we can do the complete opposite and zoom in. Let's say that the BLS [US Bureau of Labor Statistics] publishes unemployment data and that most other news outlets just publish the unemployment rate. We as data journalists are able to zoom in: We can say to readers, here is the national employment rate but also this is what it looks like for women, this is what it looks like for men, this is what it looks like for different age groups, here is what it looks like for different racial and ethnic groups. So it allows readers to explore the data more closely.

My work alternates between these two modes. I think one of my biggest critiques of outlets like *FiveThirtyEight* is that the work can sometimes be about intellectual bravado: "Here's what we can do." I'm not into that. My purpose is to serve readers and in particular the broadest community of readers, not just White men who identify as geeks. *FiveThirtyEight* readers call themselves geeks and *FiveThirtyEight* journalists call themselves that. But that is not why I got into journalism.

JG: To take one recent example of your work, could you tell us a bit more about the "Endangered Species on a Train" piece published in *The Guardian* (Figure 25.2)? How did you get into this topic, how did the project arise and how did you approach it?

MC: It was actually quite strange. It was not really inspired by the news; it was more about my personal practice of doing these illustrations and wanting to do something a bit more ambitious. Part of the reason why I started doing these illustrations is they are also really efficient: They can have such a fast turnaround, and can be made in a matter of hours if need be. I wanted to create something bigger that would take a bit more time. I started with a much bigger topic that people already feel familiar with—endangered species—but for which the existing visual language is perhaps a bit uninspiring. I took data from the International Union for Conservation of Nature (IUCN) "Red List."[1] For a lot of those numbers on endangered species they gave a range, and I chose a midpoint for each of them.

Stepping back, you could look at my illustrations as charts. The only thing that makes them charts is scale. Every illustration that I post has a sense of scale and that is what every single chart does. One of the problems with scale is that different countries and places use different scales, for example, millimetres in the United Kingdom and inches in the United States. Scales mean different things to different people. A lot of data journalists lose sight of this. What does "1 million" mean to someone? What does "1" mean to someone? All of this depends on context. When numbers are low it can be easier to get your head around this: You know what 27 means. But what does that mean?

Part of the beauty of data visualization is that it can make things feel more visceral. Another illustration that I was pretty proud of and that did really well was one where I compared the average parking space to the average solitary confinement cell (Figure 25.3). This is like a common practice for dealing with numbers in journalism: You don't say "bankers in London earn this much," you say "bankers in London earn 7,000 times what a social worker earns." All of those analogies really help people.

---

1   https://www.iucnredlist.org/

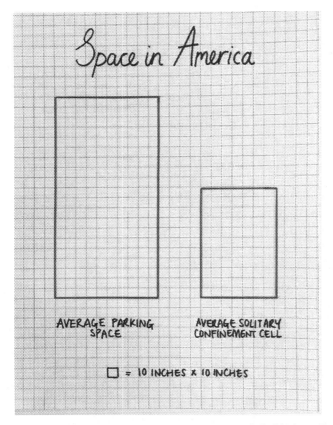

Figure 25.3. "Space in America" illustration. Source: Mona Chalabi. https://www.instagram.com/p/
BEi-v3tKvBZ/

JG: It seems that part of your practice is also to do with juxtaposition of different elements (e.g., the familiar and the disturbing). Is there also a curatorial element here?

MC: Humour also plays an important role in my work. Not that the pieces are funny, but there is often something wry in the style. The best comedy is basically saying "this is fucked up." There is always some kind of social commentary. If you can inject data journalism with a little bit of that it can be really powerful.

JG: Returning to the "Endangered Species" example as a case of making numbers relatable through humour and the use of different visual spaces of comparison, did you start with the carriage (as opposed to the chart)?

MC: First I drew the carriage, and then I drew about seven or eight of each animal. I used Photoshop to separate out the layers, to colour them and to count them. To make sure I got it correct each animal is a different layer. My first idea was to draw endangered species in different things which are all universally relatable. The New York Subway is not perfect (is it bigger or smaller than the London Tube?), but it is enough to give you a sense of scale. I started with a spreadsheet of different possibilities combining endangered species and relatable spaces. I was thinking of showing a shark in a swimming pool. But with all of the different spaces it felt a bit difficult to get your head around and once I started drawing them I realized it was going to be a really lengthy process. Rather than drawing them all in different places I would show them all in the same one, which also works better.

It is not really perfect: To fit all of the rhinos in the scale is a little bit questionable I would say (a lot of them would need to be babies rather than adults!). But it makes you feel something about the numbers. And it is also transparent about its shortcomings. When you look at a chart that *FiveThirtyEight* created, how are you, especially as a non-expert, supposed to remotely understand to what extent it is accurate? Readers are just given an ultimatum: Trust us or don't. When readers look at the illustrations of the endangered species they can look at the rhinos and think, "It is a little bit off but I get it." They have access to that critique in a way that they don't with computer generated graphics.

JG: Earlier you mentioned that you hoped your work could democratize how people engage with data. Could you say a bit more about this?

MC: Without this ability for readers to participate in making sense with data and forming their own judgements, how are journalists any better than politicians? You have right-wing papers and left-wing papers just saying: "You either trust us or you don't." But we're supposed to be empowering people to make informed decisions in their everyday lives. Empowering people is not just about saying, "These are the facts, now clearly you're supposed to go and do this." It is saying, "These are the facts; here is how we got here." It is not just journalism: I think there is a lot of work to be done in medicine as well. I'd like to do more work around how to change medical packaging. Rather than boxes saying, "Here's what you need to do," if you're going to be a really good doctor you should be able to say to the patient, "These are the risks for this medicine. These are the risks of not taking it. These are the risks of this other course of medicine. These are the risks of not taking it," so people can make decisions for themselves as no two people are alike.

I think good data visualizations should communicate uncertainty.[2] Uncertainty is part of that whole story of making an informed decision in your life. So few data journalists take the time to communicate uncertainty. So few data journalists take the time to reach out to communities that aren't geeks. Just because you don't have these particular vocabularies of statistical or computational skills does that mean that you are not smart, that you are not entitled to understand this information? Of course not. And yet some data journalists refer to so many of these terms in this off-hand way, like, "I'm not going to bother explaining this every time. You either get it or you don't." It is stupid. My approach to data journalism is based on the idea that you don't necessarily need specific vocabularies or expertise to be smart.

JG: Is there also an element of people participating in deciding what matters?

MC: Part of the reason I started the "Dear Mona" advice column was so that people could send me questions. People are constantly sending DMs on Instagram about things which matter to them, and there are many things that I wouldn't necessarily have thought of at all. There are some routes that I don't want to go down, like looking at the relation between mental health and gun control, which can stigmatize people with mental health issues and open a whole can of worms. But if I get many DMs from people who want to know about this then you wonder whether you should not just sidestep the nuance because it is complicated but should instead try to tackle it head on. So I'm constantly looking to readers to tell me what matters to them. I don't think that this is an abdication of journalistic responsibility. It is part of the democratic role of journalism and people seeing that they have a stake in the final product in every single way: In the process of creating it, in understanding it, and it is not this thing which is just given to them in a "take it or leave it" kind of way.

JG: Could you tell us a bit about the responses to your work? Have there been any unexpected or notable responses?

MC: I get all kinds of different responses to my work. Some people focus on the subject matter. So any time I do something on wage gaps, for example, I get lots of White men that are, like, "No, Black women only earn less because they work less," and you have to engage with them about how the illustrations are based on "like for like" comparisons between full-time workers, and if

---

2   Editors: See also Anderson's chapter in this book, as well as his *Apostles of Certainty: Data Journalism and the Politics of Doubt* (Oxford University Press, 2018).

there are differences in the levels they are at (e.g., senior management), that is also part of the problem. I'm always keen to focus on the critique first.

But overall I get much more support than criticism. Sometimes people respond to critiques in comments even before I get to them. People whose lives are represented in the illustrations sometimes intervene to say, "No, my personal experience bears this out." People sometimes want to see extra data. Lots of students write to say that they really want to do this (interestingly I get more female students writing to me than men). A lot of NGOs and charities write to me as they want to feel something about their data rather than thinking something about their data, and sometimes my work manages to do that. One of my pieces was cited in a US bill.

My work has been viewed and shared by a lot of people on social media who are not necessarily into data journalism per se, which is getting it in front of a new audience. Bernie Sanders shared my gun violence illustration, Miley Cyrus shared one, as did Iman, the model, and Shaun King, the civil rights activist. These are not people I know and not necessarily people who follow my work, but they see other people sharing it and it somehow ends up on their radar. It is amazing to see people engaging with it. Once someone prominent shares it, it can take on a life of its own sometimes.

Examples of the works referred to in this chapter can be found on the web at monachalabi.com and on Instagram at @monachalabi.

About the Authors

Mona Chalabi is trying to take the "numb" out of numbers and is left with lots of "ers."

Jonathan Gray is Lecturer in Critical Infrastructure Studies at the Department of Digital Humanities, King's College London, co-founder of the Public Data Lab and Research Associate at the Digital Methods Initiative, University of Amsterdam.

26. The Web as Medium for Data Visualization

Elliot Bentley

Abstract

Exploring the types of graphics made possible by the web, including interactive dataviz, games and virtual reality (VR).

Keywords: interactive graphics, data visualization, web development, JavaScript, infographics, newsgames

Not all media are created equal. A 20-episode television series is able to tell a story differently than a two-hour film, for example. In the same way, the humble web page can provide its own possibilities for data visualization.

The web was originally designed for simple, hyperlinked documents consisting of mostly text and static images. The addition of JavaScript and a slow drip of new features and tools has expanded the palette available to work with.[1]

Although traditional data visualization theory and techniques (e.g., Edward Tufte, Jacques Bertin) are still mostly applicable to graphics on the web, the unique features of the web provide vast potential for new forms of data journalism. These works are often referred to as "interactives," an awkward word that obscures some of the web's unique strengths.

Below is a list illustrating some of the ways in which graphics on the web can take advantage of their host medium.

---

1   Other "multimedia" platforms, especially Flash, provided a wealth of options long before the open web did. However, for better or worse these have since been phased out. And while all of these features—more in fact—are available in native applications, the web is far easier to work with and distribution is practically free.

Bounegru, L. and J. Gray (eds.), *The Data Journalism Handbook: Towards a Critical Data Practice.* Amsterdam: Amsterdam University Press, 2021
DOI 10.5117/9789462989511_CH26

Huge, Explorable Data Sets

A classic use of interactivity is to present the reader with a huge data set and allow them to "dive in" and explore in as much depth as they like. Sometimes this takes the shape of a giant table; other times, a big interactive map.

This format is often looked down upon nowadays, since it expects the reader to find the interesting bits themselves; but it can still be valuable if the data is juicy enough. I find that the most successful versions accept the fact they are simply tools (as opposed to being articles), such as the extremely popular *Wall Street Journal* College Rankings or *ProPublica*'s public-service news apps.[2]

Guide the Reader Through Complex Charts

A now-common format begins with a single chart and then proceeds to manipulate it—zooming in and out, travelling through time, switching out data—in order to fully explore the data set. This pairs exceptionally well with scrollytelling and is especially valuable on mobile, where there may not be enough space to show all elements of a chart at once.[3]

In the now-classic piece "A Visual Introduction to Machine Learning" (Figure 26.1), the same data points transition between multiple chart formats, helping readers keep track of how the machine learning algorithms are sorting them.[4] Another good example is "100 years of tax brackets, in one chart," a *Vox* piece that zooms in and out of a data set that might be overwhelming if presented otherwise.[5]

Up-to-the-Second Live Data

Why settle for a static data set when you can use the latest numbers of whatever you're charting? Elections, sport coverage, weather events and financial data are obvious sources of live data interesting enough to display in real time. Even more cool is providing context for these live figures in

2   https://www.wsj.com/articles/explore-the-full-wsj-the-college-rankings-11567638555,
https://www.propublica.org/newsapps/
3   https://pudding.cool/process/how-to-implement-scrollytelling/
4   http://www.r2d3.us/visual-intro-to-machine-learning-part-1/
5   https://www.vox.com/2015/10/26/9469793/tax-brackets

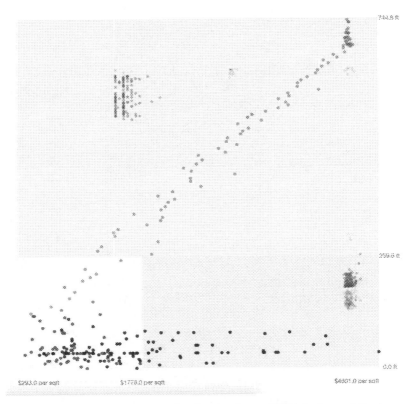

Figure 26.1. A visual introduction to machine learning. Source: R2D3. http://www.r2d3.us/visual-intro-to-machine-learning-part-1/

interesting ways—for example, showing which countries benefit from the current price of oil (Figure 26.2).

Ampp3d, a short-lived experimental pop-data journalism outlet, used live counters to bring numbers to life in interesting ways, such as the number of immigrants entering the United Kingdom, and footballer Wayne Rooney's earnings.[6] Sadly, these have since been taken offline.

Placing the Reader Within a Data Set

Another twist on the "huge data sets" idea—and one that I've found to be incredibly compelling to readers—is to show the reader where they fall in a data set, usually by asking for a couple of personal details. *The New York*

6   https://onlinejournalismblog.com/2015/05/13/the-legacy-of-ampp3d-usvsth3m-and-row-zed/

Figure 26.2. Countries that benefit from the current price of oil. Source: *Wall Street Journal*. http://graphics.wsj.com/oil-producers-break-even-prices/

Times' 2013 dialect quiz map (Figure 26.3) famously became the publication's most popular article of the year—despite only being published on December 20th.

The BBC seem to do these pretty frequently, often as a public service tool, with things like "UK fat scale calculator."[7] I like this *Quartz* piece on how people in different cultures draw circles, which opens by asking the reader to draw a circle, a compelling introduction to an otherwise (potentially) dull feature.[8]

Collecting Original Data Sets

A step beyond the previous category are projects that not only use readers' submitted data to give an immediate response, but also to compile a new data set for further analysis.

The Australian Broadcasting Corporation collaborated with political scientists on a "Vote Compass" to help readers understand their place

7   https://www.bbc.com/news/health-43697948
8   https://qz.com/994486/the-way-you-draw-circles-says-a-lot-about-you/

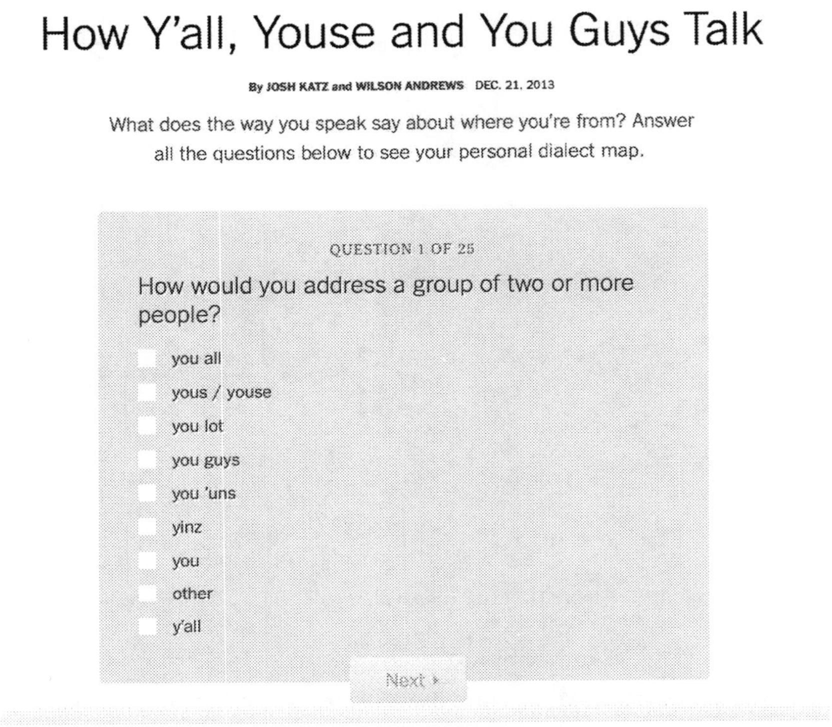

How Y'all, Youse and You Guys Talk

By JOSH KATZ and WILSON ANDREWS   DEC. 21, 2013

What does the way you speak say about where you're from? Answer
all the questions below to see your personal dialect map.

QUESTION 1 OF 25

How would you address a group of two or more
people?

you all

yous / youse

you lot

you guys

you 'uns

yinz

you

other

y'all

Next ›

Figure 26.3: *The New York Times'* 2013 dialect quiz map. Source: *The New York Times*. https://www.
nytimes.com/interactive/2014/upshot/dialect-quiz-map.html

in the political landscape—and then wrote a series of articles based on
the data.[9]

More recently, *The New York Times* used the same idea on a softer subject,
asking readers to rate *Game of Thrones* characters and plotting the results
on live charts (Figure 26.4).

The Infinite Canvas

The web is infinite in its scope and capacity, but more specifically web
pages can be as wide or tall as they like—an "infinite canvas" on which
to work. I borrowed this term from artist Scott McCloud, who argues that

---

9   https://www.abc.net.au/news/nsw-election-2015/vote-compass/, https://www.abc.net.au/
news/nsw-election-2015/vote-compass/results/

Your Estimates, and Everyone Else's

Tyrion Lannister

Introduced as "The Imp,"
Tyrion was a hard-drinking,
whoring, black sheep of the
royal family; now, he's a
respected strategist.

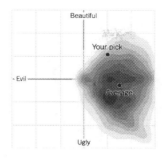

Daenerys Targaryen

A stunning beauty who feels
for the oppressed. But she has
no problem sending people to
their deaths as she conquers
kingdoms.

Figure 26.4: A plot chart rating *Game of Thrones* characters. Source: *The Upshot*. https://www.nytimes.com/interactive/2017/08/09/upshot/game-of-thrones-chart.html

there is "no reason that longform comics have to be split into pages when moving online."[10] And indeed, why should our graphics be constrained to the limits of paper either?

In *The Washington Post*'s "The Depth of the Problem," a 16K-pixel-tall graphic is used to show the depth of the ocean area being searched for missing flight MH370 (Figure 26.5).[11] Sure, this information could have been squeezed into a single screen, but it would have lacked the level of detail and emotional impact of this extremely tall graphic.

In *The Guardian*'s "How the List Tallies Europe's Migrant Bodycount," tens of thousands of migrant deaths are powerfully rendered as individual dots that appear one by one as the reader scrolls down the page.[12]

10   http://scottmccloud.com/4-inventions/canvas/index.html
11   https://www.washingtonpost.com/apps/g/page/world/the-depth-of-the-problem/931/
12   https://www.theguardian.com/world/2018/jun/20/the-list-europe-migrant-bodycount

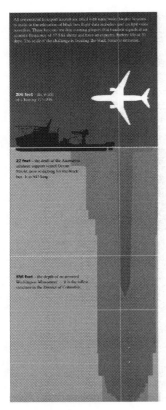

Figure 26.5. Graphic that shows the depth
of the ocean area being searched for the missing
flight MH370. Source: *The Washington Post*.
http://apps.washingtonpost.com/g/page/
world/the-depth-of-the-problem/931/

Data-Driven Games

"Newsgames," interactive experiences that borrow mechanics from video games
to explore news subjects, have existed for a while, with varying levels of success.

The Upshot's "You Draw It" series (Figure 26.6) challenges readers' assumptions by asking them to fill in a blank chart, before revealing the
answer and exploring the subject in greater depth.

Some games are more involved, perhaps asking the reader to solve a
simplified version of a real-world problem—such as how to fund the BBC—to
prove just how difficult it is.[13]

13   https://ig.ft.com/sites/2015/bbc/

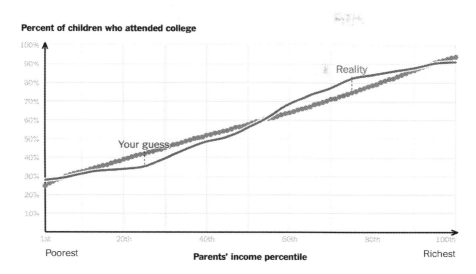

Figure 26.6. A chart from *The Upshot's* "You Draw It" series.
Source: *The Upshot.* https://www.nytimes.com/interactive/2015/05/28/upshot/you-draw-it-how-family-income-affects-childrens-college-chances.html

These could be considered toys that only present the reader with surface-level information, but done right they can provide a fresh perspective on played-out subjects. *FiveThirtyEight's* "How to Win a Trade War," in which the reader chooses a trading strategy and competes against a previous visitor to the page, brings to life the otherwise potentially dry economic theory.[14]

Live, Randomized Experiments

A related format is to allow the reader to run a live simulation in their browser. More than just an animated explainer, this introduces a degree of randomness that leads to a unique result each time and is a great way to bring abstract statistical probabilities to life.

The *Guardian* piece in Figure 26.7 simulates a measles outbreak across ten populations with varying rates of vaccination. The web graphics make the results starkly clear in a way that percentages alone could not convey. In Nathan Yau's "Years You Have Left to Live, Probably," a simple line chart

14   https://fivethirtyeight.com/features/how-to-win-a-trade-war/

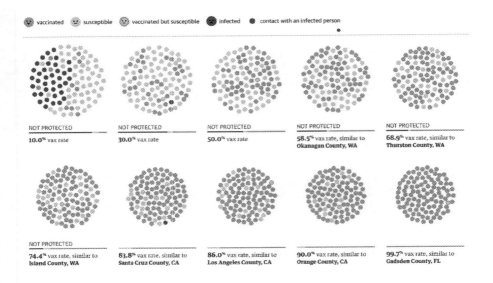

Figure 26.7: A simulation of a measles outbreak across ten populations with varying rates of vaccination. Source: *The Guardian*, https://www.theguardian.com/society/ng-interactive/2015/feb/05/-sp-watch-how-measles-outbreak-spreads-when-kids-get-vaccinated

("probability of living to next year") is made more poignant with "lives" that die at random and then pile up.[15]

These simulations don't have to use imaginary data. "The Birthday Paradox" tests the probability of shared birthdays using data from previous visitors to the page.[16]

3D, VR and AR

3D graphics and virtual reality are difficult to harness in service of data journalism, outside of maps of terrain.

Two notable experiments, both from 2015 and on the subject of financial data ("Is the Nasdaq in Another Bubble?" and "A 3-D View of a Chart That Predicts the Economic Future: The Yield Curve"), are clever novelties but failed to spark an explosion of three-dimension charts.[17] Perhaps for the best.

15   https://flowingdata.com/2015/09/23/years-you-have-left-to-live-probably/
16   https://pudding.cool/2018/04/birthday-paradox/
17   http://graphics.wsj.com/3d-nasdaq/, https://www.nytimes.com/interactive/2015/03/19/upshot/3d-yield-curve-economic-growth.html

The potential of augmented reality, in which a camera feed of the real world is overlaid with graphics, has yet to be proven.

Conclusion: How New Formats Arise

Some of the web graphics listed above are new formats that have only emerged over the past few years; some have stuck around, such as the guide through a complex chart (typically using a scrollytelling interaction pattern). Others, like three-dimensional charts, were mere flashes in the pan.

Yet it's not just taste that determines which types of graphics are in vogue on the web: Available technology and readers' consumption habits shape trends, too.

Take, for example, the widely used interactive map. In addition to being a visually attractive and easily grasped form, the proliferation and familiarity of this format was doubtless helped by tools that make them easy to create and manipulate—Google Maps and Leaflet being two of the most common.

Without any hard data to hand, it at least feels as though fewer interactive maps are being published nowadays. While it would be easy to attribute this trend to a growing realization among journalists that such interactivity (or even the map itself) can often be superfluous, new technologies likely also contributed to this drop.

A high proportion of readers now access the web using mobile phones, and interactive maps are a particularly poor experience on small touchscreens. In addition, there is a new technological solution that in many ways is superior: ai2html, a script open-sourced by *The New York Times* that generates a responsive html snippet from Adobe Illustrator files.[18] Maps built with ai2html can leverage a traditional cartographer's skill set and still have sharp, machine-readable text. The lack of interactivity in such maps is often a blessing, even if it is in many ways limiting.

This is just one example of how data journalists should be thoughtful in their use of the web's unique features. With so many possibilities to hand, it's important to carefully evaluate those and use them only when truly necessary.

18   https://github.com/newsdev/ai2html

About the Author

Elliot Bentley has worked in *The Wall Street Journal*'s graphics department since 2014 and is also the creator of open-source transcription app oTranscribe.

27. Four Recent Developments in News Graphics

Gregor Aisch and Lisa Charlotte Rost

Abstract
This chapter explores four developments we have recently seen in news graphics: "Mobile first" becomes more important, the importance of interactivity shifts, more (in-house) charting tools get developed, and data-centric online publications are on the rise.

Keywords: news graphics, mobile, charting tools, interactivity, data visualization, data journalism

The news graphics field is still young and tries to answer questions like: How do we show the bias and uncertainty in (polls) data? (Cairo & Schlossberg, 2019). How do we work together with reporters? How do we communicate complex data on fast-paced social media? (Segger, 2018). Here, we try to cover four key developments that we think are relevant for the coming years.

"Mobile First" Starts to Be Taken Seriously

"Mobile first" is a widely used buzzword, but in the fast-paced world of news graphics, mobile experiences have often remained an afterthought. Now we finally see them climb up the priority list. That has two consequences.

First, there is more thought being put in making graphics work on mobile. A note telling mobile users that "this experience works best on a desktop" becomes a faux pas. A chart needs to be responsive, to not make more than half of the users leave. But thinking inside the few pixels of a mobile box can be frustrating for graphics reporters, many of whom are used to the "luxury" of filling entire pages in print newspapers and designing full-screen desktop

Bounegru, L. and J. Gray (eds.), *The Data Journalism Handbook: Towards a Critical Data Practice*. Amsterdam: Amsterdam University Press, 2021
DOI 10.5117/9789462989511_CH27

experiences. In the best case, the limits of the small screen motivate graphics reporters to think outside of the box and become creative. We already see this happening: For example, the *Financial Times* turned their parliament seat chart 90 degrees, essentially creating a new chart type.[1]

The second consequence of mobile-first data visualization is that news developers and reporters will see "mobile" not just as a tiny screen anymore, but also as a device that is packed with sensors. This can lead to new data experiences. *The Guardian* created an app with which you can take a virtual audio tour of Rio de Janeiro, covering the same length as the marathon that took place there in 2016.[2] "Our challenge for you: Complete all 26.2 miles—or 42.2 km—of the route over the next three weeks," they write. AR and VR make similar use of our smartphones, and we see them arriving in news as well.

Interactivity Is Dead, Except When It's Not

We've seen interactivity being used less and less for simple charts in the past few years. It's now reserved for the biggest projects a newsroom will publish each year. But interactivity is not necessary for success anymore. Newsrooms like the *Financial Times*, *FiveThirtyEight* and *National Geographic* have repeatedly published charts that went viral without letting users interact with them.

We see two main reasons for a decline in interactive graphics. First, fewer people interact with charts than previously assumed.[3] Curious, Internet-savvy people—like graphics reporters—will always try to hover over a visualization. And reporters want their articles to feel more alive. But we're creating for an audience that prefers passive consumption; especially on mobile. Most people will miss content if it's hidden behind interactivity, which led many graphic reporters to decide not to hide anything in the first place.

Second, graphics arrived in the breaking news cycle. Graphics reporters have gotten faster and faster at creating visualizations, and a breaking news story will quickly have, for instance, a locator map of where an event happened. However, well-made interactivity still takes time. Often, it is left out for the sake of publishing the article faster.

We still see interactive news graphics, but their importance has shifted. Instead of adding to a story, interactivity becomes the story. We've seen great

---

1   https://ig.ft.com/italy-poll-tracker/
2   https://www.theguardian.com/sport/2016/aug/06/rio-running-app-marathon-course-riorun
3   https://vimeo.com/182590214, https://medium.com/@dominikus/the-end-of-interactive-visualizations-52c585dcafcb

examples of explorable explanations where readers can enter their personal data, such as location, income, or opinion, to then see how they fit into the greater scheme. Examples are "You Draw It: How Family Income Predicts Children's College Chances" and "Is It Better to Rent or Buy?" from *The New York Times*.[4] Both pieces are of no value for readers if they don't enter data: The value comes *through* the interaction.

Newsrooms Use More (in-House) Charting Tools

More than ever, reporters are pressured to make their articles stand out. Adding a chart is one solution, but graphics teams struggle to handle the increasingly large numbers of incoming requests. That's why we see more and more newsrooms deciding to use charting tools that make it easy to create charts, maps and tables with a few clicks. A newsroom has two options when it comes to charting tools: Use an external charting tool such as Datawrapper or Infogram, or build an in-house charting tool adjusted to internal requirements and integrated into the content management system.

Although the second option sounds like a great idea, many newsrooms will find that it uses more resources than expected. External charting tools are built by dedicated teams that will maintain the tool and offer training. Within a newsroom, all of this will often be done by the graphics or interactive team, leaving them less time for actual news projects. An in-house charting tool can become a success only if it is made a priority. The *Neue Zürcher Zeitung*, for example, has three developers that dedicate their time exclusively to developing and maintaining their charting tool Q.

Data-Centric Publications Drive Innovation and Visual Literacy

While a data-driven approach was only considered useful for individual stories a few years back, we now see entire (successful!) publications build on this idea. Often, these sites use data as a means to communicate about publication-specific topics, for example, *FiveThirtyEight* about politics and sport, *The Pudding* about pop culture and *Our World in Data* about the long-term development of humanity. Maybe the biggest difference between

4   https://www.nytimes.com/interactive/2015/05/28/upshot/you-draw-it-how-family-income-affects-childrens-college-chances.html, https://www.nytimes.com/interactive/2014/upshot/buy-rent-calculator.html

these publications and others about the same topics is the audience: It's a curious and data-orientated one, one that is not afraid of seeing a chart. As a consequence, data-centric publications can show their readership harder-to-decipher chart types such as connected scatterplots. If used well, they give a more complex, less aggregated view of the world and make comparisons visible in a way that a bar chart wouldn't be able to do.

A chapter reviewing recent developments can quickly become outdated. However, the four developments we covered have dominated debates for a few years now, and we expect them to remain relevant. This is because they are underpinned by questions with no single right answer in day-to-day news work: "Do we design a project mobile-first or go with a more complex solution that only works on desktop?", "Do we invest effort into making this visualization interactive and possibly more interesting to readers (even if only an estimated 10–20% of them will use the interactive features)?", "Do we build the visualization from scratch or use a charting tool?", "Do we create a visualization for a broader audience or for a data-savvy audience?"

The answers may differ across newsrooms, graphics teams and projects. But, increasingly, we think, the answers will converge on mobile-first and non-interactive charts and visualizations built with charting tools and for an increasingly data-literate audience.

Works Cited

Cairo, A., & Schlossberg, T. (2019, August 29). Those hurricane maps don't mean what you think they mean. *The New York Times*. https://www.nytimes.com/interactive/2019/08/29/opinion/hurricane-dorian-forecast-map.html

Segger, M. (2018, June 28). Lessons for showcasing data journalism on social media. *Medium*. https://medium.com/severe-contest/lessons-for-showcasing-data-journalism-on-social-media-17e6ed03a868

About the Authors

Gregor Aisch is a data journalist, software engineer and former graphics editor at *The New York Times* who now works as CTO of the data visualization tool Datawrapper.

Lisa Charlotte Rost is a designer who visualized data for several newsrooms (*Der Spiegel*, NPR, Bloomberg, *ZEIT Online*) before joining Datawrapper.

28. Searchable Databases as a Journalistic Product

Zara Rahman and Stefan Wehrmeyer

Abstract
Exploring the responsible data challenges and transparency opportunities of using public-facing searchable databases within a data journalism investigation.

Keywords: databases, responsible data, crowdsourcing, engagement, data journalism, transparency

A still emerging journalistic format is the searchable online database—a web interface that gives access to a data set, by newsrooms. This format is not new, but its use in data journalism projects is still relatively scarce (Holovaty, 2006).

In this chapter, we review a range of types of databases, from ones which cover topics which directly affect a reader's life, to interfaces which are created in service of further investigative work. Our work is informed by one of the co-author's work on Correctiv's Euros für Ärzte (Euros for Doctors) investigation, outlined below as an illustrative case study.[1] It is worth noting, too, that although it has become good practice to make raw data available after a data-driven investigation, the step of building a searchable interface for that data is considerably less common.

We consider the particular affordances of creating databases in journalism, but also note that they open up a number of privacy-related and ethical issues on how data is used, accessed, modified and understood. We then examine what responsible data considerations arise as a consequence of using data in this way, considering the power dynamics inherent within, as well as the

---

[1] https://correctiv.org/recherchen/euros-fuer-aerzte/ (German language)

Bounegru, L. and J. Gray (eds.), *The Data Journalism Handbook: Towards a Critical Data Practice.* Amsterdam: Amsterdam University Press, 2021
DOI 10.5117/9789462989511_CH28

consequences of putting this kind of information online. We conclude by offering a set of best practices, which will likely evolve in the future.

Examples of Journalistic Databases

Databases can form part of the public-facing aspect of investigative journalism in a number of different ways.

One type of database which has a strong personalization element is *ProPublica*'s Dollars for Docs. It compiled data on payments to doctors and teaching hospitals that were made by pharmaceutical and medical device companies.[2] This topic and approach was mirrored by Correctiv and *Der Spiegel* to create Euros für Ärzte, a searchable database of recipients of payments from pharmaceutical companies, as explained in further detail below. Both of these approaches involved compiling data from already-available sources. The goal was to increase the accessibility of said data so that readers would be able to search it for themselves to, for instance, see if their own doctor had been the recipient of payments. Both were accompanied by reporting and ongoing investigations.

Along similar lines, the *Berliner Morgenpost* built the Schul Finder to assist parents in finding schools in their area. In this case, the database interface itself is the main product.[3]

In contrast to the type of database where the data is gathered and prepared by the newsroom, another style is where the readers can contribute to the data, sometimes known as "citizen-generated" data, or simply crowdsourcing. This is particularly effective when the data required is not gathered through official sources, such as *The Guardian*'s crowdsourced database The Counted, which gathered information on people killed by police in the United States, in 2015–2016.[4] Their database used online reporting as well as reader input.

Another type of database involves taking an existing set of data and creating an interface that allows the reader to generate a report based on criteria they set. For example, the Nauru Files allows readers to view a summary of incident reports that were written by staff in Australia's detention centre on Nauru between 2013 and 2015.[5] The UK-based Bureau

2   https://projects.propublica.org/docdollars/
3   https://interaktiv.morgenpost.de/schul-finder-berlin/#/
4   https://www.theguardian.com/us-news/ng-interactive/2015/jun/01/the-counted-police-killings-us-database
5   https://www.theguardian.com/australia-news/ng-interactive/2016/aug/10/the-nauru-files-the-lives-of-asylum-seekers-in-detention-detailed-in-a-unique-database-interactive

of Investigative Journalism compiles data from various sources gathered
through their investigations, within a database called Drone Warfare.[6] The
database allows readers to select particular countries covered and the time
frame, in order to create a report with visualizations summarizing the data.

Finally, databases can also be created in service of further journalism, as a
tool to assist research. The International Consortium of Investigative Journalists created and maintain the Offshore Leaks Database, which pulls in data
from the Panama Papers, the Paradise Papers, and other investigations.[7]
Similarly, Organized Crime and Corruption Reporting Project (OCCRP)
maintains and updates OCCRP Data, which allows viewers to search over 19
million public records.[8] In both cases, the primary user of the tools is not
envisioned to be the average reader, but instead journalists and researchers
envisioned to carry out further research on whatever information is found
using these tools.

The list below summarizes the different considerations in making
databases as a news product:

- **Audience:** aimed at readers directly, or as a research database for other
  journalists
- **Timeliness:** updated on an ongoing basis, or as a one-off publication
- **Context:** forming part of an investigation or story, or the database itself
  as the main product
- **Interactivity:** readers encouraged to give active input to improve the
  database, or readers considered primarily as viewers of the data
- **Sources:** using already-public data, or making new information public
  via the database

Case Study: Euros für Ärzte (Euros for Doctors)

The European Federation of Pharmaceutical Industries and Associations
(EFPIA) is a trade association which counts 33 national associations and
40 pharmaceutical companies among its members. In 2013, the federation
decided that, starting in July 2016, member companies must publish payments to healthcare professionals and organizations in the countries they
operate (EFPIA, 2013). Inspired by *ProPublica*'s Dollars for Docs project, the
non-profit German investigative newsroom Correctiv decided to collect

6   https://www.thebureauinvestigates.com/projects/drone-war/
7   https://offshoreleaks.icij.org/
8   https://data.occrp.org/

these publications from the websites of German pharmaceutical companies and create a central, searchable database of recipients of payments from pharmaceutical companies for public viewing. They named the investigation Euros für Ärzte (Euros for Doctors).

In collaboration with the German national news outlet *Der Spiegel*, documents and data were gathered from around 50 websites and converted from different formats to consistent tabular data. This data was further cleaned and recipients of payments from multiple companies were matched. The total time for data cleaning was around ten days and involved up to five people. A custom database search interface with individual URLs per recipient was designed and published by Correctiv.[9] The database was updated in 2017 with a similar process. Correctiv also used the same methodology and web interface to publish data from Austria, in cooperation with derStandard.at and ORF, and data from Switzerland with Beobachter.ch.

The journalistic objective was to highlight the systemic influence of the pharmaceutical industry on healthcare professionals through events and organizations, and the associated conflicts of interest. The searchable database was intended to encourage readers to start a conversation with their doctor about the topic, and to draw attention to the very fact that this was happening.

On a different level, the initiative also highlighted the inadequacy of voluntary disclosure rules. Because the publication requirement was an industry initiative rather than a legal requirement, the database was incomplete—and it's unlikely that this will change without legally mandated disclosure.

As described above, the database was incomplete, meaning that a number of people who had received payments from pharmaceutical companies were missing from the database. Consequently, when users search for their doctor, an empty result can either mean the doctor received no payment or that they denied publication—two vastly different conclusions. Critics have noted that this puts the spotlight on the cooperative and transparent individuals, leaving possibly more egregious money flows in the dark. To counter that, Correctiv provided an opt-in feature for doctors who had not received payments to also appear in the database, which provides important context to the narrative, but still leaves uncertainty in the search result.

After publication, both Correctiv and *Der Spiegel* received dozens of complaints and legal threats from doctors who appeared in the database. As the data came from public, albeit difficult to find, sources, the legal team of *Der Spiegel* decided to defer most complaints to the pharma companies and only adjust the database in case of changes at the source.

9   https://correctiv.org/thema/aktuelles/euros-fuer-aerzte/

Technical Considerations of Building Databases

For a newsroom considering how to make a data set available and accessible to readers, there are various criteria to consider, such as size and complexity of the data set, internal technical capacity of the newsroom, and how readers should be able to interact with the data.

When a newsroom decides that a database could be an appropriate product of an investigation, building one requires bespoke development and deployment—a not insignificant amount of resources. Making that data accessible via a third-party service is usually simpler and requires fewer resources.

For example, in the case of Correctiv, the need to search and list around 20,000 recipients and their financial connections to pharma companies required a custom software solution. Correctiv developed the software for the database in a separate repository from its main website but in a way it could be hooked into the content management system. This decision was made to allow visual and conceptual integration into the main website and investigation section. To separate concerns, the data was stored in a relational database separate from the content database. In this case, having a process and interface for adjusting entries in the live database was crucial as dozens of upstream data corrections came in after publication.

However, smaller data sets with simple structures can be made accessible without expensive software development projects. Some third-party spreadsheet tools (e.g., Google Sheets) allow tables to be embedded. There are also numerous front-end JavaScript libraries to enhance HTML tables with searching, filtering and sorting functionalities which can often be enough to make a few hundred rows accessible to readers.

An attractive middle ground for making larger data sets accessible are JavaScript-based web applications with access to the data set via API. This setup lends itself well to running iframe-embeddable search interfaces without committing to a full-fledged web application. The API can then be run via third party services while still having full control over the styling of the front end.

Affordances Offered by Databases

Databases within, or alongside, a story, provide a number of affordances for both readers and newsrooms.

On the reader side, providing an online database allows readers to search for their own city, politician or doctor and connects the story to their own life. It provides a different channel for engagement with a story on a more personal level. Provided there are analytics running on these search queries, this also gives the newsroom more data on what their readers are interested in—potentially providing more leads for future work.

On the side of the newsroom, if the database is considered as a long-term investigative investment, it can be used to automatically cross-reference entities with other databases or sets of documents for lead generation. Similarly, if or when other newsrooms decide to make similar databases available, collaboration and increased coverage becomes much easier while reusing existing infrastructure and methodologies.

Databases also potentially offer increased optimization for search engines, thus driving more traffic to the news outlet website. When the database provides individual URLs for entities within, search engines will pick up these pages and rank them highly in their results for infrequent keyword searches related to these numerous entities—the so-called "long tail" of web searches, thus driving more traffic to the publisher's site.

Optimizing for search engines can be seen as an unsavoury practice within journalism; however, providing readers with journalistic information while they are searching for particular issues can also be viewed as a part of successful audience engagement. While the goal of the public database should not be to compete on search keywords, it will likely be a welcome benefit that drives organic traffic, and can in turn attract new readership.

Responsible Data Considerations

Drawing upon the approach of the responsible members of the data community, who work on developing best practices which take into account the ethical and privacy-related challenges faced by using data in new and different ways, we can consider the potential risks in a number of ways.[10]

First is the question of the way in which power is distributed in this situation, where a newsroom decides to publish a database containing data about people. Usually, those people have no agency or ability to veto or correct that data prior to publication. The power held by these people depends very much upon who they are—for example, a politically exposed person (PEP) included in such a database would presumably have both the

10   https://responsibledata.io/what-is-responsible-data/

expectation of such a development and adequate resources to take action, whereas a healthcare professional would probably not be expecting to be involved in an investigation. Once a database is published, visibility of the people within that database might change rapidly—for example, doctors in the Euros für Ärzte database gave feedback that one of the top web search results for their name was now their page in this database.

Power dynamics on the side of the reader or viewer are also worth considering. For whom could the database be most useful? Do they have the tools and capacity required to be able to make use of the database, or will this information be used by the already-powerful to further their interests? This might mean widening the scope of user testing prior to publication to ensure that enough context is given to properly explain the database to the desired audience, or including certain features that would make the database interface more accessible to that group.

The assumption that more data leads to decisions that are better for society has been questioned on multiple levels in recent years. Education scholar Clare Fontaine (2017) expands upon this, noting that in the United States, schools are becoming more segregated despite (or perhaps because of) an increase in data available about "school performance." She notes that "a causal relationship between school choice and rampant segregation hasn't yet been established," but she and others are working more to understand that relationship, interrogating the perhaps overly simplified relationship that more information leads to better decisions, and questioning what "better" might mean (Fontaine, 2017).

Second is the question of the database itself. A database on its own contains many human decisions; what was collected and what was left out, and how it was categorized, sorted or analyzed, for example. No piece of data is objective, although literacy and understanding of the limitations of data are relatively low, meaning that readers could well misunderstand the conclusions that are being drawn.

For example, the absence of an organization from a database of political organizations involved in organized crime may not mean that the organization does not take part in organized crime itself; it simply means that there was no data available about their actions. Michael Golebiewski and Danah Boyd (2018) refer to this absence of data as a "data void," noting that in some cases a data void may "passively reflect bias or prejudice in society." This type of absence of data in an otherwise data-saturated space also maps closely to what Brooklyn-based artist and researcher Mimi Onuoha (2016) refers to as a "missing data set," and highlights the societal choices that go into collecting and gathering data.

Third is the direction of attention. Databases can change the focus of public interest from a broader systemic issue to the actions of individuals, and vice versa. Financial flows between pharmaceutical companies and healthcare professionals are, clearly, an issue of public interest—but, on an individual level, doctors might not think of themselves as a person of public interest. The fact remains, though, that in order to demonstrate an issue as broader and systemic (as a pattern, rather than a one-off), data from multiple individuals is necessary. Some databases, such as the Euros für Ärzte case study mentioned above, also change boundaries of what, or who, is in the public interest.

Even when individuals agree to the publication of their data, journalists have to decide how long this data is of public interest and if and when it should be taken down. The General Data Protection Regulation (GDPR) will likely affect the way in which journalists should manage this kind of personal data, and what kinds of mechanisms are available for individuals to rescind consent to their data being included.

With all of these challenges, our approach is to consider how people's rights are affected by both the process and the end result of the investigation or product. At the heart is understanding that responsible data practices are ongoing approaches rather than checklists to be considered at specific points. We suggest that approaches which prioritize the rights of people reflected in the data throughout the entire investigation, from data gathering to publication, are a core part of optimizing (data) journalism for trust (Rosen, 2018).

Best Practices

For journalists thinking of building a database to share their investigation with the public, here are some best practices and recommendations. We envision these will evolve with time, and we welcome suggestions.

First, ahead of publication, develop a process for how to fix mistakes in the database. Good data provenance practices can help to find sources of errors. Second, build in a feedback channel. Particularly when individuals are unexpectedly mentioned in an investigation, there is likely to be feedback (or complaints). Providing a good user experience for them to make that complaint might help the experience. Third, either keep the database up to date, or clearly mark that it is no longer maintained. Within the journalistic context, publishing a database demands a higher level of maintenance than publishing an article. The level of interactivity that a database affords means that there is a different expectation of how up to date it is compared to an article. Fourth, allocate enough resources for maintenance over time. Keeping the data and database software up to date involves significant resources. For example, adding data from the following year to a database requires merging newer data with older data, and adding an extra time dimension to the user interface. Fifth, observe how readers are using the database. Trends in searches or use might provide leads for future stories and investigations. Finally, be transparent: It's rare that a database will be 100% "complete," and every database will have certain choices built into it. Rather than glossing over these choices, make them visible so that readers know what they're looking at.

Works Cited

EFPIA. (2013). About the EFPIA Disclosure Code. European Federation of Pharmaceutical Industries and Associations. https://efpia.eu/media/25046/efpia_about_disclosure_code_march-2016.pdf

Fontaine, C. (2017, April 20). Driving school choice. *Medium*. https://points.datasociety.net/driving-school-choice-16f014d8d4df

Golebiewski, M., & Boyd, D. (2018, May). Data voids: Where missing data can be easily exploited. *Data & Society*. https://datasociety.net/wp-content/uploads/2018/05/Data_ Society_Data_Voids_Final_3.pdf

Holovaty, A. (2006, September 6). A fundamental way newspaper sites need to change. Adrian Holovaty. http://www.holovaty.com/writing/fundamental-change/

Onuoha, M. (2016, February 3). On missing data sets. https://github.com/MimiOnuoha/missing-datasets

Rosen, J. (2018, May 14). Optimizing journalism for trust. *Medium*. https://medium.com/de-correspondent/optimizing-journalism-for-trust-1c67e81c123

About the Authors

Zara Rahman is deputy director at the Engine Room and a fellow at the Digital Civil Society Lab at Stanford University's Centre for Philanthropy and Civil Society.

Stefan Wehrmeyer is the founder of FragDenStaat.de, Germany's Freedom of Information Portal, and works as a data journalist and developer.

29. Narrating Water Conflict With Data and Interactive Comics

Nelly Luna Amancio

Abstract

How we developed an interactive comic to narrate the findings of a journalistic investigation into the water war in Peru against a big mining company.

Keywords: water conflicts, data journalism, environment, comic, interactivity, Peru

Everything in the comic *La guerra por el agua* (The war over water) is real (Figure 29.1). The main characters—Mauro Apaza and Melchora Tacure—exist, along with their fears and uncertainties. We found them on a hot September day of 2016. It was noon and there were no shadows, no wind. She was weeding the soil with her hands, he was making furrows on the rough ground. For over 70 years they've grown food on a small plot of land in the Tambo Valley, an agricultural area in southern Peru where there are proposals for a mining project. The history of this couple, like that of thousands of farmers and Indigenous communities, tells of disputes between farmers and the powerful industries working to extract one of the world's most strategic resources: Water.

How to narrate this confrontation in a country like Peru where there are more than 200 environmental conflicts and the national budget depends heavily on income from this sector? How to approach a story about tensions between precarious farmers, the interests of multinational companies and those of a government that needs to increase its tax collection? What narrative can help us to understand this? How is it possible to mobilize people around this urgent issue? These questions prompted *The War Over Water*—the first interactive comic in Peru, developed by OjoPúblico.

Bounegru, L. and J. Gray (eds.), *The Data Journalism Handbook: Towards a Critical Data Practice.* Amsterdam: Amsterdam University Press, 2021

DOI 10.5117/9789462989511_CH29

Figure 29.1. Home screen of the interactive comic The War over Water. Source: *OjoPúblico.*

The piece integrates data and visualizations into a narrative about this conflict.[1]

Why an Interactive Comic?

The project began in July 2016. We set out to narrate the conflict from an economic perspective, but to approach the reader from the perspective of two farmers, through a route that mimics an intimate trip to one of the most emblematic areas of the conflict. The interactivity of the format allows the audience to discover the sounds and dialogues of the conflict, across and beyond the strips.

We chose the story of the Tía María mining project of the Southern Copper Corporation—one of the biggest mining companies in the world, owned by one of the richest individuals in Mexico and in the world, Germán Larrea. Local opposition to this project led to violent police repression that killed six citizens.

The team that produced this comic was composed of a journalist (myself), cartoonist Jesús Cossio and web developer Jason Martínez. The three of us travelled to the Tambo Valley in Arequipa, the heart of the conflict, to interview leaders, farmers and authorities, and document the process. We took notes, photos and drawings that would later become the first sketches of the comic. Upon returning to Lima, we structured what would become the

1   https://laguerraporelagua.ojo-publico.com/en/

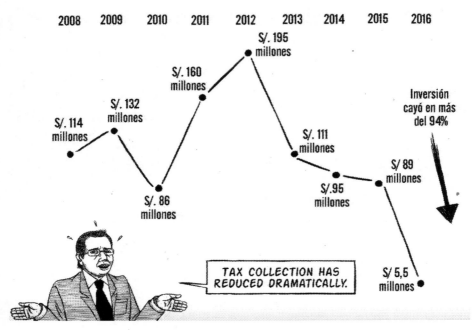

Figure 29.2. Data visualisation showing the decrease in tax collection since 2008 in Peru, as a result of the mining conflict over water. Source: *OjoPúblico*.

first prototype. Based on the prototype, we wrote the final script, worked out the interactive features, and started developing the project.

Honesty With Comics

We chose the medium of the comic because we believe that journalists should not—as cartoonist Joe Sacco (2012) puts it—"neuter the truth in the name of equal time." Sacco joined us for a presentation of the first chapter of the project and it was one of his works that inspired us: *Srebrenica*, a webcomic about the massacre in which more than 8,000 Bosnian Muslims died in 1995.

The War Over Water took eight months to develop. It is based on real events and has a narrative structure that allows the audience to experience the daily life of the characters and to surface one of the biggest dilemmas in the economy of Peru: Agriculture or mining? Is there enough water to do both?

We told the story of this conflict through the eyes and memories of Mauro and Melchora. The story is accompanied by data visualizations showing the economic dependency of the region as well as the tax privileges that mining companies have. All the scenes and the dialogue in the comic are

Figure 29.3. This is how the journalists and the illustrator of *OjoPúblico* developed the interactive script of the comic "The War over Water." Source: *OjoPúblico*.

real, products of our reporting in the area, interviews with the authorities and local people, and investigations into the finances of Southern Copper. We aimed to compose scenes from dialogues, figures, interviews and settings with honesty and precision.

From Paper to the Web

For the cartoonist Jesús Cossio, the challenge was to rethink how to work with time in an interactive comic: "While in a printed cartoon or static digital strip the idea is to make the reader stop at the impact of the images, in an interactive comic the composition and images had to be adapted to the more agile and dynamic flow of reading."

From a technological perspective, the project was a challenge for the OjoPúblico team as we had never developed an interactive comic before. We used the GreenSock Animation Platform (GSAP), a library that allowed us to make animations and transitions, as well as to standardize the scenes and timeline. This was complemented with JavaScript, CSS and HTML5.

The comic has 42 scenes and more than 120 drawings. Jesús Cossio drew each of the characters, scenes and landscapes in the script with pencil and ink. These images were then digitized and separated by layers: Backgrounds, environments, characters and elements of the drawing that had to interact with each other.

From the Web Back to Paper

The War Over Water is a transmedia experience. We have also published a print edition. With its two platforms, the comic seeks to approach different audiences. One of the greatest interests in the OjoPúblico team is the exploration of narratives and formats to tell (often complex) stories of public interest. We have previously won awards for our data investigations.

In other projects we have also used the comic format to narrate the topic of violence. In *Proyecto Memoria* (Memory project), the images tell the horror of the domestic conflict that Peru faced between 1980 and 2000. Comics provide a powerful language for telling stories with data. This is our proposal: That investigative journalists should test all possible languages to tell stories for different audiences. But above all, we want to denounce imbalances of power—in this case the management of natural resources in Peru.

Works Cited

Sacco, J. (2012). *Journalism*. Henry Holt and Co.

About the Author

Nelly Luna Amancio is an investigative journalist, editor and founder of OjoPúblico, a Peruvian media outlet that investigates power and conducts cross-border investigations in Latin America.

30. Data Journalism Should Focus on People and Stories

Winny de Jong

Abstract
The story and the people the story is about should be the sun around which journalism, including data journalism, revolve.

Keywords: storytelling, data journalism, radio, television, data publics, data visualization

As is the case with people, data journalism and journalism share more commonalities than differences.[1] Although data-driven reporting builds on different types of sources which require other skills to interrogate, the thought process is much the same. Actually, if you zoom out enough, you'll find that the processes are almost indistinguishable.

Known Unknowns

At its core, journalism is the business of making known unknowns into known knowns. The concept of knowns and unknowns was popularized by the US Secretary of Defense Donald Rumsfeld in 2002. At the time there was a lack of evidence that the Iraqi government had supplied weapons of mass destruction to terrorist groups. During a press briefing over the matter, Rumsfeld said:

[1]   Since ideas are new combinations of old elements, this essay draws on Winny's 2019 Nieman Lab prediction, a talk at the Smart News Design Conference in Amsterdam and alshetongeveer-maarklopt.nl, a Dutch website that teaches math to journalists.

Bounegru, L. and J. Gray (eds.), *The Data Journalism Handbook: Towards a Critical Data Practice.* Amsterdam: Amsterdam University Press, 2021
DOI 10.5117/9789462989511_CH30

Reports that say that something hasn't happened are always interesting to me, because as we know, there are known knowns; there are things we know we know. We also know there are known unknowns; that is to say we know there are some things we do not know. But there are also unknown unknowns—the ones we don't know we don't know. And if one looks throughout the history of our country and other free countries, it is the latter category that tend to be the difficult ones. (US Department of Defense, 2002)

Every journalistic process comes down to moving pawns over the matrix of knowns and unknowns. All journalism starts with a question—or, to follow the said matrix, with a known unknown. (You know there is something you don't know, hence the question.) When bootstrapping to move from question or hunch to publication-ready story, the ideal route is to "simply" move all pawns from known unknowns to known knowns. But as every journalist will tell you, reality tends to differ. While researching—either by interviewing people or examining documents or data sets—you are likely to find things you were not aware that you didn't know (unknown unknowns), that require answers, too. If you're lucky, you might stumble upon some things you didn't know you were familiar with (unknown knowns). Working towards your deadline, you're transforming three categories of knowledge into known knowns: Known unknowns (i.e., the questions that got you started), unknown unknowns (i.e., the questions you didn't know you should have asked), and unknown knowns (answers you didn't know you had). Unlike our governments, journalists can only proceed to action with, or publish, known knowns.

Solid Journalism

With data-driven reporting and classic bootstrapping being so indistinguish-able, surely the two should meet the same standards. Like journalism, data journalism should always be truthful, independent and free of bias. Like all other facts, data needs to be verified. So before trying to create known knowns, ask yourself: Is the data true? What does each number actually mean? What is the source? Why was the data collected? Who made the data set? How was the data table created? Are there outliers in the data? Do they make sense? And, often forgotten but, as with every interview, of significant importance: What does the source not say? While the requirements and therefore the questions are the same, the actions they result in slightly differ.

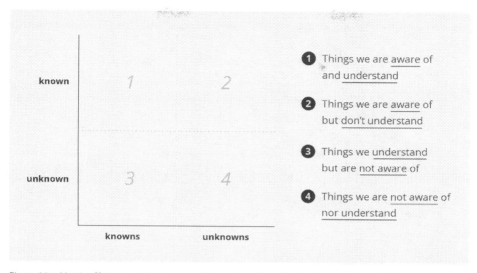

Figure 30.1. Matrix of knowns and unknowns. This matrix differs slightly from the Johari Window, which is sometimes used in cognitive psychology to help people better understand their relationship with themselves and others. Source: Lars Boogaard.

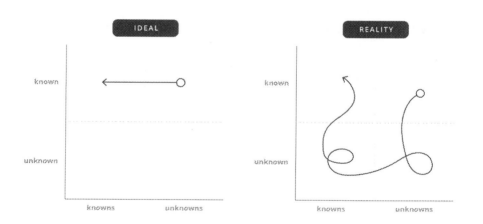

Figure 30.2. Navigating the knowns and unknowns matrix for journalism. Source: Lars Boogaard.

As Bill Kovach and Tom Rosenstiel (2007) describe in *The Elements of Journalism*, the first task of the news journalist is "to verify what information is reliable and then order it so people can grasp it efficiently." For data journalists—especially those working in television or radio—this means that the numbers they came to love do not necessarily have a place in the final production.

Figure 30.3. Still from an NOS video on how thin you need to be to become a fashion model.
Source: *NOS*.

Limited Nerdery

Obviously you should be precise while doing data analysis. But in order to keep your story "efficiently graspable," there needs to be a limit on precision—for example, the number of decimals used—in the final publication. Using "4 out of 10 people" is probably better than "41.8612%." In my experience the right amount of precision is pretty close to the precision you would use when talking about your story to non-data-nerd friends on a Saturday afternoon.

Unless your audience needs to know about the methods and tools used to be able to grasp the story, you should probably save the nerd goodies for the methodology. Because when your audience is reading, listening or watching your data-driven production they should be thinking about the story, not the data, analysis or technology that keep the story afloat. This means that the best data journalism might hardly be recognizable as such—making data journalism an invisible craft. As long as this invisibility facilitates the story, making your journalism more "efficient to grasp," it's all for the better. After all, journalism creates different maps for citizens to navigate society with, so we should make sure our maps are readable for all and read by many.

Radio and Television

When publishing data journalism stories for radio or television, less is more. In the newsroom of NOS, the largest news organization in the Netherlands, reporters talk about the number of seconds they have to tell their stories. This means that there is no time to dwell on how a story was made or why we decided to use the one data source and not the other, if that does not contribute to the story or the public's understanding of said story. In an online video on how thin you need to be to be able to become a high fashion model, we spent 20 seconds explaining our methods.[2] When you have 90 seconds to tell a story on national television, 20 seconds is a lot. In this case, less is more means no time left to explain how we went about the investigation. When time and space are limited, the story prevails above everything else.

Modest Visuals

Of course, the "less is more" adage goes for data visualizations, too. Data journalism is much like teenage sex: Everybody talks about it, yet almost nobody actually does it. When newsrooms finally add data to their toolkit, some have a tendency to kiss and tell by making data visuals for everything. Sure, I love visuals, too, especially the innovative, high-end ones—but only if they add to the story. Visualizations can add value to journalism in multiple ways. Among others they can do so by deepening the public's understanding of the story at hand and by widening the public's understanding by giving extra insight at, for example, a regional level. So act like a gentleman and don't kiss and tell. Limit yourself to value-adding data visualizations that help to get the story across. Nowadays most people combine listening to the radio and watching television with another activity. This limits their information intake: When driving, listening to news is secondary; the same goes for watching TV while cooking. So be careful not to ask too much from your audience. Again, this might make our craft an invisible one; but we're here to break news and tell stories—not to flex our dataviz (data visualization) muscles.

About People

All of this is to say that everything that truly matters—in your story, in journalism and in life at large—does not fit in a data set. It never has, and it never will. In the end it's always about people; so whatever you do, wherever

2   https://www.youtube.com/watch?v=DWRGqmywNY

you publish, talk people not data. And when you find yourself tempted to use more data, technology or news nerdery than necessary, remember that you're one of too few craftspeople in this field. That in and of itself is awesome: There is no need to underline the obvious. So simply stick to the pecking order found in the best data journalism: Form facilitates data, facilitates story. Everything and everybody needs to revolve around the story—it is our sun. Story is king.

Works Cited

Kovach, B., & Rosenstiel, T. (2007). *The elements of journalism: What newspeople should know and the public should expect.* Three Rivers Press.

US Department of Defense. (2002, February 12). DoD News Briefing—Secretary Rumsfeld and Gen. Myers [Interview transcript]. https://archive.defense.gov/Transcripts/Transcript.aspx?TranscriptID=2636

About the Author

Winny de Jong works as a data journalist at the Dutch national news broadcaster NOS and publishes the weekly *Data Journalism Newsletter* at ddj.news.

Investigating Data, Platforms and Algorithms

31. The Algorithms Beat: Angles and Methods for Investigation

Nicholas Diakopoulos

Abstract

A beat on algorithms is coalescing as journalistic skills come together with technical skills to provide the scrutiny that algorithms deserve.

Keywords: algorithms, algorithmic accountability, computational journalism, investigative journalism, algorithm studies, freedom of information (FOI)

The "Machine Bias" series from *ProPublica* began in May 2016 as an effort to investigate algorithms in society.[1] Perhaps most striking in the series was an investigation and analysis exposing the racial bias of recidivism risk assessment algorithms used in criminal justice decisions (Angwin et al., 2016). These algorithms score individuals based on whether they are a low or high risk of reoffending. States and other municipalities variously use the scores for managing pretrial detention, probation, parole and sometimes even sentencing. Reporters at *ProPublica* filed a public records request for the scores from Broward County in Florida and then matched those scores to actual criminal histories to see whether an individual had actually recidivated (i.e., reoffended) within two years. Analysis of the data showed that Black defendants tended to be assigned higher risk scores than White defendants, and were more likely to be incorrectly labelled as high risk when in fact after two years they hadn't actually been rearrested (Larson et al., 2016).

Scoring in the criminal justice system is, of course, just one domain where algorithms are being deployed in society. The "Machine Bias" series has since

[1]   https://www.propublica.org/series/machine-bias

Bounegru, L. and J. Gray (eds.), *The Data Journalism Handbook: Towards a Critical Data Practice.*
Amsterdam: Amsterdam University Press, 2021
DOI 10.5117/9789462989511_CH31

covered everything from Facebook's ad-targeting system, to geographically discriminatory auto insurance rates, and unfair pricing practices on Amazon. com. Algorithmic decision making is increasingly pervasive throughout both the public and private sectors. We see it in domains like credit and insurance risk scoring, employment systems, welfare management, educational and teacher rankings, and online media curation, among many others (Eubanks, 2018; O'Neil, 2016; Pasquale, 2015). Operating at scale and often impacting large swaths of people, algorithms can make consequential and sometimes contestable calculation, ranking, classification, association and filtering decisions. Algorithms, animated by piles of data, are a potent new way of wielding power in society.

As *ProPublica*'s "Machine Bias" series attests, a new strand of computational and data journalism is emerging to investigate and hold accountable how power is exerted through algorithms. I call this *algorithmic accountability reporting*, a re-orientation of the traditional watchdog function of journalism towards the power wielded through algorithms (Diakopoulos, 2015).[2] Despite their ostensible objectivity, algorithms can and do make mistakes and embed biases that warrant closer scrutiny. Slowly, a beat on algorithms is coalescing as journalistic skills come together with technical skills to provide the scrutiny that algorithms deserve.

There are, of course, a variety of forms of algorithmic accountability that may take place in diverse forums beyond journalism, such as in political, legal, academic, activist or artistic contexts (Brain & Mattu, n.d.; Bucher, 2018).[3] But my focus is this chapter is squarely on algorithmic accountability reporting as an independent journalistic endeavour that contributes to accountability by mobilizing public pressure. This can be seen as complementary to other avenues that may ultimately also contribute to accountability, such as by developing regulations and legal standards, creating audit institutions in civil society, elaborating effective transparency policies, exhibiting reflexive art shows, and publishing academic critiques.

2   The term *algorithmic accountability* was originally coined in: Diakopoulos, N. (2013, August 2). Sex, violence, and autocomplete algorithms. *Slate Magazine*. https://slate.com/ technology/2013/08/words-banned-from-bing-and-googles-autocomplete-algorithms.html; and elaborated in: Diakopoulos, N. (2013, October 3). Rage against the algorithms. *The Atlantic*. https://www.theatlantic.com/technology/archive/2013/10/rage-against-the-algorithms/280255/
3   For an activist/artistic frame, see: Brain, T., & Mattu, S. (n.d.). *Algorithmic disobedience*. https://samatt.github.io/algorithmic-disobedience/#/. For an academic treatment examining algorithmic power, see: Bucher, T. (2018). *If. . . then: Algorithmic power and politics*. Oxford University Press. A broader selection of the academic scholarship on critical algorithm studies can be found here: https://socialmediacollective.org/reading-lists/critical-algorithm-studies/

In deciding what constitutes the beat in journalism, it is first helpful to define what is newsworthy about algorithms. Technically speaking, an algorithm is a sequence of steps followed in order to solve a particular problem or to accomplish a defined outcome. In terms of information processes, the outcomes of algorithms are typically decisions. The crux of algorithmic power often boils down to computers' ability to make such decisions very quickly and at scale, potentially affecting large numbers of people. In practice, algorithmic accountability is not just about the technical side of algorithms, however—algorithms should be understood as composites of technology woven together with people such as designers, operators, owners and maintainers in complex sociotechnical systems (Ananny, 2015; Seaver, 2017). Algorithmic accountability is about understanding how those people exercise power within and through the system, and are ultimately responsible for the system's decisions. Oftentimes what makes an algorithm newsworthy is when it somehow makes a "bad" decision. This might involve an algorithm doing something it was not supposed to do, or perhaps not doing something it was supposed to do. For journalism, the public significance and consequences of a bad decision are key factors. What is the potential harm for an individual, or for society? Bad decisions might impact individuals directly, or in aggregate may reinforce issues like structural bias. Bad decisions can also be costly. Let's look at how various bad decisions can lead to news stories.

Angles on Algorithms

In observing the algorithms beat developed over the last several years in journalism, as well as through my own investigations of algorithms, I have identified at least four driving forces that appear to underlie many algorithmic accountability stories: (a) discrimination and unfairness, (b) errors or mistakes in predictions or classifications, (c) legal or social norm violations, and (d) misuse of algorithms by people either intentionally or inadvertently. I provide illustrative examples of each of these in the following subsections.

Discrimination and Unfairness. Uncovering discrimination and unfairness is a common theme in algorithmic accountability reporting. The story from *ProPublica* that opened this chapter is a striking example of how an algorithm can lead to systematic disparities in the treatment of different groups of people. Northpointe, the company that designed the risk assessment scores (since renamed Equivant), argued the scores were equally accurate across races and were therefore fair. But their definition of fairness failed to take into account the disproportionate volume of mistakes that affected Black people. Stories of discrimination and unfairness hinge on the definition of fairness applied, which may reflect different political suppositions (Lepri et al., 2018).

I have also worked on stories that uncover unfairness due to algorithmic systems—in particular looking at how Uber pricing dynamics may differentially affect neighbourhoods in Washington, DC (Stark & Diakopoulos, 2016). Based on initial observations of different waiting times and how those waiting times shifted based on Uber's surge pricing algorithm, we hypothesized that different neighbourhoods would have different levels of service quality (i.e., waiting time). By systematically sampling the waiting times in different census tracts over time, we showed that census tracts with more people of colour tend to have longer wait times for a car, even when controlling for other factors like income, poverty rate and population density in the neighbourhood. It is difficult to pin the unfair outcome directly to Uber's technical algorithm because other human factors also drive the system, such as the behaviour and potential biases of Uber drivers. But the results do suggest that when considered as a whole, the system exhibits disparity associated with demographics.

Errors and Mistakes. Algorithms can also be newsworthy when they make specific errors or mistakes in their classification, prediction or filtering decisions. Consider the case of platforms like Facebook and Google which use algorithmic filters to reduce exposure to harmful content like hate speech, violence and pornography. This can be important for the protection of specific vulnerable populations, like children, especially in products (such as Google's YouTube Kids) which are explicitly marketed as safe for children. Errors in the filtering algorithm for the app are newsworthy because they mean that sometimes children encounter inappropriate or violent content (Maheshwari, 2017). Classically, algorithms make two types of mistakes: False positives and false negatives. In the YouTube Kids scenario, a false positive would be a video mistakenly classified as inappropriate when actually it's totally fine for kids. A false negative is a video classified as appropriate when it is really not something you want kids watching.

Classification decisions impact individuals when they either increase or decrease the positive or negative treatment an individual receives. When an algorithm mistakenly selects an individual to receive free ice cream (increased positive treatment), you won't hear that individual complain (although when others find out, they might say it's unfair). Errors are generally newsworthy when they lead to increased negative treatment for a person, such as by exposing a child to an inappropriate video. Errors are also newsworthy when they lead to a decrease in positive treatment for an individual, such as when a person misses an opportunity. Just imagine a qualified buyer who never gets a special offer because an algorithm mistakenly excludes them. Finally, errors can be newsworthy when they cause a decrease in warranted negative attention. Consider a criminal risk assessment algorithm mistakenly labelling a high-risk individual as low-risk—a false negative. While that's great for the individual, this creates a greater risk to public safety by setting free an individual who might go on to commit a crime again.

Legal and Social Norm Violations. Predictive algorithms can sometimes test the boundaries of established legal or social norms, leading to other opportunities and angles for coverage. Consider for a moment the possibility of algorithmic defamation (Diakopoulos, 2013; Lewis et al., 2019). Defamation is defined as "a false statement of fact that exposes a person to hatred, ridicule or contempt, lowers him in the esteem of his peers, causes him to be shunned, or injures him in his business or trade."[4] Over the last several years there have been numerous stories, and legal battles, over individuals who feel they have been defamed by Google's autocomplete algorithm. An autocompletion can link an individual's or a company's name to everything from crime and fraud to bankruptcy or sexual conduct, which can then have consequences for reputation. Algorithms can also be newsworthy when they encroach on social norms like privacy. For instance, *Gizmodo* has extensively covered the "People You May Know" (PYMK) algorithm on Facebook, which suggests potential "friends" on the platform that are sometimes inappropriate or undesired (Hill, 2017b). In one story, reporters identified a case where PYMK outed the real identity of a sex worker to her clients (Hill, 2017a). This is problematic not only because of the potential stigma attached to sex work, but also out of fear of clients who could become stalkers.

Defamation and privacy violations are only two possible story angles here. Journalists should be on the lookout for a range of other legal or social norm violations that algorithms may create in various social contexts. Since algorithms necessarily rely on a quantified version of reality that only incorporates what is measurable as data they can miss a lot of the social and legal context that would otherwise be essential in rendering an accurate decision. By understanding what a particular algorithm actually quantifies about the world—how it "sees" things—journalists can inform

---

4   http://www.dmlp.org/legal-guide/defamation

critique by illuminating the missing bits that would support a decision in the richness of its full context.

Human Misuse. Algorithmic decisions are often embedded in larger decision-making processes that involve a constellation of people and algorithms woven together in a sociotechnical system. Despite the inaccessibility of some of their sensitive technical components, the sociotechnical nature of algorithms opens up new opportunities for investigating the relationships that users, designers, owners and other stakeholders may have to the overall system (Trielli & Diakopoulos, 2017). If algorithms are misused by the people in the sociotechnical ensemble, this may also be newsworthy. The designers of algorithms can sometimes anticipate and articulate guidelines for a reasonable set of use contexts for a system, and so if people ignore these in practice it can lead to a story of negligence or misuse. The risk assessment story from *ProPublica* provides a salient example. Northpointe had in fact created two versions and calibrations of the tool, one for men and one for women. Statistical models need to be trained on data reflective of the population where they will be used and gender is an important factor in recidivism prediction. But Broward County was misusing the risk score designed and calibrated for men by using it for women as well (Larson, 2016).

How to Investigate an Algorithm

There are various routes to the investigation of algorithmic power and no single approach will always be appropriate. But there is a growing stable of methods to choose from, including everything from highly technical reverse engineering and code-inspection techniques, to auditing using automated or crowdsourced data collection, or even low-tech approaches to prod and critique based on algorithmic reactions (Diakopoulos, 2017, 2019).[5] Each story may require a different approach depending on the angle and the specific context, including what degree of access to the algorithm, its data and its code is available. For instance, an exposé on systematic discrimination may lean heavily on an audit method using data collected online, whereas a code review may be necessary to verify the correct implementation of

5   For more a more complete treatment of methodological options, see: Diakopoulos, N. (2019). *Automating the news: How algorithms are rewriting the media*. Harvard University Press; see also: Diakopoulos, N. (2017). Enabling accountability of algorithmic media: Transparency as a constructive and critical lens. In T. Cerquitelli, D. Quercia, & F. Pasquale (Eds.), *Transparent data mining for big and small data* (pp. 25–43). Springer International Publishing. https://doi. org/10.1007/978-3-319-54024-5_2

an intended policy (Lecher, 2018). Traditional journalistic sourcing to talk to company insiders such as designers, developers and data scientists, as well as to file public records requests and find impacted individuals, are as important as ever. I can't go into depth on all of these methods in this short chapter, but here I want to at least elaborate a bit more on how journalists can investigate algorithms using auditing.

Auditing techniques have been used for decades to study social bias in systems like housing markets and have recently been adapted for studying algorithms (Gaddis, 2017; Sandvig et al., 2014). The basic idea is that if the inputs to algorithms are varied in enough different ways, and the outputs are monitored, then inputs and outputs can be correlated to build a theory for how the algorithm may be functioning (Diakopoulos, 2015). If we have some expected outcome that the algorithm violates for a given input this can help tabulate errors and see if errors are biased in systematic ways. When algorithms can be accessed via APIs or online web pages output data can be collected automatically (Valentino-DeVries et al., 2012). For personalized algorithms, auditing techniques have also been married to crowdsourcing in order to gather data from a range of people who may each have a unique "view" of the algorithm. AlgorithmWatch in Germany has used this technique effectively to study the personalization of Google Search results, collecting almost 6 million search results from more than 4,000 users who shared data via a browser plug-in (as discussed further by Christina Elmer in her chapter in this book).[6] *Gizmodo* has used a variant of this technique to help investigate Facebook's PYMK. Users download a piece of software to their computer that periodically tracks PYMK results locally to the user's computer, maintaining their privacy. Reporters can then solicit tips from users who think their results are worrisome or surprising (Hill & Mattu, 2018).

Auditing algorithms is not for the faint of heart. Information deficits limit an auditor's ability to sometimes even know where to start, what to ask for, how to interpret results and how to explain the patterns they are seeing in an algorithm's behaviour. There is also the challenge of knowing and defining what is expected of an algorithm, and how those expectations may vary across contexts and according to different global moral, social, cultural and legal standards and norms. For instance, different expectations for fairness may come into play for a criminal risk assessment algorithm in comparison to an algorithm that charges people different prices for an

6   https://algorithmwatch.org/filterblase-geplatzt-kaum-raum-fuer-personalisierung-bei-google-suchen-zur-bundestagswahl-2017/ (German language)

airline seat. In order to identify a newsworthy mistake or bias you must first define what normal or unbiased should look like. Sometimes that definition comes from a data-driven baseline, such as in our audits of news sources in Google search results during the 2016 US elections (Diakopoulos et al., 2018). The issue of legal access to information about algorithms also crops up and is, of course, heavily contingent on the jurisdiction (Bhandari & Goodman, 2017). In the United States, freedom of information (FOI) laws govern the public's access to government documents, but the response from different agencies for documents relating to algorithms is uneven at best (see Brauneis & Goodman, 2018; Diakopoulos, 2016; Fink, 2017). Legal reforms may be in order so that public access to information about algorithms is more easily facilitated. And if information deficits, difficult-to-articulate expectations and uncertain legal access are not challenging enough, just remember that algorithms can also be quite capricious. Today's version of the algorithm may already be different than yesterday's: As one example, Google typically changes its search algorithm 500–600 times a year. Depending on the stakes of the potential changes, algorithms may need to be monitored over time in order to understand how they are changing and evolving.

Recommendations Moving Forward

To get started and make the most of algorithmic accountability reporting, I would recommend three things. Firstly, we have developed a resource called Algorithm Tips, which curates relevant methods, examples and educational resources, and hosts a database of algorithms for potential investigation (first covering algorithms in the US federal government and then expanded to cover more jurisdictions globally).[7] If you are looking for resources to learn more and help to get a project off the ground, that could be one starting point (Trielli et al., 2017). Secondly, focus on the outcomes and impacts of algorithms rather than trying to explain the exact mechanism of their decision making. Identifying algorithmic discrimination (i.e., an output) oftentimes has more value to society as an initial step than explaining exactly how that discrimination came about. By focusing on outcomes, journalists can provide a first-order diagnostic and signal an alarm which other stakeholders can then dig into in other accountability forums. Finally, much of the published algorithmic accountability reporting I have cited here is done in teams, and with

7   http://algorithmtips.org/

good reason. Effective algorithmic accountability reporting demands all of the traditional skills journalists need in reporting and interviewing, domain knowledge of a beat, public records requests and analysis of the returned documents, and writing results clearly and compellingly, while often also relying on a host of new capabilities like scraping and cleaning data, designing audit studies, and using advanced statistical techniques. Expertise in these different areas can be distributed among a team, or with external collaborators, as long as there is clear communication, awareness and leadership. In this way, methods specialists can partner with different domain experts to understand algorithmic power across a larger variety of social domains.

Works Cited

Ananny, M. (2015). Toward an ethics of algorithms. *Science, Technology & Human Values, 41*(1), 93–117.

Angwin, J., Larson, J., Mattu, S., & Kirchner, L. (2016, May 23). Machine bias. *ProPublica*. https://www.propublica.org/article/machine-bias-risk-assessments-in-criminal-sentencing

Bhandari, E., & Goodman, R. (2017). Data journalism and the computer fraud and abuse act: Tips for moving forward in an uncertain landscape. Computation+Journalism Symposium. https://www.aclu.org/other/data-journalism-and-computer-fraud-and-abuse-act-tips-moving-forward-uncertain-landscape

Brain, T., & Mattu, S. (n.d.). Algorithmic disobedience. https://samatt.github.io/algorithmic-disobedience/

Brauneis, R., & Goodman, E. P. (2018). Algorithmic transparency for the smart city. *Yale Journal of Law & Technology, 20*, 103–176.

Bucher, T. (2018). *If... then: Algorithmic power and politics*. Oxford University Press.

Diakopoulos, N. (2013, August 6). Algorithmic defamation: The case of the shameless autocomplete. Tow Center for Journalism. https://towcenter.org/algorithmic-defamation-the-case-of-the-shameless-autocomplete

Diakopoulos, N. (2015). Algorithmic accountability: Journalistic investigation of computational power structures. *Digital Journalism, 3*(3), 398–415. https://doi.org/10.1080/21670811.2014.976411

Diakopoulos, N. (2016, May 24). We need to know the algorithms the government uses to make important decisions about us. *The Conversation*. http://theconversation.com/we-need-to-know-the-algorithms-the-government-uses-to-make-important-decisions-about-us-57869

Diakopoulos, N. (2017) Enabling Accountability of Algorithmic Media: Transparency as a Constructive and Critical Lens. In T. Cerquitelli, D. Quercia, & F. Pasquale (Eds.), *Transparent data mining for Big and Small Data* (pp. 25–44). Springer.

Diakopoulos, N. (2019). *Automating the News: How Algorithms are Rewriting the Media*. Harvard University Press.

Diakopoulos, N., Trielli, D., Stark, J., & Mussenden, S. (2018). I vote for—How search informs our choice of candidate. In M. Moore & D. Tambini (Eds.), *Digital Dominance: The power of Google, Amazon, Facebook, and Apple* (pp. 320–341). Oxford University Press. https://www.academia.edu/37432634/I_Vote_For_How_Search_Informs_Our_Choice_of_Candidate

Eubanks, V. (2018). *Automating inequality: How high-tech tools profile, police, and punish the poor*. St. Martin's Press.

Fink, K. (2017). Opening the government's black boxes: Freedom of information and algorithmic accountability. *Digital Journalism*, *17*(1). https://doi.org/10.1080/1369118X.2017.1330418

Gaddis, S. M. (2017). An introduction to audit studies in the social sciences. In M. Gaddis (Ed.), *Audit studies: Behind the scenes with theory, method, and nuance* (pp. 3–44). Springer International Publishing.

Gillespie, T., & Seaver, N. (2015, November 5). Critical algorithm studies: A reading list. *Social Media Collective*. https://socialmediacollective.org/reading-lists/critical-algorithm-studies/

Hill, K. (2017a, October). How Facebook outs sex workers. *Gizmodo*. https://gizmodo.com/how-facebook-outs-sex-workers-1818861596

Hill, K. (2017b, November). How Facebook figures out everyone you've ever met. *Gizmodo*. https://gizmodo.com/how-facebook-figures-out-everyone-youve-ever-met-1819822691

Hill, K., & Mattu, S. (2018, January 10). Keep track of who Facebook thinks you know with this nifty tool. *Gizmodo*. https://gizmodo.com/keep-track-of-who-facebook-thinks-you-know-with-this-ni-1819422352

Larson, J. (2016, October 20). Machine bias with Jeff Larson [Data Stories podcast]. https://datastori.es/85-machine-bias-with-jeff-larson/

Larson, J., Mattu, S., Kirchner, L., & Angwin, J. (2016, May 23). How we analyzed the COMPAS recidivism algorithm. *ProPublica*. https://www.propublica.org/article/how-we-analyzed-the-compas-recidivism-algorithm

Lecher, C. (2018, March 21). What happens when an algorithm cuts your health care. *The Verge*. https://www.theverge.com/2018/3/21/17144260/healthcare-medicaid-algorithm-arkansas-cerebral-palsy

Lepri, B., Oliver, N., Letouzé, E., Pentland, A., & Vinck, P. (2018). Fair, transparent, and accountable algorithmic decision-making processes. *Philosophy & Technology*, *31*(4), 611–627. https://doi.org/10.1007/s13347-017-0279-x

Lewis, S. C., Sanders, A. K., & Carmody, C. (2019). Libel by algorithm? Automated journalism and the threat of legal liability. *Journalism and Mass Communication Quarterly, 96*(1), 60–81. https://doi.org/10.1177/1077699018755983

Maheshwari, S. (2017, November 4). On Youtube Kids, startling videos slip past filters. *The New York Times.* https://www.nytimes.com/2017/11/04/business/media/youtube-kids-paw-patrol.html?_r=0

O'Neil, C. (2016). *Weapons of math destruction: How big data increases inequality and threatens democracy.* Broadway Books.

Pasquale, F. (2015). *The black box society: The secret algorithms that control money and information.* Harvard University Press.

Sandvig, C., Hamilton, K., Karahalios, K., & Langbort, C. (2014, May 22). Auditing algorithms: Research methods for detecting discrimination on Internet platforms. International Communication Association preconference on Data and Discrimination Converting Critical Concerns into Productive Inquiry, Seattle, WA.

Seaver, N. (2017). Algorithms as culture: Some tactics for the ethnography of algorithmic systems. *Big Data & Society, 4*(2). https://doi.org/10.1177/2053951717738104

Stark, J., & Diakopoulos, N. (2016, March 10). Uber seems to offer better service in areas with more White people. That raises some tough questions. *The Washington Post.* https://www.washingtonpost.com/news/wonk/wp/2016/03/10/uber-seems-to-offer-better-service-in-areas-with-more-white-people-that-raises-some-tough-questions/

Trielli, D., & Diakopoulos, N. (2017, May 30). How to report on algorithms even if you're not a data whiz. *Columbia Journalism Review.* https://www.cjr.org/tow_center/algorithms-reporting-algorithmtips.php

Trielli, D., Stark, J., & Diakopoulos, N. (2017). *Algorithm tips: A resource for algorithmic accountability in Government.* Computation + Journalism Symposium.

Valentino-DeVries, J., Singer-Vine, J., & Soltani, A. (2012, December 24). Websites vary prices, deals based on users' information. *The Wall Street Journal.* https://www.wsj.com/articles/SB10001424127887323777204578189391813881534

About the Author

Nicholas Diakopoulos is an Assistant Professor at Northwestern University School of Communication, where he directs the Computational Journalism Lab. He is the author of *Automating the News: How Algorithms are Rewriting the Media* (Harvard University Press, 2019).

32. Telling Stories With the Social Web

Lam Thuy Vo

Abstract

This chapter is a primer into investigating the social web.

Keywords: social media, misinformation, data journalism, data analysis, data visualization, bots

We have become the largest producers of data in history.[1] Almost every click online, each swipe on our tablets and each tap on our smartphone produces a data point in a virtual repository. Facebook generates data on the lives of more than 2 billion people. Twitter records the activities of more than 330 million monthly users. One MIT study found that the average American office worker was producing 5GB of data each day (Tucker, 2013). That was in 2013 and we haven't slowed down. As more and more people conduct their lives online, and as smartphones are penetrating previously unconnected regions around the world, this trove of stories is only becoming larger.

A lot of researchers tend to treat each social media user like they would treat an individual subject—as anecdotes and single points of contact. But to do so with a handful of users and their individual posts is to ignore the potential of hundreds of millions of others and their interactions with one another. There are many stories that could be told from the vast amounts of data produced by social media users and platforms because researchers and journalists are still only starting to acquire the large-scale data-wrangling expertise and analytical techniques needed to tap them.

Recent events have also shown that it is becoming crucial for reporters to gain a better grasp of the social web. The Russian interference with the 2016

---

1   Earlier versions of this chapter have been published at: https://source.opennews.org/articles/what-buzzfeed-news-learned-after-year-mining-data-/, http://www.niemanlab.org/2016/12/the-primary-source-in-the-age-of-mechanical-multiplication/

Bounegru, L. and J. Gray (eds.), *The Data Journalism Handbook: Towards a Critical Data Practice.*
Amsterdam: Amsterdam University Press, 2021
DOI 10.5117/9789462989511_CH32

US presidential elections and Brexit; the dangerous spread of anti-Muslim hate speech on Facebook in countries in Europe and in Myanmar; and the heavy-handed use of Twitter by global leaders—all these developments show that there's an ever-growing need to gain a competent level of literacy around the usefulness and pitfalls of social media data in aggregate.

How Can Journalists Use Social Media Data?

While there are many different ways in which social media can be helpful in reporting, it may be useful to examine the data we can harvest from social media platforms through two lenses.

First, social media can be used as a proxy to better understand individuals and their actions. Be it public proclamations or private exchanges between individuals—a lot of people's actions, as mediated and disseminated through technology nowadays, leave traces online that can be mined for insights. This is particularly helpful when looking at politicians and other important figures, whose public opinions could be indicative of their policies or have real-life consequences like the plummeting of stock prices or the firing of important people.

Second, the web can be seen as an ecosystem in its own right in which stories take place on social platforms (albeit still driven by human and automated actions). Misinformation campaigns, algorithmically skewed information universes and trolling attacks are all phenomena that are unique to the social web.

Case Studies

Instead of discussing these kinds of stories in the abstract, it may be more helpful to understand social media data in the context of how it can be used to tell particular stories. The following sections discuss a number of journalistic projects that made use of social media data.

Understanding Public Figures: Social Media Data for Accountability Reporting

For public figures and everyday people alike, social media has become a way to address the public in a direct manner. Status updates, tweets and posts

**Here's Where Donald
Trump Gets His News**

BuzzFeed News analyzed all
the links Donald Trump
tweeted since he launched
his presidential campaign to
determine where the
president-elect gets his news.
The analyzed tweets were
broadcast between June 1,
2015 — the month Donald
Trump announced his
presidential campaign — and
Nov. 17, 2016. Sites that were
categorized as "media" were
broadly defined as
organizations that publish
content regularly.

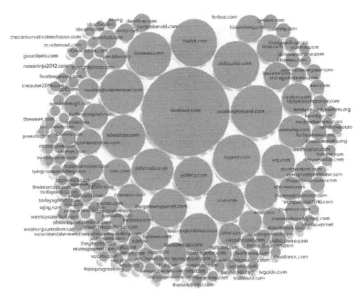

Figure 32.1. A snapshot of the media links that Trump tweeted during his presidential campaign.
Source: *BuzzFeed News*.

can serve as ways to bypass older projection mechanisms like interviews
with the news media, press releases or press conferences.

For politicians, however, these public announcements—these projections
of their selves—may become binding statements and in the case of powerful
political figures may become harbingers for policies that have yet to be put
in place.

Because a politician's job is partially to be public-facing, researching
a politician's social media accounts can help us better understand their
ideological mindset. For one story, my colleague Charlie Warzel and I collected and analyzed more than 20,000 of Donald Trump's tweets to answer
the following question: What kind of information does he disseminate and
how can this information serve as a proxy for the kind of information he
may consume?

Social data points are not a full image of who we actually are, in part due to
their performative nature and in part because these data sets are incomplete
and so open to individual interpretation. But they can help as complements:
President Trump's affiliation with *Breitbart* online, as shown in Figure 32.1,
was an early indicator for his strong ties to Steve Bannon in real life. His
retweeting of smaller conservative blogs like the Conservative Tree House
and News Ninja 2012 perhaps hinted at his distrust of "mainstream media."

Tracing Back Human Actions

While public and semi-public communications like tweets and open Facebook posts can give insights into how people portray themselves to others, there's also the kind of data that lives on social platforms behind closed walls like private messages, Google searches or geolocation data.

Christian Rudder (2014), co-founder of OKCupid and author of the book *Dataclysm*, had a rather apt description of this kind of data: These are statistics that are recorded of our behaviour when we "think that no one is watching."

By virtue of using a social platform, a person ends up producing longitudinal data of their own behaviour. And while it's hard to extrapolate much from these personal data troves beyond the scope of the person who produced them, this kind of data can be extremely powerful when trying to tell the story of one person. I often like to refer this kind of approach as a "quantified selfie," a term Maureen O'Connor coined for me when she described some of my work.

Take the story of Jeffrey Ngo, for instance. When pro-democracy protests began in his hometown, Hong Kong, in early September 2014, Ngo, a New York University student originally from Hong Kong, felt compelled to act. Ngo started to talk to other expatriate Hong Kongers in New York and in Washington, DC. He ended up organizing protests in 86 cities across the globe and his story is emblematic of many movements that originate on global outrage about an issue.

For this *Al Jazeera America* story, Ngo allowed us to mine his personal Facebook history—an archive that each Facebook user can download from the platform (Vo, 2015). We scraped the messages he exchanged with another core organizer in Hong Kong and found 10 different chat rooms in which the two and other organizers exchanged thoughts about their political activities.

The chart below (Figure 32.2) documents the ebbs and flows of their communications. First there's a spike of communications when a news event brought about public outrage—Hong Kong police throwing tear gas at peaceful demonstrators. Then there's the emergence of one chat room, the one in beige, which became the chat room in which the core organizers planned political activities well beyond the initial news events.

Since most of their planning took place inside these chat rooms, we were also able to recount the moment when Ngo first met his co-organizer, Angel Yau. Ngo himself wasn't able to recall their first exchanges but thanks to the Facebook archive we were able to reconstruct the very first conversation Ngo had with Yau.

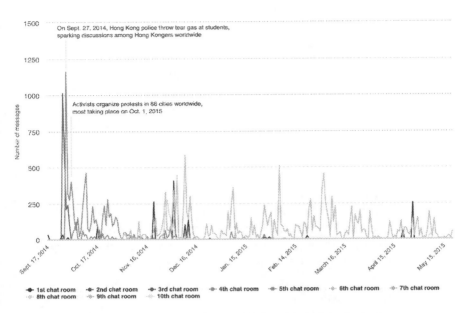

Figure 32.2. United for Democracy: Global Solidarity with Hong Kong Facebook group. Facebook data courtesy of Jeffrey Ngo. Source: *BuzzFeed News*.

While it is clear that Ngo's evolution as a political organizer is that of an individual and by no means representative of every person who participated in his movement, it is, however, emblematic of the *kind* of path a political organizer may take in the digital age.

Phenomena Specific to Online Ecosystems

Many of our interactions are moving exclusively to online platforms. While much of our social behaviour online and offline is intermingled, our online environments are still quite particular because online human beings are assisted by powerful tools.

There's bullying for one. Bullying has arguably existed as long as humankind. But now bullies are assisted by thousands of other bullies who can be called upon within the blink of an eye. Bullies have access to search engines and digital traces of a person's life, sometimes going as far back as that person's online personas go. And they have the means of amplification—one bully shouting from across the hallway is not nearly as deafening as thousands of them coming at you all at the same time. Such is the nature of trolling.

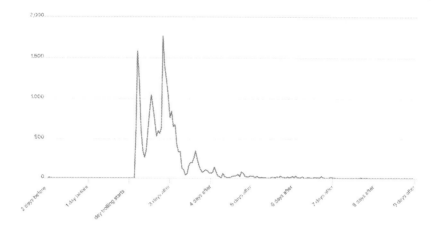

What it feels like to be trolled

After a Washington Post editor found herself at the heart of a political controversy, we analyzed and visualized 24,731 of the tweets directed at her to show you what a Twitter attack feels like. This booklet is a visualization of every Twitter mention of hers within the first 7 days of going viral.

Figure 32.3 - A chart of Doris Truong's Twitter mentions starting the day of the attack. Source: BuzzFeed News. https://www.buzzfeednews.com/article/lamvo/heres-what-it-feels-like-to-be-trolled-in-trumps-america

Washington Post editor Doris Truong, for instance, found herself at the heart of a political controversy online. Over the course of a few days, trolls (and a good amount of people defending her) directed 24,731 Twitter mentions at her. Being pummelled with vitriol on the Internet can only be ignored for so long before it takes some kind of emotional toll.

Trolling, not unlike many other online attacks, have become problems that can afflict any person now—famous or not. From Yelp reviews of businesses that go viral—like the cake shop that refused to prepare a wedding cake for a gay couple—to the ways in which virality brought about the firing and public shaming of Justine Sacco—a PR person who made an unfortunate joke about HIV and South Africans right before she took off on an intercontinental flight—many stories that affect our day-to-day life take place online these days.

Information Wars

The emergence and the ubiquitous use of social media have brought about a new phenomenon in our lives: Virality.

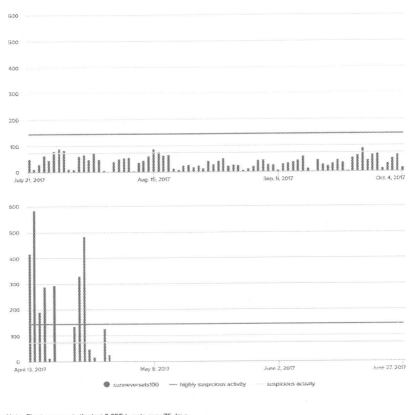

Note: Chart represents the last 2,955 tweets over 76 days.

Source: Twitter

Figure 32.4. *BuzzFeed News* compared one of its own human editors' Twitter data, @tomnamako, and the data of several accounts that displayed bot-like activity to highlight their differences in personas and behavior. The first chart above shows that the *BuzzFeed News* editor's last 2,955 tweets are evenly distributed throughout several months. His daily tweet count barely ever surpassed the mark of 72 tweets per day, which the Digital Forensics Research Lab designated as a suspicious level of activity. The second chart shows the bot's last 2,955 tweets. It was routinely blasting out a suspicious number of tweets, hitting 584 in one day. Then, it seems to have stopped abruptly. Source: *BuzzFeed News*.

Social sharing has made it possible for any kind of content to potentially be seen not just by a few hundred but by millions of people without expensive marketing campaigns or TV air time purchases.

But what that means is that many people have also found ways to game algorithms with fake or purchased followers as well as (semi-)automated accounts like bots and cyborgs (Vo, 2017a).

Bots are not evil from the get-go: There are plenty of bots that may delight us with their whimsical haikus or self-care tips. But as Atlantic Council fellow Ben Nimmo, who has researched bot armies for years, told me for a *BuzzFeed* story: "[Bots] have the potential to seriously distort any debate. . . . They can make a group of six people look like a group of 46,000 people."

The social media platforms themselves are at a pivotal point in their existence where they have to recognize their responsibility in defining and clamping down on what they may deem a "problematic bot." In the meantime, journalists should recognize the ever-growing presence of non-humans and their power online.

For one explanatory piece about automated accounts we wanted to compare tweets from a human to those from a bot (Vo, 2017b). While there's no sure-fire way to really determine whether an account is operated through a coding script and thus is not a human, there are ways to look at different traits of a user to see whether their behaviour may be suspicious. One of the characteristics we decided to look at is that of an account's activity.

For this we compared the activity of a real person with that of a bot. During its busiest hour on its busiest day the bot we examined tweeted more than 200 times. Its human counterpart only tweeted 21 times.

How to Harvest Social Data

There are broadly three different ways to harvest data from the social web: APIs, personal archives and scraping.

The kind of data that official channels like API data streams provide is very limited. Despite harbouring warehouses of data on consumers' behaviour, social media companies only provide a sliver of it through their APIs. For Facebook, researchers were once able to get data for public pages and groups but are no longer able to mine that kind of data after the company implemented restrictions on the availability of this data in response to the Cambridge Analytica scandal. For Twitter, this access is often restricted to a set number of tweets from a user's timeline or to a set time frame for search.

Then there are limitations on the kind of data users can request of their own online persona and behaviour. Some services like Facebook or Twitter will allow users to download a history of the data that constitutes their online selves—their posts, their messaging, or their profile photos—but that data archive won't always include everything each social media company has on them either.

For instance, users can only see what ads they've clicked on going three months back, making it really hard for them to see whether they may or may not have clicked on a Russia-sponsored post.

Last but not least, extracting social media data from the platforms through scraping is often against the terms of service. Scraping a social media platform can get users booted from a service and potentially even result in a lawsuit (*Facebook, Inc. v. Power Ventures, Inc.*, 2016).

For social media platforms, suing scrapers may make financial sense. A lot of the information that social media platforms gather about their users is for sale—not directly, but companies and advertisers can profit from it through ads and marketing. Competitors could scrape information from Facebook to build a comparable platform, for instance. But lawsuits may inadvertently deter not just economically motivated data scrapers but also academics and journalists who want to gather information from social media platforms for research purposes.

This means that journalists may need to be more creative in how they report and tell these stories. Journalists may want to buy bots to better understand how they act online, or reporters may want to purchase Facebook ads to get a better understanding of how Facebook works (Angwin et al., 2017).

Whatever the means, operating within and outside of the confines set by social media companies will be a major challenge for journalists as they are navigating this ever-changing cyber environment.

What Social Media Data Is *Not* Good For

It seems imperative to better understand the universe of social data also from a standpoint of its caveats.

Understanding Who *Is* and Who *Is Not* Using Social Media

One of the biggest issues with social media data is that we cannot assume that the people we hear on Twitter or Facebook are representative samples of broader populations offline.

While there are a large number of people who have a Facebook or Twitter account, journalists should be wary of thinking that the opinions expressed online are those of the general population. As a Pew study from 2018 illustrates, usage of social media varies from platform to platform (Smith

& Anderson, 2018). While more than two thirds of US adults online use YouTube and Facebook, less than a quarter use Twitter. This kind of data can be much more powerful for a concrete and specific story, whether it is examining the hate speech spread by specific politicians in Myanmar or examining the type of coverage published by conspiracy publication *Infowars* over time.

Not Every User Represents One Real Human Being

In addition to that, not every user necessarily represents a person. There are automated accounts (bots) and accounts that are semi-automated and semi-human controlled (cyborgs). And there are also users who operate multiple accounts.

Again, understanding that there's a multitude of actors out there manipulating the flow of information for economic or political gain is an important aspect to keep in mind when looking at social media data in bulk (although this subject in itself—media and information manipulation—has become a major story in its own right that journalists have been trying to tell in ever more sophisticated ways).

The Tyranny of the Loudest

Last but not least it's important to recognize that not everything or everyone's behaviour is measured. A vast amount of people often choose to remain silent. And as more moderate voices are recorded less, it is only the extreme reactions that are recorded and fed back into algorithms that disproportionately amplify the already existing prominence of the loudest.

What this means is that the content that Facebook, Twitter and other platforms algorithmically surface on our social feeds is often based on the likes, retweets and comments of those who chose to chime in. Those who did not speak up are disproportionately drowned out in this process. Therefore, we need to be as mindful of what is not measured as we are of what is measured and how information is ranked and surfaced as a result of these measured and unmeasured data points.

Works Cited

Angwin, J., Varner, M., & Tobin, A. (2017, September 14). Facebook enabled adver-tisers to reach "Jew haters." *ProPublica*. https://www.propublica.org/article/facebook-enabled-advertisers-to-reach-jew-haters

Facebook, Inc. v. Power Ventures, Inc., No. 13-17102 (United States Ninth Circuit July 12, 2016). https://caselaw.findlaw.com/summary/opinion/us-9th-circuit/2016/07/12/276979.html

Rudder, C. (2014). *Dataclysm: Who we are (When we think no one's looking)*. Fourth Estate.

Smith, A., & Anderson, M. (2018, March 1). *Social media use 2018: Demograph-ics and statistics*. Pew Research Center. https://www.pewresearch.org/internet/2018/03/01/social-media-use-in-2018/

Tucker, P. (2013, May 7). Has big data made anonymity impossible? *MIT Tech-nology Review*. https://www.technologyreview.com/2013/05/07/178542/has-big-data-made-anonymity-impossible/

Vo, L. T. (2015, June 3). The umbrella network. *Al Jazeera America*. http://projects.aljazeera.com/2015/04/loving-long-distance/hong-kong-umbrella-protest.html

Vo, L. T. (2016). The primary source in the age of mechanical multiplication. *Nieman Lab*. https://www.niemanlab.org/2016/12/the-primary-source-in-the-age-of-mechanical-multiplication/

Vo, L. T. (2017a, October 11). Twitter bots are trying to influence you. These six charts show you how to spot one. *BuzzFeed News*. https://www.buzzfeednews.com/article/lamvo/twitter-bots-v-human

Vo, L. T. (2017b, October 20). Here's what we learned from staring at social media data for a year. *BuzzFeed*. https://www.buzzfeed.com/lamvo/heres-what-we-learned-from-staring-at-social-media-data-for

Vo, L. T. (2017c, October 20). What we learned from staring at social media data for a year. *Source*. https://source.opennews.org/articles/what-buzzfeed-news-learned-after-year-mining-data-/

About the Author

Lam Thuy Vo is a senior data reporter at *BuzzFeed News* and author of *Mining Social Media: Finding Stories in Internet Data* (No Starch Press, 2019), a Python book.

33. Digital Forensics: Repurposing Google Analytics IDs

Richard Rogers

Abstract
This chapter describes a network discovery technique on the basis of websites sharing the same Google Analytics and/or AdSense IDs.

Keywords: digital methods, digital forensics, anonymous sources, network mapping, Google Analytics, data journalism

When an investigative journalist uncovered a covert network of Russian websites in July 2015 furnishing disinformation about Ukraine, not only did this revelation portend the state-sponsored influence campaigning prior to the 2016 US presidential elections,[1] it also popularized a network discovery technique for data journalists and social researchers (Alexander, 2015). Which websites share the same Google Analytics ID (see Figure 33.1)? If the websites share the same ID, it follows that they are operated by the same registrant, be it an individual, organization or media group. The journalist, Lawrence Alexander, was prompted in his work by the lack of a source behind emaidan.com.ua, a website that appears to give information about the Euromaidan protests in 2013–2014 in Ukraine that ultimately upended the pro-Russian Ukrainian president in favour of a pro-Western one. In search of the source, and "intrigued by its anonymity," Alexander (2015) dug into the website code.

---

1   A longer version of this chapter is available in Rogers, R. (2019). *Doing digital methods*. SAGE. The author would like to acknowledge the groundwork by Mischa Szpirt. For more on this approach, see Rogers, R. (2019). *Doing digital methods*. SAGE (Chapter 11), and Bounegru, L., Gray, J., Venturini, T., & Mauri, M. (Comp.) (2017). *A field guide to "fake news": A collection of recipes for those who love to cook with digital methods*. Public Data Lab (Chapter 3).

Bounegru, L. and J. Gray (eds.), *The Data Journalism Handbook: Towards a Critical Data Practice*. Amsterdam: Amsterdam University Press, 2021
DOI 10.5117/9789462989511_CH33

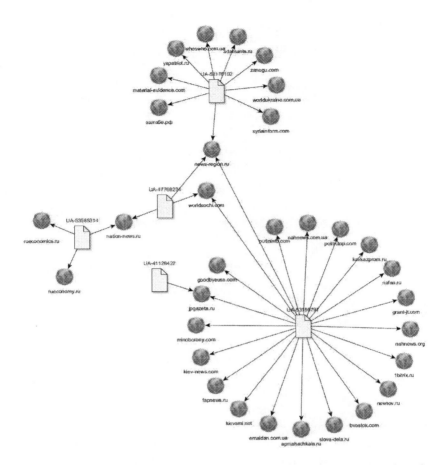

Figure 33.1. Website network discovered through (shared) Google Analytics IDs. Source: Alexander, L. (2015, July 13). Open-source information reveals pro-Kremlin web campaign. Global Voices. https://globalvoices.org/2015/07/13/open-source-information-reveals-pro-kremlin-web-campaign/

Viewing the source code of the web page, he found a Google Analytics ID, which he inserted into reverse lookup software that furnishes a list of other websites using the same ID.[2] He found a (star-shaped) network of a Google Analytics ID linked to eight other websites (in Figure 33.1 at the top of the diagram), sharing a similar anti-Ukraine narrative. One of those websites also used an additional Google Analytics ID, which led to another cluster of related websites (in Figure 33.1 at the bottom to the right), also of similar political persuasion. Examining the WHOIS records of several of

2   The lookup may also yield each website's IP address, Google AdSense ID, WHOIS domain record and other telling information.

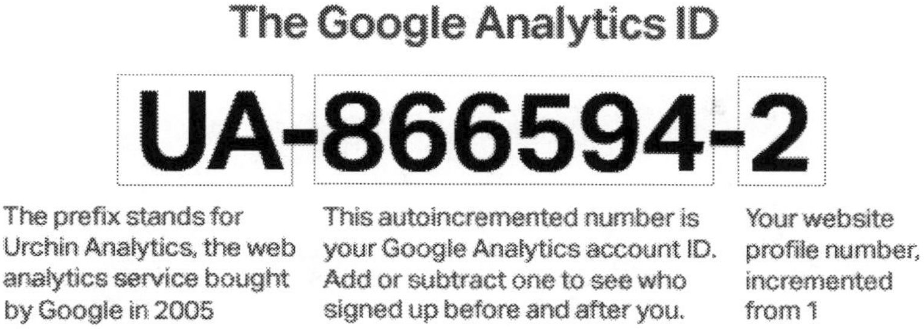

The Google Analytics ID

UA-866594-2

The prefix stands for Urchin Analytics, the web analytics service bought by Google in 2005

This autoincremented number is your Google Analytics account ID. Add or subtract one to see who signed up before and after you.

Your website profile number, incremented from 1

Figure 33.2. Google Analytics ID. Source: Baio, A. (2011, November 15). Think you can hide, anonymous blogger? Two words: Google analytics. Wired. https://www.wired.com/2011/11/goog-analytics-anony-bloggers/

these domains, he found an associated email address, and subsequently a person's profile and photo on VKontakte, the Russian social networking site. The name of this person he then found on a leaked list of employees from the Internet Research Agency in St Petersburg, known as the workplace of the Russian government-sponsored "troll army" (Chen, 2015; Toler, 2015). Drawing links between data points, Alexander put a name and face on a so-called Russian troll. He also humanized the troll, somewhat, by pointing to his Pinterest hobby page, where there is posted a picture of Russian space achievements. The troll is a Cosmonaut space fan, too.

Employing so-called "open-source intelligence" (OSINT) tools as discovery techniques (and also digital methods in the sense of repurposing Google Analytics and reverse lookup software), Alexander and other journalists make and follow links in code, public records, databases and leaks, piecing it all together for an account of "who's behind" particular operations (Bazzell, 2016). "Discovery" is an investigative or even digital forensics approach for journalistic mining and exposure, where one would identify and subsequently strive to contact the individual, organization or media group to interview them, and grant them an opportunity to account for their work.[3] The dual accountings—the journalist's discovery and the discovered's explanation—constitute the story to be told. The purpose is to make things public, to wring out of the hairy code of websites the covert political work being undertaken, and have this particular proof be acknowledged (Latour, 2005).

Google Analytics ID detective work has a lineage in the practice of unmasking anonymous online actors through exploits, or entry points to personally

---

3   Digital forensics has its roots in the investigation of corporate fraud through techniques such as "data carving," which enable the retrieval of deleted files.

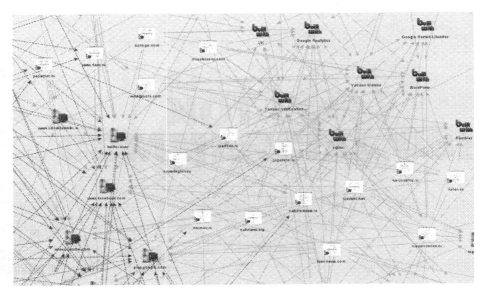

Figure 33.3. Embedded digital objects on websites, depicted as network diagram. Source: Alexander, L. (2015, July 13). Open-source information reveals pro-Kremlin web campaign. Global Voices. https://globalvoices.org/2015/07/13/open-source-information-reveals-pro-kremlin-web-campaign/.

identifiable data that have not been foreseen by its creators. Mining Google Analytics IDs for network discovery and mapping is also a repurposing exercise, using the software in unintended fashion for social research. The originator of the technique, Andy Baio, a journalist at *Wired* magazine, tells the story of an anonymous blogger posting highly offensive material, who had covered his tracks in the "usual ways": "hiding personal info in the domain record, using a different IP address from his other sites, and scrubbing any shared resources from his WordPress install" (Baio, 2011). Baio ID'd him because the blogger shared a Google Analytics ID with other websites he operated in full view. The cautionary tale about this discovery and unmasking technique concludes with Baio providing a safety guide for other anonymous bloggers *with a just cause*, such as those monitoring Mexican drug cartels, whose discovery could lead to danger or even loss of life. Here one also could test the robustness of the anonymity, and inform the journalists working undercover online of any vulnerabilities or potential exploits.

By way of conclusion, I offer a research protocol for network discovery using Google Analytics IDs, summarized in the list below:

Curate a list of websites that do not provide their sources.
Locate Google Analytics and AdSense IDs.

Insert URL list into reverse lookup software such as dnslytics.com.
Seek websites that share the same IDs.
Thematically group and characterize the websites sharing IDs.
Consider network visualization using Gephi.

Works Cited

Alexander, L. (2015, July 13). Open-source information reveals pro-Kremlin web campaign. *Global Voices*. https://globalvoices.org/2015/07/13/open-source-information-reveals-pro-kremlin-web-campaign/

Baio, A. (2011, November 15). Think you can hide, anonymous blogger? Two words: Google analytics. *Wired*. https://www.wired.com/2011/11/goog-analytics-anony-bloggers/

Bazzell, M. (2016). *Open source intelligence techniques: Resources for searching and analyzing online information* (5th ed.). CreateSpace Independent Publishing Platform.

Chen, A. (2015, June 2). The agency. *The New York Times Magazine*. https://www.nytimes.com/2015/06/07/magazine/the-agency.html

Latour, B. (2005). From realpolitik to dingpolitik—An introduction to making things public. In B. Latour & P. Weibel (Eds.), *Making things public: Atmospheres of democracy* (pp. 14–41). MIT Press. http://www.bruno-latour.fr/node/208.html

Toler, A. (2015, March 14). Inside the Kremlin troll army machine: Templates, guidelines, and paid posts. *Global Voices*. https://globalvoices.org/2015/03/14/russia-kremlin-troll-army-examples/

About the Author

Richard Rogers is Professor of New Media and Digital Culture in Media Studies at the University of Amsterdam and director of the Digital Methods Initiative as well as the Netherlands Research School for Media Studies.

34. Apps and Their Affordances for Data Investigations

Esther Weltevrede

Abstract
Exploring app–platform relations for data investigations.

Keywords: apps, social media platforms, digital methods, data infrastructures, data journalism, data investigations

Recently, Netvizz, a tool to extract data from Facebook, lost access to Facebook's Page Public Content Access feature. This seems to have terminated the precarious relationship its developer, the digital methods researcher Bernhard Rieder, has maintained with the Facebook API over the past nine years.[1] The end of Netvizz is symptomatic of a larger shift in digital research and investigations where platforms are further restricting data collection through their application programming interfaces (APIs) and developer policies. Even though the actual effectiveness of the Cambridge Analytica methods are questioned (Lomas, 2018; Smout & Busvine, 2018), the scandal prompted a debate on privacy and data protection in social media and in turn Facebook responded by further restricting access to data from their platforms.

Since the initial announcement in March 2018,[2] the staggered implementation of data access restrictions by Facebook within its larger family of apps has made visible the vast network of third-party stakeholders that have come to rely on the platform for a wide variety of purposes. Apps stopped working, advertising targets have been restricted, but the party most severely hit seems to be digital researchers. This is because apps that

1   http://thepoliticsofsystems.net/?s=netvizz
2   https://about.fb.com/news/2018/03/cracking-down-on-platform-abuse/

Bounegru, L. and J. Gray (eds.), *The Data Journalism Handbook: Towards a Critical Data Practice.*
Amsterdam: Amsterdam University Press, 2021
DOI 10.5117/9789462989511_CH34

have data collection as their primary purpose are no longer allowed. Digital researchers resisted these changes (Bruns, 2018) by arguing that they would be to the cost of research in the interest of the public good. The list of references to the Netvizz article (Rieder, 2013) comprise over 450 publications, which in reality easily exceed that amount—just consider the many student research projects making use of the tool. Similarly, an ad hoc inventory by Bechmann of studies that "could not have existed without access to API data"[3] comprises an impressive list of journalism, social science and other digital research publications.

Reflecting on the impact data access restrictions have on digital research, authors have contextualized these developments and periodized the past decade as "API-based research" (Venturini & Rogers, 2019) or "API-related research" (Perriam et al., 2020). These are defined as approaches to digital research based on the extraction of data made available by online platforms through their APIs. Certainly, APIs—with their data ready-made for social research—have lowered the threshold for research with social media data, not to mention that they allowed a generation of students to experiment with digital research. No technical skills are required, and for web data standards, the data is relatively clean. API-based research has also been critiqued from the onset, most notably because of APIs' research affordances driven by convenience, affecting the researchers' agency in developing relevant research questions (Marres, 2017).

This chapter picks up on recent calls for "post-API research" by Venturini and Rogers (2019) and the Digital Methods Initiative and focuses on the opportunities that arise in response to recent developments within social media ecosystems.[4] Digital research, in the sense employed in this chapter, is defined by the methodological principle of "following the medium," responding to and interfacing methods with developments in the digital environment. In what follows I approach the recent API restrictions by arguing for the renewed need for, and potential of, creative and inventive explorations of different types of sociotechnical data that are key in shaping the current platform environments. I continue by picking up on the opportunities that have been identified by digital researchers, and adding to that by proposing a methodological perspective to study app–platform relations. In doing so I hope to offer data journalists interested in the potential of social data for storytelling (see, e.g., the chapter by Lam Thuy Vo in this volume), some

---

3   https://docs.google.com/document/d/15YKeZFSUc1jo3b4lW9YXxGmhYEnFx3TSy68qCrX9BEI/edit

4   https://wiki.digitalmethods.net/Dmi/WinterSchool2020

starting points for approaching investigations with and about platforms and their data in the current post-API moment.

Digital methods have in common that they utilize a series of data collection and analysis techniques that optimize the use of native digital data formats. These emerge with the introduction of digital media in social life. Digital methods researchers develop tools inspired by digital media to be able to handle these data formats in methodologically innovative ways. The history of digital methods can therefore also be read as narrating a history of key data formats and data structures of the Internet; they are adaptive to changes of the media and include these in analysis. In what follows, I would like to contribute to post-API research approaches by proposing a perspective to study platforms as data infrastructures from an app–platform perspective. The impact the data access restrictions have on the larger media ecosystems attest to the fact that advanced, nuanced knowledge of platform infrastructures and their interplay with third-party apps is direly needed. It demonstrates the need for a broadened data infrastructure literacy (Gray et al., 2018), in addition to knowledge about how third-party companies and apps operate in social media environments.

Apps and Platforms-as-Infrastructure

The platform data restrictions are part and parcel of developments of social media into platforms-as-infrastructure. These developments highlight the evolution of digital ecosystems' focus on corporate partnerships (Helmond et al., 2019). After a year of negative coverage following the platform's role in elections, Zuckerberg posted a note sketching out the platform's changing perspective from "connecting people" to building a "social infrastructure" (Helmond et al., 2019; Hoffmann et al., 2018).[5] The notion of social infrastructure both highlights social activities as the platform's core product to connect and create value for the multiple sides of the market, as well as the company's shift from a social network into a data infrastructure, extending the platform to include their websites and the larger family of 70 apps (Nieborg & Helmond, 2019).[6] This infrastructural turn marks a next step in the platform's ability to extend their data infrastructure into third-party apps, platforms and websites, as well as facilitating inwards integrations.

---

5   https://www.facebook.com/notes/mark-zuckerberg/building-global-community/10154544292806634/

6   https://www.appannie.com/en/

Even though platforms-as-infrastructure receive increasing attention (Plantin et al., 2018), as do individual apps, how apps operate on and between data infrastructures is understudied and often unaccounted for. Yet apps continually transform and valorize everyday practices within platform environments. I use a relational definition of apps by focusing on third-party apps, defined as applications built on a platform by external developers, not owned or operated by the platform. When an app connects to a platform, access is granted to platform functions and data, depending on the permissions. Apps also enable their stakeholders—for example, app stores, advertisers or users—to integrate and valorize them in multiple, simultaneous ways. In other words, apps have built-in tendencies to be related to, and relate themselves within different operative data infrastructures. This specfic position of third-party apps makes them particularly appropriate for studies into our platform-as-infrastructure environments.

Social media platforms pose methodological challenges, because, as mentioned, access to user-generated data is increasingly limited, which challenges researchers to consider what "social data" is anew and open up alternative perspectives. Contrary to how social media platforms offer access to user-generated data for digital research, structured via APIs, app data sources are increasingly characterized by their closed source or proprietary nature. Even though obfuscation is a widely used technique in software engineering (Matviyenko et al., 2015), efforts that render code and data illegible or inaccessible have a significant impact on digital research. These increased challenges posed by platform and app environments to circumvent or sidetrack empirical research are what colleagues and I have termed "infrastructural resistance" (Dieter et al., 2019). Instead, the data formats available for digital research today are characterized by heterogeneous data formats ranging from device-based data (e.g., GPS), software libraries (e.g., software development kits, SDKs) and network-connections (e.g., ad networks). Apps can collect user-generated data, but mostly do not offer access via open APIs, hence there is an absence of ready-made data for data investigations.

In what follows I present three different bottom-up data explorations through which digital researchers and journalists can actively invoke different "research affordances" (Weltevrede, 2016) and use these to advance or initiate an inquiry. Research affordances attune to the action possibilities within software from the perspective of, and aligned with, the interests of the researcher. This approach allows the development of inventive digital methods (Lury & Wakeford, 2012; Rogers, 2013). These require the rethinking of the technical forms and formats of app–platform relationships by exploring their analytical opportunities. The explorations draw on recent research colleagues and I undertook, taking inspiration from but also noting challenges and making suggestions towards the type of inquiries these data sources afford to increase our understanding of the platform-as-infrastructure environment.

Fake Social Infrastructures

The first exploration considers fake followers and their relation to Facebook's social infrastructure. Increasing attention is being paid to the extent of fake followers in social media environments from both platforms and digital research. From the perspective of the platforms, the fake follower market is often excluded in discussions of platforms as multisided markets; the fake follower market is not considered a "side" and certainly not part of the "family." Fake followers establish an unofficial infrastructure of relations, recognized by the platforms as undesirable misuses. They are unintended by the platforms, but work in tandem with and by virtue of platform mechanisms. Moreover, these practices decrease the value of the key product, namely social activity.

Colleagues and I investigated the run-up to the Brexit referendum on Twitter by focusing on the most frequently used apps in that data set (Gerlitz & Weltevrede, 2019) (see Figure 34.1). A systematic analysis of these apps and their functionalities provides insight into the mechanisms of automated and fake engagements within the platform's governance structure. In an ongoing project with Johan Lindquist, we are exploring a set of over 1,200 reselling platforms that enable the buying and selling of fake engagements on an extensive range of platforms. These initial explorations show how fake followers technically relate to platforms, both official third-party apps connecting through the API, as well as through an infrastructure of platforms unofficially connecting to social media platforms. What these initial explorations have shown is that research will have to accommodate a variety of data of automated and fake origin. Automated and fake accounts cannot (only) be treated as type or actor but as *practice*, that is situated and emerging in relation to the affordances of the medium. As shown in the case of Twitter, an account does not necessarily represent a human user, as it is accomplished in distributed and situated ways, just as a tweet is not a tweet, commonly understood as a uniquely typed post (Gerlitz & Weltevrede, 2019).

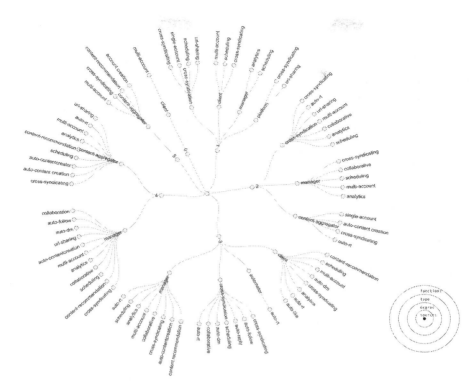

Figure 34.1. Automation functions. The dendrogram visualises the hierarchy of sources, degrees of automation, types of sources and their functions in the Brexit data set, 17–23 June 2016. Source: Gerlitz, C., & Weltevrede, E. (2019). What happens to ANT, and its emphasis on the socio-material grounding of the social, in digital sociology? In A. Blok, I. Farias, & C. Roberts (Eds.), Companion to Actor-Network Theory. Routledge. https://doi.org/10.4324/9781315111667-38

App–Platform Relations

The second exploration considers app stores as data infrastructures for apps. Today, the main entry point to apps—for developers and users—is via app stores, where users can search for individual apps or demarcate collections or genres of apps. Building on methods from algorithm studies (Rogers, 2013; Sandvig et al., 2014), one can engage with the technicity of "ranking cultures" (Rieder et al., 2018), for example, in Google Play and the App Store. Such an undertaking concerns both algorithmic and economic power as well as their societal consequences. It can be used to gain knowledge about their ranking mechanisms and an understanding of why this matters for the circulation of cultural content.

The app stores can also be used to demarcate collections or genres of apps to study app–platform relations from the perspective of apps. In

Table 34.1: Detected App–Platform Relations per Source Set

Relation	Facebook	Instagram	Snapchat	Twitter
Brand (mentions)	1,449 (34.96%)	2,945 (80.03%)	614 (12.17%)	1,107 (21.80%)
Legal (mentions)	302 (7.29%)	318 (8.65%)	268 (5.31%)	305 (6.01%)
Technical (mentions)	61 (1.47%)	62 (1.68%)	70 (1.39%)	114 (2.24%)
Technical (libraries, SDK)*	83 (33.20%)	0 (0%)	0 (0%)	40 (16.13%)
Technical (HTTP requests)	156 (62.40%)	89 (35.60%)	12 (4.80%)	102 (41.13%)

*Only for Google Play search results (N = 998)
Note. The Technical (libraries, SDKs) and Technical (HTTP requests) categories indicate apps that engage in an "official" relationship with the social medium through their APIs. From Gerlitz et al. (2019).

"Regramming the Platform" (Gerlitz et al., 2019), colleagues and I investigated over 18,500 apps and the different ways in which apps relate themselves to platform features and functionalities. One of the key findings of this study is that app developers find creative solutions to navigate around the official platform APIs, thereby also navigating around the official governance systems of platforms (Table 34.1). The app-centric approach to platforms-as-infrastructure provides insights into the third-party apps developed on the peripheries of social media platforms, the practices and features supported and extended by those apps, and the messy and contingent relations between apps and social media platforms (Gerlitz et al., 2019).

Third-Party Data Connections

The third exploration considers app software and how it relates to data infrastructures of external stakeholders. With this type of exploration it is possible to map out how the app as a software object embeds external data infrastructures as well as the dynamic data flows in and out of apps (Weltevrede & Jansen, 2019). Apps appear to us as discrete and bounded objects, whereas they are by definition data infrastructural objects, relating themselves to platforms to extend and integrate within the data infrastructure.

In order to activate and explore the inbound and outbound data flows, we used a variation on the "walkthrough method" (Light et al., 2016). Focusing on data connections, the resulting visualization shows which data is channelled into apps from social media platforms and the mobile platform (Figure 34.2). In a second step, we mapped the advertising networks, cloud services, analytics and other third-party networks the apps connect to in order to monetize app data, improve functionality or distribute hosting to external

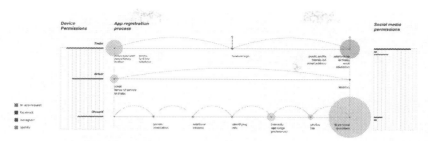

Figure 34.2. Interface walkthrough of data flows during the registration process. Source: Infrastructures of intimate data: Mapping the inbound and outbound data flows of dating apps. Computational Culture, 7. http://computationalculture.net/infrastructures-of-intimate-data-mapping-the-inbound-and-outbound-data-flows-of-dating-apps/

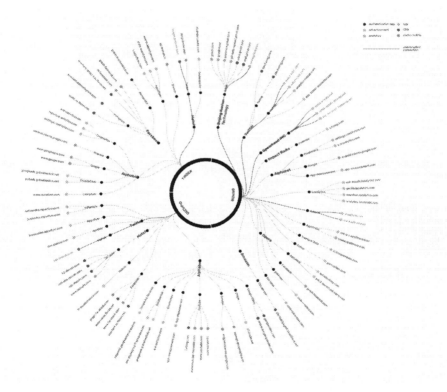

Figure 34.3. Network connections established between dating apps Tinder, Grindr and OKCupid and their third parties. Source: Infrastructures of intimate data: Mapping the inbound and out-bound data flows of dating apps. Computational Culture, 7. http://computationalculture.net/infra-structures-of-intimate-data-mapping-the-inbound-and-outbound-data-flows-of-dating-apps/

parties, among others (Figure 34.3). Mapping data flows in and out of apps provides critical insight into the political economy of the circulation and recombination of data: The data connections that are established, how they are triggered and which data types are being transferred to which parties.

Conclusion

Platforms and apps are so fundamentally woven into everyday life that they often go unnoticed without any moment of reflection. This tendency to move to the background is precisely the reason why digital researchers, data journalists and activists should explore how they work and the conditions which underpin their creation and use. It is important to improve data infrastructure literacy in order to understand how they are related to different platforms and networks, how they operate between them, and how they involve a diversity of often unknown stakeholders.

In the aftermath of the Cambridge Analytica scandal, data ready-made for social investigations accessible through structured APIs is increasingly being restricted by platforms in response to public pressure. In this chapter, I have suggested that, as a response, researchers, journalists and civil society groups should be creative and inventive in exploring novel types of data in terms of their affordances for data investigations. I have explored three types of data for investigating apps. There are, moreover, multiple opportunities to further expand on this. It should be stressed that I have mainly addressed apps, yet this might offer inspiration for investigations into different data-rich environments, including smart cities and the Internet of things. A more nuanced understanding of the data infrastructures that increasingly shape the practices of everyday life remains an ongoing project.

Works Cited

Bruns, A. (2018, April 25). Facebook shuts the gate after the horse has bolted, and hurts real research in the process. *Internet Policy Review*. https://policyreview. info/articles/news/facebook-shuts-gate-after-horse-has-bolted-and-hurts-real-research-process/786

Dieter, M., Gerlitz, C., Helmond, A., Tkacz, N., Van der Vlist, F. N., & Weltevrede, E. (2019). Multi-situated app studies: Methods and propositions: *Social Media + Society*. https://doi.org/10.1177/2056305119846486

Gerlitz, C., Helmond, A., Van der Vlist, F. N., & Weltevrede, E. (2019). Regramming the platform: Infrastructural relations between apps and social media. *Computational Culture, 7.* http://computationalculture.net/regramming-the-platform/

Gerlitz, C., & Weltevrede, E. (2019). What happens to ANT, and its emphasis on the socio-material grounding of the social, in digital sociology? In A. Blok, I. Farias, & C. Roberts (Eds.), *Companion to actor–network theory* (pp. 345–356). Routledge. https://doi.org/10.4324/9781315111667-38

Gray, J., Gerlitz, C., & Bounegru, L. (2018). Data infrastructure literacy. *Big Data & Society, 5*(2), 1–13. https://doi.org/10.1177/2053951718786316

Helmond, A., Nieborg, D. B., & Van der Vlist, F. N. (2019). Facebook's evolution: Development of a platform-as-infrastructure. *Internet Histories, 3*(2), 123–146. https://doi.org/10.1080/24701475.2019.1593667

Hoffmann, A. L., Proferes, N., & Zimmer, M. (2018). "Making the world more open and connected": Mark Zuckerberg and the discursive construction of Facebook and its users. *New Media & Society, 20*(1), 199–218. https://doi.org/10.1177/1461444816660784

Light, B., Burgess, J., & Duguay, S. (2016). The walkthrough method: An approach to the study of apps. *New Media & Society, 20*(3), 881–900. https://doi.org/10.1177/1461444816675438

Lomas, N. (2018, April 24). Kogan: "I don't think Facebook has a developer policy that is valid." *TechCrunch.* https://social.techcrunch.com/2018/04/24/kogan-i-dont-think-facebook-has-a-developer-policy-that-is-valid/

Lury, C., & Wakeford, N. (2012). *Inventive methods: The happening of the social.* Routledge.

Marres, N. (2017). *Digital sociology: The reinvention of social research.* Polity Press.

Matviyenko, S., Ticineto Clough, P., & Galloway, A. R. (2015). On governance, blackboxing, measure, body, affect and apps: A conversation with Patricia Ticineto Clough and Alexander R. Galloway. *The Fibreculture Journal, 25*, 10–29. http://twentyfive.fibreculturejournal.org/fcj-179-on-governance-blackboxing-measure-body-affect-and-apps-a-conversation-with-patricia-ticineto-clough-and-alexander-r-galloway/

Nieborg, D. B., & Helmond, A. (2019). The political economy of Facebook's platformization in the mobile ecosystem: Facebook Messenger as a platform instance. *Media, Culture & Society, 41*(2), 196–218. https://doi.org/10.1177/0163443718818384

Perriam, J., Birkbak, A., & Freeman, A. (2020). Digital methods in a post-API environment. *International Journal of Social Research Methodology, 23*(3), 277–290. https://doi.org/10.1080/13645579.2019.1682840

Plantin, J.-C., Lagoze, C., Edwards, P. N., & Sandvig, C. (2018). Infrastructure studies meet platform studies in the age of Google and Facebook. *New Media & Society, 20*(1), 293–310. https://doi.org/10.1177/1461444816661553

Rieder, B. (2013). Studying Facebook via data extraction: The Netvizz application. In *Proceedings of the 5th Annual ACM Web Science Conference* (pp. 346–355). https://doi.org/10.1145/2464464.2464475

Rieder, B., Matamoros-Fernández, A., & Coromina, Ò. (2018). From ranking algorithms to "ranking cultures": Investigating the modulation of visibility in YouTube search results. *Convergence, 24*(1), 50–68. https://doi.org/10.1177/1354856517736982

Rogers, R. (2013). *Digital methods*. MIT Press.

Sandvig, C., Hamilton, K., Karahalios, K., & Langbort, C. (2014, May 22). Auditing algorithms: Research methods for detecting discrimination on Internet platforms. International Communication Association preconference on Data and Discrimination Converting Critical Concerns into Productive Inquiry, Seattle, WA.

Smout, A., & Busvine, D. (2018, April 24). Researcher in Facebook scandal says: My work was worthless to Cambridge Analytica. *Reuters*. https://www.reuters.com/article/us-facebook-privacy-cambridge-analytica-idUSKBN1HV17M

Venturini, T., & Rogers, R. (2019). "API-based research" or how can digital sociology and journalism studies learn from the Cambridge Analytica data breach. *Digital Journalism, 7*(4), 532–540. https://doi.org/10.1080/21670811.2019.1591927

Weltevrede, E. (2016). *Repurposing digital methods: The research affordances of platforms and engines* [Doctoral dissertation], University of Amsterdam.

Weltevrede, E., & Jansen, F. (2019). Infrastructures of intimate data: Mapping the inbound and outbound data flows of dating apps. *Computational Culture, 7*. http://computationalculture.net/infrastructures-of-intimate-data-mapping-the-inbound-and-outbound-data-flows-of-dating-apps/

About the Author

Esther Weltevrede is an Assistant Professor of New Media and Digital Culture and coordinator of the Digital Methods Initiative at the University of Amsterdam, where she explores the various research affordances of digital media, with a specific interest in methodological innovations in the study of the infrastructures of social media platforms and third parties.

35. Algorithms in the Spotlight: Collaborative Investigations at *Der Spiegel*

Christina Elmer

Abstract

Using several examples from German media, this chapter provides insights into collaborative projects that investigate algorithms and summarizes the most important lessons learned.

Keywords: algorithms, algorithmic accountability, data journalism, crowdsourcing, transparency, collaboration

The demand for transparency around algorithms is not new in Germany. In 2012, *Der Spiegel* columnist Sascha Lobo called for the mechanics of the Google search algorithm to be disclosed (Lobo, 2012), even if this would harm the company. The reason was that Google can shape how we view the world, for example through the autocomplete function, as a prominent case in Germany illustrated. In this case, the wife of the former federal president had taken legal action against Google because problematic terms were suggested in the autocomplete function when her name was searched for. Two years later, the German minister of justice repeated this appeal, which was extended again by the federal chancellor in 2016: Algorithms should be more transparent, Angela Merkel demanded (Kartell, 2014; Reinbold, 2016).

In the past few years, the topic of algorithmic accountability has been under constant discussion at *Der Spiegel*—but initially only as an occasion for reporting, not in the form of our own research or analysis project. There may be two primary reasons why the German media began experimenting in this area later than their colleagues in the United States. First, journalists in Germany do not have such strong freedom of information rights and

Bounegru, L. and J. Gray (eds.), *The Data Journalism Handbook: Towards a Critical Data Practice*. Amsterdam: Amsterdam University Press, 2021

DOI 10.5117/9789462989511_CH35

instruments at their disposal. Second, data journalism does not have such a long tradition as in the United States. *Der Spiegel* has only had its own data journalism department since 2016 and is slowly but steadily expanding this area. It is, of course, also possible for newsrooms with smaller resources to be active in this field—for example, through cooperation with organizations or freelancers. In our case, too, all previous projects in the area of algorithmic accountability reporting have come about in this way. This chapter will therefore focus on collaborations and the lessons we have learned from them.

Google, Facebook and Schufa: Three Projects at a Glance

Our editorial team primarily relies on cooperation when it comes to the investigation of algorithms. In the run-up to the 2017 federal elections, we joined forces with the NGO AlgorithmWatch to gain insights into the personalization of Google search results.[1] Users were asked to install a plug-in that regularly performed predefined searches on their computer. A total of around 4,400 participants donated almost six million search results and thus provided the data for an analysis that would challenge the filter bubble thesis—at least regarding Google and the investigated area.

For this project, our collaborators from AlgorithmWatch approached *Der Spiegel*, as they were looking for a media partner with a large reach for crowdsourcing the required data. While the content of the reporting was entirely the responsibility of our department covering Internet- and technology-related topics, the data journalism department supported the planning and methodological evaluation of the operation. Furthermore, the backup of our legal department was essential in order to implement the project in a way which was legally bulletproof. For example, data protection issues had to be clarified within the reporting and had to be fully comprehensible for all participants involved in the project.

Almost at the same time, *Der Spiegel* collaborated with *ProPublica* to deploy their AdCollector in Germany in the months before the elections (Angwin & Larson, 2017). The project aimed to make transparent how German parties target Facebook users with ads. Therefore, a plug-in collected the political ads that a user sees in her stream and revealed those ads that are not displayed to her. For this project, *Der Spiegel* joined forces with other German media outlets such as *Süddeutsche Zeitung* and *Tagesschau*—an

---

1   https://algorithmwatch.org/filterblase-geplatzt-kaum-raum-fuer-personalisierung-bei-google-suchen-zur-bundestagswahl-2017/ (German language)

unusual constellation of actors who usually are in competition with each other. In this case it was necessary to reach as many people as possible to serve the public interest. The results could also be published as journalistic stories, but our primary focus was transparency. After two weeks, around 600 political advertisements had been collected and made available to the public.

ProPublica's Julia Angwin and Jeff Larson introduced the idea of a collaboration at the annual conference of the German association of investigative journalists, Netzwerk Recherche in Hamburg, where they held a session on algorithmic accountability reporting. The idea was developed from the very beginning in collaboration with technical and methodology experts from multiple departments in the newsroom of *Der Spiegel*. The exchange with our previous partner, the non-profit AlgorithmWatch, was also very valuable for us in order to shed light on the legal background and to include it in our research. After the conference, we expanded the idea further through regular telephone conferences. Our partners from the other German media outlets became involved at later stages as well.

In 2018, *Der Spiegel* contributed to a major project to investigate an extremely powerful algorithm in Germany—the Schufa credit report. The report is used to assess the creditworthiness of private individuals. The report should indicate the probability that someone can pay their bills, pay the rent or service a loan. It can therefore have far-reaching implications for a person's private life and a negative effect on society as a whole. For example, it is conceivable that the score may increase social discrimination and unequal treatment of individuals, depending on the amount of data that is available about them. Incorrect data or mix-ups could be fatal for individuals. The algorithm's underlying scoring is not transparent. Which data is taken into account in which weighting is not known. And those affected often have no knowledge of the process. This makes Schufa a controversial institution in Germany—and projects like OpenSCHUFA absolutely vital for public debate on algorithmic accountability, in our opinion.[2]

The project was mainly driven by the NGOs Open Knowledge Foundation (OKFN) and AlgorithmWatch. *Der Spiegel* was one of two associated partners, together with Bayerischer Rundfunk (Bavarian Broadcasting). The idea for this project came up more or less simultaneously, with several parties involved. After some successful projects with the NGOs AlgorithmWatch and

2   http://www.openschufa.de/ (German language)

OKFN as well as with the data journalism team of Bayerischer Rundfunk, *Der Spiegel* was included in the initial discussions.

The constellation posed special challenges. For the two media teams, it was important to work separately from the NGOs in order to ensure their independence from the crowdfunding process in particular. Therefore, although there were, of course, discussions between the actors involved, neither an official partnership nor a joint data evaluation were possible. This example emphasizes how important it is for journalists to reflect on their autonomy, especially in such high-publicity topics.

Making OpenSCHUFA known was one of the central success factors of this project. The first step was to use crowdfunding to create the necessary infrastructure to collect the data, which was obtained via crowdsourcing. The results were jointly evaluated by the partners in the course of the year in anonymized form. The central question behind it is: Does the Schufa algorithm discriminate against certain population groups, and does it increase inequality in society? According to the results, it does. We found that the score privileged older and female individuals, as well as those who change their residence less frequently. And we discovered that different versions of algorithms within the score generated different outcomes for people with the same attributes, a type of discrimination that was not previously known regarding this score.

These results would not have been possible without the participation of many volunteers and supporters. The crowdfunding campaign was largely successful, so that the financing of the software could be secured within the framework.[3] And within the subsequent crowdsourcing process, about 2,800 people sent in their personal credit reports. This sample was, of course, not representative, but nevertheless sufficiently diverse to reveal the findings described.

Impact and Success Indicators

Both the Facebook and the Google investigations were rather unspectacular in terms of findings and confirmed our hypotheses. Political parties apparently hardly used Facebook's targeting options and the much-cited Google filter bubble was not found in our crowdsourcing experiment in Germany. But for us the value of these projects lay in increasing our readers' literacy around functionalities and risks of algorithms in society.

3   https://www.startnext.com/openschufa (German language)

The reach of our articles was an indicator that we had succeeded in making the topic more widely known. The introductory article at the start of the Schufa project reached a large audience (around 335,000 readers).[4] The reading time was also clearly above the typical one—with an average of almost three minutes. In addition, the topic was widely discussed in public arenas and covered by many media outlets and conferences.

The topic has also been debated in political circles. After the publication of the Schufa investigations, the German minister of consumer protection called for more transparency in the field of credit scoring. Every citizen must have the right to know which essential features have been included in the calculation of their creditworthiness and how these are weighted, she demanded.

What about impact on everyday reality? As a first step, it was important for us to contribute to establishing the topic in the public consciousness. So far, we have not seen any fundamentally different way political actors deal with algorithms that have broader societal consequences.

Nevertheless, the topic of algorithmic accountability reporting is very important to us. This is because in Europe we still have the opportunity to debate the issue of algorithms in society and to shape how we want to deal with it. It is part of our function as journalists to provide the necessary knowledge so that citizens can understand and shape the future of algorithms in society. As far as possible, we also take on the role of a watchdog by trying to make algorithms and their effects transparent, to identify risks and to confront those responsible. To achieve this, we have to establish what might otherwise be considered unusual collaborations with competitors and actors from other sectors. We hope that such alliances will ultimately increase the pressure on legislation and transparency standards in this area.

More effort and resources need to be dedicated to algorithmic accountability investigations and "The Markup" has published some very exciting research in this area. Further experimentation is very much needed, partly because there is still scope for action in the regulation of algorithms. The field of algorithmic accountability reporting has only begun to develop in recent years. And it will have to grow rapidly to meet the challenges of an increasingly digitized world.

---

4   The majority of these, however, came to the article via internal channels like our homepage. This was different in the case of another article, the field report featuring the author's personal story, which was read by around 220,000 people. A fifth of them reached the article via social media channels, which is well above the average. So it seems that we were able to reach new target groups with this topic.

Organizing Collaborative Investigations

Running collaborative investigations takes a whole set of new or less used skills in the newsroom. This includes the analysis of large data sets and the programming of specific procedures, but also the management of projects. The latter is too easily overlooked and will be described in more detail here, with concrete examples from our previous work.

Working together in diverse constellations not only makes it easier to share competencies and resources, it also allows a clear definition of roles. As a media partner, *Der Spiegel* positioned itself in these collaborations more as a neutral commentator, not too deeply involved in the project itself. This allowed the editors to remain independent and thus justify the trust of their readers. They continued to apply their quality criteria to reporting within the project—for example, by always giving any subject of their reporting the opportunity to comment on accusations. Compared to the NGOs involved, these mechanisms may slow media partners down more than they are comfortable with, but at the same time they ensure that readers are fully informed by their reports—and that these will enrich public debate in the long term.

Reaching agreement about these roles in advance has proven to be an important success criterion for collaborations in the field of algorithmic accountability. A common timeline should also be developed at an early stage and language rules for the presentation of the project on different channels should be defined. Because, after all, a clear division of roles can only work if it is communicated consistently. This includes, for example, a clear terminology on the roles of the different partners in the project and the coordination of disclaimers in the event of conflicts of interest.

Behind the scenes, project management methods should be used prudently, project goals should be set clearly and available resources have to be discussed. Coordinators should help with the overall communication and thus give the participating editors the space they need for their investigations. To keep everyone up to date, information channels should be kept as simple as possible, especially around the launch of major project stages.

Regarding editorial planning, the three subject areas were challenging. Although in general relevance and news value were never questioned, special stories were needed to reach a broad readership. Often, these stories focused on the personal effects of the algorithms examined. For example, incorrectly assigned Schufa data made it difficult for a colleague from the *Der Spiegel* editorial team to obtain a contract with an Internet provider. His experience report impressively showed what effects the Schufa algorithm can have on a personal level and thus connected with the reality of our audience's lives (Seibt, 2018).

Thus, we tailored the scope of our reporting to the interests of our audience as far as possible. Of course, the data journalists involved were also very interested in the functioning of the algorithms under investigation—an interest that is extremely useful for research purposes. However, only if these details have a relevant influence on the results of the algorithms can they become the subject of reporting—and only if they are narrated in a way that is accessible for our readers.

Internally in the editorial office, support for all three projects was very high. Nevertheless, it was not easy to free up resources for day-to-day reporting in the daily routine of a news-driven editorial team—especially when the results of our investigations were not always spectacular.

Lessons Learned

By way of conclusion, I summarize what we have learned from these projects.

Collaborate where possible. Good algorithmic accountability investigations are only possible by joining forces with others and creating teams with diverse skill sets. This is also important given both the scarcity of resources and legal restrictions that most journalists have to cope with. But since these projects bring together actors from different fields, it is crucial to discuss beforehand the underlying relevance criteria, requirements and capabilities.

Define your goals systematically. Raising awareness of the operating principles of algorithms can be a first strong goal in such projects. Of course, projects should also try to achieve as much transparency as possible. At best we would check whether algorithms have a discriminatory effect—but project partners should bear in mind that this is a more challenging goal to attain, one that requires extensive data sets and resources.

Exercise caution in project implementation. Depending on the workload and the day-to-day pressure of the journalists involved, you might even need a project manager. Be aware that the project timeline may sometimes conflict with reporting requirements. Take this into account in communicating with other partners and, if possible, prepare alternatives for such cases.

Invest in research design. To set up a meaningful design that produces useful data, you might need specialized partners. Close alliances with scientists from computer science, mathematics and related disciplines are particularly helpful for investigating some of the more technical aspects of algorithms. Furthermore, it may also be useful to cooperate with social and cultural researchers to gain a deeper understanding of classifications and norms that are implemented in them.

Protect user data. Data donations from users may be useful to investigate algorithms. In such crowdsourcing projects legal support is indispensable in order to ensure data protection and to take into account the requirements of the national laws and regulations. If your company has a data protection officer, involve them in the project early on.

Works Cited

Angwin, J., & Larson, J. (2017, September 7). Help us monitor political ads online. *Pro-Publica.* https://www.propublica.org/article/help-us-monitor-political-ads-online

Kartell, S. vor. (2014, September 16). Maas hätte gerne, dass Google geheime Such-formel offenlegt. *Der Spiegel.* https://www.spiegel.de/wirtschaft/unternehmen/google-heiko-maas-fordert-offenlegung-von-algorithmus-a-991799.html

Lobo, S. (2012, September 11). Was Bettina Wulff mit Mettigeln verbindet. *Der Spiegel.* https://www.spiegel.de/netzwelt/netzpolitik/google-suchvorschlaege-was-bettina-wulff-mit-mettigeln-verbindet-a-855097.html

Reinbold, F. (2016, October 26). Warum Merkel an die Algorithmen will. *Der Spiegel.* https://www.spiegel.de/netzwelt/netzpolitik/angela-merkel-warum-die-kanzlerin-an-die-algorithmen-von-facebook-will-a-1118365.html

Seibt, P. (2018, March 9). Wie ich bei der Schufa zum "deutlich erhöhten Risiko" wurde. *Der Spiegel.* https://www.spiegel.de/wirtschaft/service/schufa-wie-ich-zum-deutlich-erhoehten-risiko-wurde-a-1193506.html

About the Author

Christina Elmer established the data journalism section and fosters in-novation projects in the editorial R&D team at *Der Spiegel* and is a board member of Netzwerk Recherche.

Organizing Data Journalism

36.   The #ddj Hashtag on Twitter

Eunice Au and Marc Smith

Abstract
How we used the social network analysis and visualization package
NodeXL to examine what the global data journalism community tweets
about.

Keywords: #ddj, Twitter, social network analysis, data journalism, social
media, data analysis

Picking a single term to track the data journalism field is not easy. Data
journalists use a myriad of hashtags in connection with their work, such as
#datajournalism, #ddj, #dataviz, #infographics, and #data. When the Global
Investigative Journalism Network (GIJN)—an international association
of investigative journalism organizations that supports the training and
sharing of information among investigative and data journalists—first
started to report on conversations around data journalism on Twitter
six years ago, the most popular hashtag appeared to be #ddj (data-driven
journalism).[1]

The term "data-driven journalism" itself is controversial as it can be
argued that journalism is not driven by data; data merely informs, or is a
tool used for journalism. Data consists of structured facts and statistics
that require journalists to filter, analyze and discover patterns in order to
produce stories. Just as one would not call a profile piece "interview-driven
journalism" or an article based on public documents "document-driven
journalism," great data journalism stories use data as only one of their
components.

---

[1]   https://gijn.org/

Bounegru, L. and J. Gray (eds.), *The Data Journalism Handbook: Towards a Critical Data Practice*.
Amsterdam: Amsterdam University Press, 2021
DOI 10.5117/9789462989511_CH36

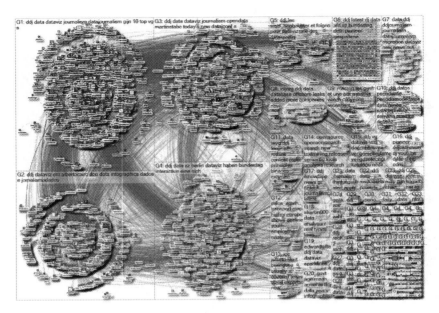

Figure 36.1. #ddj mapping on Twitter from January 1, 2018, to August 13, 2018. Source: NodeXL.

The Role of #ddj

Aside from these considerations, the widespread use of the #ddj hashtag among data journalism communities has made it a prominent resource for sharing projects and activities around the world. Data journalists use the hashtag to promote their work and broadcast it to wider international audiences.

The hashtag also helps facilitate discussions on social media, where members of the data journalism community can search, discover and share content using the hashtag. Discussions embracing the #ddj hashtag range from election forecasting and misinterpretation of probability graphs, to data ethics and holding artificial intelligence to account.

The Birth of Top 10 #ddj

GIJN's weekly Top 10 #ddj series started in January 2014 when one of us first tweeted a #ddj network graph (Smith, 2014). The graph, which mapped tweets mentioning the hashtag #ddj, including replies to those tweets, was created using NodeXL, a social network analysis and visualization package that builds on the Excel spreadsheet software. These network graphs reveal the patterns of interconnection that emerge from activities such as replying, @mentioning and retweeting. These patterns highlight key people, groups and topics being discussed.

As an international investigative journalism organization, GIJN is always looking for ways to raise awareness about what is happening in the fields of investigative and data journalism. When GIJN's executive director, David Kaplan, saw Smith's network graph, he proposed to use the map to produce a weekly Top 10 #ddj to showcase popular and interesting examples of data journalism. (He and Smith also tried a weekly round-up of investigative journalism, but no single hashtag came close to doing the job that #ddj does for data journalism.) Although GIJN follows the network graph's suggested findings closely, some human curation is necessary to eliminate duplicates and to highlight the most interesting items.

Since the birth of the series, we have assembled more than 250 snapshots of the data journalism community's discussions featuring the #ddj hashtag over the past six years (GIJN, n.d.). The series now serves as a good quick summary for interested parties who cannot follow every #ddj tweet. Our use of the term "snapshot" is not simply a metaphor. This analysis gives us a picture of the data journalism Twitter community, in the same way that photojournalism depicts real crowds on the front pages of major news outlets.

The Evolution of #ddj Twitter Traffic

To get a sense of how Twitter traffic using #ddj has evolved, we did a very basic and rough analysis of the #ddj data we collected from 2014 to 2019. We selected a small sample of eight weeks in February and March from each of the six years, or 48 weeks. There was a variety of content being shared and engaged with and the most popular items included analysis and think pieces, awards, grants, events, courses, jobs, tools, resources, and investigations. The types of content shared remained consistent over the years.

In 2014, we saw articles that discussed a burgeoning data journalism field. This included pieces arguing that data journalism is needed because it fuels accountability and insights (Howard, 2014), and predicting that analyzing data is the future for journalists (Arthur, 2010). In later years, we observed new topics being discussed, such as artificial intelligence, massive data leaks and collaborative data investigations. There were also in-depth how-to pieces, where data journalists started offering insights into their data journalism processes (Grossenbacher, 2019) and sharing how to best utilize databases (Gallego, 2018), rather than debating whether the media

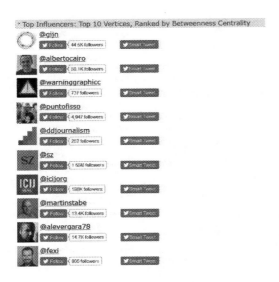

Figure 36.2. Example of top influencers (from January 1, 2018 to August 13, 2018). Source: NodeXL.

industry should incorporate data journalism into its newsrooms. We also noticed that among the investigations shared there were often analyses of elections, immigration, pollution, climate and football.

GIJN's weekly #ddj round-up not only highlights the most popular tweets and URLs, but also lists the central participants of the #ddj discussion. Some of the usual suspects at the centre of #ddj discussions include data journalism experts Edward Tufte, Alberto Cairo, Martin Stabe, Nate Silver and Nathan Yau, along with data teams from Europe and North America, including those at *Le Telegramme, Tages-Anzeiger, Berliner Morgenpost, FiveThirtyEight,* the *Financial Times,* and The Upshot from *The New York Times.* Their work can at times be educational and inspiring and trigger further debate. The data journalism community can also take advantage of and network with these influencers.

A number of other hashtags often accompany #ddj, as Connected Action's mapping reveals, allowing members of the community to seek out similar stories.

By far, the most common hashtags to appear alongside #ddj were #dataviz, #visualization, #datajournalism, #opendata, #data and #infographics. This signals to us that those who are in this field particularly care not just about the availability of public data, but also the way in which data is creatively presented and visualized for readers.

However, the NodeXL #ddj mapping is by no means representative of the entire field as it analyzes only people who tweet. Furthermore, those who

Top Hashtags in Tweet in Entire Graph:
[22540] ddj 🖉
[6765] dataviz 🖉
[1783] datajournalism 🖉
[1578] opendata 🖉
[1517] vg 🖉
[1253] data 🖉
[1080] infographics 🖉
[589] opensource 🖉
[541] datajournalismawards 🖉
[534] journalism 🖉

Figure 36.3. Example of top related hashtags (from January 1, 2018 to August 13, 2018). Source: NodeXL.

generally have more followers on Twitter and garner more retweets tend to feature more prominently in our round-up.

We have also noticed that the majority of the top tweets usually come from Europe and the Americas, particularly Germany and the United States, with some smatterings of tweets from Asia and Africa. This could be due to the skew of the user base on Twitter, because other regions have relatively less robust data journalism communities, or because data journalism communities in other regions do not organize through the same Twitter hashtags or do not organize on Twitter at all.

Over the past year, we observed that some work by prominent data journalism organizations that was widely shared on Twitter did not appear in our network graph. This could possibly be due to people not using the hashtag #ddj when tweeting the story, or using other hashtags or none at all. We suspect that Twitter's expansion of the tweet character count from 140 to 280 in November 2017 might also have helped people to choose lengthier hashtags such as #datajournalism.

Fun #ddj Discoveries

While what we find is often powerful journalism and beautiful visualizations, sometimes it is also just plain funny. By way of conclusion, we briefly discuss some of the more entertaining items we have discovered using the #ddj hashtag in the past year.

In an adorable and clever visual essay, Xaquín G. V. (2017) showed what people in different countries tend to search for the most when they want to fix something. In many warmer countries, it is fridges, for North Americans and East Asians it is toilets, while people in northern and eastern Europe seem to need information on how to fix light bulbs. Next, a chart, found among the Smithsonian's Sally L. Steinberg Collection of Doughnut Ephemera, argues that the size of the doughnut hole has gradually shrunk over the years (Edwards, 2018). In a different piece, graphic designer Nigel Holmes illustrated and explained oddly wonderful competitions around the world, from racing snails to carrying wives, in a book called *Crazy Competitions* (Yau, 2018).

In another piece in our collection, women worldwide already know that the pockets on women's jeans are impractically tiny, and *The Pudding* has provided the unequivocal data and analysis to prove it (Diehm & Thomas, 2018). Finally, is there such a thing as peak baby-making seasons? An analysis by Visme of United Nations' data on live births seems to suggest so. They found a correlation between three different variables: The top birth months, seasons of the year and the latitude of the country (distance from the equator) that may have influence on mating rhythms in different countries (Chibana, n.d.).

Works Cited

Arthur, C. (2010, November 22). Analysing data is the future for journalists, says Tim Berners-Lee. *The Guardian*. https://www.theguardian.com/media/2010/nov/22/data-analysis-tim-berners-lee

Chibana, N. (n.d.). Do humans have mating seasons? This heat map reveals the surprising link between birthdays and seasons. *Visual Learning Center by Visme*. https://visme.co/blog/most-common-birthday/

Diehm, J., & Thomas, A. (2018, August). Pockets. *The Pudding*. https://pudding.cool/2018/08/pockets/

Edwards, P. (2018, June 1). Have donut holes gotten smaller? This compelling vintage chart says yes. *Vox*. https://www.vox.com/2015/9/20/9353957/donut-hole-size-chart

Gallego, C. S. (2018, January 23). How to investigate companies found in the offshore leaks database. ICIJ. https://www.icij.org/blog/2018/01/investigate-companies-found-offshore-leaks-database/

GIJN. (n.d.). Top 10 in data journalism archives. Global Investigative Journalism Network. https://gijn.org/series/top-10-data-journalism-links/

Grossenbacher, T. (2019, March 8). (Big) data journalism with Spark and R. https://timogrossenbacher.ch/2019/03/big-data-journalism-with-spark-and-r/

Howard, A. (2014, March 3). Data-driven journalism fuels accountability and insight in the 21st century. *TechRepublic*. https://www.techrepublic.com/article/data-driven-journalism-fuels-accountability-and-insight-in-the-21st-century/

Smith, M. (2014, January 22). First NodeXL #ddj network graph. Twitter. https://twitter.com/marc_smith/status/425801408873385984

Xaquín G. V. (2017, September 1). How to fix a toilet and other things we couldn't do without search. http://how-to-fix-a-toilet.com/

Yau, N. (2018, May 21). Nigel Holmes new illustrated book on Crazy Competitions. *FlowingData*. https://flowingdata.com/2018/05/21/nigel-holmes-new-illustrated-book-on-crazy-competitions/

About the Authors

Eunice Au is programme coordinator at the Global Investigative Journalism Network, where she produces a weekly Top 10 #ddj round-up of the most popular tweets on data journalism.

Marc Smith is a sociologist building and applying tools to study social media networks.

37. Archiving Data Journalism

Meredith Broussard

Abstract
This chapter discusses the challenges of archiving data journalism projects and the steps that data teams can take to ensure their projects are preserved for the future.

Keywords: data journalism, archival practices, archives, digital archives, broken links, web archiving

In the first edition of *The Data Journalism Handbook*, published in 2012, data journalism pioneer Steve Doig wrote that one of his favourite data stories was the "Murder Mysteries" project by Tom Hargrove.[1] In the project, which was published by the Scripps Howard News Service, Hargrove looked at demographically detailed data about 185,000 unsolved murders and built an algorithm to suggest which murders might be linked. Linked murders could indicate a serial killer at work. "This project has it all," Doig wrote. "Hard work, a database better than the government's own, clever analysis using social science techniques, and interactive presentation of the data online so readers can explore it themselves."

By the time of the second edition of *The Data Journalism Handbook*, six years later, the URL to the project was broken (projects.scrippsnews.com/magazine/murder-mysteries). The project was gone from the web because its publisher, Scripps Howard, was gone. The Scripps Howard News Service had gone through multiple mergers and restructurings, eventually merging with Gannett, publisher of the *USA Today* local news network.

We know that people change jobs and media companies come and go. However, this has had disastrous consequences for data journalism projects

---

1   http://www.murderdata.org/

Bounegru, L. and J. Gray (eds.), *The Data Journalism Handbook: Towards a Critical Data Practice.* Amsterdam: Amsterdam University Press, 2021
DOI 10.5117/9789462989511_CH37

(for more on this issue see, e.g., Boss & Broussard, 2017; Broussard, 2014, 2015a, 2015b; Fisher & Klein, 2016).

Data projects are more fragile than "plain" text-and-images stories that are published in the print edition of a newspaper or magazine.

Ordinarily, link rot is not a big deal for archivists; it is easy to use Lexis-Nexis or ProQuest or another database provider to find a copy of everything published by, say, *The New York Times* print edition on any day in the 21st century. But for data stories, link rot indicates a deeper problem. Data journalism stories are not being preserved in traditional archives. As such, they are disappearing from the web. Unless news organizations and libraries take action, future historians will not be able to read everything published by *The Boston Globe* on any given day in 2017. This has serious implications for scholars and for the collective memory of the field. Journalism is often referred to as the "first draft of history." If that first draft is incomplete, how will future scholars understand the present day? Or, if stories disappear from the web, how will individual journalists maintain personal portfolios of work?

This is a human problem, not just a computational problem. To understand why data journalism is not being archived for posterity, it helps to start with how "regular" news is archived. All news organizations use software called a content management system (CMS), which allows the organization to schedule and manage the hundreds of pieces of content it creates every day and also imposes a consistent visual look and feel on each piece of content published. Historically, legacy news organizations have used a different CMS for the print edition and for the web edition. The web CMS allows the news organization to embed ads on each page, which is one of the ways that the news organization makes money. The print CMS allows print page designers to manage different versions of the print layout and then send the pages to the printer for printing and binding. Usually, video is in a different CMS. Social media posts may or may not be managed by a different application like SocialFlow or Hootsuite. Archival feeds to Lexis-Nexis and the other big providers tend to be hooked up to the print CMS. Unless someone at the news organization remembers to hook up the web CMS, too, digital-first news is not included in the digital feeds that libraries and archives get. This is a reminder that archiving is not neutral, but depends on deliberate human choices about what matters (and what doesn't) for the future.

Most people ask at this point, "What about the Internet Archive?" The Internet Archive is a treasure, and the group does an admirable job of capturing snapshots of news sites. Their technology is among the most advanced digital archiving software. However, their approach does not capture everything. The Internet Archive only collects publicly available web pages. News organizations that require logins, or which include paywalls as part of their financial strategy, cannot be automatically preserved in the Internet Archive. Web pages that are static content, or plain HTML, are the easiest to preserve. These pages are easily captured in the Internet Archive. Dynamic content, such as JavaScript or a data visualization or anything that was once referred to as "Web 2.0," is much harder to preserve, and is not often stored in the Internet Archive. "There are many different kinds of dynamic pages, some of which are easily stored in an archive and some of which fall apart completely," reads an Internet Archive FAQ. "When a dynamic page renders standard html, the archive works beautifully. When a dynamic page contains forms, JavaScript, or other elements that require interaction with the originating host, the archive will not contain the original site's functionality."

Dynamic data visualizations and news apps, currently the most cutting-edge kinds of data journalism stories, cannot be captured by existing web archiving technology. Also, for a variety of institutional reasons, these types of stories tend to be built outside of a CMS. So, even if it were possible to archive data visualizations and news apps (which it generally is not using this approach), any automated feed would not capture them because they are not inside the CMS.

It's a complicated problem. There aren't any easy answers. I work with a team of data journalists, librarians and computer scientists who are trying to develop tech to solve this thorny problem. We are borrowing methods from reproducible scientific research to make sure people can read today's news on tomorrow's computers. We are adapting a tool called ReproZip that collects the code, data and server environment used in computational science experiments. We think that ReproZip can be integrated with a tool such as Webrecorder.io in order to collect and preserve news apps, which are both stories and software. Because web- and mobile-based data journalism projects depend on and exist in relation to a wide range of other media environments, libraries, browser features and web entities (which may also continually change), we expect that we will be able to use ReproZip to collect and preserve the remote libraries and code that allow complex data journalism objects to function on the web. It will take another year or two to prove our hypothesis.

In the meantime, there are a few concrete things that every data team can do to make sure their data journalism is preserved for the future.

Take a video. This strategy is borrowed from video game preservation. Even when a video game console is no more, a video play-through can show the game in its original environment. The same is true of data journalism stories. Store the video in a central location with plain text metadata that describes what the video shows. Whenever a new video format emerges (as when VHS gave way to DVD, or DVD was replaced by streaming video), upgrade all of the videos to this new format.

Make a scaled-down version for posterity. Libraries like Django-bakery allow dynamic pages to be rendered as static pages. This is sometimes called "baking out." Even in a database with thousands of records, each dynamic record could be baked out as a static page that requires very little maintenance. Theoretically, all of these static pages could be imported into the organization's content management system. Baking out doesn't have to happen at launch. A data project can be launched as a dynamic site, then it can be transformed into a static site after traffic dies down a few months later. The general idea is to adapt your work for archiving systems by making the simplest possible version, then make sure that simple version is in the same digital location as all of the other stories published around the same time.

Think about the future. Journalists tend to plan to publish and move on to the next thing. Instead, try planning for the sunset of your data stories at the same time that you plan to launch them. Matt Waite's story "Kill All Your Darlings" on Source, the OpenNews blog, is a great guide to how to think about the life cycle of a data journalism story. Eventually, you will be promoted or will move on to a new organization. You want your data journalism to survive your departure.

Work with libraries, memory institutions and commercial archives. As an individual journalist, you should absolutely keep copies of your work. However, nobody is going to look in a box in your closet or on your hard drive, or even on your personal website, when they look for journalism in the future. They are going to look in Lexis-Nexis, ProQuest or other large commercial repositories. To learn more about commercial preservation and digital archiving, Kathleen Hansen and Nora Paul's book *Future-Proofing the News: Preserving the First Draft of History* (2017) is the canonical guide for understanding the news archiving landscape as well as the technological, legal and organizational challenges to preserving the news.

Works Cited

Boss, K., & Broussard, M. (2017). Challenges of archiving and preserving born-digital news applications. *IFLA Journal, 43*(2), 150–157. https://doi.org/10.1177/0340035216686355

Broussard, M. (2014, April 23). Future-proofing news apps. *MediaShift*. http://mediashift.org/2014/04/future-proofing-news-apps/

Broussard, M. (2015a). Preserving news apps present huge challenges. *Newspaper Research Journal, 36*(3), 299–313. https://doi.org/10.1177/0739532915600742

Broussard, M. (2015b, November 20). The irony of writing about digital preservation. *The Atlantic.* https://www.theatlantic.com/technology/archive/2015/11/the-irony-of-writing-about-digital-preservation/416184/

Fisher, T., & Klein, S. (2016). A conceptual model for interactive databases in news. GitHub. https://github.com/propublica/newsappmodel

About the Author

Meredith Broussard is an Associate Professor at the Arthur L. Carter Journalism Institute of New York University and the author of *Artificial Unintelligence: How Computers Misunderstand the World* (MIT Press, 2018).

38. From *The Guardian* to Google News Lab: A Decade of Working in Data Journalism

Simon Rogers

Abstract

A personal narrative of the last decade of data journalism through the lens of the professional journey of one of its acclaimed figures.

Keywords: data journalism, *The Guardian*'s Datablog, WikiLeaks, open data, transparency, spreadsheets

When I decided I wanted to be a journalist, somewhere between the first and second years of primary school, it never occurred to me that would involve data. Now, working with data every day, I realize how lucky I was. It certainly was not the result of carefully calibrated career plans. I was just in the right place at the right time. The *way* it happened says a lot about the state of data journalism in 2009. I believe it also tells us a lot about data journalism in 2019.

Adrian Holovaty, a developer from Chicago who had worked at *The Washington Post* and started EveryBlock, a neighbourhood-based news and discussion site, came to give a talk to the newsroom in the Education Centre of *The Guardian* on Farringdon Road in London. At that time I was a news editor at the print paper (then the centre of gravity), having worked online and edited a science section. The more Holovaty spoke about using data to both tell stories and help people understand the world, the more something triggered in me. Not only could I be doing this, but it actually reflected what I *was* doing more and more. Maybe I could be a journalist who worked with data. A "data journalist."

Working as a news editor with the graphics desk gave me the opportunity to work with designers who changed how I see the world, in Michael

Bounegru, L. and J. Gray (eds.), *The Data Journalism Handbook: Towards a Critical Data Practice*. Amsterdam: Amsterdam University Press, 2021.
DOI 10.5117/9789462989511_CH38

Robinson's talented team. And as the portfolio of visuals grew, it turned out that I had accumulated a lot of numbers: Matt McAlister, who was launching *The Guardian*'s open API, described it as "the motherlode." We had GDP data, carbon emissions, government spending data and much more cleaned up, all saved as Google spreadsheets and ready for use the next time we needed it.

What if we just published this data in an open data format? No PDFs, just interesting accessible data, ready to use, by anyone. And that's what we did with *The Guardian*'s Datablog—at first with 200 distinct data sets: Crime rates, economic indicators, war zone details, and even fashion week and Doctor Who villains. We started to realize that data could be applied to everything. It was still a weird thing to be doing. "Data editor" was hardly a widespread job—very few newsrooms had any kind of data team at all. In fact, just using the word "data" in a news meeting would elicit sniggers. This wasn't "proper" journalism, right?

But 2009 was the start of the open data revolution: US government data hub data.gov had been launched in May of that year with just 47 data sets. Open data portals were being launched by countries and cities all over the world, and campaigners were demanding access to ever more. Within a year, we had our readers helping to crowdsource the expenses of thousands of MPs. Within the same period, the UK government had released its ultimate spending data set: COINS (Combined Online Information System) and *The Guardian* team had built an interactive explorer to encourage readers to help explore it.[1] Once stories were produced from that data, however, the ask became, "How can we get more of this?"

There wasn't long to wait. The answer came from a then-new organization based in Sweden with what could charitably be described as a radical transparency agenda: WikiLeaks. Whatever you feel about WikiLeaks today, the impact of the organization on the recent history of data journalism cannot be overstated. Here was a massive dump of thousands of detailed records from the war zones of Afghanistan first, followed by Iraq. It came in the form of a giant spreadsheet, one too big for the investigations team at *The Guardian* to handle initially.

It was larger than the Pentagon Papers, that release of files during the Vietnam War which shed light on how the conflict was really going. The records were detailed too—including a list of incidents with casualty counts, geo locations, details and categories. We could see the rise in IED attacks in Iraq, for instance, and how perilous the roads around the country had

1   https://www.theguardian.com/politics/coins-combined-online-information-system

become. And when that data was combined with the traditional reporting skills of seasoned war reporters, the data changed how the world saw the wars.

It wasn't hard to produce content that seemed to have an impact across the whole world. The geodata in the spreadsheets lent itself to mapping, for instance, and there was a new free tool which could help with that: Google Fusion Tables. So we produced a quick map of every incident in Iraq in which there had been at least one death. Within 24 hours, a piece of content which took an hour to make was being seen around the world as users could explore the war zone for themselves in a way which made it seem more real. And because the data was structured, graphics teams could produce sophisticated, rich visuals which provided more in-depth reporting.

And by the end of 2011—the year before this book was first published— the "Reading the Riots" project had applied the computer-assisted reporting techniques of Phil Meyer in the 1960s to an outbreak of violence across England (Robertson, 2011). Meyer had applied social science techniques to reporting on the Detroit riots of the late 1960s. A team led by *The Guardian*'s Paul Lewis did the same to the outbreak of unrest across England that year and incorporated data as a key part of that work. These were front-page, data-based stories.

But there was another change happening to the way we consume information, and it was developing fast. I can't remember hearing the word "viral" outside health stories before 2010. The same is not true today and the rise of data journalism also coincided with the rise of social media. We were using tweets to sell stories to users across the globe and the resultant traffic led to more users looking for these kinds of data-led stories. A visual or a number could be seen in seconds by thousands. Social media transformed journalism but the amplification of data journalism was the shift which propelled it from niche to mainstream.

For one thing, it changed the dynamic with consumers. In the past, the words of a reporter were considered sacrosanct; now you are just one voice among millions. Make a mistake with a data set and 500 people would be ready to let you know. I can recall having long (and deep) conversations on Twitter with designers around colour schemes for maps—and changing what I did because of it. Sharing made my work better.

In fact that spirit of collaboration is something that still persists in data journalism today. The first edition of this book was, after all, initially developed by a group of people meeting at the Mozilla Festival in London—and as events around data started to spring up, so did the opportunities for data journalists to work together and share skill sets. If the Iraq and WikiLeaks releases were great initial examples of cross-Atlantic cooperation, then see how those exercises grew into pan-global reporting involving hundreds of reporters. The Snowden leaks and the Panama Papers were notable for how reporters coordinated around the world to share their stories and build off each other's work.[2]

Just take an exercise like Electionland, which used collaborative reporting techniques to monitor voting issues in real time on election day. I was involved, too, providing real-time Google data and helping to visualize those concerns in real time. To this date, Electionland is the biggest single-day reporting exercise in history, with over a thousand journalists involved on the day itself. There's a direct line from Electionland to what we were doing in those first few years.

My point is not to list projects but to highlight the broader context of those earlier years, not just at *The Guardian,* but in newsrooms around the world. *The New York Times*, the *Los Angeles Times, La Nación* in Argentina: Across the world journalists were discovering new ways to work by telling data-led stories in innovative ways. This was the background to the first edition of this book. *La Nación* in Argentina is a good example of this. A small team of enthused reporters taught themselves how to visualize with Tableau (at that time a new tool) and combined this with freedom of information reports to kickstart a world of data journalism in Latin and South America.

Data journalism went from being the province of a few loners to an established part of many major newsrooms. But one trend became clear even then: Whenever a new technique is introduced in reporting, data would not only be a key part of it but data journalists would be right there in the middle of it. In a period of less than three years, crowdsourcing became an established newsroom tool, and journalists found data, used databases to manage huge document dumps, published data sets and applied data-driven analytical techniques to complex news stories.

This should not be seen as an isolated development within the field of journalism. These were just the effects of huge developments in international transparency beyond the setting up of open data portals. These included campaigns such as those run by Free Our Data, the Open Knowledge Foundation and civic tech groups to increase the pressure on the UK government to open up news data sets for public use and provide APIs for anyone to explore. They also included increased access to powerful free data visualization and cleaning tools, such as OpenRefine, Google Fusion Tables, Many Eyes,

---

2   For more on large-scale collaborations around the Panama Papers, see Díaz-Struck, Gallego and Romera's chapter in this volume.

Datawrapper, Tableau Public and more. Those free tools combined with access to a lot of free public data facilitated the production of more and more public-facing visualizations and data projects. Newsrooms, such as *The Texas Tribune* and *ProPublica*, started to build operations around this data.

Can you see how this works? A virtuous circle of data, easy processing, data visualization, more data, and so on. The more data is out there, the more work is done with the data the greater pressure there is for more data to be released. When I wrote the piece "Data Journalism Is the New Punk" it was making that point: We were at a place where creativity could really run free (Rogers, 2012). But also where the work would eventually become mainstream.

Data can't do everything. As Jonathan Gray (2012) wrote: "The current wave of excitement about data, data technologies and all things data-driven might lead one to suspect that this machine-readable, structured stuff is a special case." It is just one piece of the puzzle of evidence that reporters have to assemble. But as there is more and more data available, that role changes and becomes even more important. The ability to access and analyze huge data sets was the main attraction for my next career move.

In 2013, I got the chance to move to California and join Twitter as its first data editor—and it was clear that data had entered the vocabulary of mainstream publishing, certainly in the United States and Europe. A number of data journalism sites sprouted within weeks of each other, such as *The New York Times'* Upshot and Nate Silver's *FiveThirtyEight*. Audiences out there in the world were becoming more and more visually literate and appreciative of sophisticated visualizations of complex topics. You will ask what evidence I have that the world is comfortable with data visualizations? I don't have a lot beyond my experience that producing a visual which garners a big reaction online is harder than it used to be. Where we all used to react with "oohs and aahs" to visuals, now it's harder to get beyond a shrug.

By the time I joined the Google News Lab to work on data journalism in 2015, it had become clear that the field has access to greater and larger data sets than ever before. Every day, there are billions of searches, a significant proportion of which have never been seen before. And increasingly reporters are taking that data and analyzing it, along with tweets and Facebook likes.[3] This is the exhaust of modern life, turned around and given back to us as insights about the way we live today.

Data journalism is now also more widespread than it has ever been. In 2016, the Data Journalism Awards received a record 471 entries. But the 2018

---

3   For further perspectives on this, see the "Investigating Data, Platforms and Algorithms" section.

awards received nearly 700, over half from small newsrooms, and many from across the world. And those entries are becoming more and more innovative. Artificial intelligence, or machine learning, has become a tool for data journalism, as evidenced by Peter Aldhous' work at *Buzzfeed* (Aldhous, 2017). Meanwhile access to new technologies like virtual and augmented reality open up possibilities for telling stories with data in new ways. As someone whose job is to imagine how data journalism could change—and what we can do to support it—I look at how emerging technologies can be made easier for more reporters to integrate into their work. For example, we recently worked with design studio Datavized to build TwoTone, a visual tool to translate data into sound.[4]

What does a data journalist at Google do? I get to tell stories with a large and rich collection of data sets, as well as getting to work with talented designers to imagine the future of news data visualization and the role of new technologies in journalism. Part of my role is to help explore how new technologies can be matched with the right use cases and circumstances in which they are appropriate and useful. This role also involves exploring how journalists are using data and digital technologies to tell stories in new ways. For example, one recent project, *El Universal*'s "Zones of Silence," demonstrated the use of AI in journalism, using language processing to analyze news coverage of drug cartel murders and compare them to the official data, the gap between the two being areas of silence in reporting. I helped them do it, through access to AI APIs and design resources.

The challenges are great, for all of us. We all consume information in increasingly mobile ways, which brings its own challenges. The days of full-screen complex visualizations have crashed against the fact that more than half of us now read the news on our phones or other mobile devices (a third of us read the news on the toilet, according to a Reuters news consumption study (Newman et al., 2017)). That means that increasingly newsroom designers have to design for tiny screens and dwindling attention spans.

We also have a new problem that can stop us learning from the past. Code dies, libraries rot and eventually much of the most ambitious work in journalism just dies. *The Guardian*'s MPs' expenses, EveryBlock and other projects have all succumbed to a vanishing institutional memory. This problem of vanishing data journalism is already subject to some innovative approaches (as you can see from Broussard's chapter in this book). In the long run, this requires proper investment and it remains to be seen if the community is sufficiently motivated to make it happen.

4   https://twotone.io/

And we face a wider and increasingly alarming issue: Trust. Data analysis has always been subject to interpretation and disagreement, but good data journalism can overcome that. At a time when belief in the news and a shared set of facts are in doubt every day, data journalism can light the way for us, by bringing facts and evidence to light in an accessible way.

So, despite all the change, some things are constant in this field. Data journalism has a long history,[5] but in 2009, data journalism seemed an important way to get at a common truth, something we could all get behind. Now that need is greater than ever before.

Works Cited

Aldhous, P. (2017, August 8). We trained a computer to search for hidden spy planes. This is what it found. *BuzzFeed News*. https://www.buzzfeednews.com/article/peteraldhous/hidden-spy-planes

Gray, J. (2012, May 31). What data can and cannot do. *The Guardian*. https://www.theguardian.com/news/datablog/2012/may/31/data-journalism-focused-critical

Newman, N., Fletcher, R., Kalogeropoulos, A., Levy, D. A. L., & Nielsen, R. K. (2017). *Digital News Report 2017*. Reuters Institute for the Study of Journalism. https://reutersinstitute.politics.ox.ac.uk/sites/default/files/Digital%20News%20Report%202017%20web_0.pdf

Robertson, C. (2011, December 9). Reading the riots: How the 1967 Detroit riots were investigated. *The Guardian*. https://www.theguardian.com/uk/video/2011/dec/09/reading-the-riots-detroit-meyer-video

Rogers, S. (2012, May 24). Anyone can do it. Data journalism is the new punk. *The Guardian*. https://www.theguardian.com/news/datablog/2012/may/24/data-journalism-punk

About the Author

Simon Rogers is data editor on the News Lab team at Google, based in San Francisco, he is director of the Sigma Data Journalism Awards and teaches Data Journalism at Medill-Northwestern University.

---

5   See, for example, the chapters by Anderson and Cohen in this volume.

39. Data Journalism's Ties With Civic Tech

Stefan Baack

Abstract

How data journalism overlaps with other forms of data work and data culture.

Keywords: civic tech, gatekeeping, professional boundaries, data journalism, freedom of information (FOI), databases

While computer-assisted reporting was considered a practice exclusive to (investigative) journalists, data journalism is characterized by its entanglements with the technology sector and other forms of data work and data culture. Compared to computer-assisted reporting, the emergence of data journalism in the United States and in Europe intersected with several developments both within and outside newsrooms. These include: The growing availability of data online, not least due to open data initiatives and leaks; newsrooms hiring developers and integrating them within the editorial team to better cope with data and provide interactive web applications; and the emergence of various "tech for good" movements that are attracted to journalism as a way to use their technological skills for a "public good." This has contributed to an influx of technologists into newsrooms ever since data journalism emerged and became popular in the 2000s in the West and elsewhere. However, the resulting entanglements between data journalists and other forms of data work are distinct in different regions. Moreover, data journalism is connected to new, entrepreneurial forms of journalism that have emerged in response to the continued struggle of media organizations to develop sustainable business models. These new types of media organizations, for example, non-profit newsrooms like *ProPublica* or venture-backed news start-ups like *BuzzFeed*, tend to question traditional boundaries of journalism in their aspiration to "revive" or "improve" journalism, and

Bounegru, L. and J. Gray (eds.), *The Data Journalism Handbook: Towards a Critical Data Practice.*
Amsterdam: Amsterdam University Press, 2021
DOI 10.5117/9789462989511_CH39

technology and data often play a key role in these efforts (see Usher, 2017; Wagemans et al., 2019).

The entanglements between data journalism and other forms of data work and data cultures create new dependencies, but also new synergies that enable new forms of collaboration across sectors. Here I want to use the close relationship between data journalism and civic tech as an example because in many places both phenomena emerged around the same time and mutually shaped each other from an early stage. Civic tech is about the development of tools that aim to empower citizens by making it easier for them to engage with their governments or to hold them accountable. Examples of civic tech projects are OpenParliament, a parliamentary monitoring website that, among other things, makes parliamentary speeches more accessible; WhatDoTheyKnow, a freedom of information website that helps users to submit and find freedom of information requests; and FixMyStreet, which simplifies the reporting of problems to local authorities.[1]

Civic technologists and data journalists share some important characteristics. First, many practitioners in both groups are committed to the principles of open-source culture and promote sharing, the use of open-source tools and data standards. Second, data journalists and civic technologists heavily rely on data, be it from official institutions, via crowdsourcing or via other sources. Third, while differing in their means, both groups aspire to provide a public service that empowers citizens and holds authorities accountable. Because of this overlapping set of data skills, complementary ambitions and joint commitment to sharing, civic technologists and data journalists easily perceive each other as complementary. In addition, support from media organizations, foundations such as the Knight Foundation, and grassroots initiatives such as Hacks/Hackers, have created continuous exchanges and collaborations between data journalists and civic technologists.

The Tension Between Expanding and Reinforcing the Journalistic "Core"

Based on a case study in Germany and the United Kingdom that examined how data journalists and civic technologists complement each other, we can describe their entanglements as revolving around two core practices:

---

1   Openparliament.ca, WhatDoTheyKnow.com, FixMyStreet.com

Facilitating and gatekeeping (Baack, 2018). Facilitating means enabling others to take actions themselves, while gatekeeping refers to the traditional journalistic role model of being a gatekeeper for publicly relevant information. To illustrate the difference, parliamentary monitoring websites developed by civic technologists are intended to enable their users to *inform themselves*, for example, by searching through parliamentary speeches (facilitating), but not to *pro-actively push* information to them that is deemed relevant by professionals (gatekeeping). Facilitating is about individual empowerment, while gatekeeping is about directing public debate and having impact.

What characterizes the entanglements between data journalists and civic technologists is that practices of facilitating and gatekeeping are complementary and can mutually reinforce each other. For example, civic tech applications not only facilitate ordinary citizens; data journalists can use them for their own investigations. Investigations by journalists, on the other hand, can draw attention to particular issues and encourage people to make use of facilitating services. Moreover, information rights are essential for both facilitating and gatekeeping practices, which creates additional synergies. For example, data journalists can use their exclusive rights to get data that they then share with civic technologists, while journalists can profit from civic tech's advocacy for stronger freedom of information rights and open data policies.

New entrepreneurial forms of journalism play a particular role in the relationship between data journalism and civic tech, as they are more open towards expanding traditional gatekeeping with civic tech's notion of facilitating. For example, *ProPublica* has developed several large, searchable databases intended not only to facilitate the engagement of ordinary citizens with their governments, but also to aid journalistic investigations by reporters in local newsrooms who do not have the resources and expertise to collect, clean and analyze data themselves. Another non-profit newsroom from Germany, Correctiv, has taken a similar approach and integrated the freedom of information website of the Open Knowledge Foundation Germany into some of its applications. This integration enabled users to directly request further information that is automatically added back to Correctiv's database once obtained.[2]

While these examples illustrate that there is a growing number of organizations that expand traditional notions of journalism by incorporating practices and values from other data cultures, there is also the opposite: Data journalists that react to the similarities in practices and aspirations

---

2   Correctiv.org

with other fields of data work by embracing their professional identity as gatekeepers and storytellers. Those journalists do not necessarily reject civic tech, but their response is a greater specialization of journalism, closer to notions of traditional, investigative journalism.

The Opportunities of Blurry Boundaries

In sum, data journalism's entanglements with other fields of data work and data culture contribute to a greater diversification of how "journalism" is understood and practiced, be it towards an expansion or a reinforcement of traditional values and identities. Both journalists themselves and research-ers can consider data journalism as a phenomenon embedded in broader technological, cultural and economic transformations. I have focused on the entanglements between data journalists and civic technologists in this chapter, but I would like to point out two key lessons for data journalists that are relevant beyond this particular case.

Benefitting from blurry boundaries. Journalists tend to describe a lack of professional boundaries towards other fields as problematic, but the synergies between civic technologists and data journalists demonstrate that blurry boundaries can also be an advantage. Rather than perceiving them primarily as problematic, data journalists also need to ask whether there are synergies with other fields of data work, and how to best benefit from them. Importantly, this does not mean that journalists necessarily have to adopt practices of facilitating themselves. While there are examples of that, journalists who reject this idea can still try to find ways to benefit without sacrificing their professional identity.

Embracing diversity in professional journalism. The findings of my study reflect how "journalism" is increasingly delivered by a variety of different, more specialized actors. This diversification is raising concerns for some of the journalists I interviewed. For them, media organizations that adopt practices of facilitating might weaken their notion of "hard," investigative journalism. However, journalists need to acknowledge that it is unlikely that there will be a single definite form of journalism in the future.

In sum, a stronger awareness of both the historical and contemporary ties to other forms of data work and data culture can help journalists to reflect on their own role and to be better aware of not just new dependencies, but also potential synergies that can be used to support and potentially expand their mission.

Works Cited

Baack, S. (2018). Practically engaged. The entanglements between data journalism and civic tech. *Digital Journalism*, 6(6), 673–692. https://doi.org/10.1080/21670 811.2017.1375382

Usher, N. (2017). Venture-backed news start-ups and the field of journalism. *Digital Journalism*, 5(9), 1116–1133. https://doi.org/10.1080/21670811.2016.1272064

Wagemans, A., Witschge, T., & Harbers, F. (2019). Impact as driving force of journalistic and social change. *Journalism*, 20(4), 552–567. https://doi. org/10.1177/1464884918770538

About the Author

Stefan Baack is a media researcher associated with the Weizenbaum Institute for the Networked Society and a research and data analyst at the Mozilla Foundation.

40. Open-Source Coding Practices in Data Journalism

Ryan Pitts and Lindsay Muscato

Abstract
This chapter discusses the challenges of open-source coding for journalism and the features that successful projects share.

Keywords: open source, programming, coding, journalism, tool development, code libraries

Imagine this: A couple of journalists work together to scrape records from government websites, transform those scraped documents into data, analyze that data to look for patterns and then publish a visualization that tells a story for readers. Some version of this process unfolds in newsrooms around the world every single day. In many newsrooms, each step relies at least in part on open-source software, piecing together community-tested tools into a workflow that is faster than any way we could do it before.

But it is not just open-source software that has become part of today's data journalism workflow, it is also the *philosophy* of open source. We share knowledge and skills with one another, at events and through community channels and social media. We publish methodologies and data, inviting colleagues to correct our assumptions and giving readers reason to trust our results. Such open, collaborative approaches can make our journalism better.[1] Every time we seek feedback or outside contributions, we make our work more resilient. Someone else might spot a problem with how we used data in a story or contribute a new feature that makes our software better.

---

[1]   See also the chapters by Leon and Mazotte for different perspectives on the role of open-source practices and philosophies in data journalism.

Bounegru, L. and J. Gray (eds.), *The Data Journalism Handbook: Towards a Critical Data Practice*. Amsterdam: Amsterdam University Press, 2021
DOI 10.5117/9789462989511_CH40

These practices can also have broader benefits beyond our own projects and organizations. Most of us will never dive into a big project using nothing but tools we have built ourselves and techniques we have pioneered alone. Instead, we build on the work of other people, learning from mentors, listening at conferences and learning how projects we like were made.

At OpenNews, we have worked with journalists on open-source projects, supported developer collaborations, and written *The Field Guide to Open Source in the Newsroom*.[2] In this chapter we reflect on some of the things we have learned about the role of open-source practices in data journalism, including common challenges and features of successful projects.

Common Challenges

Working openly can be rewarding and fun, and you can learn more in the process—but it is not always simple! Planning for success means going in clear-eyed about the challenges that open-source projects often face.

Making the case. It can feel hard to persuade editors, legal teams and others that "giving away" your work is a good idea. There may be legal, business, reputational and sustainability concerns. In response, we have been working with journalists to document the benefits of open-sourcing tools and process, including stronger code, community goodwill and increased credibility.[3]

People move on, and so does technology. When a key member of a team takes another job, the time they have available to maintain and advocate for an open-source project often goes with them. For example, a few years ago, *The New York Times* released Pourover, a JavaScript framework that powered fast, in-browser filtering of gigantic data sets. Pourover was widely shared and began to build a community. But one of the primary developers took a job elsewhere, and the team started looking at newer tools to solve similar problems. That is by no means a knock on Pourover's code or planning—sometimes a project's lifespan is just different than you had imagined.

Pressures of success. It sounds counterintuitive, but finding out that people are really excited about something you built can create work you are not ready for. Sudden, explosive popularity adds pressure to keep building, fix bugs and respond to community contributions. Elliot Bentley wrestled with all these things after releasing oTranscribe, a web app he wrote to solve

2   https://opennews.org/, http://fieldguide.opennews.org/
3   http://fieldguide.opennews.org/en/latest/Chapter01-Choosing-Open-Source/

a problem in his day job: Transcribing audio interviews. A few months later he had tens of thousands of active users and questions about the future of the project.

Features of Successful Projects

There are many great examples of open source in journalism—from projects released by one newsroom and adopted by many others, to those that are collaborations from the start. The most successful efforts we have seen share one or more qualities, which we describe below.

They solve a problem that you run into every day. Odds are, someone else is running into the same roadblock or the same set of repetitive tasks as you are. In covering criminal justice nationwide, the Marshall Project watches hundreds of websites for changes and announcements. Visiting a list of URLs over and over again is not a good use of a reporter's time, but it is a great use of a cloud server. Klaxon keeps an eye on those websites and sends an alert whenever one changes—it's so fast that the newsroom often has information even before it is officially announced.[4] That kind of tracking is useful for all kinds of beats, and when the Marshall Project solved a problem for their reporters, they solved it for other organizations, too. By releasing Klaxon as an open-source project, its developers help reporting in dozens of newsrooms and receive code contributions in return that make their tool even better.

They solve a problem that is not fun to work on. NPR's data/visuals team needed a way to make graphics change dimensions along with the responsive pages they were embedded on. It is a critical feature as readers increasingly use mobile devices to access news content, but not necessarily a fun problem to work on. When NPR released Pym.js, an open-source code library that solved the problem, it did not take long to find widespread adoption across the journalism community.

They have great documentation. There is a huge difference between dumping code onto the Internet and actually explaining what a project is for and how to use it. Deadlines have a tendency to make writing documentation a low priority, but a project can't thrive without it. New users need a place to get started, and you, too, will thank yourself when you revisit your own work later on. Wherewolf is a small JavaScript service you can use to figure out where an address is located inside a set of boundaries (e.g., school

4   https://newsklaxon.org/

districts or county borders). Although the code has not needed an update for a while, the user community is still growing, at least in part because its documentation is thorough and full of examples.

They welcome contributors. The California Civic Data Coalition has a suite of open-source tools that help reporters use state campaign-finance data. The project began as a collaboration between a few developers in two newsrooms, but it has grown thanks to contributions from students, interns, civic data folks, interested citizens and even journalists with no coding experience at all. This didn't happen by accident: The initiative has a roadmap of features to build and bugs to fix, they create tickets with tasks for different levels of expertise, and they show up at conferences and plan sprints that welcome everyone.

There are many ways to measure success for an open-source newsroom project. Are you looking to build a community and invite contributions? Do you need a way to get extra eyes on your work? Or did you make something that solves a problem for you, and it just feels good to save other people the same heartache? You get to decide what success looks like for you. No matter what you choose, developing a plan that gets you there will have a few things in common: Being clear about your goal so you can create an honest roadmap for yourself and set the right expectations for others; writing friendly, example-driven documentation that brings new people onboard and explains decision making down the road; adopting a collaborative way of working that welcomes people in. You'll learn so much by doing, so get out there and share!

About the Authors

Ryan Pitts is programme lead for technology at OpenNews, a non-profit team that connects newsroom developers, designers and data analysts with resources (and each other!) in ways that make journalism more equitable and collaborative.

Lindsay Muscato is an editor, writer and project manager in journalism, most recently with OpenNews and currently with Vox Media.

41. Data Feudalism: How Platforms Shape Cross-border Investigative Networks

Ştefan Cândea

Abstract

Data feudalism: How platforms shape cross-border investigative journalism and pave the way for its colonization.

Keywords: cross-border investigation, political economy of network-ing, sociotechnological access control, radical sharing, data feudalism, platforms

The platformization of cross-border investigative journalism is a growing phenomenon, endorsed by the same techno-positivism as the current trend of the platformization of society (Dijck et al., 2018). Platforms to host data for cross-border investigations began to gain prominence around 2010, in the context of doing investigations with leaked data. Perhaps the most notable example of a platform-based large-scale journalistic collaboration is the Pulitzer Prize-winning Panama Papers.

In order to organize data querying and reporting for the 500 journalists involved in the Panama Papers investigation, the International Consortium of Investigative Journalists (ICIJ) developed a platform called Global I-Hub (Wilson-Chapman, 2017).[1] Ryle (2017) describes the platform as "specially developed technology.... used to interrogate and distribute information, connect journalists together in an online newsroom and ensure that the journalists work as one global team." It is called "the ICIJ virtual office ... a Facebook for journalists" by both editorial and research staff of the ICIJ (Hare, 2016; Raab, 2016).

---

[1]   For a different perspective on the I-Hub platform, see Díaz-Struck, Gallego and Romera's chapter in this book.

Bounegru, L. and J. Gray (eds.), *The Data Journalism Handbook: Towards a Critical Data Practice*. Amsterdam: Amsterdam University Press, 2021.
DOI 10.5117/9789462989511_CH41

Data and cross-border investigations are supposed to be a perfect match and to empower independent journalistic collaborations (Coronel, 2016; Houston, 2016). Organizations such as the ICIJ, the Organised Crime and Corruption Reporting Project (OCCRP), and others, offer a hand-picked group of hundreds of journalists around the world, free (or, better said, subsidized) access to exclusive data sets available for querying on a private electronic platform, inaccessible to the outside world. They also offer a platform to publish and advertise the stories produced by these journalists.

For these organizations, using such platforms enables achieving scale and efficiency. For individual journalists, having exclusive and secure access in a single place to data troves of leaks, scraped company records, results of FOIA requests, archives, reporter notes, past stories, digitized prosecution files and court records—to name just a few—is a nirvana. This is especially true for those working in isolation and lacking the resources to travel and to store and process data.

While acknowledging these short-term benefits, critical research into how such investigative platforms are shaping the position and work of individual journalists who are using them and the networks they are part of, is yet to be developed.

There are consequences to having very few actors running such platforms and large numbers of journalists depending on them in the cross-border journalism realm. One of these could be understood as what in the landscape of "big tech" has been called a "hyper-modern form of feudalism" based on data ownership (Morozov, 2016). This concept draws attention to how total control of users' data and interactions is placed in the hands of a few companies who face no competition.

This model raises a number of concerns. An important one is access control. Access to such platforms is for many good reasons behind many layers of security and not every journalist can gain access. The essential question is who decides about who is included and excluded, and what the rules governing these decisions, and any tensions and conflicts that might emerge from them, are. Participation in such platforms is typically governed by a basic non-disclosure agreement or a partnership agreement, where the duties of the journalist or the media outlet receiving access are listed in detail, usually with scarce reference to their rights. Such systems and their governing schemes are not designed with co-ownership principles in mind, but rather as centrally owned structures, with surveillance of user activities and policing of agreement breaches as built-in features.

Moreover, adopting this model in investigative journalism, just as in the rest of the "sharing economy," runs the risk of generating a precariat within the realm of investigative journalism. Suggestive of this risk are the self-descriptions of some of the organizations running these platforms. For example, the OCCRP is describing itself as the "AirBnb or Uber of journalists" who want to do "great cross-border investigations" (OCCRP, 2017).

Indeed, often journalists are working without pay on data leaks owned by these organizations, having to pay for access to this data with their stories, and at any time running the risk of being removed from the platform. In spite of these unfavourable conditions, journalists increasingly have to be active on such platforms to stay in the game.

For these reasons, the business model for a major investigative network intermediary today may be seen as resembling that of a gig economy digital platform. Access to the platform can be revoked at any time, governance is not open for discussion, surveillance of user activity is built-in and "money is best kept out of the equation" (Buzenberg, 2015). The unpaid work and "radical sharing" interactions of hundreds of journalists are "sold" to donors, without profits being shared back. The ownership of the data leaks and the information exchange enriching such leaks is also not shared with users. Data produced by the information exchanged among users is only shared back under the form of features that would make the platform more efficient and thus would bring more interactions, more users and by extension more donors. The real cost of services is unknown to users.

What can be done to remedy this current trend in the investigative journalism world? A key first step is to acknowledge that platform-based data sharing in investigative journalism networks needs to be accompanied by discussions of governance rules and technology design, as well as co-ownership of data and digital tools. These networks need to develop and adopt public codes of conduct and to have accountability mechanisms in place to deal with abuses of any kind. The absence of these may amplify the precarious work conditions of individual journalists, instead of disrupting legacy media actors.

Secondly, the goal should not be to scale up a small number of cross-border investigative networks to thousands of people each. Rather, the goal should be to find a good model that can be applied to a multitude of independent networks that may collaborate with each other. So instead of a single network of 150 media partners, a more desirable approach would be to have ten networks of 15 partners each. The latter would be commensurate with the principles of a healthy media system, including fair competition and media pluralism. Without such approaches, the participatory potential of cross-border investigative networks will fail to materialize and, fuelled by a network effect, a few platforms will consolidate into a global investigative data-feudalism system.

Works Cited

Buzenberg, W. E. (2015, July 6). Anatomy of a global investigation: Collaborative, data-driven, without borders. Shorenstein Center. https://shorensteincenter.org/anatomy-of-a-global-investigation-william-buzenberg/

Coronel, S. (2016, June 20). Coronel: A golden age of global muckraking at hand. Global Investigative Journalism Network. https://gijn.org/2016/06/20/a-golden-age-of-global-muckraking/

Dijck, J. van, Poell, T., & Waal, M. de. (2018). *The platform society: Public values in a connective world*. Oxford University Press.

Hare, K. (2016, April 4). How ICIJ got hundreds of journalists to collaborate on the Panama Papers. Poynter. https://www.poynter.org/reporting-editing/2016/how-icij-got-hundreds-of-journalists-to-collaborate-on-the-panama-papers/

Houston, B. (2016, April 14). Panama papers showcase power of a global movement. Global Investigative Journalism Network. https://gijn.org/2016/04/13/panama-papers-showcase-power-of-a-global-movement/

Morozov, E. (2016, April 24). Tech titans are busy privatising our data. *The Guardian*. https://www.theguardian.com/commentisfree/2016/apr/24/the-new-feudalism-silicon-valley-overlords-advertising-necessary-evil

OCCRP. (2017). *2016 Annual Report*. OCCRP. https://www.occrp.org/documents/AnnualReport2017.pdf

Raab, B. (2016, April 8). Behind the Panama Papers: A Q&A with International Consortium of Investigative Journalists director Gerard Ryle. Ford Foundation. https://www.fordfoundation.org/ideas/equals-change-blog/posts/behind-the-panama-papers-a-qa-with-international-consortium-of-investigative-journalists-director-gerard-ryle/

Ryle, G. (2017, November 5). Paradise Papers: More documents, more reporters, more revelations. ICIJ. https://www.icij.org/blog/2017/11/more-documents-more-journalists-and-bigger-revelations/

Wilson-Chapman, A. (2017, August 29). Panama Papers a "notable security success." ICIJ. https://www.icij.org/blog/2017/08/panama-papers-notable-security-success/

About the Author

Ștefan Cândea is a doctoral researcher at CAMRI, University of Westminster, a member of the International Consortium of Investigative Journalists (ICIJ) and the coordinator of European Investigative Collaborations (EIC).

42. Data-Driven Editorial? Considerations for Working With Audience Metrics

Caitlin Petre

Abstract

Drawing on Caitlin Petre's ethnographic study of Chartbeat, Gawker Media and *The New York Times*, this chapter explores the role of metrics in contemporary news production and offers recommendations to newsrooms incorporating metrics into editorial practice.

Keywords: metrics, analytics, newsrooms, journalism practice, ethnography, editorial practice

On August 23, 2013, the satirical news site *The Onion* published an op-ed purporting to be written by CNN digital editor Meredith Artley, titled "Let Me Explain Why Miley Cyrus' VMA Performance Was Our Top Story This Morning."[1] The answer, the piece explained matter-of-factly, was "pretty simple":

> It was an attempt to get you to click on CNN.com so that we could drive up our web traffic, which in turn would allow us to increase our advertising revenue. There was nothing, and I mean nothing, about that story that related to the important news of the day, the chronicling of significant human events, or the idea that journalism itself can be a force for positive change in the world. . . . But boy oh boy did it get us some web traffic. (Artley, 2013)

---

[1] This piece has been excerpted and adapted from "The Traffic Factories: Metrics at Chartbeat, Gawker Media, and The New York Times," originally published by the Tow Center for Digital Journalism at the Columbia University Graduate School of Journalism in 2015. Republished with permission.

Bounegru, L. and J. Gray (eds.), *The Data Journalism Handbook: Towards a Critical Data Practice.* Amsterdam: Amsterdam University Press, 2021
DOI 10.5117/9789462989511_CH42

The piece went on to mention specific metrics like page views and bounce rates as factors that motivated CNN to give the Cyrus story prominent home page placement.

Of course, Artley did not actually write the story, but it hit a nerve in media circles nonetheless—especially since a story on Cyrus' infamous performance at the MTV Video Music Awards had occupied the top spot on CNN.com and, as the real Meredith Artley later confirmed, did bring in the highest traffic of any story on the site that day. The fake op-ed can be interpreted not only as a condemnation of CNN, but also as a commentary on the sorry state of news judgement in the era of web metrics.

Media companies have always made efforts to collect data on their audiences' demographics and behaviour. But the tracking capabilities of the Internet, as well as the ability to store and parse massive amounts of data, mean that audience metrics have grown far more sophisticated in recent years. In addition to the aforementioned page views and bounce rates, analytics tools track variables like visitors' return rates, referral sites, scroll depths and time spent on a page. Much of this data is delivered to news organizations in real time.

Metrics dashboards are now virtually ubiquitous in contemporary news-rooms, and heated debates about how and when they should be consulted are nearly as widespread as the metrics themselves. It is not surprising that metrics have become a hot-button issue in journalism. Their presence invites a number of ever-present tensions in commercial news media to come crashing into the foreground. Among them: What is the fundamental mission of journalism, and how can news organizations know when they achieve that mission? How can media companies reconcile their profit imperative with their civic one? To the extent that the distinction between journalist and audience is still meaningful, what kind of relationship should journalists have with their readers? Audience metrics have become ubiquitous in news organizations, but there has been little empirical research on how the data is produced or how it affects newsroom culture and journalists' daily work.

With the support of Columbia University's Tow Center for Digital Journal-ism, I undertook a long-term ethnographic research project to understand how the use of metrics changes reporters' behaviour and what this means for journalism. My key research questions included the following:

First, How are metrics produced? That is, how do the programmers, data scientists, designers, product leads, marketers and salespeople who make and sell these tools decide which aspects of audience behaviour should be measured and how to measure them? What ideas—about both those whose behaviour they are measuring (news consumers) and those who will be using their tool (journalists)—are embedded in these decisions? How do analytics firms communicate the value of metrics to news organizations?

Second, How are metrics interpreted? Despite their opposing stances, arguments that metrics are good or bad for journalism have one thing in common: They tend to assume that the meaning of metrics is clear and straightforward. But a number on its own does not mean anything without a conceptual framework with which to interpret it. Who makes sense of metrics, and how do they do it?

Third, How are metrics actually used in news work? Does data inform the way newsrooms assign, write and promote stories? In which ways, if any, is data a factor in personnel decisions such as raises, promotions and layoffs? Does data play more of a role in daily work or long-term strategy? And how do the answers to these questions differ across organizational contexts?

To answer these questions, I conducted an ethnographic study of the role of metrics in contemporary news by examining three case studies: Chartbeat, Gawker Media, and *The New York Times*. Through a combination of observation and interviews with product managers, data scientists, reporters, bloggers, editors and others, my intention was to unearth the assumptions and values that underlie audience measures, the effect of metrics on journalists' daily work, and the ways in which metrics interact with organizational culture. In what follows I will summarize some of my central discoveries.

First, analytics dashboards have important emotional dimensions that are too often overlooked. Metrics, and the larger "big data" phenomenon of which they are a part, are commonly described as a force of rationalization: That is, they allow people to make decisions based on dispassionate, objective information rather than unreliable intuition or judgement. While this portrayal is not incorrect, it is incomplete. The power and appeal of metrics are significantly grounded in the data's ability to elicit particular feelings, such as excitement, disappointment, validation and reassurance. Chartbeat knew that this emotional valence was a powerful part of the dashboard's appeal, and the company included features to engender emotions in users. For instance, the dashboard was designed to communicate deference to journalistic judgement, cushion the blow of low traffic and provide opportunities for celebration in newsrooms.

Second, the impact of an analytics tool depends on the organization using it. It is often assumed that the very presence of an analytics tool will change how a newsroom operates in particular ways. However, I found that organizational context was highly influential in shaping if and how metrics influence the production of news. For instance, Gawker Media and *The*

New York Times are both Chartbeat clients, but the tool manifests in vastly different ways in each setting. At Gawker, metrics were highly visible and influential. At *The Times*, they were less so, and often used to corroborate decisions editors had already made. This suggests that it is impossible to know how analytics are affecting journalism without examining how they are used in particular newsrooms.

Finally, for writers, a metrics-driven culture can be simultaneously a source of stress and reassurance. It is also surprisingly compatible with a perception of editorial freedom. While writers at Gawker Media found traffic pressures stressful, many were far more psychologically affected by online vitriol in comments and on social media. In a climate of online hostility or even harassment, writers sometimes turned to metrics as a reassuring reminder of their professional competence. Interestingly, writers and editors generally did not perceive the company's traffic-based evaluation systems as an impediment to their editorial autonomy. This suggests that journalists at online-only media companies like Gawker Media may have different notions of editorial freedom and constraint than their legacy media counterparts.

By way of conclusion, I make the following recommendations to news organizations. First, news organizations should prioritize strategic thinking on analytics-related issues (i.e., the appropriate role of metrics in the organization and the ways in which data interacts with the organization's journalistic goals). Most journalists were too busy with their daily assignments to think extensively or abstractly about the role of metrics in their organization, or which metrics best complemented their journalistic goals. As a result, they tended to consult, interpret and use metrics in an ad hoc way. But this data is simply too powerful to implement on the fly. Newsrooms should create opportunities—whether internally or by partnering with outside researchers—for reflective, deliberate thinking removed from daily production pressures about how best to use analytics.

Second, when choosing an analytics service, newsroom managers should look beyond the tools and consider which vendor's strategic objectives, business imperatives and values best complement those of their newsroom. We have a tendency to see numbers—and, by extension, analytics dashboards—as authoritative and dispassionate reflections of the empirical world. When selecting an analytics service, however, it is important to remember that analytics companies have their own business imperatives.

Third, when devising internal policies for the use of metrics, newsroom managers should consider the potential effects of traffic data not only on editorial content, but also on editorial workers. Once rankings have a prominent place on a newsroom wall or website, it can be difficult to limit their influence. Traffic-based rankings can drown out other forms of evaluation, even when that was not the intention.

Finally, although efforts to develop better metrics are necessary and worthwhile, newsrooms and analytics companies should be attentive to the limitations of metrics. As organizational priorities and evaluation systems are increasingly built on metrics, there is danger in conflating what is quantitatively measurable with what is valuable. Not everything can—or should—be counted. Newsroom, analytics companies, funders and media researchers might consider how some of journalism's most compelling and indispensable traits, such as its social mission, are not easily measured. At a time when data analytics are increasingly valorized, we must take care not to equate what is quantifiable with what is valuable.

Works Cited

Artley, M. (2013, August 26). Let me explain why Miley Cyrus' VMA performance was our top story this morning. *The Onion.* https://www.theonion.com/let-me-explain-why-miley-cyrus-vma-performance-was-our-1819584893

About the Author

Caitlin Petre is an Assistant Professor of Journalism & Media Studies at Rutgers University. Her work examines the social and political implications of an increasingly data-saturated world.

Learning Data Journalism Together

43. Data Journalism, Digital Universalism and Innovation in the Periphery

Anita Say Chan

Abstract

The "myth of digital universalism" manifests not only in the means by which it keeps public narratives and imaginations fixed exclusively around so-called "centres" of innovation, but in the means by which it simultaneously discourages attention to digital dynamics beyond such centres—a dynamic conjuring colonial relations to data and the periphery that reporters and scholars of global digital cultures alike must be wary of reproducing.

Keywords: digital universalism, centre, periphery, colonial relations, decolonial computing, local innovation

"Digital universalism" is the pervasive but mistaken framework shaping global imaginaries around the digital that presumes that a single, universal narrative propelled by "centres" of innovation can accurately represent the forms of digital development underway across the globe today. It presumes, that is, that the given centres of contemporary "innovation" and technological design will inevitably determine the digital future that comes to spread across the world for the majority of the "digital rest." And it resonates through the casual presumption that the best, most "legitimate" sites from which to study and observe technological transformation, digital productivity and practice, or information-based innovation and inquiry, are from such centres. Foremost among them: The labs, offices and research sites nestled in Silicon Valley and their dispersed equivalents in other innovation capitals worldwide that concentrate elite forms of digital expertise.

It is from such centres that digital culture presumably originates and has its purest form and manifestation—only to be replicated elsewhere; there

Bounegru, L. and J. Gray (eds.), *The Data Journalism Handbook: Towards a Critical Data Practice*. Amsterdam: Amsterdam University Press, 2021.
DOI 10.5117/9789462989511_CH43

that visions for digital futuricity in its most accurate or ideal approximations emerge; and there that technological advancements—and thus digital cultural advancements—are dominantly understood to be at their most dynamic, lively and inspired. It assumes, in other words, that digital culture—despite its uniquely global dimensions—does indeed have more "authentic" and productive sites from which to undertake its study and observe its dynamics.

As a young researcher studying and writing about digital cultural activism and policy in Peru and Latin America from the early 2000s onward, it shaped my experience in fundamental ways, most regularly in the routine and seemingly innocent question I heard: "Why go to Peru or Latin America to study digital culture?" Weren't there "better" sites from which to study digital cultures, and wouldn't my time be better invested attending to and documenting activity in a site like Silicon Valley?

For such questioners, Peru inevitably evoked the idea of a mountainous South American nation that once served as the heart of the Inca civilization: Home to Machu Picchu, high stretches of the Andes mountain range, and large populations of Quechua- and Aymara-speaking communities. This Peru might be known as an ideal space from which to peer into past tradition, native culture or the plethora of nature's bounty—but it had little to tell us, the thinking went, about the dynamics of contemporary digital culture, high technological flows or their associated future-oriented developments. Places such as Peru might unlock a path strewn with the relics and treasures of a technological past we'd have to literally struggle *not* to forget, while sites like Silicon Valley are where the secrets to a technological future whose path we had yet to fully tread would inevitably come to be unlocked.

Quietly asserted in such a question then, is a casual certainty around the idea that the digital futures imagined by select populations of technologists in elite design centres can speak for the global rest, and the present currently unfolding in innovation centres must surely be the future of the periphery.

The power of the "myth of digital universalism" thus manifests not only in the means by which it keeps public narratives and imaginations fixed exclusively around established centres of innovation, but in the means by which it simultaneously discourages attention to digital dynamics beyond such centres. It therein narrows the diversity and global circulation of narratives around *actual* digital dynamics occurring across a range of locales, invisibilizes diverse forms of digital generativity, and artificially amplifies and reinforces a representation of "innovation" capitals as exclusive sites of digital productivity.

There is a particular colonial notion of the periphery conjured here that reporters and scholars of global digital cultures alike must be wary of reproducing: That is, of the "periphery" as mere agents of global counterfeit or zones of diffusion for a future invented prior and elsewhere. Indeed, the periphery is hardly so passive or uninventive. Lively and dynamic outdoor markets or Internet cafes filled with used, recycled and reassembled computers and parts are innovations of the Global South that extended low-cost Internet access and scaled out global and local media content circulation to diverse populations in rural and urban zones alike. These technological hacks and local improvisations are an everyday part of the periphery's technology landscape whose vibrancy is only partly captured by comparing it to formalized commercial chains of digital goods or computer and Internet suppliers. As the social scientists Daniel Miller and Don Slater (2001) observed in their study of Trinidad, "the Internet is not a monolithic cyberspace," but exists instead as a globally expansive technology with various local realities, adoptive practices and cultural politics that surround its varying localizations. There have been, indeed, more ways than one to imagine what digital practice and connection could look like.

In Peru, evidence of lively digital cultures that brought a range of distinct actors and interests into unexpected and often contradictory proximity was readily visible. Apparent collectives of free software advocates, who had helped to bring the first UN-sponsored conference on free software use in Latin America—a landmark event—to the ancient Incan capital of Cuzco in 2003, sought to reframe the adoption of open technologies. They sought to reframe it as not just an issue of individual liberty and free choice, as it had been for free/libre and open-source software (FLOSS) advocacy in the United States, but of cultural diversity, state transparency and political sovereignty from the monopolistic power of transnational corporations in the Global South.

"Digital innovation" classrooms installed in rural schools by the state would later be converted into the largest network of deployment sites for MIT's high-profile One Laptop per Child (OLPC) initiative just several years later, all in the name of enabling universal digital inclusion. And intellectual property (IP) titles newly and aggressively applied by state programmes to "traditional" goods promised to convert rural producers and artisans into new classes of export-ready "information workers" as part of the nation's growing information society-based initiatives.

FLOSS advocates and high-tech activists in Cuzco, state-promoted "innovation classrooms" in rural schools, and traditional artisans as new global "information workers" were not the conventional interests or protagonists that emerged from most tales spun in centres of digital culture. To watch their stories unfold was to watch the details of each spill over the edges of the existing frameworks and dominant narratives of digital culture. Global imaginaries around IT in the new millennium, after all, have made Silicon Valley hackers, the obsessions and aspirations of high-tech engineers, and the strategic enterprise of competitive technology entrepreneurs, the stuff of popular Hollywood films and obsessively followed Twitter accounts. These are a cast of increasingly recognizable actors, heroes and villains. But to capture the dynamic engagements and fraught experiments in digital culture in Peru requires attention to a host of other stakes, agents and developments—ones that in working around the digital tried to build new links and exchanges between spaces of the rural and the urban, the high-tech and the traditional, and distinct orientations around the global with intensive commitments to the local.

Data journalists today have a growing host of digital tools and technological resources to witness, capture and recall digital cultures and activities across a range of local sites around the world. Even before the wave of social protests in the Middle East starting in early 2011, networked digital media extended new global broadcast capabilities for movements that adopted strategic uses of social media in contexts as diverse as Mexico (Schulz, 2007), Iran (Burns & Eltham, 2009; Grossman, 2009), the Philippines (Uy-Tioco, 2003; Vicente, 2003) and Ukraine (Morozov, 2010).

In the wake of the 2011 Arab Spring—movements from Spain's 15-M Indignados, to the North American Occupy, made strategic uses of hashtag organizing and activism on social media platforms. More recently, movements from the US-launched #MeToo and #BlackLivesMatter run alongside global mobilizations from Latin America's #NiUnaMenos, to the Nigerian-launched #BringBackOurGirls, Australia's #Sosblakaustralia, Canadian First Nations' #IdleNoMore mobilizations and Hong Kong's #UmbrellaRevolution.

Such movements' expanding user-generated media streams multiply civic data practices and decentre the dominant applications of "big data" on social media platforms that bias towards forms of market-oriented profiling. They instead leverage data practices for new forms of narrative capacity that break from established centres of media and news production while lending their data archives—and online evidence of the global extensions of their publics—to geographically dispersed documentarians, reporters and organizers alike.

But the growth of digital resources and data repositories—from online "data" archives by social movements on social media platforms, to parallel forms of creative data activism—creates new risks for data journalists as well. Foremost among these is a risk from the seductive capacity of big data and social media platforms to leverage the abundance of data and information they collect as a means to convince audiences that their extensive data trackings compile and create the best possible form of documenting present human activity and social experience—as well as assessing and *predicting* the future of their political or economic ramifications.

The temporal presumptiveness of digital universalists' projection that the forms of digital "present" cultivated in innovation centres today can and will accurately represent the digital futures of global peripheries finds a new complement in data industries' self-assured claims for the predictive capacities of algorithmic data processing. Such pronouncements remain, even despite the evident contemporary failures of mainstream political data analysts, social media companies and news pundits in the West to accurately predict the major global political disruptions of recent years—from the 2016 US presidential election, to Brexit, to the Cambridge Analytica scandal, to the "surprise" rise of the alt-right movements across the West.

Today's data journalists should be vigilantly wary of enabling data tracings and archives—regardless of how extensive and impressively large they may be—to serve as the sole or dominant form of documenting, speaking for and assessing the diverse forms of social realities that the public relies on them to channel. Parallel with growing calls from Latin American and postcolonial scholars for broadening research and documentation methods to expand what and who represents information, technology and new media cultures under a "decolonial computing" framework (Chan, 2018), data journalists critical of digital universalist frameworks should aim too to consciously diversify data sources and decentre methods that would privilege "big data" as the exclusive or most legitimate key to mapping empirical events and social realities. Moves towards a "decolonization of knowledge" underscore the significance of the diverse ways through which citizens and researchers in the Global South are engaging in bottom-up data practices.[1] These practices leverage an emphasis on community practices and human-centred means of assessing and interpreting data—for social change, as well as speaking for the resistances to uses of big data that increase oppression, inequality and social harm.

Data journalists critical of digital universalism's new extensions in data universalism should take heart to find allies and resonant concerns for developing accountable and responsible data practices with scholars in critical data studies, algorithm studies, software and platform studies, and postcolonial computing. This includes a reinforced rejection of data funda-mentalism (Boyd & Crawford, 2012) and technological determinism that still surrounds mainstream accounts of algorithms in application. It also entails a fundamental recentring of the human within datafied worlds and data

---

1   For more on this see Kukutai and Walter's chapter in this book.

industries—that resists the urge to read big data and "algorithms as fetishized objects . . . and firmly resist[s] putting the technology in the explanatory driver's seat" (Crawford, 2016). It also involves treating data infrastructures and the underlying algorithms that give political life to them intentionally as both ambiguous and approachable—to develop methodologies that not only explore new empirical and everyday settings for data politics—whether airport security, credit scoring, hospital and patient tracking, or social media across a diversity of global sites—but also find creative ways to make data productive for analysis (Gillespie, 2013; Ziewitz, 2016).

Finally, it is perhaps worth a reminder that conserving the given centres of digital innovation as the exclusive sites of digital invention or the making of data futures, of course, also neglects another crucial detail—that the centres of the present were once on the periphery, too. To focus on centres as inventing models that simply come to be adopted and copied elsewhere presumes the perfect, continual extension of replicative functions and forces. It fails to account for the possibility of change within the larger system—the destabilizations and realignments of prior centres—and so, too, the realignments of prior peripheries.

The "surprise" of the 2011 Arab Spring and its influence across a range of global sites in the West and non-West like, much like the recent rise of non-Western digital markets and economic competitors in nations labelled "developing" less than two decades ago, and the destabilization of powerful Western democracies today, are reminders that the stability of established powers and the permanence of centre–periphery relations can questioned. Far from merely lagging behind or mimicking centres, dynamic activities from the periphery suggest how agents once holding minor status can emerge instead as fresh sources of distinct productivity. Their diverse threads unsettle the unspoken presumption that a single, universal narrative could adequately represent the distinct digital futures and imaginaries emerging across a range of local sites today.

Works Cited

Boyd, D., & Crawford, K. (2012). Critical questions for big data. *Information, Communication & Society*, 15(5), 662–679. https://doi.org/10.1080/1369118X.2012.678878

Burns, A., & Eltham, B. (2009). Twitter free Iran: An evaluation of Twitter's role in public diplomacy and information operations in Iran's 2009 election crisis. In P. Franco & M. Armstrong (Eds.), *Record of the Communications Policy & Research Forum 2009* (pp. 322–334). Network Insight Institute.

Chan, A. (2018). Decolonial computing and networking beyond digital universalism. *Catalyst*, 4(2). https://doi.org/10.28968/cftt.v4i2.29844

Crawford, K. (2016). Can an algorithm be agonistic? Ten scenes from life in calculated publics. *Science, Technology, & Human Values*, 41(1), 77–92. https://doi.org/10.1177/0162243915589635

Gillespie, T. (2013). The relevance of algorithms. In T. Gillespie, P. J. Boczkowski, & K. A. Foot (Eds.), *Media technologies: Essays on communication, materiality, and society* (pp. 167–193). MIT Press.

Grossman, L. (2009, June 17). Iran's protests: Why Twitter is the medium of the movement. *Time*. http://content.time.com/time/world/article/0,8599,1905125,00.html

Miller, D., & Slater, D. (2001). *The Internet: An ethnographic approach*. Berg Publishers.

Morozov, E. (2010). *The net delusion: The dark side of Internet freedom*. Public Affairs.

Schulz, M. (2007). The role of the Internet in transnational mobilization: A case study of the Zapatista movement, 1994–2005. In M. Herkenrath (Ed.), *Civil society: Local and regional responses to global challenges* (pp. 129–156). Transaction Publishers.

Uy-Tioco, C. (2003, October 11). The cell phone and EDSA 2: The role of a communication technology in ousting a president. Critical Themes in Media Studies Conference.

Vicente, R. (2003). The cell phone and the crowd: Messianic politics in the contemporary Philippines. *Public Culture*, 24(47), 3–36. https://doi.org/10.1080/01154451.2003.9754246

Ziewitz, M. (2016). Governing algorithms: Myth, mess, and methods. *Science, Technology, & Human Values*, 41(1), 3–16. https://doi.org/10.1177/0162243915608948

About the Author

Anita Say Chan is Associate Professor at the School of Information Sciences and College of Media, and Faculty Fellow at the National Center for Supercomputing Applications at the University of Illinois, Urbana–Champaign, and Faculty Fellow at the Data & Society Research Institute in New York.

44. The Datafication of Journalism: Strategies for Data-Driven Storytelling and Industry–Academy Collaboration

Damian Radcliffe and Seth C. Lewis

Abstract

How are journalism and academia responding to the datafication of their professions, and how can they collaborate more effectively on data-driven work?

Keywords: journalism, academia, collaboration, datafication, data work, researcher–journalist collaborations

We live in a world driven and informed by data. Data increasingly influences how policy and political decisions are made (Höchtl et al., 2016; Kreiss, 2016), informs the design and functionality of the cities we live in (Glaeser et al., 2018), as well as shapes the types of news, products and information that we have access to—and consume—in the digital age (Diakopoulos, 2019; Lewis, 2017; Lewis & Westlund, 2015; Thurman et al., 2019; Usher, 2016; Zamith, 2018). The full power and potential of data, for good or ill, is only just beginning to be realized (Couldry & Mejias, 2019; O'Neil, 2016; Schroeder, 2018).

Governments, universities and news media have long made use of data and statistics to find patterns and explain the world. But with the growth in digital devices and the massive trace data they produce—about our clicks, likes, shares, locations, contacts and more—the sheer volume of data generated, as well as the increase in computing power to harness and analyze such data at scale, is staggering. Making sense of all that data, in many cases, is arguably the biggest challenge, and is deeply fraught with ethical determinations along the way (Crawford et al., 2014). It is a riddle that

Bounegru, L. and J. Gray (eds.), *The Data Journalism Handbook: Towards a Critical Data Practice.* Amsterdam: Amsterdam University Press, 2021

DOI 10.5117/9789462989511_CH44

policy makers, businesses, researchers, activists, journalists and others are contending with—and one that will not be so easily resolved by "big-data solutions" or, in vogue today, the glittering promise of artificial intelligence (Broussard, 2018; Broussard et al., 2019).

In this chapter, building on our respective observations of practice (Radcliffe) and research (Lewis) regarding data and journalism, we outline how the worlds of journalism and academia are responding to the datafication of their professions as well as the broader datafication of public life. Ultimately, our aim is to offer recommendations for how these two fields, which historically have shared a rather uneasy relationship (Carlson & Lewis, 2019; Reese, 1999), might more productively work together on data-centric challenges.

The poet John Donne wrote that "no man is an island." In a data-driven world, no profession should be either.

Journalism and Data-Driven Storytelling: Five Strategic Considerations

The use of data to tell stories, and make sense of the world around us, is not wholly new.[1]

In Victorian England, physician John Snow produced a map that plotted cholera cases in central London. It enabled him to identify a pump on Broad Street as the cause of a particularly fatal, and geographically focused, outbreak of the disease in 1855 (see Figures 44.1 and 44.2). Snow's influential analysis does not look too dissimilar from disease maps produced with modern tools of data analysis and visualization.

In another example, Florence Nightingale's visualizations "of the causes of mortality in the army in the East" ("Worth a Thousand Words," 2013) helped to demonstrate the role that sanitation (or lack thereof) played in causing the death of British soldiers fighting in the Crimean War (see Figure 44.3). Her designs still feel remarkably contemporary.

Alongside these efforts, around the same time, Horace Greeley's work for *The New York Tribune* in the mid-19th century exposed how a number of elected officials (including a young Abraham Lincoln) were claiming expenses greater than they were eligible for (Klein, 2015). Although the world has moved on (Greeley's work focused on distances typically travelled by horseback), this type of important investigative work continues to be a journalistic staple (Larcinese & Sircar, 2017; see also Barrett, 2009; "A

---

1   See Anderson's chapter in this book for a look at different genealogies of data journalism.

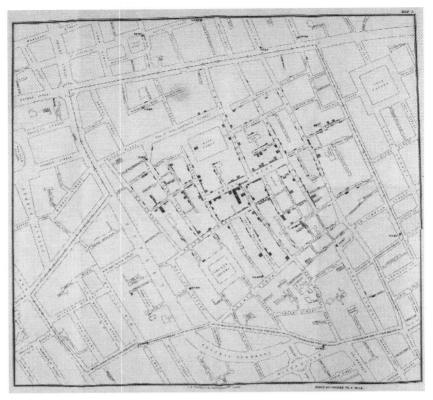

Figure 44.1. Map of London produced by physician John Snow, plotting cholera cases in central London in 1855. Source: British Library. https://www.bl.uk/collection-items/john-snows-map-showing-the-spread-of-cholera-in-soho-london-1855.

Chronology of the Senate Expenses Scandal," 2016; "Expenses Scandal an Embarrassing Start," 2017; "MPs' Expenses: Full List," 2009; "Q&A: MP Expenses," 2009; Rayner, 2009; "Senate Expenses Scandal," n.d.).

These historic examples, coupled with more contemporary case studies (such as those identified by the annual Data Journalism Awards), can act as powerful sources of inspiration for journalists.[2] They demonstrate how data-driven approaches may be used to hold authority to account (ICIJ, n.d.), highlight important social injustices (Lowenstein, 2015), as well as visualize and showcase the extraordinary ("2016 Year in Review," 2016).

While data has long been a part of journalism, as reflected in the emergence of "computer-assisted reporting" during the late 20th century, recent

2   https://www.datajournalismawards.org/. See also Loosen's discussion of the awards in her chapter in this book.

38   THE CHOLERA NEAR GOLDEN SQUARE

therefore, determined to return to Baljik, taking with him the *Trafalgar* and *Albion*, also badly affected.

"The crew of the *Britannia* were at once sent away from the ship, in small parties, into the numerous transports that remained idle ; and it appears that, by this procedure, the epidemic influences operating among them have been greatly moderated, if not extirpated."

The most terrible outbreak of cholera which ever occurred in this kingdom, is probably that which took place in Broad Street, Golden Square, and the adjoining streets, a few weeks ago. Within two hundred and fifty yards of the spot where Cambridge Street joins Broad Street, there were upwards of five hundred fatal attacks of cholera in ten days. The mortality in this limited area probably equals any that was ever caused in this country, even by the plague ; and it was much more sudden, as the greater number of cases terminated in a few hours. The mortality would undoubtedly have been much greater had it not been for the flight of the population. Persons in furnished lodgings left first, then other lodgers went away, leaving their furniture to be sent for when they could meet with a place to put it in. Many houses were closed altogether, owing to the death of the proprietors ; and, in a great number of instances, the tradesmen who remained had sent away their families : so that in less than six days from the commencement of the outbreak, the most afflicted streets were deserted by more than three-quarters of their inhabitants.

There were a few cases of cholera in the neighbourhood of Broad Street, Golden Square, in the latter part of August ; and the so-called outbreak, which commenced in the night between the 31st August and the 1st September, was, as in all similar instances, only a violent increase of the malady. As soon as I became acquainted with the

Figure 44.2. Text of an 1855 newspaper story documenting cholera cases in central London. Source: British Library. https://www.bl.uk/learning/images/makeanimpact/publichealth/large12734.html

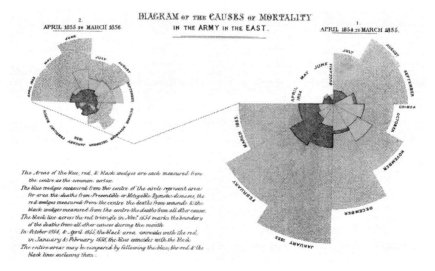

Figure 44.3. "Diagram of the causes of mortality in the army in the East," by Florence Nightingale. Source: Wikimedia. https://upload.wikimedia.org/wikipedia/commons/1/17/Nightingale-mortality.jpg

developments in the availability and accessibility of data-driven techniques have amplified opportunities for distinctly data-driven journalism (for a history, see Anderson, 2018; for an overview of data journalism, see Gray et al., 2012). It is against this backdrop that news organizations around the world—particularly the best-resourced ones, but increasingly smaller newsrooms as well—are using data to inform their journalistic work, both in telling stories with data (Hermida & Young, 2019) as well as in using data (in the form of digital audience metrics) to influence story selection as well as to measure and improve the impact of their work (Zamith, 2018).

Here are five key messages for newsrooms and journalists looking to do more with data:

Data alone does not tell stories. We still need journalists. For all of the data we have access to, we still need journalists to make sense of it, by providing context and interrogating the data in the same way as any other source.

As Steve Johnson (2013) of Montclair State University has noted: "Readers don't care about the raw data. They want the story within the data." Commenting on data about lower Manhattan provided by an early open-data portal, EveryBlock, he observed:

> There were reports on what graffiti the city said it had erased each month, by neighborhoods. But what was missing was context, and photos. If I'm a reporter doing a story on graffiti, I want to show before and after photos, AND, more importantly, I want to know whether the city is successfully fighting the graffiti artists, i.e., who is winning. The raw data didn't provide that. (Johnson, 2013)

More recent "data dumps" such as the Paradise Papers and Panama Papers also emphasize this point. In this instance, sources had to be cross-referenced and contextualized—a time-consuming process that took many journalists months to do. However, without this interrogation of the sources by journalists (as opposed to concerned citizens), the full impact of the data could not be realized. These principles are as applicable at the local level as they are in stories of national and international import (Radcliffe, 2013).

Data, in itself, is seldom the story. It needs to be unpacked and its implications explained, if the full meaning behind it is to be understood.

You don't have to go it alone. Collaboration is often key. Collaboration has been a watchword of the networked age, and a key element in the ongoing blending of journalism and technology sensibilities—including the integration of "hacks" (journalists) and "hackers" (coders) (Lewis & Usher, 2014, 2016) as well as the broader interplay of news organizations and their communities around shared concerns. The essence of such "networked journalism" (Beckett, 2010; Van der Haak et al., 2012) or "relational journalism" (Boczkowski & Lewis, 2018; Lewis, 2019) is the underlying belief that more might be accomplished through cooperative activity.

This approach is applicable to many beats and stories, including those involving large volumes of data. As *The Guardian* showed in their 2009 analysis of British MPs' expenses, concerned citizens and members of the public can work in tandem with journalists to analyze data sets and provide tips ("MPs' Expenses: *The Guardian*," 2009; Rogers, 2009a, 2009b). More recently, research by Stanford's James T. Hamilton (2016) and others (Sambrook, 2018) has identified the importance of collaboration—both across organizations and in the deployment of different disciplines—for many newsrooms, when it comes to producing high-quality, high-impact investigative journalism.

The amount of data that many new organizations are contending with, coupled with ongoing challenging economic circumstances, means that partnerships, the use of specialists, volunteers and wide-ranging skill sets, are often a necessity for many newsrooms. And, a collaborative approach is increasingly essential from both a financial and journalistic standpoint.

How you present your data matters. Journalists have access to a wide range of tools, techniques and platforms through which to present data and tell stories accordingly.[3] As a result, it is important to determine which tools are most appropriate for the story you are trying to tell.

Data visualizations, graphs, infographics, charts, tables and interactives—all can help to convey and drive home a story. But which one (or ones) you use can make all the difference.[4]

As our colleague Nicole Dahmen has noted, one way to do this is through data visualization. "Visuals catch audience attention . . . [and] . . . are processed 60 times faster than text" (as cited in Frank et al., 2015). When used well, they can help to bring a story alive in a manner that text alone cannot.

The Washington Post's online feature "The Depth of the Problem," which shows how deep in the ocean the black box from the missing Malaysia Airlines flight 370 could be, is a good example of this ("The Depth of the Problem," n.d.; see Figure 26.5). The reader scrolls down the page to 1,250 feet, the height of the Empire State Building; past 2,600 feet, the depth of giant squids; and below 12,500 feet, where the *Titanic* sits; to 15,000 feet, where the black box was believed to be.

---

3   https://www.journaliststoolbox.org/2018/03/11/online_journalism/
4   See https://www.import.io/post/8-fantastic-examples-of-data-journalism/ for eight stories which use different techniques and consider swapping them.

"You're not just reading how deep that plane is," Dahmen has said. "You can see and engage and really experience and understand how deep they suspect that plane to be."

Determining your approach may be influenced by both the story you want to tell and the data literacy and preferences of your audience. Either way, your data-driven stories should be well designed so that audiences do not struggle to understand what is being shown or how to interact with the data (Radcliffe, 2017b, 2017c).

Place your work in a wider context. Alongside these considerations, journalists working with data also need to be cognizant of wider developments, in terms of the consumption of content and attitudes towards journalism.

Think mobile: In 2012, the Pew Research Center found that over half of those who owned a smartphone or a tablet accessed news content on those devices (Mitchell et al., 2012; "News Consumption on Digital Devices," 2017); just four years later, more than seven in ten Americans (72%) reported getting news via mobile (Mitchell et al., 2016). As mobile news consumption continues to grow, so too it is imperative that news organizations provide a positive mobile experience for all of their content, including data-rich material.

Make it personal: In an era of personalization and algorithmically generated media experiences, this can include creating opportunities for audiences to interrogate data and understand what it means for them. *ProPublica*'s Dollars for Docs investigation (Tigas et al., 2019), which enables patients to see the payments made by pharmaceutical and medical device companies to their doctors, is one example of this technique in action.

Protecting your sources: Journalists need to know how to protect data as well as how to analyze it. Protecting yourself, and your sources, may well require a new approach—including new skill sets—to handling sensitive data and whistleblowers (Keeble-Gagnere, 2015). Encryption coupled with anonymity (as witnessed in the Panama Papers) is one way to do this.

Harnessing new technologies: Blockchain is just one tool that may protect and support data and investigative work (IJNET, 2016). As Walid Al-Saqaf of Södertörn University (Sweden) (as cited in Bouchart, 2018) has explained: "Blockchain preserves data permanently and prevents any manipulation or fraud. That means that if governmental data is there it can't be removed or changed once it is published." Machine learning is another technology already being used in this space, and one which will only grow (Bradshaw, 2017).

Rebuilding public trust: With trust in journalism at near-record lows, it is incumbent on all journalists to work towards remedying this (Knight Foundation, 2018; Nicolau & Giles, 2017). For those working with data, this means being transparent about the data you are working with, providing links to the original sources, and ensuring that original data files are available for download. Showing your work—what Jay Rosen (2017) calls "the new terms for trust in journalism"—allows readers to see the raw materials you worked with (and interpreted), and thereby opens a door to transparency-based trust in news.

The influence of data on your work is/will be wider than you might think. Finally, it is impossible to overlook the role that data also plays in shaping acts of journalism. We need to remember that the datafication of journalism is not just influencing data storytelling but also the wider journalistic profession (Anderson, 2018; Usher, 2016).

Analytics tools such as Google Analytics, Chartbeat and Omniture are omnipresent in newsrooms, giving journalists more information about the reading habits of their audiences than ever before. These quantitative insights, coupled with qualitative insights (see, e.g., programs like Metrics for News, developed by the American Press Institute), are informing the work of newsrooms large and small.

As highlighted in white papers published by Pars.ly[5] and in recent academic research (Belair-Gagnon & Holton, 2018; Cherubini & Nielsen, 2016; Ponsford, 2016; Radcliffe et al., 2017; Zamith, 2018), it's clear that data is playing a pivotal role both in the positioning of stories (including literally how they are placed on homepages and promoted on social media) and in the decision making around what stories get covered.

Levi Pulkkinen, a Seattle-based reporter and editor and former senior editor of the *Seattle Post-Intelligencer*, argues that much of this data suggests that newsrooms need to do some things differently. "I think there's a hesitancy in the newspaper industry among reporters to not recognize that what the metrics are telling us is that we need to change the content," Pulkkinen (as cited in Radcliffe, 2017a) says, indicating that public affairs reporting (among other beats) may be ripe for change. "They like when we can tell them a whole story, or tell them an important story . . . but they don't need us to just act as a kind of stenographer of government" (as cited in Radcliffe, 2017a).

Moving Forward: Five Ideas for Industry–Academy Collaboration

Data is shaping and informing acts of journalism across virtually all newsrooms and reporting beats. It can be a tool for telling specific stories—as exemplified among established players such as *The Guardian* and newer

5 https://www.parse.ly/resources/case-studies/

entities such as *FiveThirtyEight* and *Quartz* (Ellis, 2015; Seward, 2016)—as well as an important source for editorial and resource-driven decision making.

But beyond discrete stories and strategies, data portends a larger sea change in journalism. For better or worse, an embrace of quantification may well have major implications for what have been described as the Four Es of big data and journalism: Epistemology (what journalism knows), expertise (how journalism expresses that knowledge), economics (journalism's market value) and ethics (journalism's social values) (Lewis & Westlund, 2015). The data-related implications are therefore far-reaching—for how we teach, practice and research journalism.

We believe that, too often, the worlds of academia and news industry fail to recognize the generative potential that could come through greater collaboration between them (much like our point about collaborative journalism, above). As both parties grapple with the possibilities afforded by datafication, we contend that closer relationships between journalists and academics could be mutually beneficial. Below we outline five starting points to explore.

More partnerships between classrooms and newsrooms. The work undertaken by Paul Bradshaw offers a clear indication of how to do this. As part of the new MA in Data Journalism offered at Birmingham City University in the UK, Paul and his students have partnered with a number of news organizations, such as *The Daily Telegraph* (Bradshaw, 2018), the BBC, ITN, the *Manchester Evening News*, *The Guardian* and the Centre for Investigative Journalism.[6] To extend this teaching-based partnership to improve research, these news organizations could open up their data journalism processes to (participant) observation by ethnographers, with the expectation that such scholarship would lead not only to peer-reviewed academic publication but also to public-facing reports that are intended for industry—like the kind produced by the Tow Center for Digital Journalism and the Reuters Institute for the Study of Journalism.

Undertake classroom projects with potential news value. Jan Goodey, a journalism lecturer at Kingston University in west London, has also demonstrated the ability to turn class projects into tangible reporting, having identified some potential conflicts of interest in UK local government. Their research—which included submitting, tracking and analyzing 99 separate FOI requests—revealed that these bodies were investing pension funds in fracking companies, while at the same time also acting as arbiters for planning proposals submitted by this nascent industry (Goodey & Milmo,

6   http://bcu.ac.uk/media/courses/data-journalism-ma-2018-19

2014). In some cases, students and their professors may have a longer time horizon to explore data projects, thus allowing them to do forms of data journalism that are elusive for journalists overwhelmed by ceaseless daily deadlines.

Reverse-engineer these relationships. Given the resource challenges that most newsrooms face, journalists could more frequently approach students and academics with stories that could benefit from their help. Arizona State University's Steve Doig, who won a 1993 Pulitzer Prize for Public Service at *The Miami Herald*,[7] for a series which showed how weakened building codes and poor construction practices exacerbated damage caused by Hurricane Andrew a year before, actively consults on computer-assisted reporting problems.[8] He won the George Polk Award (2012) for Decoding Prime, an analysis of suspect hospital billing practices for the California Watch investigative organization.[9] His is an advising and consultancy model—with faculty and potential student involvement—that others could emulate.

Open the door to researchers and independent critique. Journalists are known to rely on academics as frequent sources for news stories, but they are often less comfortable opening themselves up to academic scrutiny. Compounding this problem are increasingly strident organizational directives against taking surveys or speaking to researchers without permission from upper management. But, just as journalists need good source material to do their work, for academics to do good research *about* journalism requires their having better access than they presently do. This is especially pertinent as researchers seek to understand what datafication means for journalism (Baack, 2015)—for how journalists use metrics (Belair-Gagnon & Holton, 2018; Christin, 2018; Ferrer-Conill & Tandoc, 2018), for how they tell stories in new ways (Hermida & Young, 2019; Toff, 2019; Usher, 2016) and so on. A little less defensiveness on the part of news organizations could go a long way towards developing a mutually beneficial relationship: Researchers get better access to understanding how data fits in journalism, and in turn news organizations can gain independent evaluations of their work and thus better appraise, from a critical distance, how they are doing.

Ensure your research is accessible. On the flip side, academics could do much more to ensure the openness and accessibility of their work. By now, dozens of academic studies have been produced regarding the "datafication

7   http://www.pulitzer.org/winners/miami-herald
8   https://www.flickr.com/photos/juggernautco/sets/72157607210036175/
9   https://cronkite.asu.edu/about/faculty-and-leadership/faculty/doigbio

of journalism," with a particular emphasis on the evolution of tools for data storytelling and its impact on journalistic ethics and approaches (for an overview, see Ausserhofer et al., 2020). These studies could have tremendous relevance for news organizations. But too often they are locked behind academic journal paywalls, obscured by the overuse of jargon and altogether situated in such a way that makes it hard for journalists to access, let alone understand, the transferable lessons in this research. Where possible, industry outreach and engagement could be an integral part of the publication process, so that the benefits of these insights resonate beyond the journals—such as through rewritten briefs or short explainers for trade-press venues, such as Nieman Journalism Lab, or websites designed to disseminate academic work to lay audiences, such as *The Conversation*.

Conclusion

Data journalism, in the words of famed data journalist Simon Rogers (2012), now data editor at Google, is "a great leveler." Because of its emergent character, virtually anyone can try it and become proficient in it. "Data journalism is the new punk," he says (Rogers, 2012). This means that "many media groups are starting with as much prior knowledge and expertise as someone hacking away from their bedroom" (Rogers, 2012).[10]

Data journalism, of course, has a long history, with antecedents in forms of science and storytelling that have been around for more than a century (Anderson, 2018).[11] But as a nascent "social world" (Lewis & Zamith, 2017) within journalism—a space for sharing tools, techniques and best practices across news organizations and around the globe—data journalism is at a particular inflection point, amid the broader datafication of society in the 21st century.

There is a corresponding opportunity, we argue, for critical self-reflection: For examining what we know about data journalism so far, for outlining what remains to be explored, and particularly for pursuing a path that recognizes the mutual dependence of journalism as practice and pedagogy, industry and academy. For journalism to make sense of a world awash in data requires better recognizing, self-critically, the limitations and generative possibilities of data-driven approaches—what they reveal, what they don't and how they can be improved.

10　See also Simon Rogers' chapter in this book.
11　See also Anderson's chapter in this book.

Works Cited

2016 year in review: Highlights and heartbreaks. (2016, December 29). *Los Angeles Times*. https://www.latimes.com/local/california/la-me-updates-best-year-review-2016-htmlstory.html#every-shot-kobe-bryant-ever-took-all-30-699-of-them

Anderson, C. W. (2018). *Apostles of certainty: Data journalism and the politics of doubt*. Oxford University Press.

Ausserhofer, J., Gutounig, R., Oppermann, M., Matiasek, S., & Goldgruber, E. (2020). The datafication of data journalism scholarship: Focal points, methods, and research propositions for the investigation of data-intensive newswork. *Journalism*, *21*,(7) 950–973. https://doi.org/10.1177/1464884917700667

Baack, S. (2015). Datafication and empowerment: How the open data movement re-articulates notions of democracy, participation, and journalism. *Big Data & Society*, *2*(2), 2053951715594634. https://doi.org/10.1177/2053951715594634

Barrett, D. (2009, May 17). MPs' expenses: How they milk the system. *The Telegraph*. https://www.telegraph.co.uk/news/newstopics/mps-expenses/5335101/MPs-expenses-how-they-milk-the-system.html

Beckett, C. (2010). *The value of networked journalism*. POLIS, London School of Economics and Political Science.

Belair-Gagnon, V., & Holton, A. E. (2018). Boundary work, interloper media, and analytics in newsrooms. *Digital Journalism*, *6*(4), 492–508. https://doi.org/10.1080/21670811.2018.1445001

Boczkowski, P. J., & Lewis, S. C. (2018). The center of the universe no more: From the self-centered stance of the past to the relational mindset of the future. In P. J. Boczkowski & Z. Papacharissi (Eds.), *Trump and the media* (pp. 177–185). MIT Press. https://doi.org/10.7551/mitpress/11464.003.0028

Bouchart, M. (2018, February 1). A data journalist's new year's resolutions. *Medium*. https://medium.com/data-journalism-awards/a-data-journalists-new-year-s-resolutions-474ef92f7e8f

Bradshaw, P. (2017, December 14). Data journalism's AI opportunity: The 3 different types of machine learning & how they have already been used. *Online Journalism Blog*. https://onlinejournalismblog.com/2017/12/14/data-journalisms-ai-opportunity-the-3-different-types-of-machine-learning-how-they-have-already-been-used/

Bradshaw, P. (2018, February 15). Wanted: MA Data Journalism applicants to partner with *The Telegraph*. Medium. https://medium.com/@paulbradshaw/wanted-ma-data-journalism-applicants-to-partner-with-the-telegraph-8abd154260f3

Broussard, M. (2018). *Artificial unintelligence: How computers misunderstand the world*. MIT Press.

Broussard, M., Diakopoulos, N., Guzman, A. L., Abebe, R., Dupagne, M., & Chuan, C.-H. (2019). Artificial intelligence and journalism. *Journalism & Mass Communication Quarterly, 96*(3), 673–695. https://doi.org/10.1177/1077699019859901

Carlson, M., & Lewis, S. C. (2019). Temporal reflexivity in journalism studies: Making sense of change in a more timely fashion. *Journalism, 20*(5), 642–650. https://doi.org/10.1177/1464884918760675

Cherubini, F., & Nielsen, R. K. (2016). *Editorial analytics: How news media are developing and using audience data and metrics* (SSRN Scholarly Paper ID 2739328). Social Science Research Network. https://doi.org/10.2139/ssrn.2739328

Christin, A. (2018). Counting clicks: Quantification and variation in web journalism in the United States and France. *American Journal of Sociology, 123*(5), 1382–1415. https://doi.org/10.1086/696137

A chronology of the Senate expenses scandal. (2016, July 13). *CBC News.* https://www.cbc.ca/news/politics/senate-expense-scandal-timeline-1.3677457

Couldry, N., & Mejias, U. A. (2019). Data colonialism: Rethinking big data's relation to the contemporary subject. *Television & New Media, 20*(4), 336–349. https://doi.org/10.1177/1527476418796632

Crawford, K., Gray, M. L., & Miltner, K. (2014). Critiquing big data: Politics, ethics, epistemology. *International Journal of Communication, 8*, 1663–1672. https://ijoc.org/index.php/ijoc/article/view/2167

The depth of the problem. (n.d.). *The Washington Post.* https://www.washingtonpost.com/apps/g/page/world/the-depth-of-the-problem/931/

Diakopoulos, N. (2019). *Automating the news: How algorithms are rewriting the media.* Harvard University Press.

Ellis, J. (2015, June 23). Quartz maps a future for its interactive charts with Atlas. Nieman Lab. https://www.niemanlab.org/2015/06/quartz-maps-a-future-for-its-interactive-charts-with-atlas/

Expenses scandal an embarrassing start to 2017 for Australia's embattled Prime Minister. (2017, January 13). *The Indian Express.* https://indianexpress.com/article/world/expenses-scandal-an-embarrassing-start-to-2017-for-australias-embattled-prime-minister/

Ferrer-Conill, R., & Tandoc, E. C. (2018). The audience-oriented editor. *Digital Journalism, 6*(4), 436–453. https://doi.org/10.1080/21670811.2018.1440972

Frank, A., Yang, Y., & Radcliffe, D. (2015, December 18). The mainstreaming of data reporting and what it means for journalism schools. *Journalism.co.uk.* https://www.journalism.co.uk/news/the-mainstreaming-of-data-journalism-and-what-it-means-for-journalism-schools/s2/a593608/

Glaeser, E. L., Kominers, S. D., Luca, M., & Naik, N. (2018). Big data and big cities: The promises and limitations of improved measures of urban life. *Economic Enquiry, 56*(1), 114–137. https://www.hbs.edu/faculty/Pages/item.aspx?num=51012

Goodey, J., & Milmo, C. (2014, April 27). Exclusive: Local authorities have "conflict of interest" on fracking investments. *The Independent.* http://www.independent. co.uk/news/uk/politics/exclusive-local-authorities-have-conflict-of-interest-on-fracking-investments-9294590.html

Gray, J., Chambers, L., & Bounegru, L. (Eds.). (2012). *The data journalism handbook: How journalists can use data to improve the news.* O'Reilly Media.

Hamilton, J. T. (2016). *Democracy's detectives: The economics of investigative journalism.* Harvard University Press.

Hermida, A., & Young, M. L. (2019). *Data journalism and the regeneration of news.* Routledge.

Höchtl, J., Parycek, P., & Schöllhammer, R. (2016). Big data in the policy cycle: Policy decision making in the digital era. *Journal of Organizational Computing and Electronic Commerce, 26*(1–2), 147–169. https://doi.org/10.1080/10919392.2015.1125187

ICIJ. (n.d.). The Panama Papers: Exposing the rogue offshore finance industry. https://www.icij.org/investigations/panama-papers/

IJNET. (2016, August 5). How blockchain technology can boost freedom of the press. International Journalists' Network. https://ijnet.org/en/story/how-blockchain-technology-can-boost-freedom-press

Johnson, S. (2013, February 8). Sorry EveryBlock, you never learned how to write a headline. *The Hudson Eclectic.* https://hudsoneclectic.com/2013/02/08/sorry-everyblock-you-never-learned-how-to-write-a-headline/

Keeble-Gagnere, G. (2015, November 5). Encryption for the working journalist: Communicating securely. *Journalism.co.uk.* https://www.journalism.co.uk/news/encryption-for-the-working-journalist/s2/a580914/

Klein, S. (2015, March 17). Antebellum data journalism: Or, how big data busted Abe Lincoln. *ProPublica.* https://www.propublica.org/nerds/antebellum-data-journalism-busted-abe-lincoln

Knight Foundation. (2018, June 26). 10 reasons why Americans don't trust the media. *Medium.* https://medium.com/trust-media-and-democracy/10-reasons-why-americans-dont-trust-the-media-d0630c125b9e

Kreiss, D. (2016). *Prototype politics: Technology-intensive campaigning and the data of democracy.* Oxford University Press.

Larcinese, V., & Sircar, I. (2017). Crime and punishment the British way: Accountability channels following the MPs' expenses scandal. *European Journal of Political Economy, 47,* 75–99. https://doi.org/10.1016/j.ejpoleco.2016.12.006

Lewis, S. C. (2017). Digital journalism and big data. In B. Franklin & S. Eldridge (Eds.), *The Routledge companion to digital journalism studies* (pp. 126–135). Routledge.

Lewis, S. C. (2019). Lack of trust in the news media, institutional weakness, and relational journalism as a potential way forward. *Journalism, 20*(1), 44–47. https://doi.org/10.1177/1464884918808134

Lewis, S. C., & Usher, N. (2014). Code, collaboration, and the future of journalism: A case study of the hacks/hackers global network. *Digital Journalism*, 2(3), 383–393. https://doi.org/10.1080/21670811.2014.895504

Lewis, S. C., & Usher, N. (2016). Trading zones, boundary objects, and the pursuit of news innovation: A case study of journalists and programmers. *Convergence*, 22(5), 543–560. https://doi.org/10.1177/1354856515623865

Lewis, S. C., & Westlund, O. (2015). Big data and journalism: Epistemology, expertise, economics, and ethics. *Digital Journalism*, 3(3), 447–466. https://doi.org/10.1080/21670811.2014.976418

Lewis, S. C., & Zamith, R. (2017). On the worlds of journalism. In P. J. Boczkowski & C. W. Anderson (Eds.), *Remaking the news: Essays on the future of journalism scholarship in the digital age* (pp. 111–128). MIT Press.

Lowenstein, J. K. (2015, February 13). How I used data-driven journalism to reveal racial disparities in U.S. nursing homes. *Storybench*. https://www.storybench.org/how-i-used-data-driven-journalism-to-reveal-racial-disparities-in-u-s-nursing-homes/

Mitchell, A., Gottfried, J., Barthel, M., & Shearer, E. (2016, July 7). *The modern news consumer: News attitudes and practices in the digital era*. Pew Research Center. https://www.journalism.org/2016/07/07/pathways-to-news/

Mitchell, A., Rosenstiel, T., & Christian, L. (2012). Mobile devices and news consumption: Some good signs for journalism. In Pew Research Center (Ed.), *The state of the news media: An annual report on American journalism*. https://www.pewresearch.org/wp-content/uploads/sites/8/2017/05/State-of-the-News-Media-Report-2012-FINAL.pdf

MPs' expenses: Full list of MPs investigated by *The Telegraph*. (2009, May 8). *The Telegraph*. https://www.telegraph.co.uk/politics/0/mps-expenses-full-list-mps-investigated-telegraph/

MPs' expenses: *The Guardian* launches major crowdsourcing experiment. (2009, June 23). *The Guardian*. https://www.theguardian.com/gnm-press-office/crowdsourcing-mps-expenses

News consumption on digital devices. (2017, August 21). Pew Research Center. https://www.journalism.org/2012/03/18/mobile-devices-and-news-consumption-some-good-signs-for-journalism/5-news-consumption-on-digital-devices/

Nicolau, A., & Giles, C. (2017, January 16). Public trust in media at all time low, research shows. *Financial Times*. https://www.ft.com/content/fa332f58-d9bf-11e6-944b-e7eb37a6aa8e

O'Neil, C. (2016). *Weapons of math destruction: How big data increases inequality and threatens democracy*. Crown.

Ponsford, D. (2016, July 31). "Heartbroken" reporter Gareth Davies says *Croydon Advertiser* print edition now "thrown together collection of clickbait." *Press Gazette*. https://www.pressgazette.co.uk/heartbroken-reporter-gareth-davies-says-croydon-advertser-print-edition-now-thrown-together-collection-of-clickbait/

Q&A: MP expenses row explained. (2009, June 18). *BBC News*. http://news.bbc.co.uk/2/hi/uk_news/politics/7840678.stm

Radcliffe, D. (2013). Hyperlocal media and data journalism. In J. Mair & R. L. Keeble (Eds.), *Data journalism: Mapping the future* (pp. 120–132). Abramis Academic Publishing.

Radcliffe, D. (2017a). Local journalism in the Pacific Northwest: Why it matters, how it's evolving, and who pays for it (SSRN Scholarly Paper ID 3045516). Social Science Research Network. https://papers.ssrn.com/abstract=3045516

Radcliffe, D. (2017b). Data journalism in the US: Three case studies and ten general principles for journalists. In J. Mair, R. L. Keeble, & M. Lucero (Eds.), *Data journalism: Past, present and future* (pp. 197–210). Abramis Academic Publishing.

Radcliffe, D. (2017c, November 28). 10 key principles for data-driven storytelling. *Journalism.co.uk*. https://www.journalism.co.uk/news/10-key-principles-for-data-driven-storytelling/s2/a713879/

Radcliffe, D., Ali, C., & Donald, R. (2017). *Life at small-market newspapers: Results from a survey of small-market newsrooms*. Tow Center for Digital Journalism. https://doi.org/10.7916/D8XP7BGC

Rayner, G. (2009, May 8). MPs' expenses: Ten ways MPs play the system to cash in on expenses and allowances. *The Telegraph*. https://www.telegraph.co.uk/news/newstopics/mps-expenses/5293498/MPs-expenses-Ten-ways-MPs-play-the-system-to-cash-in-on-expenses-and-allowances.html

Reese, S. D. (1999). The progressive potential of journalism education: Recasting the academic versus professional debate. *Harvard International Journal of Press/Politics*, 4(4), 70–94. https://doi.org/10.1177/1081180X9900400405

Rogers, S. (2009a, June 18). How to crowdsource MPs' expenses. *The Guardian*. https://www.theguardian.com/news/datablog/2009/jun/18/mps-expenses-houseofcommons

Rogers, S. (2009b, June 19). MPs' expenses: What you've told us. So far. *The Guardian*. http://www.theguardian.com/news/datablog/2009/sep/18/mps-expenses-westminster-data-house-of-commons

Rogers, S. (2012, May 24). Anyone can do it. Data journalism is the new punk. *The Guardian*. https://www.theguardian.com/news/datablog/2012/may/24/data-journalism-punk

Rosen, J. (2017, December 31). Show your work: The new terms for trust in journalism. *PressThink*. https://pressthink.org/2017/12/show-work-new-terms-trust-journalism/

Sambrook, R. (Ed.). (2018). *Global teamwork: The rise of collaboration in investigative journalism*. Reuters Institute for the Study of Journalism.

Schroeder, R. (2018). *Social theory after the Internet: Media, technology, and globalization*. UCL Press.

Senate expenses scandal. (n.d.). *HuffPost Canada*. https://www.huffingtonpost.ca/news/senate-expenses-scandal/

Seward, Z. M. (2016, May 10). Atlas is now an open platform for everyone's charts and data. *Quartz*. https://qz.com/679853/atlas-is-now-an-open-platform-for-everyones-charts-and-data/

Thurman, N., Lewis, S. C., & Kunert, J. (2019). Algorithms, automation, and news. *Digital Journalism*, *7*(8), 980–992. https://doi.org/10.1080/21670811.2019.1685395

Tigas, M., Jones, R. G., Ornstein, C., & Groeger, L. (2019, October 17). Dollars for docs. *ProPublica*. https://projects.propublica.org/docdollars/

Toff, B. (2019). The "Nate Silver effect" on political journalism: Gatecrashers, gatekeepers, and changing newsroom practices around coverage of public opinion polls. *Journalism*, *20*(7), 873–889. https://doi.org/10.1177/1464884917731655

Usher, N. (2016). *Interactive journalism: Hackers, data, and code*. University of Illinois Press.

Van der Haak, B., Parks, M., & Castells, M. (2012). The future of journalism: Networked journalism. *International journal of communication*, *6*, 2923–2938.

Worth a thousand words. (2013, October 7). *The Economist*. https://www.economist.com/christmas-specials/2013/10/07/worth-a-thousand-words

Zamith, R. (2018). Quantified audiences in news production: A synthesis and research agenda. *Digital Journalism*, *6*(4), 418–435. https://doi.org/10.1080/21670811.2018.1444999

About the Authors

Damian Radcliffe is the Carolyn S. Chambers Professor in Journalism, a Professor of Practice, and an affiliate of the Department for Middle East and North Africa Studies (MENA), at the University of Oregon.

Seth C. Lewis (PhD, University of Texas at Austin) is the founding holder of the Shirley Papé Chair in Emerging Media in the School of Journalism and Communication at the University of Oregon and is a visiting fellow with the Reuters Institute for the Study of Journalism and with Green Templeton College at the University of Oxford.

45. Data Journalism by, about and for Marginalized Communities

Eva Constantaras

Abstract

Data journalism has a role to play in empowering marginalized communities to combat injustice, inequality and discrimination.

Keywords: data journalism, marginalized communities, injustice, inequality, discrimination, empowerment

I do data journalism in countries where things are widely considered to be going badly—as in not just a rough patch, not just a political hiccup, but entire political and economic systems failing. In such places, one reads that corruption has paralyzed the government, citizens are despondent and civil society is under siege. Things are going terribly. Producing data journalism in some of the most impoverished, uneducated and unsafe parts of the world has brought me to an important conclusion. Injustice, inequality and discrimination are ubiquitous, insidious and overlooked in most countries. Journalists I work with have unflinchingly embraced new tools to, for the first time, measure just how bad things are, who is suffering as a result, whose fault it is and how to make things better. In these contexts, journalists have embraced data as a means to influence policy, mobilize citizens and combat propaganda. Despite the constraints on free press, data journalism is seen as a means to empowerment.

This chapter explores data journalism by, about and for marginalized communities. By attending to different aspects of injustice, inequality and discrimination, and their broader consequences on the lives of marginalized communities, we render them visible, measurable and maybe even solvable. These stories engage journalists deeply rooted in marginalized communities. They tap into issues that groups which face institutional discrimination care about to foster citizen engagement. They are disseminated through local

Bounegru, L. and J. Gray (eds.), *The Data Journalism Handbook: Towards a Critical Data Practice.*
Amsterdam: Amsterdam University Press, 2021
DOI 10.5117/9789462989511_CH45

Figure 45.1. Data journalists in Pakistan develop initial wireframes with their data findings.
Source: *Internews*.

mass media to reach large numbers of people and pressure governments into making better decisions for the whole country. In what follows I will discuss five kinds of data journalism stories that attend to the interests and concerns of marginalized communities in Afghanistan, Pakistan, Kenya, Kyrgyzstan and the Balkans.

Why Are People Going Hungry if Our Country Has Enough Resources to Feed Everyone?

In Kenya, donors were funding exactly the wrong food programmes. A 12-minute television story by NTV's Mercy Juma about Turkana, an isolated, impoverished region of Northern Kenya, revealed that malnutrition in children is a growing problem as drought and famine become more frequent and intense. Money goes to emergency food aid, not long-term drought mitigation. The same money spent on one year of emergency food aid could fund a food sustainability programme for the entire county and its nearly one million residents, according to draft policies in parliament. Juma threatened to pull her story when editors wanted to edit out the data: Her story depended on engaging donors, enraging citizens and embarrassing the government mostly through television, but also in print and a summary online (Juma, 2014).

Figure 45.2. A print version of Mercy Juma's television special on food security in Turkana. Source: *Internews*.

She convinced donors with the strength of her data. She sourced climate, agricultural and health data from government ministries, public health surveys, donor agencies and the Kenyan Red Cross. The USAID Kenya mission saw the data visualization demonstrating that one year of USAID emergency food aid could fund the entire Kenya Red Cross food sustainability strategy for Turkana. She demonstrated the health impact of delays on children, and the stark contrast with countries growing food in deserts. She was invited to present her findings at the USAID office in Nairobi and, in 2015, USAID's agriculture and food security strategy shifted from humanitarian aid to sustainable agriculture.[1]

She won over public opinion with the intimate documentation of families starving in Turkana. She spent three days with the families featured in the piece along with a Turkana translator and videographer. The station phone was ringing off the hook before the story finished airing, with Kenyans seeking to donate money to the families featured in the story. Due to the massive reaction to the story from individuals and organizations alike, within hours the station established a relief fund for Turkana County. This and follow-up stories on the desperate famine situation in Northern Kenya prompted daily attention in the Kenyan media, which has historically shown

1   https://www.usaid.gov/kenya/agriculture-and-food-security

a lack of interest in the plight of the isolated and impoverished regions of Northern Kenya. Her main audience connected to a strong, human story and not the data that would suggest donations could be more wisely invested in development.

The government succumbed to public and donor pressure. The Drought Monitoring Committee asked Juma to share data from her story because they claimed they were not aware that the situation had become so desperate, although the same department had tried to charge her for access to the data when she began her investigation. Based on Juma's water shortage data, the Ministry of Water plans to travel to Turkana to dig more boreholes. The government, through the Ministry of Planning and Devolution, released Sh2.3 billion ($27 million) to go towards relief distribution in Turkana County, a development that Juma followed closely. Due to the massive reaction to the story from individuals and organizations, food sustainability legislation that redirected aid was finally introduced into the Senate in May that year.[2] Juma has continued to produce data-driven features on the disconnect between public perception, donor programmes and policy, including in "Teen Mums of Kwale," an investigation on the impact of contraceptive use on teen pregnancy rates in a conservative part of the country ("#TeenMumsOfKwale," 2016).

How Do We Ensure Our Justice System Is Protecting the Marginalized?

In Afghanistan, the *Pajhwok Afghan News* data team used data to probe the impact of two policies lauded as key for progress towards justice in the country: Afghanistan's Law on the Elimination of Violence Against Women (2009), and the Afghanistan National Drug Control Strategy (2012–2016). It found two unexpected casualties of these policies: Abused women and rural labourers. Although Afghanistan does not have an access to information law, many agencies that receive donor funding, including the women's affairs and counternarcotics ministries, are contractually obliged to make that data available.

Five years after the domestic violence law took effect, *Pajhwok Afghan News* wanted to track the fate of abusers and the abused. The team obtained the data on the 21,000 abuse cases from the Ministry of Women's Affairs and several UN agencies tasked with tracking cases, from registration, to final verdicts and mediation. They found that in the worst country in the world to be a woman, the widely lauded law has channelled women through a

2   http://kenyalaw.org/kl/fileadmin/pdfdownloads/bills/2014/TheFoodSecurityBill2014.pdf

local mediation process entrenched in traditional chauvinism, that usually lands her right back with her abuser (Munsef & Salehai, 2016). Two years later, Human Rights Watch published a study confirming PAN's findings, namely that law and mediation have failed Afghan women (United Nations Assistance Mission in Afghanistan, 2018). Even if more women had access to the court system, which boasts a high rate of conviction for abusers, there remains the thorny issue of what to do with divorced women in a society where women do not work.

Similar practical challenges arise in the enforcement of Afghanistan's drug strategy. The United Nations Office of Drugs and Crime was granted rare access to prisoners convicted of drug charges and handed over the raw survey data to the *Pajhwok* team. Analysis of survey findings revealed that the policy has seen mostly poor and illiterate drivers and farmers being imprisoned, while most drug kingpins walk free (Barakzai & Wardak, 2016). Most also reported that they planned to go right back to labouring in the drug trade once they are released as it is the only way to support their families in isolated rural areas.

These stories served a threefold purpose for the *Pajhwok* data team: To reality check policies developed from a Western legal lens, to highlight the consequences of economic marginalization by both gender and location, and to provide data-driven public interest content in Dari, Pashtu and English for a diverse audience.

How Do We Ensure Quality Education for Everyone?

Access to education, often regarded as a great equalizer, has allowed marginalized communities to quantify the government's failure to provide basic public services and push local leaders towards reform. In a series of stories, developer-cum-journalist Abdul Salam Afridi built a beat around education access among the disadvantaged, which landed him on the shortlist for the Data Journalism Awards for his portfolio. In his first story, he used official government education statistics and nationwide education survey data to show that parents in the remote tribal region of the Khyber Pass, who out of desperation were sending growing numbers of children to private schools, were making a bad investment. His story showed that most graduating students in both public and private schools fail basic standardized tests (Afridi, 2017a). Further stories on public education in the Khyber Pass and the Federally Administered Tribal Areas, where Salam himself is from, probe the reasons behind the failing schools (Afridi, 2017b, 2018).

Another story based on student rosters for the national vocational training programme and national job listings revealed a huge gap between skills and market demand. The investigation revealed that the country is training IT specialists and beauticians when it needs drivers and steel workers. Thus over half of their alumni are left unemployed, largely because of who is behind the project. Funded by the German government development fund, GiZ, the Pakistan government did its own analysis, came to the same conclusion, and quickly overhauled the programme, adding new course offerings aligned with more needed jobs skills (Afridi, 2017c).

An inherent advantage to data-driven beat reporting among marginalized communities is that the journalist can stay on the story after the initial scandal is forgotten. What these stories also have in common is that they use data not just to report the problem, but also what can be done about it. These journalists gathered data to measure the problem, the impact, the causes and the solution. Globally, there is a push for accessible data journalism by, about and for marginalized communities to win their trust and engage them in civic life.

Data Journalism Under Constraints

Much of the division in academia about the long-term viability of data journalism stems from a split over whether its aim is to produce high profile interactive products or fact-based public interest reporting. Journalists in developing countries use data to answer basic questions about institutionalized gender discrimination, prejudicial justice systems and wilful neglect of the hungry, and to deliver that information to as many people as they can. They do this knowing that these problems are complicated and policies are still very unlikely to change as a result. Data journalists in the West, with access to better resources, data and free media, and a more responsive government, are often not seizing the opportunity to ensure that in such tumultuous times, we are addressing the information needs of marginalized citizens and holding government accountable.

Most of these problems were invisible in the past and will become invisible again if journalists stop counting. Data journalism at its best is by, about and for those who society has decided do not count. Luckily civil society, activists, academics, governments and others are working together to do a better job of counting those who have been left out. Journalists have a vital role in ensuring that these are problems people are talking about and working to fix. Everything was terrible, is terrible and will be terrible unless we keep counting and talking. Year after year, we need to count the hungry, the abused, the imprisoned, the uneducated, the unheard, because everywhere on earth, things are terrible for someone.

Works Cited

Afridi, A. S. (2017a, February 18). In KP, parents still prefer private over public schools. *News Lens Pakistan.* http://www.newslens.pk/in-kp-parents-still-prefer-private-over-public-schools/

Afridi, A. S. (2017b, June 16). Half of FATA schools functioning in dire straits. *News Lens Pakistan.* http://www.newslens.pk/half-fata-schools-functioning-dire-straits/

Afridi, A. S. (2017c, September 16). TVET Reform programmes targeting wrong skills. *News Lens Pakistan.* http://www.newslens.pk/tvet-reform-programmes-targeting-wrong-skills/

Afridi, A. S. (2018, March 2). Despite huge investment the outlook of Education in KP remains questionable. *News Lens Pakistan.* http://www.newslens.pk/despite-huge-investment-outlook-education-in-kp/

Barakzai, N. A., & Wardak, A. (2016, September 28). Most jailed drug offenders are poor, illiterate. *Pajhwok Afghan News.* https://www.pajhwok.com/en/2016/09/28/most-jailed-drug-offenders-are-poor-illiterate

Juma, M. (2014, January 28). When will Kenya have enough to feed all its citizens? *Daily Nation.* https://www.nation.co.ke/lifestyle/dn2/When-will-Kenya-have-enough-to-feed-all-its-citizens-/957860-2163092-p8mgj9z/index.html

Munsef, A. Q., & Salehai, Z. (2016, May 11). Cases of violence against women: Is mediation the best option? *Pajhwok Afghan News.* https://www.pajhwok.com/en/2016/05/11/cases-violence-against-women-mediation-best-option

#TeenMumsOfKwale: Primary school girls in Kwale using contraceptives to prevent unwanted pregnancies. (2016, October 2). *NTV Kenya.* https://www.youtube.com/watch?v=xMx5lRHbw3g

United Nations Assistance Mission in Afghanistan. (2018). *Injustice and impunity: Mediation of criminal offences of violence against women.* United Nations Office of the High Commissioner for Human Rights. https://unama.unmissions.org/sites/default/files/unama_ohchr_evaw_report_2018_injustice_and_impunity_29_may_2018.pdf

About the Author

Eva Constantaras is a data journalist who specializes in establishing data teams in media houses in the Global South.

46. Teaching Data Journalism

Cheryl Phillips

Abstract

Teaching data journalism begins with teaching critical thinking.

Keywords: critical thinking, data journalism education, programming, collaboration, data practice, researcher–journalist collaborations

At Texas State University, Professor Cindy Royal teaches web development.[1] A few thousand miles east, at the University of Florida, Mindy McAdams, the Knight Chair of Journalism Technologies and the Democratic Process, and Associate Professor Norman Lewis, teach a variety of classes from coding to traditional data journalism and app development. Alberto Cairo, the Knight Chair of Visual Journalism at the School of Communication at the University of Miami, teaches an entire programme focused on data visualization.

Go north and students at Columbia University and CUNY take classes taught by practicing data journalists from NBC and *The New York Times*, learning the basics of investigative reporting along with data analysis. At the University of Maryland, media law classes regularly go through the process of submitting public records requests for journalism projects. In Nebraska, Matt Waite teaches students to visualize data using Legos. At Stanford University, we teach basic data analysis, coding in Python and R and basic data visualization, more for understanding than presentation.

Data journalism professors—many of whom got their start as practitioners—teach in a variety of ways across the world (and the examples above

---

1   Credit for this chapter is due to Charles Berret, co-author of *Teaching Data and Computational Journalism*, published with support from Columbia University and John S. and James L. Knight Foundation.

Bounegru, L. and J. Gray (eds.), *The Data Journalism Handbook: Towards a Critical Data Practice*. Amsterdam: Amsterdam University Press, 2021
DOI 10.5117/9789462989511_CH46

are just from programmes in the United States). Which programme is true data journalism? Trick question: All of them are. So how to teach?

The same way we teach any type of journalism class. Any specialization—from sports journalism to business reporting or science reporting—has domain-specific skills and knowledge that must be learned. Yet each rests on the fundamentals of journalism.

In the same way, data journalism education should begin with the fundamentals. By that, I don't mean learning spreadsheets, although I do think it can be ideal for understanding many basic tenets of data journalism. There's nothing like understanding the inherent messiness of entered data by having students embark on a class exercise that involves entering information into little boxes on a computer screen. I also don't mean learning a particular way of coding, from Python to R, although I do think both languages have many benefits. There's nothing like seeing a student run a line of code and get a result that would take four or more steps in a spreadsheet.

Learning about data journalism begins with understanding how to think critically about information and how it can be collected, normalized and analyzed for journalistic purposes. It begins with figuring out the story, and asking the questions that get you there.

And journalism educators likely already know the form those questions can take:

- Who created the data?
- What is the data supposed to include?
- When was the data last updated?
- Where in the world does the data represent?
- Why do we need this data to tell our story?
- How do we find the answers to the questions we want to ask of this data?

So, build the curricula using spreadsheets, or SQL, or Python, or R. It doesn't matter. Just as it doesn't matter that I once knew something called Paradox for DOS. What matters is knowing the steps to take with collecting and analyzing data. Visualization is key both in analyzing and presenting, but if visual analysis for understanding comes first—then presentation follows more easily.

This chapter contains a variety of approaches and starting points regarding how to teach data journalism, based on who you are, what level of programme you have and how you can build collaborative efforts. After introducing the "suitcase" approach to teaching data journalism, it explores one-course models, flipped classroom models, integrated models and experiments in co-teaching across different disciplines.

One Course Is All You Can Do: Packing the Suitcase

When we go car camping, we always make the joke that we pack everything, including the kitchen sink. The trick is knowing what you can pack and what would overload you to the point of unproductiveness. That kitchen sink is actually a small, foldable, cloth-based bowl.

If you are teaching just one class, and you are the solo data journalism educator—don't try to pack in too much, including data analysis with spreadsheets and Structured Query Language (SQL), data processing using Python, analysis using R and data visualization design using D3, all in one quarter or semester.

Pick the tools that are vital. Consider making the class at least partly project-based. Either way, walk through the steps. Do it again and keep it simple. Keep the focus on the journalism that comes out of using the tools you do select.

In 2014 and 2015, Charles Berret of Columbia University and I conducted a survey and extensive interviews with data journalists and journalism educators. Most of those who teach data journalism reported that beginning with a spreadsheet introduces the concept of structured data to students in a way that is easy to grasp.

Another step is to ramp up the complexity to include other valuable techniques in data journalism: Moving beyond sorts and filters and into "group by" queries, or joining disparate data sets to find patterns otherwise undiscovered.

But that doesn't mean adding a myriad number of new tools, or even picking the newest tool. You can introduce students to that next level using whatever technology works for you and your institution's journalism programme. If it's a university programme where every student has MS Access, then use that, but go behind the point-and-click interface to make sure that students understand the Structured Query Language behind each query. Or use MySQL. Or use Python in a Jupyter Notebook. Or use R and R Studio, which has some great packages for SQL-like queries.

The goal is to teach the students journalism while helping them to understand what needs to happen and that there are many ways of achieving similar operations with data in the service of telling a story.

Again, keep it simple. Don't make students jump through hoops for tech tools. Use the tools to make journalism more powerful and easier to do. To go back to that car camping analogy, pack just what you need into your class. Don't bring the chainsaw if all you need is a hatchet, or a pocketknife.

But also, once you have the one class established, think beyond that one-class model. Think about ways to build in data journalism components throughout the department or school. Find shared motivation with other classes. Can you work with colleagues who are teaching a basic news reporting class to see where they might be interested in having their students learn a bit more about integrating data?

Some journalism professors have experimented with "flipped classroom" models to balance skills instruction, critical thinking and theoretical reflection. Students can take tutorials at their own pace and focus on problem-solving with instructors during class as well as learning other methods for tackling a variety of data journalism challenges. Professor McAdams from the University of Florida follows a flipped classroom model for her designing web apps class, for example.

One benefit for this type of classroom is that it accounts for journalists of many different skill levels. In some instances, a journalism class may draw interest from a student who is adept at computer science, and, at the same time, a student who has never used a spreadsheet.

But teaching data journalism goes beyond flipped classrooms. It means thinking about other ways to teach data journalism concepts. At SRCCON, a regular unconference, Sarah Cohen, the Knight Chair in Data Journalism at Arizona State University, and a Pulitzer Prize-winning journalist most recently at *The New York Times*, advocated using other analogue activities to engage students. Cohen and Waite, a professor of practice at the University of Nebraska, were introducing the idea of a common curriculum with modules that can be used by educators everywhere. The goal is to create a system where professors don't have to build everything from scratch. At the conference in summer 2018, they led a group of participants in contributing possible modules for the effort. "We are trying not to have religion on that stuff [tools]," Cohen told the group, instead arguing that the focus should be on the "fundamental values of journalism and the fundamental values of data analysis."

Now, a GitHub repo is up and going with contributors adding to and tweaking modules for use in data journalism education.[2] The repo also offers links to other resources in teaching data journalism, including this handbook.

A few possibilities for modules include interpreting polls or studies. Basic numeracy is an important component of journalism courses. Finding data online is another quick hit that can boost any class.

It also doesn't mean you have to give up all your free time for the cause. Build a module or tutorial once and it can be used over and again by others.

2   https://github.com/datajtext/DataJournalismTextbook

Or tap into the many free tutorials already out there. The annual conferences held by Investigative Reporters and Editors (IRE) and the National Institute for Computer-Assisted Reporting (NICAR) yield even more tutorials for their members on everything from pivot tables to scraping and mapping.

I guest-teach once a quarter for a colleague on finding data online. The benefits include creating a pipeline of students interested in exploring data journalism and being part of a collegial atmosphere with fellow faculty.

If possible, consider building modules that those colleagues could adopt. Environmental journalists could do a module on mean temperatures over time using a spreadsheet, for example. Doing so has one other potential benefit: You are showing your colleagues the value of data journalism, which may also help to build the case for a curriculum that systematically integrates these practices and approaches.

More on an Integrated Model, or Teaching Across Borders

A fully integrated model means more than one person is invested in teaching the concepts of data journalism. It also has potential to reach beyond the bounds of a journalism programme. At Stanford, we launched the Stanford Open Policing Project and partnered with Poynter to train journalists in analyzing policing data. Professors in engineering and journalism have worked together to teach classes that cross boundaries and educate journalism students, law students and computer science students. This is important because the best collaborative teams in newsrooms include folks from multiple disciplines. More recently, academic institutions are not only adopting such integrated models, but producing work that reaches into newsrooms and teaching students at the same time.

Just this month, the Scripps Howard Foundation announced it is providing two $3 million grants to Arizona State University and the University of Maryland, which will launch investigative reporting centres.[3] Those centres will train students and produce investigative work, taking on the role of publisher as well as trainer.

Classes that have a mission and that move beyond the classroom are more compelling to students and can provide a more engaging learning experience. One of the most successful classes I have been a part of is the Law, Order &

---

3   To learn more about the grants for launching investigative journalism centres, see Boehm, J. (2018, August 6). Arizona State University, University of Maryland get grants to launch investigative journalism centers, *AZCentral*. https://amp.azcentral.com/amp/902340002

Algorithms class taught in spring 2018 by myself and Assistant Engineering Professor Sharad Goel. The class title is Goel's, but we added a twist. My watchdog class by the same name met in concert with Goel's class. Between the two classes, we taught computer science and engineering students, law students and journalism students. The student teams produced advanced statistical analysis, white papers and journalism out of their projects. Goel and I each lectured in our own area of expertise. I like to think that I learned something about the law and how algorithms can be used for good and for ill, and that Prof. Goel learned a little something about what it takes to do investigative and data journalism.

As for the students, the project-based nature of the class meant they were learning what they needed to accomplish the goals of their team's project. What we avoided was asking the students to learn so much in the way of tools or techniques that they would only see incremental progress. We tried to pack in just what was necessary for success, kind of like those car camping trips.

About the Author

Cheryl Phillips teaches data journalism at Stanford University and is the founder of Big Local News (biglocalnews.org), a collaborative data-sharing effort and platform for journalists.

47. Organizing Data Projects With Women and Minorities in Latin America

Eliana A. Vaca Muñoz

Abstract

This chapter discusses organizing data projects with women and minorities in Latin America.

Keywords: analogue dataviz, minorities, women, Latin America, data journalism education, data visualization

Chicas Poderosas (Powerful Girls) is a transnational network of journalists, designers and developers working to develop digital media projects by and for women and marginalized communities throughout Latin America. As a designer with Chicas Poderosas, my work explores the role that design can play as an agent of culture and diversity, including through interdisciplinary and participatory research to explore cultural heritage, identity, the appropriation of territories, and the recognition of women and vulnerable populations.

This chapter examines the organization of several Chicas Poderosas initiatives in Colombia and Central America. As social and cultural inequalities in Colombia widen, it is important for minorities to be heard, to share their knowledge and to be treated as equals. To this end, the Chicas Colombia team has conducted a series of collaborative workshops focusing on data journalism and associated digital media practices. In the following sections I examine two methods that we used to facilitate participation in these workshops: Analogue data collection and analogue data visualization. These approaches may be relevant to the practices and cultures of data journalism in communities and regions where connectivity, devices and technological literacies cannot be taken for granted.

Bounegru, L. and J. Gray (eds.), *The Data Journalism Handbook: Towards a Critical Data Practice.* Amsterdam: Amsterdam University Press, 2021

DOI 10.5117/9789462989511_CH47

Analogue Data Collection

In May 2016, Chicas Colombia went to Villa España in Quibdó, Chocó, to work with women and teenagers belonging to the AJODENIU (Association of Displaced Youth) collective. Since 2002 this group has worked to defend the interests and rights of children displaced from Chocó, Río Sucio, Bojayá and Urabá. These regions are all difficult to access, with no Internet and few support services available. Therefore, the workshops began with analogue techniques to collect qualitative data. With this data, we worked to construct stories on issues such as forced displacement and teenage pregnancy, by recording spoken and written narratives.[1]

Building on these approaches, we worked with the United Nations Development Programme in Honduras in September 2018 to create a workshop with the Observatorios de Municipales de Convivencia y Seguridad Ciudadana (Municipal Observatories for Coexistence and Citizen Security). They worked with data on violent deaths of men and women and were interested in presenting data disaggregated by gender. Two of the goals were to create emotional pathways to initiate conversations with the community around these difficult topics through participatory activities, and to use limited resources to share sensitive and important data.

At these workshops the initial steps are ice-breaking activities with simple and funny questions (Figure 47.1). At the Honduras workshop there were difficulties in discussing violence with participants due to different societal norms as well as language barriers. Thus, we focused the workshop on different exploratory data-gathering activities to surface different conceptions and experiences of violence. We used drawings, pictures and photographs to create posters together. Participants could add stickers to these as a way to gather data—including on the way they envisaged themselves, on their understanding of rights and on how they had experienced different kinds of domestic violence (e.g., physical, psychological, economic) in their own lives.

Analogue Data Visualization

In an effort to better understand the issues plaguing Indigenous communities, in 2017 we planned interactive workshops with the Embera Tribe of the Vigía del Fuerte region. The workshops sought to provide a window into

---

1   https://chicaspoderosas.org/2016/11/22/the-pacific-counts-chicas-poderosas-quibdo-colombia/

Figure 47.1. "I'm so creative?": analogue data collection activity. Source: Eliana Vaca.

their lives in spite of language barriers. Historically, interactions between the tribe and outsiders have been largely male-dominated, so we prioritized accessing the female populations in order to gauge their levels of education and facilitate discussions regarding empowerment.

In the absence of modern technologies, we explored traditional expressions of culture as a means to more meaningfully access the lives of our participants. These expressions included traditional practices such as weaving, beading and craftwork (Figure 47.2).

In September 2018 in Honduras, we ran a workshop around the question of how to "humanize" data, conducting resiliency projects with victims and populations at risk. We designed low-cost analogue data visualization workshops with empathetic design techniques using scissors, papers, stickers, post-its and balloons. These served to facilitate the sharing of sensitive information with relevant organizations to better support these communities, as well as teaching different methods that vulnerable and low-literacy populations could use to share data about their lives, experiences and issues. For example, we worked with participants to create analogue visualizations about murders and femicides by region, type and age.

In another workshop in Belize we explored different collaborative approaches to visualizing data about crime and violence. We originally set out to see how data from the Belize Violence Observatory could be used to coordinate different kinds of collective responses. While participants had

Figure 47.2. An example of analogue visualisation with beading where different colours represent different languages spoken and the amount of beads represents fluency in each. Source: Eliana Vaca.

high levels of literacy, the technological resources and connectivity were much more precarious, making it difficult to use basic online visualization tools. This raised many questions and challenges about online data visualization practices, which are often taken for granted, but which would not work in the settings we were in—again suggesting the relevance of analogue approaches to data visualization using more readily available materials.

About the Author

Eliana A. Vaca Muñoz is a designer who specializes in developing projects that involve human behaviour and anthropology methodologies to create human-centred design solutions.

Situating Data Journalism

48. Genealogies of Data Journalism

C. W. Anderson

Abstract

This chapter takes a critical and historical look at data journalism.

Keywords: genealogy, data journalism, history, uncertainty, computational journalism, precision journalism

Introduction

Why should anyone care about the history of data journalism? Not only is "history" a rather academic and abstract topic for most people, it might seem particularly remote for working data journalists with a job to do. Journalists, working under tight deadlines and with a goal of conveying complicated information quickly and understandably to as many readers as possible, can be understandably averse to wasting too much time on self-reflection. More often than not, this reluctance to "navel-gaze" is an admirable quality; when it comes to the practices and concepts of data journalism and computational reporting, however, a hostility towards historical thinking can be a detriment that hampers the production of quality journalism itself.

Data journalism may be the most powerful form of collective journalistic sense making in the world today. At the very least, it may be the most positive and positivistic form of journalism. This *power* (the capacity of data journalism to create high-quality journalism, along with the rhetorical force of the data journalism model), *positivity* (most data journalists have high hopes for the future of their particular subfield, convinced it is on the rise) and *positivism* (data reporters are strong believers in the ability of method-guided research to capture real and provable facts about the world) create what I would call an empirically self-assured profession. One consequence of this self-assurance, I would argue, is that it can also create a Whiggish assumption that data journalism is always improving and improving the world. Such an

Bounegru, L. and J. Gray (eds.), *The Data Journalism Handbook: Towards a Critical Data Practice*. Amsterdam: Amsterdam University Press, 2021
DOI 10.5117/9789462989511_CH48

attitude can lead to arrogance and a lack of critical self-reflexivity, and make journalism more like the institutions it spends its time calling to account.

In this chapter I want to argue that a better attention to history can actually improve the day-to-day workings of data journalism. By understanding that their processes and practices have a history, data journalists can open their minds to the fact that things in the present could be done differently because they might have once been otherwise. In particular, data journalists might think harder about how to creatively represent uncertainty in their empirical work. They might consider techniques through which to draw in readers of different political sensibilities and persuasions that go beyond simply stating factual evidence. They might, in short, open themselves up to what science and technology studies scholars and historians Catherine D'Ignazio and Lauren Klein have called a form of "feminist data visualization," one that rethinks binaries, embraces pluralism, examines power and considers context (D'Ignazio & Klein, 2020; see also D'Ignazio's chapter in this book). To accomplish these changes, data journalism, more than most forms of journalistic practice, should indeed inculcate this strong historical sensibility due to the very nature of its own power and self-assurance. No form of history is better equipped to lead to self-reflexivity, I would argue, than the genealogical approach to conceptual development pioneered by Michel Foucault and embraced by some historians of science and scholars in science and technology studies.

"Genealogy," as defined by Foucault, who himself draws on the earlier work of Nietzsche, is a unique approach to studying the evolution of institutions and concepts over time and one that might be distinguished from history as such. Genealogical analysis does not look for a single, unbroken origin of practices or ideas in the past, nor does it try to understand how concepts developed in an unbroken and evolutionary line from yesterday to today. Rather, it focuses more on *discontinuity* and *unexpected changes* than it does on the presence of the past in the present. As Nietzsche noted, in a passage from the *Genealogy of Morals* quoted by Foucault:

> The "development" of a thing, a practice, or an organ has nothing to do with its progress towards a single goal, even less is it the logical and shortest progress reached with the least expenditure of power and resources. Rather, it is the sequence of more or less profound, more or less mutually independent processes of overpowering that take place on that thing, together with the resistance that arises against that overpowering each time, the changes of form which have been attempted for the purpose of defense and reaction, as well as the results of successful counter-measures. Form is fluid; the "meaning," however, is even more so. (Foucault, 1980)

A "genealogy of data journalism," then, would uncover the ways that data journalism evolved in ways that its creators and practitioners never anticipated, or in ways that may have even been contrary to their desires. It would look at the ways that history surprises us and sometimes leads us in unexpected directions. This approach, as I argued earlier, would be particularly useful for working data journalists of today. It would help them understand, I think, that they are *not* working in a predefined tradition with a venerable past; rather, they are mostly making it up as they go along in ways that are radically contingent. And it would prompt a useful form of critical self-reflexivity, one that might help mitigate the (understandable and often well-deserved) self-confidence of working data journalists and reporters.

I have attempted to write such a genealogical account in my book, *Apostles of Certainty: Data Journalism and the Politics of Doubt* (Anderson, 2018). In the pages that follow, I want to summarize some of the main findings of the book and discuss ways that its lessons might be helpful for the present day. I want to conclude by arguing that journalism, particularly of the datafied kind, could and should do a better job demonstrating what it does not know, and that these gestures towards uncertainty would honour data journalism's origins in the critique of illegitimate power rather than the reification if it.

Data Journalism Through Time: 1910s, 1960s and 2010s

Can journalists use data—along with other forms of quantified information such as paper documents of figures, data visualizations, and charts and graphs—in order to produce better journalism? And how might that journalism assist the public in making better political choices? These were the main questions guiding *Apostles of Certainty: Data Journalism and the Politics of Doubt*, which tried to take a longer view of the history of news. With stops in the 1910s, the 1960s, and the present, the book traces the genealogy of data journalism and its material and technological underpinnings, and argues that the use of data in news reporting is inevitably intertwined with national politics, the evolution of computable databases and the history of professional scientific fields. It is impossible to understand journalistic uses of data, I argue in the book, without understanding the oft-contentious relationships between social science and journalism. It is also impossible to disentangle empirical forms of public truth telling without first understanding the remarkably persistent progressive belief that the publication of empirically verifiable information will lead to a more just and prosperous world. *Apostles of Certainty* concluded that this intersection of technology and professionalism has led to a better journalism but not necessarily to a better politics. To fully meet the demands of the digital age, journalism must be more comfortable expressing empirical doubt as well as certitude. Ironically, this "embrace of doubt" could lead journalism to become more like science, not less.

The Challenge of Social Science

The narrative of *Apostles of Certainty* grounds itself in three distinct US time periods which provide three different perspectives on the development of data journalism. The first is the so-called "Progressive Era," which was a period of liberal political ascendancy accompanied by the belief that both the state *and* ordinary citizens, informed by the best statistics available, could make the world a more just and humane place. The second moment is the 1950s and 1960s, when a few journalism reformers began to look to quantitative social science, particularly political science and sociology, as a possible source of new ideas and methods for making journalism more empirical and objective. They would be aided in this quest by a new set of increasingly accessible databases and powerful computers. The third moment is the early 2010s, when the cutting edge of data journalism has been supplemented by "computational" or "structured" journalism. In the current moment of big data and "deep machine learning," these journalists claim that journalistic objectivity depends less on external referents but rather emerges from within the structure of the database itself.

In each of these periods, data-oriented journalism both *responded to* but also defined itself *in partial opposition to* larger currents operating within social science more generally, and this relationship to larger political and social currents helped inform the choice of cases I focused on in this chapter. In other words, I looked for inflection points in journalism history that could help shed light on larger social and political structures, in addition to journalism. In the Progressive Era,[1] traditional news reporting largely rejected sociology's emerging focus on social structures and depersonalized contextual information, preferring to retain their individualistic focus on powerful personalities and important events. As journalism and sociology professionalized, both became increasingly comfortable with making structural claims, but it was not until the 1960s that Philip Meyer and the

---

1   In the United States the time period known as the "Progressive Era" lasted from the 1880s until the 1920s, and is commonly seen as a great era of liberal reform and an attempt to align public policy with the industrial era.

reformers clustered around the philosophy of Precision Journalism began to hold up quantitative sociology and political science as models for the level of exactitude and context to which journalism ought to aspire. By the turn of the 21st century, a largely normalized model of data journalism began to grapple with doubts about replicability and causality that were increasingly plaguing social science; like social science, it began to experiment to see if "big data" and non-causal forms of correlational behaviouralism could provide insights into social activity.

Apostles of Certainty thus argues implicitly that forms of journalistic expertise and authority are never constructed in isolation or entirely internally to the journalistic field itself. Data journalism did not become data journalism for entirely professional journalistic reasons, nor can this process be analyzed solely through an analysis of journalistic discourse or "self-talk." Rather, the type of expertise that in the 1960s began to be called data journalism can only be understood *relationally*, by examining the manner in which data journalists responded to and interacted with their (more authoritative and powerful) social scientific brethren. What's more, this process cannot be understood solely in terms of the actions and struggles of humans, either in isolation or in groups. Expertise, according to the model I put forward in *Apostles of Certainty*, is a networked phenomenon in which professional groupings struggle to establish jurisdiction over a wide variety of discursive *and* material artefacts. Data journalism, to put it simply, would have been impossible without the existence of the database, but the database as mediated through a particular professional understanding of what a database was and how it could be deployed in ways that were properly journalistic (for a more general attempt at this argument about the networked nature of expertise, see Anderson, 2013). It is impossible to understand journalistic authority without also understanding the authority of social science (and the same thing might be said about computer science, anthropology or long-form narrative non-fiction). Journalistic professionalism and knowledge can never be understood solely by looking at the field of journalism itself.

The Persistence of Politics

Data journalism must be understood genealogically and in relation to adjacent expert fields like sociology and political science. All of these fields, in turn, must be analyzed through their larger conceptions of politics and how they come to terms with the fact that the "facts" they uncover are "political" whether they like it or not. Indeed, even the desire for factual knowledge is itself a political act. Throughout the history of data journalism, I argue in *Apostles of Certainty*, we have witnessed a distinct attempt to lean on the neutrality of social science in order to enact what can only be described as progressive political goals. The larger context in which this connection is forged, however, has shifted dramatically over time. These larger shifts should temper any enthusiasm that what we are witnessing in journalism is a teleological unfolding of journalistic certainty as enabled by increasingly sophisticated digital devices.

In the Progressive Era, proto-data journalists saw the gathering and piling up of quantitative facts as a process of social and political enlightenment, a process that was nonetheless free of any larger political commitments. By collecting granular facts about city sanitation levels, the distribution of poverty across urban spaces, statistics about church attendance and religious practice, labour conditions, and a variety of other bits of factual knowledge—and by transmitting these facts to the public through the medium of the press—social surveyors believed that the social organism would gain a more robust understanding of its own conditions of being. By gaining a better understanding of itself, society would improve, both of its own accord and by spurring politicians towards enacting reformist measures. In this case, factual knowledge about the world spoke for itself; it simply needed to be gathered, visualized and publicized, and enlightenment would follow. We might call this a "naïve and transparent" notion of what facts are—they require no interpretation in and of themselves, and their accumulation will lead to positive social change. Data journalism, at this moment, could be political without explicitly stating its politics.

By the time of Philip Meyer and the 1960s, this easy congruence between transparent facts and politics had been shattered. Journalism was flawed, Meyer and his partisans argued throughout the 1950s and 1960s, because it mistook objectivity for simply collecting a record of what all sides of a political issue might think the truth might be and allowing the reader to make their own decisions about what was true. In an age of social upheaval and political turmoil, journalistic objectivity needed to find a more robust grounding, and it could find its footing on the terrain of objective social science. The starting point for journalistic reporting on an issue should not be the discursive claims of self-interested politicians but rather the cold, hard truth gleaned from an analysis of relevant data with the application of an appropriate method. Such an analysis would be *professional but not political*; by acting as a highly professionalized cadre of truth-tellers, journalists could cut through the political spin and help plant the public on the terrain of objective truth. The directions this truth might lead, on the other hand, were of no concern. Unlike the earlier generation of blissfully and naively progressive data journalists, the enlightened consequences of data were not a foregone conclusion.

Today I would argue that a new generation of computational journalists has unwittingly reabsorbed some of the political and epistemological beliefs of their Progressive Era forbearers. Epistemologically, there is an increasing belief amongst computational journalists that digital facts in some way "speak for themselves," or at least these facts will do so when they have been properly collected, sorted and cleaned. At scale, and when linked to larger and internally consistent semantic databases, facts generate a kind of *correlational excess* in which troubles with meaning or causality are washed away through a flood of computational data. Professionally, data journalists increasingly understand objectivity as emerging from within the structure of the database itself rather than as part of any larger occupational interpretive process. Politically, finally, I would argue that there has been the return of a kind of "crypto-progressivism" amongst many of the most studiously neutral data journalists, with a deep-seated political hope that more and more data, beautifully visualized and conveyed through a powerful press, can act as a break on the more irrational or pathological political tendencies increasingly manifest within Western democracies. Such, at least, was the hope before 2016 and the twin shocks of Brexit and Donald Trump.

Certainty and Doubt

The development of data journalism in the United States across the large arc of the 20th century should be seen as one in which increasingly exact claims to journalistic professional certitude coexisted uneasily with a dawning awareness that all facts, no matter what their origins, were tainted with the grime of politics. These often-contradictory beliefs are evident across a variety of data-oriented fields, of course, not simply just in journalism. In a 2017 article for *The Atlantic*, for instance, science columnist Ed Yong grappled with how the movement towards "open science" and the growing replicability crisis could be used by an anti-scientific Congress to demean and defund scientific research. Yong quoted Christie Aschwanden, a science reporter at *FiveThirtyEight*: "It feels like there are two opposite things that the public thinks about science," she tells Yong.

> [Either] it's a magic wand that turns everything it touches to truth, or that it's all bullshit because what we used to think has changed. . . . The truth

is in between. Science is a process of uncertainty reduction. If you don't show that uncertainty is part of the process, you allow doubt-makers to take genuine uncertainty and use it to undermine things. (Yong, 2017)

These thoughts align with the work of STS scholar Helga Nowotny (2016), who argues in *The Cunning of Uncertainty* that "the interplay between overcoming uncertainty and striving for certainty underpins the wish to know." The essence of modern science—at least in its ideal form—is not the achievement of certainty but rather the fact that it so openly states the provisionality of its knowledge. Nothing in science is set in stone. It admits to often know little. It is through this, the most modern of paradoxes, that its claims to knowledge become worthy of public trust.

One of the insights provided by this genealogical overview of the development and deployment of data journalism, I would argue, is that data-oriented journalists have become obsessed with increasing exactitude and certainty at the expense of a humbler understanding of provisionality and doubt. As I have tried to demonstrate, since the middle of the 20th century journalists have engaged in an increasingly successful effort to render their knowledge claims more certain, contextual and explanatory. In large part, they have done this by utilizing different forms of evidence, particularly evidence of the quantitative sort. Nevertheless, it should be clear that this heightened professionalism—and the increasing confidence of journalists that they are capable of making contextualized truth claims—has not always had the democratic outcomes that journalists expect. Modern American political discourse has tried to come to grips with the uncertainty of modernity by engaging a series of increasingly strident claims to certitude. Professional journalism has not solved this dilemma; rather it has exacerbated it. To better grapple with the complexity of the modern world, I would conclude, journalism ought to rethink the means and mechanisms by which it conveys its own provisionality and uncertainty. If done correctly, this could make journalism more like modern science, rather than less.

Works Cited

Anderson, C. W. (2013). Towards a sociology of computational and algorithmic journalism. *New Media & Society*, *15*(7), 1005–1021. https://doi.org/10.1177/1461444812465137

Anderson, C. W. (2018). *Apostles of certainty: Data journalism and the politics of doubt*. Oxford University Press.

D'Ignazio, C., & Klein, L. F. (2020). *Data feminism*. MIT Press.

Foucault, M. (1980). *Power/knowledge: Selected interviews and other writings, 1972–1977*. Vintage.

Nowotny, H. (2016). *The cunning of uncertainty*. Polity Press.

Yong, E. (2017, April 5). How the GOP could use science's reform movement against it. *The Atlantic*. https://www.theatlantic.com/science/archive/2017/04/reproducibility-science-open-judoflip/521952/

About the Author

C. W. Anderson is Professor of Media and Communication at the University of Leeds and author of *Rebuilding the News: Metropolitan Journalism in the Digital Age* (Temple University Press, 2013) and *Apostles of Certainty: Data Journalism and the Politics of Doubt* (Oxford University Press, 2018).

49. Data-Driven Gold Standards: What the Field Values as Award-Worthy Data Journalism

Wiebke Loosen

Abstract

This chapter explores the relationship between the datafication of society and a datafied journalism and introduces awards as a means to study the evolution of data journalism.

Keywords: Data Journalism Awards, datafication, datafied journalism, data society, journalism research, co-creation

Introduction: Journalism's Response to the Datafication of Society

Perhaps better than in the early days of data journalism, we can understand the emergence of this new reporting style today as one journalistic response to the datafication of society (Loosen, 2018). Datafication refers to the ever-growing availability of data that has its roots in the digitalization of our (media) environment and the digital traces and big data that accrue with living in such an environment (Dijck, 2014). This process turns many aspects of our social life into computerized data—data that is to various ends aggregated and processed algorithmically. Datafication leads to a variety of consequences and manifests itself in different ways in politics, for instance, than it does in the financial world or in the realm of education. However, what all social domains have in common is that we can assume that they will increasingly rely on an ever more diverse range and greater amount of data in their (self-)sense-making processes.

Situating the datafication of journalism in relation to the datafication of wider society helps us to look beyond data journalism, to recognize

Bounegru, L. and J. Gray (eds.), *The Data Journalism Handbook: Towards a Critical Data Practice*. Amsterdam: Amsterdam University Press, 2021

DOI 10.5117/9789462989511_CH49

it as "only" one occurrence of datafication in journalism, and to better understand journalism's transformation towards a more and more data-based, algorithmicized, metrics-driven or even automated practice (Loosen, 2018). In particular, this includes the objects and topics that journalism is supposed to cover, or, put differently, journalism's function as an observer of society. The more the fields and social domains that journalism is supposed to cover are themselves "datafied," the more journalism itself needs to be able to make sense of and produce data to fulfil its societal role. It is this relationship that is reflected in contemporary data journalism which relies on precisely this increased availability of data to expand the repertoire of sources for journalistic research and for identifying and telling stories.

Awards: A Means to Study What Is Defined and Valued as Data Journalism

One way of tracing the evolution of data journalism as a reporting style is to look at its output. While the first studies in journalism research tended to focus more on the actors involved in its production and were mainly based on interviews, more and more studies have recently been using content analysis to better understand data journalism on the basis of its products (Ausserhofer et al., 2020). Journalism awards are a good empirical access point for this purpose for several reasons. Firstly, award submissions have already proved to be useful objects for the analysis of genres and aspects of storytelling (e.g., Wahl-Jorgensen, 2013). Secondly, data journalism is a diffuse object of study that makes it not only difficult, but, rather, preconditional, to identify respective pieces for a content analysis. The sampling of award nominees, in turn, avoids starting with either a too narrow or too broad definition—this strategy is essentially a means of observing self-observation in journalism, as such pieces represent what the field itself regards as data journalism and believes are significant examples of this reporting style. Thirdly, nominations for internationally oriented awards are likely to influence the development of the field as a whole as they are highly recognized, are considered to be a kind of gold standard and, as such, also have a cross-border impact. In addition, looking at international awards allows us to investigate a sample that covers a broad geographical and temporal range.

However, it is also important to keep in mind that studying (journalism) awards brings with it different biases. The study we are drawing from here is based on an analysis of 225 nominated pieces (including 39 award-winning pieces) for the Data Journalism Awards (DJA)—a prize annually awarded by the Global Editors Network[1]—in the years 2013 to 2016 (Loosen et al., 2020). This means that our sample is subject to a double selection bias: At first it is self-selective, since journalists have to submit their contributions themselves in order to be nominated at all. In the second step, a more or less annually changing jury of experts will decide which entries will actually be nominated. In addition, prizes and awards represent a particular form of "cultural capital," which is why award-winning projects can have a certain signal effect for the field as a whole and serve as a model for subsequent projects (English, 2002). This also means that awards not only represent the field (according to certain standards), but also constitute it. That is, in our case, by labelling content as data journalism, the awards play a role in gathering together different practices, actors, conventions and values. They may be considered, then, to have not just an *award-making function* but also a *field-making function*. This means that award-worthy pieces are always the result of a kind of "co-construction" by applicants and jurors and their mutually shaped expectations. Such effects are likely to be particularly influential in the case of data journalism as it is still a relatively new reporting style with which all actors in the field are more or less experimenting.

Evolving but Not Revolutionizing: Some Trends in (Award-Worthy) Data Journalism

Studies that analyze data-driven pieces generally demonstrate that the evolution of data journalism is by no means a revolution in news work. As a result, they challenge the widespread belief that data-driven journalism is revolutionizing journalism by replacing traditional methods of news discovery and reporting. Our own study broadly concurs with what other empirical analyses of "daily" data journalism samples have found (Loosen et al., 2020). These only represent fairly limited data collections, but they do at least allow us to trace some developments and perhaps, above all, some degree of consistency in data journalism output.

In terms of who is producing data-driven journalism on an award-worthy level, results show that the "gold standard" for data journalism, that is, worthy of peer recognition, is dominated by newspapers and their online departments. Over the four years we analyzed, they represent by far the largest group among all nominees as well as among award-winners (total:

1   https://www.globaleditorsnetwork.org/about-us/, https://www.datajournalismawards.org/

43.1%; DJA awarded: 37.8%). The only other prominent grouping comprises organizations involved in investigative journalism such as *ProPublica* and the International Consortium of Investigative Journalists (ICIJ), which were awarded significantly more often than not. This might reflect the awards' inherent bias towards established, high-profile actors, echoing findings from other research that data journalism above a certain level appears to be an undertaking for larger organizations that have the resources and editorial commitment to invest in cross-disciplinary teams made up of writers, programmers and graphic designers (Borges-Rey, 2020; Young et al., 2018). This is also reflected in the team sizes. Of the 192 projects in our sample that had a byline, they named on average just over five individuals as authors or contributors, and about a third of projects were completed in collaboration with external partners who either contributed to the analysis or designed visualizations. This seems particularly true for award-winning projects that our analysis found were produced by larger teams than those only nominated (M = 6.31, SD = 4.7 vs M = 4.75, SD = 3.8).

With regards to the geographies of data journalism that receives recognition in this competition, we can see that the United States dominates: Nearly half of the nominees come from the United States (47.6%), followed at a distance by Great Britain (12.9%) and Germany (6.2%). However, data journalism appears to be an increasingly global phenomenon, as the number of countries represented by the nominees grew with each year, amounting to 33 countries from all five continents in 2016.

Data journalism's reliance on certain sources influences the topics it may or may not cover. As a result, data journalism can neglect those social domains for which data is not regularly produced or accessible. In terms of topics covered, DJA nominees are characterized by an invariable focus on political, societal and economic issues, with almost half the analyzed pieces (48.2%) covering a political topic. The small share of stories on education, culture and sports—in line with other studies—might be unrepresentative of data journalism in general and instead result from a bias towards "serious" topics inherent in industry awards. However, this may also reflect the availability or unavailability of data sources for different domains and topics or, in the case of our sample, the applicants' self-selection biases informed by what they consider worthy of submission and what they expect jurors to appreciate. In order to gain more reliable knowledge on this point of crucial importance, an international comparative study that relates data availability and accessibility to topics covered by data reporting in different countries would be required. Such a study is still absent from the literature but could shed light on which social domains and topics are covered by which analytical methods and based on which data sources. Such an approach would also provide valuable insight to the other side of this coin: The blind spots in data-driven coverage due to a lack of (available) data sources.

One recurring finding in content-related research on data journalism is that it exhibits a "dependency on pre-processed public data" from statistical offices and other governmental institutions (Borges-Rey, 2020; Tabary et al., 2016; Young et al., 2018). This is also true of data-driven pieces at an award-worthy level: We observed a dependence on data from official institutions (almost 70% of data sources) and other non-commercial organizations such as research institutes and NGOs, as well as data that are publicly available, at least on request (almost 45%). This illustrates, on the one hand, that data journalism is making sense of the increased availability of data sources, but, on the other, that it also relies heavily on this availability: The share of self-collected, scraped, leaked and requested data is substantially smaller. Nonetheless, data journalism has been continually linked to investigative reporting, which has "led to something of a perception that data journalism is all about massive data sets, acquired through acts of journalistic bravery and derring-do" (Knight, 2015; Parasie, 2015; Royal & Blasingame, 2015). Recent cases such as the Panama Papers have contributed to that perception.[2] However, what this case also shows is that some complex issues of global importance are embedded in data that require transnational cooperation between different media organizations. Furthermore, it is likely that we will see more of these cases as soon as routines can be further developed to continuously monitor international data flows, for example, in finance, not merely as a service, but also as deeper and investigative background stories. That could stimulate a new kind of *investigative data-based real-time journalism*, which constantly monitors certain finance data streams, for example, and searches for anomalies.

Interactivity counts as a quality criterion in data journalism, but interactivity is usually implemented with a relatively clear set of features—here our results are also in harmony with other studies and what is often described as a "lack of sophistication" in data-related interactivity (Young et al., 2018). Zoomable maps and filter functions are most common, perhaps because of a tendency to apply easy-to-use and/or freely available software solutions, which results in less sophisticated visualizations and interactive features. However, award-winning projects are more likely to provide at least one interactive feature and integrate a higher number of different visualizations. The trend towards rather limited interactive options might also reflect

2   https://panamapapers.icij.org/

journalists' experiences with low audience interest in sophisticated interactivity (such as gamified interactivity opportunities or personalization tools that make it possible to tailor a piece with customized data). At the same time, however, interactive functions as well as visualizations should at best support the storytelling and the explanatory function of an article—and this requires solutions adapted to each data-driven piece.

A summary of the developmental trends over the years shows a somewhat mixed pattern, as the shares and average numbers of the categories under study were mostly stable over time or, if they did change, they did not increase or decrease in a linear fashion. Rather, we found erratic peaks and lows in individual years, suggesting the trial-and-error evolution one would expect in a still emerging field such as data journalism. As such, we found few consistent developments over the years: A significantly growing share of business pieces, a consistently and significantly increasing average number of different kinds of visualizations, and a (not statistically significant, but) constantly growing portion of pieces that included criticism (e.g., on the police's wrongful confiscation methods) or even calls for public intervention (e.g., with respect to carbon emissions). This share grew consistently over the four years (2013: 46.4% vs 2016: 63.0%) and was considerably higher among award winners (62.2% vs 50.0%). We can interpret this as an indication of the high appreciation of the investigative and watchdog potential of (data) journalism and, perhaps, as a way of legitimizing this emerging field.

From Data Journalism to Datafied Journalism—and Its Role in the Data Society

Data journalism represents the emergence of a new journalistic sub-field that is co-evolving in parallel with the datafication of society—a logical step in journalism's adaptation to the increasing availability of data. However, data journalism is no longer a burgeoning phenomenon; it has, in fact, firmly positioned itself within mainstream practice. A noteworthy indicator of this can again be found when looking at the Data Journalism Awards. The 2018 competition introduced a new category called "innovation in data journalism," which suggests that data journalism is no longer regarded as an innovative field in and of itself, but is looking for novel approaches in contemporary practice.[3]

---

3   https://www.datajournalismawards.org/categories/

We can expect data journalism's relevance and proliferation to co-evolve alongside the increasing datafication of society as a whole—a society in which sense making, decisions and all kinds of social actions increasingly rely on data. Against this background, it is not too difficult to see that the term "data journalism" will become superfluous in the not too distant future because journalism as a whole, as well as the environment of which it is part, is becoming increasingly datafied. Whether this prognosis is confirmed or not: The term "data journalism," just as the term "data society," still sensitizes us to fundamental transformation processes in journalism and beyond. This includes how and by what means journalism observes and covers (the datafied) society, how it self-monitors its performance, how it controls its reach and audience participation, and how it (automatically) produces and distributes content. In other words, contemporary journalism is characterized by its transformation towards a more data-based, algorithmicized, metric-driven or even automated practice.

However, data is not a "raw material"; it does not allow direct, objective or otherwise privileged access to the social world (Borgman, 2015). This way of understanding data is all the more important for a responsible data journalism as the process of society's datafication advances. Advancing datafication and data-driven journalism's growing relevance may also set incentives for other social domains to produce or make more data available (to journalists), and we are likely to see the co-evolution of a "data PR," that is, *data-driven public relations* produced and released to influence public communications for its own purposes. This means that routines for checking the quality, origin and significance of data are becoming increasingly important for (data) journalism, and raise the question of why there may be no data available on certain facts or developments.

In summary, I can organize our findings according to seven "Cs"—seven challenges and underutilized capacities of data journalism that may also be useful for suggesting modified or alternative practices in the field.

Collection. Investigative and critical data journalism must overcome its dependency on publicly accessible data. More effort needs to be made in gaining access to data and collecting them independently.

Collaboration. Even if the "everyday" data-driven piece is becoming increasingly easier to produce, more demanding projects are resource- and personnel-intensive, and it is to be expected that the number of globally relevant topics will increase. These will require data-based investigations across borders and media organizations, and, in some cases, collaboration with other fields such as science or data activism.

Crowdsourcing. The real interactive potential of data journalism lies not in increasingly sophisticated interactive features but in crowdsourcing approaches that sincerely involve users or citizens as collectors, categorizers and co-investigators of data (Gray, 2018).

Co-Creation. Co-creation approaches, common in the field of software development, can serve as a model for long-term data-driven projects. In such cases, users are involved in the entire process, from finding a topic to developing one and maintaining it over a longer period.

Competencies. Quality data journalism requires teams with broad skill sets. The role of the journalist remains important, but journalists increasingly need a more sophisticated understanding of data, data structures and analytical methods. Media organizations, in turn, need resources to recruit data analysts who are increasingly desirable in many other industries.

Combination. Increasingly complex data requires increasingly sophisticated analysis. Methods that combine data sources and look at these data from a variety of perspectives could help paint more substantial pictures of social phenomena and strengthen data journalism's analytical capacity.

Complexity. Complexity includes not only the data itself, but its increasing importance for various social areas and political decision making. In the course of these developments, data journalism will increasingly be confronted with data PR and "fake data."

What does this mean? Taking into account what we already know about (award-winning) data journalism in terms of what kinds of data journalism are valued, receiving wide public attention and contributing to a general appreciation of journalism, what kinds of data journalism do we really want? In this regard, I would argue that responsible data journalism in the data society is one that: Investigates socially relevant issues and makes the data society understandable and criticizable by its own means; is aware of its own blind spots while asking why there are data deficiencies in certain areas and whether this is a good or a bad sign; actively tries to uncover data manipulation and data abuse; and, finally, keeps in mind, explains and emphasizes the character of data as "human artefacts" that are by no means self-evident collections of facts, but are often collected in relation to very particular conditions and objectives (Krippendorff, 2016).

At the same time, however, this means that data journalism's peculiarity, its dependency on data, is also its weakness. This limitation concerns the availability of data, its reliability, its quality and its manipulability. A responsible data journalism should be reflexive about its dependency on data—and it should be a core subject in the discussion on ethics in data journalism. These conditions indicate that data journalism is not only a new style of reporting, but also a means of intervention that challenges and questions the data society, a society loaded with core epistemological questions that confront journalism's assumptions about *what* we (can) know and *how* we know (through data).

These questions become more urgent as more and increasingly diverse data is incorporated at various points in the "circuit of news": As a means of journalistic observation and investigation, as part of production and distribution routines, and as a means of monitoring the consumption activities of audiences. It is in these ways that datafied journalism is affecting: (a) *journalism's way of observing the world* and constructing the news from data, (b) the very core of journalism's performance in *facilitating the automation of content production*, (c) the *distribution and circulation of journalism's output* within an environment that is shaped by algorithms and their underlying logic to process data, and (d) what is *understood as newsworthy* to increasingly granularly measured audience segments.

These developments present (data) journalism with three essential responsibilities: To critically observe our development towards a datafied society, to make it understandable through its own means, and to make visible the limits of what can and should be recounted and seen through the lens of data.

Works Cited

Ausserhofer, J., Gutounig, R., Oppermann, M., Matiasek, S., & Goldgruber, E. (2020). The datafication of data journalism scholarship: Focal points, methods, and research propositions for the investigation of data-intensive newswork. *Journalism*, *21*(7), 950–973. https://doi.org/10.1177/1464884917700667

Borges-Rey, E. (2020). Towards an epistemology of data journalism in the devolved nations of the United Kingdom: Changes and continuities in materiality, performativity and reflexivity: *Journalism*, *21*(7), 915–932. https://doi.org/10.1177/1464884917693864

Borgman, C. L. (2015). *Big data, little data, no data: Scholarship in the networked world*. The MIT Press.

Dijck, J. van. (2014). Datafication, dataism and dataveillance: Big data between scientific paradigm and ideology. *Surveillance & Society*, *12*(2), 197–208. https://doi.org/10.24908/ss.v12i2.4776

English, J. F. (2002). Winning the culture game: Prizes, awards, and the rules of art. *New Literary History*, *33*(1), 109–135. https://www.jstor.org/stable/20057712

Gray, J. (2018, August 8). *New project:* What can citizen-generated data do? Research collaboration around UN Sustainable Development Goals. Jonathan Gray. https://jonathangray.org/2018/08/08/what-can-citizen-generated-data-do/

Knight, M. (2015). Data journalism in the UK: A preliminary analysis of form and content. *Journal of Media Practice, 16,* 55–72. https://doi.org/10.1080/14682753.2015.1015801

Krippendorff, K. (2016). Data. In K. B. Jensen & R. T. Craig (Eds.), *The international encyclopedia of communication theory and philosophy, vol. 1: A–D* (pp. 484–489). Wiley Blackwell. https://doi.org/10.1002/9781118766804.wbiect104

Loosen, W. (2018). *Four forms of datafied journalism. Journalism's response to the datafication of society.* (Communicative Figurations Working Paper No. 18). https://www.kofi.uni-bremen.de/fileadmin/user_upload/Arbeitspapiere/CoFi_EWP_No-18_Loosen.pdf

Loosen, W., Reimer, J., & De Silva-Schmidt, F. (2020). Data-driven reporting: An on-going (r)evolution? An analysis of projects nominated for the Data Journalism Awards 2013–2016. *Journalism, 21*(9), 1246–1263. https://doi.org/10.1177/1464884917735691

Parasie, S. (2015). Data-driven revelation? *Digital Journalism, 3*(3), 364–380. https://doi.org/10.1080/21670811.2014.976408

Royal, C., & Blasingame, D. (2015). Data journalism: An explication. *#ISOJ, 5*(1), 24–46. https://isojjournal.wordpress.com/2015/04/15/data-journalism-an-explication/

Tabary, C., Provost, A.-M., & Trottier, A. (2016). Data journalism's actors, practices and skills: A case study from Quebec. *Journalism: Theory, Practice & Criticism, 17*(1), 66–84. https://doi.org/10.1177/1464884915593245

Wahl-Jorgensen, K. (2013). The strategic ritual of emotionality: A case study of Pulitzer Prize–winning articles. *Journalism: Theory, Practice & Criticism, 14*(1), 129–145. https://doi.org/10.1177/1464884912448918

Young, M. L., Hermida, A., & Fulda, J. (2018). What makes for great data journalism? A content analysis of Data Journalism Awards finalists 2012–2015. *Journalism Practice, 12*(1), 115–135. https://doi.org/10.1080/17512786.2016.1270171

About the Author

Wiebke Loosen is a senior journalism researcher at the Leibniz Institute for Media Research/Hans-Bredow-Institut (HBI) in Hamburg, as well as a Professor at the University of Hamburg.

50. Beyond Clicks and Shares: How and Why to Measure the Impact of Data Journalism Projects

Lindsay Green-Barber

Abstract

This chapter argues that data journalism is uniquely positioned to have an impact on individuals, networks and institutions, and strategies for measuring the impact of this work are proposed.

Keywords: impact, social science, impact measurement, analytics, data journalism, audience engagement

Journalism and Impact

While many journalists balk at the idea of journalistic impact, in fact contemporary journalism, as a profession, is built on a foundation of impact: To inform the public so we can be civically engaged and hold the powerful to account. And while journalists worry that thinking about, talking about, strategizing for and measuring the positive (and negative) impact of their work will get too close to crossing the red line from journalism into advocacy, practitioners and commentators alike have spent many column inches and pixels hand-wringing about the negative effects of "fake news," misinformation and partisan reporting on individuals, our society and democracy. In other words, while journalists want to avoid talking about the impact of their work, they recognize the serious social, political and cultural impacts of "fake news."

What's more, prior to the professionalization of journalism in the late 19th and early 20th centuries, journalism was a practice in influence, supported by political parties and produced with the express goal of supporting

Bounegru, L. and J. Gray (eds.), *The Data Journalism Handbook: Towards a Critical Data Practice*. Amsterdam: Amsterdam University Press, 2021
DOI 10.5117/9789462989511_CH50

the party and ensuring its candidates were elected (Pitt & Green-Barber, 2017). Thus, in a historical perspective, journalism's professionalization and embrace of (the myth of) neutrality are actually quite new (Groseclose & Milyo, 2005; Hamilton, 2004). And journalism's striving for "neutrality" was not a normative decision, but rather a function of changing economic models and a need to appeal to the largest possible audience in order to generate revenue (Hamilton, 2004).

Given the concurrent and intimately related crises of the news industry business model and lack of public trust in media in the United States and Western Europe, one might argue that journalism's turn away from acknowledging its impact has been an abdication of responsibility, at best, and a failure, at worst.

But there are signs of hope. In recent years, some media organizations have begun to embrace the fact that they are influential in society. The proliferation of non-profit media, often supported by mission-driven philanthropic foundations and individuals, has created a Petri dish for impact experimentation. Many commercial media have also come around to the idea that communicating the positive impact of their work with audiences is a strategy for building trust and loyalty, which will hopefully translate into increases in revenue. For example, in 2017, *The Washington Post* added "Democracy Dies in Darkness" to its masthead, embracing (and advertising) its role in our political system. And CNN created an "Impact Your World" section on its website, connecting world events, its reporting, stories of "impact" and pathways for audience members to take action, from hashtag campaigns to donations.[1]

Media organizations have also begun to try new strategies to maximize the positive impact of their work, as well as to use research methods and metrics different from those used for advertising to understand the effectiveness of these strategies. While, in some cases, digital metrics can be useful proxies for impact measurement, advertising metrics like unique page views or even more advanced analytics like time spent on a page are meant to measure the reach of content without consideration of the effects of this content on an individual.

I would like to propose a framework for media impact that is a change in the status quo as a result of an intervention and that includes four types of impact: On individuals, on networks, on institutions and on public discourse. These types of impact are interrelated. For example, as journalism often assumes, reporting can increase individuals' level of knowledge about an

---

1   https://edition.cnn.com/specials/impact-your-world

issue, resulting in them voting in a particular way and ultimately affecting institutions. Or, a report may have immediate effects on institutions, such as a firing or a restructuring, which then trickles down to impact individuals. However, impact that is catalyzed by journalism often takes time and involves complex social processes.

Different types of journalism are better equipped for different types of impact. For example, James T. Hamilton shows that investigative reporting can save institutions money by uncovering malfeasance, corruption or wrongdoing and spurring change. And documentary film has proven to be particularly effective in generating new and/or strengthened advocacy networks to promote change (Green-Barber, 2014).

The remainder of this chapter explores the relationship between data journalism and impact, demonstrating how data journalism can contribute to various types of social change. It then suggests methods for how data journalism's effectiveness might be measured, and what journalists and news organizations can do with this information.

Why Data Journalism

While journalists employ data journalism for many reasons, there are two that come to the fore: First, to provide credible evidence to support claims made in storytelling; and second, to present information to audiences as data, rather than text-based narrative. The practice of data journalism is built on a foundational value judgement that data is credible, and, by extension, that a journalistic product that includes data reporting is credible—and potentially more so than it would be without.

Data reporting that is used to communicate information as static numbers, data, charts, graphs or other visuals is similar to other journalistic formats (i.e., text, video, audio) in that it is essentially a linear form of communicating selected information to an audience. Data reporting that is made available to audiences through a news interactive is a unique form of storytelling in that it assumes an audience member will interact with the data, ask their own questions and search for answers in the data at hand. Thus, the "story" depends upon the user as much as it does on the journalism.

Even this rough-hewn version of data journalism implicates all four types of impact.

Individuals

Data journalism tends to focus on individual audience members as the potential unit for change, providing audiences with credible information so that they may become more knowledgeable and, by extension, make more informed decisions. And while data journalism as a scaffolding for traditional, linear storytelling increases audience trust in the content, news or data interactives provide the greatest potential for data journalism to have an impact at the level of individuals.

With a data interactive, that is, a "big interactive database that tells a news story," a user can generate their own question and query the data to look for answers (Klein, 2012). Media companies often assume that data interactives will allow audiences to do deep dives and explore data, find relevant information, and tell stories. In an analysis of data interactives by one news organization, the author of this chapter found that the most successful data apps, meaning those that were highly trafficked and deeply explored, were part of a full editorial package that included other content, offered the ability to look up geographically local or relevant data, had a high degree of interactivity, were aesthetically pleasing and well-designed, and loaded quickly (Green-Barber, 2015b).

ProPublica's Dollars for Docs is a classic example of data journalism in that it accesses significant amounts of data, in this case about pharmaceutical and medical device companies' payments to doctors, structures the data, and presents it to audiences as an interactive database with the goal to inspire individuals to conduct their own research and possibly take action.[2] The project instructs audiences to "use this tool" to search for payments to their doctors, and, in a sidebar, says, "Patients, Take Action. We want to know how you've used or might use this information in your day to day lives. Have you talked to your doctor? Do you plan to? Tell us."[3]

Networks

Data journalism provides credible information that can be used by networks (formal and/or informal) to strengthen their positions and work. For example, advocacy organizations often use data reporting to bolster their claims in

---

2   https://projects.propublica.org/docdollars/

3   https://propublica.forms.fm/was-the-dollars-for-docs-information-helpful-tell-us-how-you-will-use-it/forms/2249<

public appeals or in legal proceedings, especially in cases where the data is not publicly available. Journalism's practice of requesting access to data that is not available in the public realm, analyzing this data and publishing the findings, absorbs costs that would otherwise be insurmountable for individuals or networks (Hamilton, 2016).

Institutions

Data journalism can generate reporting that institutions work hard to keep hidden, as they are evidence of corruption, malfeasance, wrongdoing and/or incompetence. When this information comes to light, there is pressure on institutions to reform—resulting from the threats associated with elections on politicians, or market forces on publicly held companies.

For example, the International Consortium of Investigative Journalists' Panama Papers collaborative investigation analyzed more than 11.5 million records to uncover "politicians from more than 50 countries connected to offshore companies in 21 tax havens."[4] This investigation led to the resignation of politicians, such as Iceland's prime minister, Sigmundur Gunnlaugsson, investigations of others, like Pakistan's former prime minister, Nawaz Sharif (who was sentenced to ten years in jail in 2018), and countless other institutional responses.

Public discourse

Because data journalism can often be broken down into smaller parts, whether geographically, demographically or by other factors, the data can be used to tell different stories by different media. In this way, data journalism can be localized to generate a shift in public conversation about issues across geographic locations, demographic groups or other social boundaries.

The Center for Investigative Reporting has published national interactive data sets about the US Department of Veterans Affairs (VA), one with average wait times for veterans trying to access medical care at VA hospitals, and a second with the number of opiates being prescribed to veterans by VA systems. In both cases, local journalism organizations used the data sets as the baseline to do local reporting about the issues.

---

4   https://www.icij.org/investigations/panama-papers/

So, How Can Data Journalists Strategize for Impact?

You have done the hard work: You got access to data, you crunched the numbers, you structured the data and you have an important story to tell. Now what?

A high-impact strategy for data journalism might follow the following five steps:

Set goals. What might happen as a result of your project? Who or what has the power and/or incentive to address any wrongdoing? Who should have access to the information you are bringing to light? Ask yourself these questions to decide what type or types of impact are reasonable for your project.

Content. Once you have goals for your project, identify the important target audiences for the work. What source of news and information do these audiences trust? How might they best access the information? Do they need an interactive, or will a linear story be more effective?

Engagement. How will you and your news organization engage with audiences, and how will audiences engage with your work? For example, if you have identified a news organization other than your own as a trusted source of information for a target audience, collaborate. If your data interactive has important information for an NGO community, hold a webinar explaining how to use it.

Strategic research. Depending upon your goals and content and engagement plans, select the appropriate research methods and/or indicators in order to track progress and understand what is working and what is not working. While media often refer to "measuring" the impact of their work, I prefer the term "strategic research," as both qualitative and quantitative research methods should be considered. The sooner you can identify research methods and indicators, the better your information will be. (The subsequent section discusses measurement options in greater depth.)

Repeat. You have invested time and resources in your data journalism reporting, content, engagement and measurement. What worked? What will you change next time? What questions are still outstanding? Share these learnings with your team and the field to push the next project further ahead.

How Do We "Measure" the Impact of Our Work?

As alluded to earlier, media impact research has been dominated by advertising metrics. However, ad metrics, like page views, time on page and bounce rate are potential proxies for some impact. They are meant to measure the total exposure of content to individuals without concern for their opinions about the issues, whether or not they have learned new information, or their intent to take action based upon the content. When considering the impact of content on individuals, networks, institutions and public discourse, however, there are other innovative qualitative and quantitative methods that can be used to better understand success and failure in this area. This section explores a handful of promising research methods for understanding the impact of data journalism.

Analytics. Media metrics can be used as proxies for desired outcomes, such as increased awareness or increased knowledge. However, media companies should be intentional and cautious when attributing change to analytics. For example, if a data journalism project has as its goal to spur institutional change, unique page views are not an appropriate metric of success; mentions of the data by public officials in documents would be a better indicator.

Experimental research. Experimental research creates constant conditions under which the effects of an intervention can be tested. The Center for Media Engagement at the University of Texas at Austin has conducted fascinating experimental research about the effects of news homepage layout on audience recall and affect, and of solutions-oriented reporting on audience affect for news organizations. Technology companies are constantly testing the effects of different interactive elements on users. Journalism organizations can do the same to better understand the effects of data interactives on users, whether in partnership with universities or by working directly with researchers in-house from areas like marketing, business development and audience engagement.

Surveys. Surveys, while not the most leading-edge research method, are a proven way to gather information from individuals about changes in interest, knowledge, opinion and action. Organizations can be creative with survey design, making use of technology that allows for things like return visit-triggered pop-ups or tracking newsletter click-through to generate a survey pool of potential respondents.

Content analysis. Content analysis is a research method used to determine changes in discourse, over time. This method can be employed to any text-based corpus, making it extremely flexible. For example, when an organization produces content with the goal of influencing national public discourse, it could conduct a post-project content analysis on the top ten national newspapers to determine the influence of its stories. If the goal is to influence state legislature, an organization can use post-project content analysis on publicly available legislative agendas (Green-Barber, 2015a). Or, if the goal is to make data available to advocacy networks, post-project content analysis could be used to analyze an organization's newsletters.

Content analysis can be conducted in at least three ways. At the most basic level, a news organization can search for a project's citations in order to document where and when it has been cited. For example, many reporters create Google News Alerts using a keyword from their reporting, together with their surname, in order to determine in what other outlets a project is picked up. This is not methodologically sound, but it provides interesting information and can be used to do a gut check about impact. This process may also generate additional questions about a project's impact that are worth a deeper dive. Many organizations use news clipping services like Google News Alerts or Meltwater for this purpose.

Rigorous content analysis would identify key words, data and/or phrases in a project, then analyze their prevalence pre- and post-publication in a finite corpus of text to document change. Computational text analysis goes a step further and infers shifts in discourse by advanced counting and analysis techniques. These more rigorous content analysis methods likely require a news organization to partner with trained researchers.

Looking Ahead: Why Journalists Should Care about the Impact of Data Journalism

To stay relevant, journalism must not only accept that it has an impact on society, but embrace that fact. By working to understand the ecosystem of change in which journalism functions, and its specific role within this system, the industry can work to maximize its positive impact and demonstrate its value to audiences.

Data journalists, with their understanding of the value and importance of both quantitative and qualitative data, are well positioned for this endeavour. By articulating the goals of data journalism projects, developing creative audience engagement and distribution strategies, and building sophisticated methods for measuring success into these projects, reporters can lead this movement from within.

Works Cited

Green-Barber, L. (2014). Waves of change: The case of rape in the fields. The Center for Investigative Reporting. https://www.documentcloud.org/documents/1278731-waves-of-change-the-case-of-rape-in-the-fields.html

Green-Barber, L. (2015a). Changing the conversation: The VA backlog. The Center for Investigative Reporting. https://s3.amazonaws.com/uploads-cironline-org/uploaded/uploads/VA+Backlog+White+Paper+11.10.14.pdf

Green-Barber, L. (2015b). What makes a news interactive successful? Preliminary lessons from the Center for Investigative Reporting. The Center for Investigative Reporting. https://s3-us-west-2.amazonaws.com/revealnews.org/uploads/CIR+News+Interactives+White+Paper.pdf

Groseclose, T., & Milyo, J. (2005). A measure of media bias. *The Quarterly Journal of Economics, 120*(4), 1191–1237. https://doi.org/10.1162/003355305775097542

Hamilton, J. T. (2004). *All the news that's fit to sell: How the market transforms information into news.* Princeton University Press.

Hamilton, J. T. (2016). *Democracy's detectives: The economics of investigative journalism.* Harvard University Press.

Klein, S. (2012). News apps at ProPublica. In J. Gray, L. Chambers, & L. Bounegru (Eds.), *The data journalism handbook: How journalists can use data to improve the news* (pp. 185–186). O'Reilly Media.

Pitt, F., & Green-Barber, L. (2017). *The case for media impact: A case study of ICIJ's radical collaboration strategy.* Tow Center for Digital Journalism. https://doi.org/10.7916/D85Q532V

About the Author

Lindsay Green-Barber is the founder of Impact Architects, a consulting firm dedicated to developing high impact journalism, media and communication strategies, and to using rigorous social science research methods to understand the impact of this work.

51. Data Journalism: In Whose Interests?

Mary Lynn Young and Candis Callison

Abstract
This chapter asks whose interests are served by data journalism projects and questions the imagined audiences, particularly in regard to recent crime-related data journalism that purports to serve the public good. It draws on the work of Indigenous scholars who suggest that refusal, misrepresentation, colonialism and data collection are persistent challenges for journalism and require better ethical diagnostics.

Keywords: colonialism, Indigenous, data journalism, crime content, ethics, science and technology studies

One of the early significant contributions to data journalism in the United States was chicagocrime.org, an online map of Chicago layered with crime statistics (Anderson, 2018; Holovaty, 2005, 2008). According to its founder, Adrian Holovaty, chicagocrime.org, which launched in 2005, was one of the

> original map mashups, combining crime data from the Chicago Police Department with Google Maps. It offered a page and RSS feed for every city block in Chicago and a multitude of ways to browse crime data—by type, by location type (e.g., sidewalk or apartment), by ZIP code, by street/ address, by date, and even by an arbitrary route. (Holovaty, 2008)[1]

A few years later, the *Los Angeles Times* launched the journalism blog Homicide Report, which drew from police data to generate homicide blog posts about each of the more than 900 homicides in the county. Both projects

---

[1] It was an early iteration of the eulogized community data journalism site, EveryBlock, which was launched by Holovaty in 2008, and acquired by *MSNBC.com* in 2009 (Holovaty, A. (2013, 7 February). RIP EveryBlock. Adrian Holovaty. http://www.holovaty.com/writing/ rip-everyblock/).

Bounegru, L. and J. Gray (eds.), *The Data Journalism Handbook: Towards a Critical Data Practice.* Amsterdam: Amsterdam University Press, 2021
DOI 10.5117/9789462989511_CH51

utilized crime data and geography in major metropolitan US centres. And both provide insight into persistent critiques and challenges related to the aims and impacts of data-driven journalism, and journalism in general.

Holovaty's motives for launching chicagocrime.org were in keeping with journalism's goals of generating local "news you can use" along with its increasingly technical identity and focus on "cool technical things" (Holovaty, 2005). The goals of Homicide Report's founder, *Los Angeles Times* journalist Jill Leovy, were more critical. Leovy wanted to account for all homicides in Los Angeles County in order to deconstruct traditional journalism norms and practices that saw only certain homicides covered (Leovy, 2008; Young & Hermida, 2015).[2] In a 2015 interview with National Public Radio's *Fresh Air*, Leovy articulated her motives for launching the Homicide Report as a response to structural bias in the news, and her frustration that newspaper reporting on crime "paled to the reality so much":

> The newspaper's job is to cover unusual events, and when it comes to homicide, that always ends up meaning that you're covering the very low edges of the bell curve. And you're never the bulge in the middle because that's implicitly the routine homicides, even though, of course, a homicide is never routine. Those homicides have gone on in the same form, in the same ways, for so long in America, particularly American cities, that they are the wallpaper of urban life. They are taken for granted, and it's very difficult to make them into a narrative and a story that works for a newspaper. (Leovy, 2015)

By combining her experience as a crime journalist with the endless, less hierarchical space of digital journalism (compared to a newspaper front page) and access to public data, Leovy (2008) envisioned a news report that represented information about all the killings in the county, "mostly of young Latinos and, most disproportionately, of young Black men," with as much equivalence as possible (Leovy, 2015). According to Leovy (2008), the response was powerful: "Readers responded strongly. 'Oh my God,' began one of the first posts by a reader. 'The sheer volume is shocking,' wrote another. 'Almost like they're disposable people,' wrote a third."

As novel articulations of a growing subspecialty, these examples of data journalism received commendation and acclaim for innovation. The site, chicagocrime.org, according to Holovaty (2008), was even part of an exhibit at the Museum of Modern Art in New York. But questions about whose

---

2   It was later re-envisioned as an algorithmic journalism blog.

interests and who was the imagined audience of these signature projects and others that purport to share data in the interests of the public good have remained largely silent.

Science and technology studies (STS) scholars have repeatedly demonstrated how harmful relationships between vulnerable populations and certain kinds of data can and do persist even while technology is heralded as new and transformative (Nelson, 2016; Reardon, 2009; TallBear, 2013).

Data journalism's positivist orientation (Coddington, 2019) is implicated as well despite extensive critique about the social construction of race and the role of technology in replicating White supremacy (Benjamin, 2019; Noble, 2018). In addition, studies of journalism representations, norms, practices, economics and crime news indicate a long history of racialization, social control, harm and ongoing colonialism(s) (Anderson & Robertson, 2011; Callison & Young, 2020; Ericson et al., 1991; Hamilton, 2000; Schudson, 2005; Stabile, 2006).

This chapter briefly explores what structures are being supported and whose data is more likely to be gathered—or not—while raising questions about journalists' need to be able to incorporate an "ethics of refusal" as they decide whether and how to employ data journalism (Simpson, 2014; TallBear, 2013). As Butler argues, "there are ways of distributing vulnerability, differential forms of allocation that make some populations more subject to arbitrary violence than others" (Butler, 2004).

We draw from Coddington (2014, 2019) for our definition of data journalism as quantitative journalism consisting of three forms: Data journalism, computational journalism and computer-assisted reporting. Persistent critiques of scientific practices and societal institutions that bring together research and data collection rationales, new technologies, and social issues, are relevant to all three forms of data journalism, as are questions about vulnerability and whose interests are being supported.

STS and Indigenous studies scholar TallBear studied genomic research among Indigenous populations in the US and found that many of the stereotypes and colonial narratives associated with the notion of "vanishing Indians" were part of the rationale for research in addition to statements about potential identity (i.e., knowing about migration and connectedness of ancestors) and health benefits. She points out that,

> While the notion of genetic connectedness may have replaced that of racial hierarchy in the lexicon of mainstream science, relations of power, difference, and hierarchy remain integral to our broader culture, to our institutions and structures, and to the culture in which science gets done and which science helps produce. (TallBear, 2007, p. 413)

What TallBear argues is that undergirding scientific notions of machinic or lab-based objectivity are institutional prerogatives, historical and ongoing relations with communities, and cultural frameworks that drive both rationales for research and articulations of intended benefits. The questions of "in whose interest and why" must always be asked—and in some cases, research and/or data mining analyses are worth refusing because meaning-making processes are predicated on entrenched notions of race, gender and class. What TallBear calls "the colonial assumptions and practices that continue to inform science," we would argue, similarly inform journalism and, by extension, data journalism (TallBear, 2007, p. 423).

Indigenous peoples have also been subject to contending with extensive anthropological and government archives and consistent media misrepresentations and stereotypes (Anderson & Robertson, 2011) in the service of varied forms and histories of settler colonialism (Tuck & Yang, 2012; Wolfe, 2006). Hence, the stakes for data journalism specifically as an extension of notions of machine-based objectivity are profound. In Simpson's (2014) critique of anthropology, she suggests that Mohawk communities regularly engage in forms of refusal when it comes to both contending with such archives and participating in research centred on settler colonial institutions and frameworks. Refusal in Simpson's framework is multidirectional: A refusal to be eliminated, a refusal to internalize the misrepresentations of your identity, culture and lands, and a refusal to conform to expectations of difference such that state or other (we add in this case, media) recognition is conveyed on you or your group.

Such arguments by Indigenous scholars pose direct challenges to intentions, rationales and practices of data journalism, as they centre questions of history and power. These questions pertain not just to the state, but also to the role of journalism in maintaining social orders that support state aims and goals *and* structures and ideologies such as patriarchy, settler colonialism and White supremacy (Callison & Young, 2020).

A further complication for Indigenous communities is that both data and accurate media representations are almost always difficult to locate—as well as the fact that data is a reflection of the institutional contexts in which the data is gathered, archived and accessed.[3] Ericson's critique of police statistics as not reflecting the social reality of crime but rather the "cultural, legal, and social constructs produced . . . for organizational purposes" (Ericson, 1998, p. 93) is relevant for journalists focused solely on data wrangling. For example, Laguna Pueblo journalist Jenni Monet (2020)

---

3   For more on these issues, see Kukutai and Walter's chapter in this volume.

characterizes Indigenous communities in the United States as "Asterisk nations," which are those for whom no data exists. Especially in Alaska, many social data charts will have an asterisk saying there is no data for Alaska natives. Digital media, like Facebook, offer hopeful alternative platforms that might be seen as a tool for journalism to engage Indigenous audiences and their concerns and to create meaningful and accurate representations that address structural inequities and data gaps (Monet, 2018). Again then, the question of whether and how to participate revolves around who benefits, what processes are utilized in data collection and whose meaning-making processes prevail.

For journalism, broadly speaking, meaning-making processes are often linked to issues of dissent, deviance, conflict, or "the behaviour of a thing or person straying from the norm" (Ericson, 1998, p. 84) within a positivist orientation. Journalism's role in social ordering has had and continues to have material impacts and harmful effects on populations constructed as deviant (Callison & Young, 2020; Rhodes, 1993; Stabile, 2006). Stabile's historical study of crime news in the United States, which includes newspapers, television coverage of crime and radio programmes, and the relationship of crime news to race, articulates the impact of norms of deviance on structurally vulnerable populations within an ideological context of White supremacy and for-profit journalism. She focuses on race and gender as they "are among the most important sites for struggles over the historical meaning assigned to deviance" (Stabile, 2006, p. 5), arguing that media supports the "processes of criminalization" of Black men by the state and its agents such as the police (Stabile, 2006, p. 3). An example is how media amplify and reinforce police data-gathering practices by focusing on specific crimes, such as carjackings, offenders and victims. She finds an "acquisitive and violent white society that flourished in the USA, in which fictions of white terror have consistently displaced the materialities of white terrorism" (Stabile, 2006, p. 2). Here Carey's (1974) analysis of journalism as about generating enemies and allies might be understood as also relevant to the profession's institutional relationships to capitalism and the state in North America, which include state genocide and ongoing colonialisms. Combined with journalism's allergy to the notion that facts and knowledge are socially constructed, journalism—and news in particular—becomes the fascia by which discourses of social ordering have been and are co-generated, replicated and also potentially transformed (Dumit & O'Connor, 2016).

On these critical points, the literatures from journalism, criminology, STS and other disciplines raise a set of urgent concerns that have been underaddressed with regards to data journalism. Scholars have spent more time on typologies (Coddington, 2019), the state of data journalism (Heravi, 2017), and effects of data journalism on broader journalistic epistemologies, cultures, practices and identities (Anderson, 2018; Borges-Rey, 2020; Gynnild, 2014; Lewis & Usher, 2014; Young & Hermida, 2015) than on its wider effects and consequences. Few scholars have raised questions related to power, with the exception of research by Borges-Rey (2016, 2020), who integrates a political economy analysis of the growth of data journalism in the United Kingdom.

However, data journalism can point to some impacts, such as in this statement from Holovaty:

> A lot of good has come out of chicagocrime.org. At the local level, countless Chicago residents have contacted me to express their thanks for the public service. Community groups have brought print-outs of the site to their police-beat meetings, and passionate citizens have taken the site's reports to their aldermen to point out troublesome intersections where the city might consider installing brighter street lights. (Holovaty, 2008)

In this case, community groups have taken the data and created their own meaning and rationale for action. But how this works on a larger scale, in rural areas far from the centres of power and media, in communities already disproportionately surveilled, and in cases where communities are not well represented in newsrooms that remain predominantly White in both Canada and the United States, requires a broader set of ethical diagnostics (Callison & Young, 2020). Given these examples and evidence from critical literatures outside of journalism studies, potential harm could and should take priority over norms such as "news you can use" and technologically fuelled experimentations. The way journalists cover crime news from a data perspective requires deep understanding of the consequences as well as problems of considering intentions that are only internal to journalism, evidence of success and rationales of innovation.[4] Ethical diagnostics need to better account for the notion of refusal, the long histories of misrepresentation and service to colonialism by journalism, and the uneven processes by which meaning-making and data collection occur. In whose interests and why become essential questions for journalists in considering how, where, and for whom data journalism is making a contribution.

4   See Loosen's chapter in this volume.

Works Cited

Anderson, C. W. (2018). *Apostles of certainty: Data journalism and the politics of doubt.* Oxford University Press.

Anderson, M. C., & Robertson, C. L. (2011). *Seeing red: A history of natives in Canadian newspapers.* University of Manitoba Press.

Benjamin, R. (2019). *Race after technology: Abolitionist tools for the New Jim Code.* Polity Press.

Borges-Rey, E. (2016). Unravelling data journalism: A study of data journalism practice in British newsrooms. *Journalism Practice, 10*(7), 833–843. https://doi.org/10.1080/17512786.2016.1159921

Borges-Rey, E. (2020). Towards an epistemology of data journalism in the devolved nations of the United Kingdom: Changes and continuities in materiality, performativity and reflexivity. *Journalism, 21*(7), 915–932. https://doi.org/10.1177/1464884917693864

Butler, J. (2004). *Precarious life: The powers of mourning and violence.* Verso.

Callison, C., & Young, M. L. (2020). *Reckoning: Journalism's limits and possibilities.* Oxford University Press.

Carey, J. W. (1974). The problem of journalism history. *Journalism History, 1*(1), 3–27. https://doi.org/10.1080/00947679.1974.12066714

Coddington, M. (2014). Clarifying journalism's quantitative turn. *Digital Journalism, 3*, 331–348. https://doi.org/10.1080/21670811.2014.976400

Coddington, M. (2019). Defining and mapping data journalism and computational journalism: A review of typologies and themes. In S. Eldridge & B. Franklin (Eds.), *The Routledge handbook of developments in digital journalism studies* (pp. 225–236). Routledge. https://doi.org/10.4324/9781315270449-18

Dumit, J., & O'Connor, K. (2016). The senses and sciences of fascia: A practice as research investigation. In L. Hunter, E. Krimmer, & P. Lichtenfels (Eds.), *Sentient performativities of embodiment: Thinking alongside the human* (pp. 35–54). Rowman & Littlefield.

Ericson, R. (1998). How journalists visualize fact. *The Annals of the American Academy of Political and Social Science, 560*, 83–95. https://doi.org/10.1177/0002716298560001007

Ericson, R., Baranek, P. M., & Chan, J. B. L. (1991). *Representing order: Crime, law, and justice in the news media.* University of Toronto Press.

Gynnild, A. (2014). Journalism innovation leads to innovation journalism: The impact of computational exploration on changing mindsets. *Journalism, 15*(6), 713–730. https://doi.org/10.1177/1464884913486393

Hamilton, J. T. (2000). *Channeling violence: The economic market for violent television programming.* Princeton University Press.

Heravi, B. (2017, August 1). State of data journalism globally: First insights into the global data journalism survey. *Medium*. https://medium.com/ucd-ischool/state-of-data-journalism-globally-cb2f4696ad3d

Holovaty, A. (2005, May 18). Announcing chicagocrime.org. Adrian Holovaty. http://www.holovaty.com/writing/chicagocrime.org-launch/

Holovaty, A. (2008, January 31). In memory of chicagocrime.org. Adrian Holovaty. http://www.holovaty.com/writing/chicagocrime.org-tribute/

Leovy, J. (2008, February 4). Unlimited space for untold sorrow. *Los Angeles Times*. https://www.latimes.com/archives/la-xpm-2008-feb-04-me-homicide4-story.html

Leovy, J. (2015, January 25). "Ghettoside" explores why murders are invisible in Los Angeles [interview with Dave Davies]. *Fresh Air*. https://www.npr.org/2015/01/26/381589023/ghettoside-explores-why-murders-are-invisible-in-los-angeles

Lewis, S. C., & Usher, N. (2014). Code, collaboration, and the future of journalism: A case study of the hacks/hackers global network. *Digital Journalism*, *2*(3), 383–393. https://doi.org/10.1080/21670811.2014.895504

Monet, J. (2020, October 30). Native American voters could decide key Senate races while battling intense voter suppression. *Democracy Now!* https://www.democracynow.org/2020/10/30/jenni_monet_indigenous_sovereignty_2020

Monet, J. (2018b, March 23). #DeleteFacebook? Not in Indian Country. *Yes! Magazine*. https://www.yesmagazine.org/social-justice/2018/03/23/deletefacebook-not-in-indian-country

Nelson, A. (2016). *The social life of DNA: Race, reparations, and reconciliation after the genome*. Beacon Press

Noble, S. (2018). *Algorithms of oppression*. NYU Press.

Reardon, J. (2009). *Race to the finish: Identity and governance in an age of genomics*. Princeton University Press.

Rhodes, J. (1993). The visibility of race and media history. *Critical Studies in Mass Communication*, *10*(2), 184–190. https://doi.org/10.1080/15295039309366859

Schudson, M. (2005). Autonomy from what? In R. Benson & E. Neveu (Eds.), *Bourdieu and the journalistic field* (pp. 214–223). Polity Press.

Simpson, A. (2014). *Mohawk interruptus: Political life across the borders of settler states*. Duke University Press.

Simpson, A. (2016). The state is a man: Theresa Spence, Loretta Saunders and the gender of settler sovereignty. *Theory & Event*, *19*(4). https://muse.jhu.edu/article/633280

Stabile, C. (2006). *White victims, Black villains: Gender, race and crime news in US culture*. Routledge.

TallBear, K. (2007). Narratives of race and indigeneity in the genographic project. *The Journal of Law, Medicine & Ethics*, *35*(3), 412–424. https://doi.org/10.1111/j.1748-720X.2007.00164.x

TallBear, K. (2013). *Native American DNA: Tribal belonging and the false promise of genetic science*. University of Minnesota Press.

Tuck, E., & Yang, K. (2012). Decolonization is not a metaphor. *Decolonization: Indigeneity, Education & Society, 1*(1), 1–40.

Wolfe, P. (2006). Settler colonialism and the elimination of the native. *Journal of Genocide Research, 8*(4), 387–409. https://doi.org/10.1080/14623520601056240

Young, M. L., & Hermida, A. (2015). From Mr. and Mrs. Outlier to central tendencies. *Digital Journalism, 3*(3), 381–397. https://doi.org/10.1080/21670811.2014.976409

About the Authors

Mary Lynn Young is an Associate Professor in the School of Journalism, Writing, and Media, University of British Columbia.

Candis Callison is an Associate Professor in the School of Journalism, Writing, and Media and the Institute for Critical Indigenous Studies at the University of British Columbia.

52. Data Journalism With Impact

Paul Bradshaw

Abstract

Data journalism with impact: How and why impact is measured, how that has changed, and the factors shaping impact.

Keywords: impact, engagement, data journalism, analytics, investigative journalism, data quality

If you have not seen *Spotlight* (2015), the film about *The Boston Globe*'s investigation into institutional silence over child abuse, then you should watch it right now. More to the point—you should watch right through to the title cards at the end.[1]

A list scrolls down the screen. It details the dozens and dozens of places where abuse scandals have been uncovered since the events of the film, from Akute, Nigeria, to Wollongong, Australia. But the title cards also cause us to pause in our celebrations: One of the key figures involved in the scandal, it says, was reassigned to "one of the highest ranking Roman Catholic churches in the world."

This is the challenge of impact in data journalism: Is raising awareness of a problem "impact"? Does the story have to result in penalty or reward? Visible policy change? How important is impact? And to whom?

These last two questions are worth tackling first. Traditionally, impact has been important for two main reasons: Commercial and cultural. Commercially, measures of impact such as brand awareness and high audience figures can contribute directly to a publication's profit margin through advertising (increasing both price and volume) and subscription/copy sales (Rusbridger, 2018). Culturally, however, stories with impact have also given

---

[1]   https://www.imdb.com/title/tt1895587/quotes/qt3112625?mavIsAdult=false&mavCanonic alUrl=, https%3A%2F%2Fwww.imdb.com%2Ftitle%2Ftt1895587%2Fquotes

Bounegru, L. and J. Gray (eds.), *The Data Journalism Handbook: Towards a Critical Data Practice*. Amsterdam: Amsterdam University Press, 2021

DOI 10.5117/9789462989511_CH52

news organizations and individual journalists "bragging rights" among their peers. Both, as we shall see, have become more complicated.

Measurements of impact in journalism have, historically, been limited: Aggregate sales and audience figures, a limited pool of industry prizes, and the occasional audience survey were all that publishers could draw on. Now, of course, the challenge lies not only in a proliferation of metrics, but in a proliferation of business models, too, with the expansion of non-profit news provision in particular leading to an increasing emphasis on impact and discussion about how that might be measured (Schlemmer, 2016). Furthermore, the ability to measure impact on a story-by-story basis has meant it is no longer editors who are held responsible for audience impact, but journalists, too.

Measuring Impact by the Numbers

Perhaps the easiest measure of impact is sheer *reach*: Data-driven interactives like the BBC's "7 Billion People and You: What's Your Number?"[2] engaged millions of readers in a topical story; while at one point in 2012 Nate Silver's data journalism was reaching one in five visitors to *The New York Times* (Byers, 2012).

Some will sneer at such crude measures—but they are important. If journalists were once criticized for trying to impress their peers at the expense of their audience, modern journalism is at least expected to prove that it can connect with that audience. In most cases this proof is needed for advertisers, but even publicly funded universal news providers like the BBC need it, too, to demonstrate that they are meeting requirements for funding.

Engagement is reach's more sophisticated relation, and here data journalism does well, too: At one editors' conference for newspaper publisher Reach, for example, it was revealed that simply adding a piece of data visualization to a page can increase dwell time (the amount of time a person spends on a page) by a third. Data-driven interactivity can transform the dullest of subjects: In 2015 the same company's David Higgerson noted that more than 200,000 people put their postcodes into an interactive widget by their data team based on deprivation statistics—a far higher number, he pointed out, "than I would imagine [for] a straight-forward 'data tells us x' story" (Higgerson, 2015).

Engagement is particularly important to organizations who rely on advertising (rates can be increased where engagement is high), but also to

2   https://www.bbc.com/news/world-15391515

those for whom subscriptions, donations and events are important: These tend to be connected with engagement, too.

The expansion of non-profit funding and grants often comes with an explicit requirement to monitor or demonstrate impact which is about more than just reach. *Change* and *action*, in particular—political or legal—are often referenced. The International Consortium of Investigative Journalists (ICIJ), for example, highlight the impact of their Panama Papers investigation in the fact that it resulted in "at least 150 inquiries, audits or investigations . . . in 79 countries," alongside the more traditional metric of almost 20 awards, including the Pulitzer Prize (Fitzgibbon & Díaz-Struck, 2016; "ICIJ's Awards," n.d.). In the United Kingdom, a special place is reserved in data journalism history for the MPs' expenses scandal. This not only saw *The Telegraph* newspaper leading the news agenda for weeks, but also led to the formation of a new body: The Independent Parliamentary Standards Authority (IPSA). The body now publishes open data on politicians' expense claims, allowing them to be better held to account and leading to further data journalism.

But policy can be much broader than politics. The lending policies of banks affect millions of people, and were famously held to account in the late 1980s in the US by Bill Dedman in his Pulitzer Prize-winning "Colour of Money" series of articles. In identifying racially divided loan practices ("redlining"), the data-driven investigation also led to political, financial and legal change, with probes, new financing, lawsuits and the passing of new laws among the follow-ups.[3]

Fast-forward 30 years and you can see a very modern version of this approach: *ProPublica*'s "Machine Bias" series shines a light on algorithmic accountability, while the Bureau Local tapped into its network to crowd-source information on algorithmically targeted "dark ads" on social media (McClenaghan, 2017). Both have helped contribute to change in a number of Facebook's policies, while *ProPublica*'s methods were adopted by a fair housing group in establishing the basis for a lawsuit against the social network (Angwin & Tobin, 2018; "Improving Enforcement and Promoting Diversity," 2017; Jalonick, 2017). As the policies of algorithms become increasingly powerful in our lives—from influencing the allocation of police, to Uber pricing in non-White areas—holding these to account is becoming as important as holding more traditional political forms of power to account, too (Chammah, 2016; Stark, 2016).

What is notable about some of these examples is that their impact relies upon—and is partly demonstrated by—collaboration with others. When

3   http://powerreporting.com/color/

the Bureau Local talk about impact, for example, they refer to the numbers of stories produced by members of its grassroots network, inspiring others to action, while the ICIJ lists the growing scale of its networks: "LuxLeaks (2014) involved more than 80 reporters in 26 countries. Swiss Leaks (2015) more than 140 reporters in 45 countries" (Cabra, 2017). The figure rises to more than 370 reporters in nearly 80 countries for the Panama Papers investigation: A hundred media organizations publishing 4,700 articles (Blau, 2016).

What is more, the data gathered and published as a result of investigations can become a source of impact itself: The Offshore Leaks database, the ICIJ points out, "is used regularly by academics, NGOs and tax agencies" (Cabra, 2017).

There is something notable about this shift from the pride of publishing to winning plaudits for acting as facilitators and organizers and database managers. As a result, collaboration has become a skill in itself: Many non-profit organizations have community or project management roles dedicated to building and maintaining relationships with contributors and partners, and journalism training increasingly reflects this shift, too.

Some of this can be traced back to the influence of early data journalism culture: Writing about the practice in Canada in 2016, Alfred Hermida and Mary Lynn Young (2017) noted "an evolving division of labor that prioritizes inter-organizational networked journalism relationships." And the influence was recognized further in 2018 when the Reuters Institute published a book on the rise of collaborative journalism, noting that "collaboration can become a story in itself, further increasing the impact of the journalism" (Sambrook, 2018).

Changing What We Count, How We Count It and Whether We Get It Right

Advanced technical skills are not necessarily required to create a story with impact. One of the longest-running data journalism projects, the Bureau of Investigative Journalism's "Drone Warfare" project, has been tracking US drone strikes for over five years.[4] Its core methodology boils down to one word: Persistence.[5] On a weekly basis Bureau reporters have turned "free text" reports into a structured data set that can be analyzed, searched and queried. That data—complemented by interviews with sources—has been

4   https://www.thebureauinvestigates.com/projects/drone-war
5   https://www.thebureauinvestigates.com/explainers/our-methodology

used by NGOs and the Bureau has submitted written evidence to the UK Parliament's Defence Committee.[6]

Counting the uncounted is a particularly important way that data journalism can make an impact—indeed, it is probably fair to say that it is data journalism's equivalent of "giving a voice to the voiceless." "The Migrants' Files," a project involving journalists from over 15 countries, was started after data journalists noted that there was "no usable database of people who died in their attempt to reach or stay in Europe" (The Migrants' Files, n.d.). Its impact has been to force other agencies into action: The International Organization for Migration and others now collect their own data.

Even when a government appears to be counting something, it can be worth investigating. While working with the BBC England Data Unit on an investigation into the scale of library cuts, for example, I experienced a moment of panic when I saw that a question was being asked in Parliament for data about the issue ("Libraries Lose a Quarter of Staff as Hundreds Close," 2016). Would the response scoop the months of work we had been doing? In fact, it didn't—instead, it established that the government itself knew less than we did about the true scale of those cuts, because they hadn't undertaken the depth of investigation that we had.

And sometimes the impact lies not in the mere existence of data, but in its representation: One project by the Mexican newspaper *El Universal*, "Ausencias Ignoradas" (Ignored absences), puts a face to over 4,500 women who have gone missing in the country in a decade (Crosas Batista, 2016). The data was there, but it hadn't been broken down to a "human" level. *Libération*'s "Meurtres conjugaux, des vies derrière les chiffres" does the same thing for domestic murders of women, and Ceyda Ulukaya's "Kadin Cinayetleri" project has mapped femicides in Turkey.[7]

When Data Is Bad: Impacting Data Quality

Some of my favourite projects as a data journalist have been those which highlighted, or led to the identification of, flawed or missing data. In 2016 the BBC England Data Unit looked at how many academy schools were following rules on transparency: We picked a random sample of a hundred

---

6   https://publications.parliament.uk/pa/cm201314/cmselect/cmdfence/772/772vw08.htm
7   https://www.liberation.fr/apps/2018/02/meurtres-conjugaux-derriere-les-chiffres/ (French language), http://kadincinayetleri.org/ (Turkish language), http://datadrivenjournalism.net/featured_projects/kadincinayetleri.org_putting_femicide_on_the_map<

academies and checked to see if they published a register of all their governors' interests, as required by official rules. One in five academies failed to do so—and as a result the regulator Ofcom took action against those we'd identified ("Academy Schools Breach Transparency Rules," 2016). But were they serious about ensuring this would continue? Returning to the story in later years would be important in establishing whether the impact was merely short-term, or more systemic.

Sometimes the impact of a data journalism project is a by-product—only identified when the story is ready and responses are being sought. When the Bureau Local appeared to find that 18 councils in England had nothing held over in their reserves to protect against financial uncertainty, and sought a response, it turned out the data was wrong. No one noticed the incorrect data, they reported. "Not the councils that compiled the figures, nor the Ministry of Housing, Communities and Local Government, which vetted and then released [them]" (Davies, 2018). Their investigation has added to a growing campaign for local bodies to publish data more consistently, more openly and more accurately.

Impact Beyond Innovation

As data journalism has become more routine, and more integrated into ever-complex business models, its impact has shifted from the sphere of innovation to that of delivery. As data editor David Ottewell wrote of the distinction in 2018:

> Innovation is getting data journalism on a front page. Delivery is getting it on the front page day after day. Innovation is building a snazzy interactive that allows readers to explore and understand an important issue. Delivery is doing that, and getting large numbers of people to actually use it; then building another one the next day, and another the day after that. (Ottewell, 2018)

Delivery is also, of course, about impact beyond our peers, beyond the "wow" factor of a striking dataviz or interactive map—on the real world. It may be immediate, obvious and measurable, or it may be slow-burning, under the radar and diffuse. Sometimes we can feel like we did not make a difference—as in the case of *The Boston Globe*'s Catholic priest—but change can take time: Reporting can sow the seeds of change, with results coming years or decades later. The Bureau Local and BBC do not know if council or schools data will be more reliable in future—but they do know that the spotlight is on both to improve.

Sometimes shining a spotlight and accepting that it is the responsibility of others to take action is all that journalism can do; sometimes it takes action itself, and campaigns for greater openness. To this data journalism adds the ability to force greater openness, or create the tools that make it possible for others to take action.

Ultimately, data journalism with impact can set the agenda. It reaches audiences that other journalism does not reach and engages them in ways that other journalism does not. It gives a voice to the voiceless and shines a light on information which would otherwise remain obscure. It holds data to account and speaks truth to its power.

Some of this impact is quantifiable, and some has been harder to measure—and any attempt to monitor impact should bear this in mind. But that does not mean that we should not try.

Works Cited

Academy schools breach transparency rules. (2016, November 18). *BBC News*. https://www.bbc.com/news/uk-england-37620007

Angwin, J., & Tobin, A. (2018, March 27). Fair housing groups sue Facebook for allowing discrimination in housing ads. *ProPublica*. https://www.propublica.org/article/facebook-fair-housing-lawsuit-ad-discrimination

Blau, U. (2016, April 6). How some 370 journalists in 80 countries made the Panama Papers happen. Nieman Reports. https://niemanreports.org/articles/how-some-370-journalists-in-80-countries-made-the-panama-papers-happen/

Byers, D. (2012, November 6). 20% of NYT visitors read 538. *Politico*. https://www.politico.com/blogs/media/2012/11/nate-silver-draws-of-nyt-traffic-148670.html

Cabra, M. (2017, November 29). How ICIJ went from having no data team to being a tech-driven media organization. ICIJ. https://www.icij.org/blog/2017/11/icij-went-no-data-team-tech-driven-media-organization/

Chammah, M. (2016, February 3). Policing the future. The Marshall Project. https://www.themarshallproject.org/2016/02/03/policing-the-future

Crosas Batista, M. (2016, June 22). How one Mexican data team uncovered the story of 4,000 missing women. *Online Journalism Blog*. https://onlinejournalismblog.com/2016/06/22/mexico-data-journalism-ausencias-ignoradas/

Davies, G. (2018, May 2). Inaccurate and unchecked: Problems with local council spending data. The Bureau of Investigative Journalism. https://www.

thebureauinvestigates.com/blog/2018-05-02/inaccurate-and-unchecked-problems-with-local-council-spending-data

Fitzgibbon, W., & Díaz-Struck, E. (2016, December 1). Panama Papers have had historic global effects—And the impacts keep coming. ICIJ. https://www.icij.org/investigations/panama-papers/20161201-global-impact/

Hermida, A., & Young, M. L. (2017). Finding the data unicorn. *Digital Journalism*, 5(2), 159–176. https://doi.org/10.1080/21670811.2016.1162663

Higgerson, D. (2015, October 14). How audience metrics dispel the myth that readers don't want to get involved with serious stories. David Higgerson. https://davidhiggerson.wordpress.com/2015/10/14/how-audience-metrics-dispel-the-myth-that-readers-dont-want-to-get-involved-with-serious-stories/

ICIJ's awards. (n.d.). ICIJ. https://www.icij.org/about/awards/

Improving enforcement and promoting diversity: Updates to ads policies and tools. (2017, February 8). About Facebook. https://about.fb.com/news/2017/02/improving-enforcement-and-promoting-diversity-updates-to-ads-policies-and-tools/

Jalonick, M. C. (2017, October 27). Facebook vows more transparency over political ads. *The Seattle Times*. https://www.seattletimes.com/business/facebook-vows-more-transparency-over-political-ads/

Libraries lose a quarter of staff as hundreds close. (2016, March 29). *BBC News*. https://www.bbc.com/news/uk-england-35707956

McClenaghan, M. (2017, May 18). Campaigners target voters with Brexit "dark ads." The Bureau of Investigative Journalism. https://www.thebureauinvestigates.com/stories/2017-05-18/campaigners-target-voters-brexit-dark-ads

The Migrants' Files. (n.d.). http://www.themigrantsfiles.com/

Ottewell, D. (2018, March 28). The evolution of data journalism. *Medium*. https://towardsdatascience.com/the-evolution-of-data-journalism-1e4c2802bc3d

Rusbridger, A. (2018, August 31). Alan Rusbridger: Who broke the news? *The Guardian*. https://www.theguardian.com/news/2018/aug/31/alan-rusbridger-who-broke-the-news

Sambrook, R. (Ed.). (2018). *Global teamwork: The rise of collaboration in investigative journalism*. Reuters Institute for the Study of Journalism.

Schlemmer, C. (2016). *Speed is not everything: How news agencies use audience metrics*. Reuters Institute for the Study of Journalism. https://reutersinstitute.politics.ox.ac.uk/our-research/speed-not-everything-how-news-agencies-use-audience-metrics

Stark, J. (2016, May 2). Investigating Uber surge pricing: A data journalism case study. Global Investigative Journalism Network. https://gijn.org/2016/05/02/investigating-uber-surge-pricing-a-data-journalism-case-study/

About the Author

Paul Bradshaw runs the MA in Data Journalism and the MA in Multi-platform and Mobile Journalism at Birmingham City University, and fits in work as a consulting data journalist with the BBC England Data Unit alongside writing books and training journalists at a range of news organizations.

53. What Is Data Journalism For? Cash, Clicks, and Cut and Trys

Nikki Usher

Abstract

The financial incentives and the unintended consequences of commercial data journalism are addressed.

Keywords: journalism, datafication, misinformation, political economy, elections, experimentation

The daily refreshing of *FiveThirtyEight*'s interactive 2016 election map forecasts was all but ritual among my fellow Washingtonians, from politicians to journalists to students to government workers and beyond. Some of this ilk favoured *The New York Times*' Upshot poll aggregator; the more odds-minded of them, *Real Clear Politics*, and those with more exotic tastes turned to *The Guardian*'s US election coverage. For these serial refreshers, all was and would be right with the world so long as the odds were ever in Hillary Clinton's favour in the US presidential election's version of the Hunger Games, the bigger the spread, the better.

We know how this story ends. Nate Silver's map, even going into election day, had Hillary Clinton likely to win by 71.4%. Perhaps it's due time to get over the 2016 US election, and after all, obsession with election maps is perhaps a particularly American pastime, due to the regular cycle of national elections—although that is not to say that a worldwide audience is not also paying attention (N. P. Lewis & Waters, 2018). But until link rot destroys the map, it is there, still haunting journalists and Clinton supporters alike, providing fodder for Republicans to remind their foes that the "lamestream media" is "fake news." Politics aside, the 2016 US presidential election should not be forgotten by data journalists: Even if the quantification was correct to anyone's best knowledge, the failures in mapping and visualization have

Bounegru, L. and J. Gray (eds.), *The Data Journalism Handbook: Towards a Critical Data Practice*. Amsterdam: Amsterdam University Press, 2021

DOI 10.5117/9789462989511_CH53

become one more tool through which to dismantle journalists' claim to epistemic authority (or more simply, their claim to be "authorized knowers").

Yes, it is unfair to conflate data journalism with electoral prediction—it certainly is far more than that, particularly from a global vantage point, but it sometimes seems that this is what data journalism's ultimate contribution looks like: Endless maps, clickable charts, calculators prone to user error, oversimplification, and marginalization regardless of the rigor of the computation and statistical prowess that produced them. With the second edition of this handbook now in your hands, we can declare that data journalism has reached a point of maturation and self-reflection, and, as such, it is important to ask, "What is data journalism for?"

Data journalism, as it stands today, still only hints at the potential it has offered to reshape and reignite journalism. The first edition of this handbook began as a collaborative project, in a large group setting in 2011 at a Mozilla Festival, an effort I observed but quickly doubted would ever actually materialize into a tangible result (I was wrong); this second edition is now being published by the University of Amsterdam Press and distributed in the United States by the University of Chicago Press with solicited contributors, suggesting the freewheeling nature of data journalism has been exchanged somewhat in return for professionalism, order and legitimacy. And indeed, this is the case: Data journalism is mainstream, taught in journalism schools, and normalized into the newsroom (Usher, 2016). Data journalism has also standardized and, as such, has changed little over the past five to seven years; reviews of cross-national data journalism contests reveal limited innovation in form and topic (most often: politics), with maps and charts still the go-to (Loosen et al., 2020). Interactivity is limited to what is considered "entry-level techniques" by those in information visualization (Young et al., 2018); moreover, data journalism has not gone far enough to visualize "dynamic, directed, and weighted graphs" (Stoiber et al., 2015). Data journalists are still dealing with preprocessed data rather than original "big data"—and this data is "biggish," at best—government data rather than multilevel data in depth and size of the sort an Internet service provider might collect.

This critique I offer flows largely from a Western-centred perspective (if not a US-centred perch), but that does not undermine the essential call to action I put forward: Data journalists are still sitting on a potentially revolutionary toolbox for journalism that has yet to be unleashed. The revolution, however, if executed poorly, only stands to further undermine both the user experience and the knowledge-seeking efforts of news consumers, and, at worst, further seed distrust in news. If data journalism just continues to look like it has looked for the past five to ten years, then data journalism does little to advance the cause of journalism in the digital and platform era. Thus, to start asking this existential question ("What is data journalism for?"), I propose that data journalists, along with less-data-focused-but-web-immersed journalists who work in video, audio and code, as well as the scholars who poke and prod them, need to rethink data journalism's origin story, its present rationale and its future.

Data Journalism in the United States: The Origin Story

The origin story is the story we tell ourselves about how and why we came to be, and is more often than not viewed through rose-tinted glasses and filled with more braggadocio than it is reality. The origin story of data journalism in the United States goes something like this: In the primordial pre-data journalism world, data journalism existed in an earlier form, as computer-assisted reporting, or was called that in the United States, which offered an opportunity to bring social science rigor to journalism.

In the mythos of data journalism's introduction to the web, data journalists would become souped-up investigative journalists empowered with the superior computational prowess of the 21st century who set the data (or documents) free in order to help tell stories that would otherwise not be told. But beyond just investigating stories, data journalists were also somehow to save journalism with their new web skills, bringing a level of transparency, personalization and interactivity to news that news consumers would appreciate, learn from and, of course, click on. Stories of yesteryear's web, as it were, would never be the same. Data journalism would right wrongs and provide the much-needed objective foundation that journalism's qualitative assessments lacked, doing it at a scale and with a prowess unimaginable prior to our present real-time interactive digital environment replete with powerful cloud-based servers that offload the computational pressure from any one news organization. Early signs of success would chart the way forward, and even turn ordinary readers into investigative collaborators or citizen scientists, such as with *The Guardian*'s coverage of the MPs' expenses scandal or the "Cicada Tracker" project of the New York City public radio station WNYC, which got a small army of area residents to build soil thermometers to help chart the arrival of the dreaded summer instincts. And this inspired orchestration of journalism, computation, crowds, data and technology would continue, pushing truth to justice.

The Present: The "Hacker Journalist" as Just Another (Boring) Newsroom Employee

The present has not moved far past the origin story that today's data journalists have told themselves, neither in vision nor in reality. What has emerged has become two distinct types of data journalism: The "investigative" data journalism that carries the noble mantle of journalism's efforts forward, and daily data journalism, which can be optimized for the latest viral click interest, which might mean anything from an effort at ASAP journalistic cartography to turning public opinion polling or a research study into an easily shareable meme with the veneer of journalism attached. Data journalism, at best, has gotten boring and overly professional, and, at worst, has become another strategy to generate digital revenue.

It is not hyperbole to say that data journalism could have transformed journalism as we know it—but hitherto it has not. At the 2011 MozFest, a headliner hack of the festival was a plug-in of sorts that would allow anyone's face to become the lead image of a mock-up of *The Boston Globe* home page. That was fun and games, but *The Boston Globe* was certainly not going to just allow user-generated content, without any kind of pre-filtering, to actually be used on its home page. Similarly, during the birth of the first *Data Journalism Handbook*, the data journalist was the "hacker journalist," imagined as coming from technology into journalism or at least using the spirit of open source and hacking to inspire projects that bucked at the conventional processes of institutional journalism and provided room for experimentation, imperfection and play—tinkering for the sake of leading to something that might not be great in form or content, but might well hack journalism nonetheless (S. C. Lewis & Usher, 2013). In 2011, the story was of outsiders moving into journalism, but in 2018, the story is of insiders professionalizing programming in journalism, so in five years the spirit of innovation and invention has become decidedly corporate, decidedly white-collar and decidedly less fun (S. C. Lewis & Usher, 2016).

Boring is OK, and it serves a role. Some of the professionalization of data journalism has been justified with the "data journalist as hero" self-perception—data journalists as those who, thanks to a different set of values (e.g., collaboration, transparency) and skills (visualization, assorted computational skills) could bring truth to power in new ways. The Panama and Paradise Papers are perhaps one of the best expressions of this vision. But investigative data journalism requires time, effort and expertise that goes far beyond just data crunching, and includes many other sources of more traditional data, primarily interviews, on-location reporting and documents.

Regularly occurring, groundbreaking investigative journalism is an oxymoron, although not for lack of effort: The European Data Journalism Network, the United States' Institute for NonProfit News and the Global Investigative Journalism Network all showcase the vast network of would-be investigative efforts. The truth is that a game-changer investigation is not easy to come by, which is why we can generally name these high-level successes on about ten fingers and the crowdsourced investigative success of *The Guardian's* MPs' expenses example from 2010 has yet to be replaced by anything newer.

What's past is prologue when it comes to data journalism. "Snow Fall," *The New York Times'* revolutionary immersive storytelling project that won a Pulitzer Prize in 2012, emerged in December 2017 as "Deliverance from 27,000 Feet" or "Everest." Five years later, *The New York Times* featured yet another long-form story about a disaster on a snowy mountain, just a different one (but by same author, John Branch). In those five years, "Snowfall" or "Snowfalled" became shorthand within *The New York Times* and outside it for adding interactive pizzazz to a story; after 2012, a debate raged not just at *The Times* but in other US and UK newsrooms as to whether data journalists should be spending their time building templating tools that could auto-Snowfall any story, or work on innovative one-off projects (Usher, 2016). Meanwhile, "Snow Fall," minimally interactive at best in 2012, remained minimally interactive at best in its year-end 2017 form.

"But wait," the erstwhile data journalist might proclaim. "'Snow Fall' isn't *data journalism*—maybe a fancy trick of some news app developers, but there's no data in 'Snow Fall'!" Herein lies the issue: Maybe data journalists don't think "Snow Fall" is data journalism, but why not? *What is data journalism for if it is not to tell stories in new ways with new skills that take advantage of the best of the web?*

Data journalism also cannot just be for maps or charts, either, nor does mapping or charting data give data journalism intellectual superiority over immersive digital journalism efforts. What can be mapped is mapped. Election mapping in the United States aside, the ethical consequences of quantifying and visualizing the latest available data into clickable coherence needs critique. At its most routine, data journalism becomes the vegetables of visualization. This is particularly true given the move towards daily and regular demand for data journalism projects. Perhaps it's a new labour statistic, city cycling data, recycling rates, the results of an academic study, visualization because it can be visualized (and maybe, will get clicked on more). At worst, data journalism can oversimplify to the point of dehumanizing the subject of the data that their work is supposed to illuminate. Maps of migrants and their flows across Europe take on the form of interactive arrows or genderless person icons. As human geographer Paul Adams argues, digital news cartography has rendered the refugee crisis into a disembodied series of clickable actions, the very opposite of what it could as journalism do to make unknown "refugees" empathetic and more than a number (Adams, 2017). Before mapping yet another social problem or academic study, data journalists need to ask: To what end are we mapping and charting (or charticle-ing for that matter)?

And somewhere between "Snow Fall" and migration maps lies the problem: *What is data journalism for*? The present provides mainly evidence of professionalization and isomorphism, with an edge of corporate incentive that data journalism is not just to aid news consumers with their understanding of the world but also to pad the bottom lines of news organizations. Surely that is not all data journalism can be.

The Future: How Data Journalism Can Reclaim Its Worth (and Be Fun, Too)

What is data journalism for? Data journalism needs to go back to its roots of change and revolution, of inspired hacking and experimentation, of a self-determined vision of renegades running through a tired and uninspired industry to force journalists to confront their presumed authority over knowledge, narrative and distribution. Data journalists need to own up to their hacker inspiration and hack the newsroom as they once promised to do; they need to move past a focus on profit and professionalism within their newsrooms. Reclaiming outsider status will bring us closer to the essential offering that data journalism promised: A way to think about journalism differently, a way to present journalism differently, and a way to bring new kinds of thinkers and doers into the newsroom, and beyond that, a way to reinvigorate journalism.

In the future, I imagine data journalism as unshackled from the term "data" and instead focused on the word "journalism." Data journalists presumably have skills that the rest of the newsroom or other journalists do not: The ability to understand complicated data or guide a computer to do this for them, the ability to visualize this data in a presumably meaningful way, and the ability to code. Data journalism, however, must become what I have called interactive journalism—data journalism needs to shed its vegetable impulse of map and chart cranking as well as its scorn of technologies and skills that are not data-intensive, such as 360 video, augmented reality and animation. In my vision of the future, there will be a lot more of the BBC's "Secret Life of the Cat" interactives and *The New York Times'* "Dialect Quizzes"; there will be more projects that combine 360 video or VR with data, like Dataverse's effort funded by the Journalism 360 immersive news initiative. There will be a lot less election mapping and cartography that illustrates the news of the day, reducing far-away casualties to clickable lines and flows. Hopefully, we will see the end of the new trend towards interactives showing live-time polling results, a new fetish of top news outlets in the United States. Rather, there will be a lot more originality, fun, and inspired breaking of what journalism is supposed to look like and what it is supposed to do. Data journalism is for accountability, but it is also for fun and for the imagination; it gains its power not just because an MP might resign or a trend line becomes clearer, but also because ordinary people see the value of returning to news organizations and to journalists because journalists fill a variety of human information needs—for orientation, for entertainment, for community, and beyond.

And to really claim superior knowledge about data, data journalists intent on rendering data knowable and understandable need to collect this data on their own—data journalism is not just for churning out new visualizations of data gathered by someone else. At best, churning out someone else's data makes the data providers' assumptions visible; at worst, data journalism becomes as stenographic as a press release for the data provider. Yet many data journalists do not have much interest in collecting their own data and find it outside the boundaries of their roles; as *The Washington Post* data editor Steven Rich explained, in a tweet, the *Post* "and others should not have to collect and maintain databases that are no-brainers for the government to collect. This should not be our fucking job" (Rich, 2018). At the same time, however, the gun violence statistics Rich was frustrated by having to maintain are more empowering than he realized: Embedded in government data are assumptions and decisions about what to collect that need sufficient inquiry and consideration. The data is not inert, but filled with presumptions about what facts matter. Journalists seeking to take control over the domain of facticity need to be able to explain why the facts are what they are, and, in fact, the systematic production of fact is how journalists have claimed their epistemic authority for most of modern journalism.

What data journalism is for, then, is for so much more than it is now—it can be for fun, play and experimentation. It can be for changing how stories get told and can invite new ways of thinking about them. But it also stands to play a vital role in re-establishing the case for journalism as truth-teller and fact-provider; in creating and knowing data, and being able to explain the process of observation and data collection that led to a fact. Data journalism might well become a key line of defence about how professional journalists can and do gather facts better than any other occupation, institution or ordinary person ever could.

Works Cited

Adams, P. (2017). Migration maps with the news: Guidelines for ethical visualization of mobile populations. *Journalism Studies, 19*(1), 1–21. https://doi.org/10.1080/1 461670X.2017.1375387

Lewis, N. P., & Waters, S. (2018). Data journalism and the challenge of shoe-leather epistemologies. *Digital Journalism, 6*(6), 719–736. https://doi.org/10.1080/21670 811.2017.1377093

Lewis, S. C., & Usher, N. (2013). Open source and journalism: Toward new frameworks for imagining news innovation. *Media, Culture & Society, 35*(5), 602–619. https:// doi.org/10.1177/0163443713485494

Lewis, S. C., & Usher, N. (2016). Trading zones, boundary objects, and the pursuit of news innovation: A case study of journalists and programmers. *Convergence, 22*(5), 543–560. https://doi.org/10.1177/1354856515623865

Loosen, W., Reimer, J., & De Silva-Schmidt, F. (2020). Data-driven reporting: An on-going (r)evolution? An analysis of projects nominated for the Data Journalism Awards 2013–2016. *Journalism, 21*(9), 1246–1263. https://doi. org/10.1177/1464884917735691

Rich, S. (2018, February 15). The @washingtonpost and others should not have to collect and maintain databases that are no-brainers for the government to collect. This should not be our fucking job. Twitter. https://twitter.com/ dataeditor/status/964160884754059264

Stoiber, C., Aigner, W., & Rind, A. (2015). Survey on visualizing dynamic, weighted, and directed graphs in the context of data-driven journalism. In *Proceedings of the International Summer School on Visual Computing* (pp. 49–58).

Usher, N. (2016). *Interactive journalism: Hackers, data, and code*. University of Illinois Press.

Young, M. L., Hermida, A., & Fulda, J. (2018). What makes for great data journalism? A content analysis of Data Journalism Awards finalists 2012–2015. *Journalism Practice, 12*(1), 115–135. https://doi.org/10.1080/17512786.2016.1270171

About the Author

Nikki Usher is an Associate Professor at the University of Illinois at Urbana–Champaign and is the author of *Interactive Journalism: Hackers, Data, and Code* (University of Illinois Press, 2016).

54. Data Journalism and Digital Liberalism

Dominic Boyer

Abstract

How the rise of data journalism intersects with political liberalism.

Keywords: liberalism, sedentary journalism, screenwork, lateral messaging, autological individuality, data journalism

The past 30 years have witnessed a massive transformation of the journalistic profession and the organizational culture of news-making. The causes and effects of that transformation are too complex to detail here. Suffice it to say that the model of print and terrestrial broadcasting that still seemed quite robust as late as the 1990s has been almost fully replaced by a digital-first model of news media created by the rise of the Internet, search engines and social media as dominant communication and information systems, and by the widespread financialization and privatization of news media driven by the economic philosophy of "neoliberalism." As this volume argues, proliferating digital data streams and tokens are now the default condition of journalistic practice. All journalism is now, to some extent, "data journalism." In my 2013 book *The Life Informatic* I described this process as "the lateral revolution," suggesting that we have witnessed an ecological shift from the dominance of radial (e.g., largely monodirectional, hub-to-spoke) infrastructures of news media to lateral (e.g., largely pluridirectional, point-to-point) infrastructures (Boyer, 2013). As Raymond Williams (1974) observed in his brilliant historical study of the rise of television, electronic media have exhibited both radial and lateral potentialities since the 18th century. Where these potentialities have been unlocked and institutionalized has always been guided by social and political circumstances beyond the technologies themselves. There was a prototype fax machine over a century

Bounegru, L. and J. Gray (eds.), *The Data Journalism Handbook: Towards a Critical Data Practice.* Amsterdam: Amsterdam University Press, 2021

DOI 10.5117/9789462989511_CH54

before there was an obvious social need for such a technology and so its formal "invention" was delayed accordingly. Broadcasting systems ranging from radio to television first became socially necessary, Williams (1974) argues, once what he terms the "mobile privatization" of Western society had advanced to the point that it was difficult for government and industry to locate and communicate with citizen-consumers other than by "blanket" radial messaging over a whole terrain. The lesson for our contemporary situation is simply that we should not assume that the recent data revolution in news journalism is solely or even primarily driven by new technologies and infrastructures like the Internet. We should rather be attentive to how news media have evolved (and continue to evolve) within a more complex ecology of social forces.

Williams' approach informed the concept of "digital liberalism" that I developed in *The Life Informatic* to capture a hunch that I developed during my fieldwork with news journalists in the late 2000s that there was a symbiotic relationship between the digital information practices of news journalists and the broader neoliberalization of society and the economy since the 1980s. I was, for example, interested in the increasing importance of screenwork among news journalists. One might consider screenwork as an infrastructural precondition for the rise of data journalism. Screenwork first emerged as an aspect of news-making in the 1970s and 1980s, driven by organizational initiatives in news media and elsewhere in Western corporate culture to harness personal computers and office-based digital information systems to generate new production efficiencies. In the news industry, computerization was originally viewed as a means of improving word-processing speed and reducing labour costs through the automation of composition and some copyediting work. But in the process of institutionalization, computers rapidly became involved in every aspect of news production from marketing to layout to archiving, creating new opportunities for automating tasks previously accomplished directly by humans and for concentrating remaining production tasks in the hands of fewer news workers. Veteran journalists who recalled work life before computerization frequently told me how much larger the support staff had been, how much more time they now spent at their desks, and how their individual workloads had increased.

It is true that news journalism has always had its sedentary side. Typewriting, for example, also involved seated production; as did telephone use before cellular systems. The crucial difference between previous forms of sedentary journalism and its contemporary variant is how screenwork currently channels an unprecedented number of key journalistic tasks (e.g., word processing, text editing, archival research, breaking news monitoring, surveillance of the competition, and intra-office communication and coordination) through a single interface with a normally fixed location. The combined importance of smartphone use and fast-time social media like Twitter for news journalism has made mobile screenwork at least as important as desktop screenwork, but it has done little to change the phenomenon of journalists being "glued to their screens." Few would dispute now that the screen interface has become a central aspect of journalistic practice. Almost everything journalists do, almost every source of information, almost every professional output involves their engagement with one or more screens.

This co-location of critical tasks creates convenience but also distraction. Many journalists report feeling overwhelmed by the sheer number and speed of the data streams they have to manage. It is important to recognize that the experience of data journalism is frequently an anxious one. In my field research, journalistic screen workers frequently reported having to rely on other trusted news sources for judgements (for example, as to news value) because their own abilities were so overtaxed. It is easy to see how screenwork contributes to the much-maligned "herd mentality" of contemporary news, with distracted, overwhelmed journalists often relying on each other for real-time guidance while data streams move on at breakneck pace.

Knowing that the dominance of screenwork did not emerge in a vacuum, this is where a parallel investigation of neoliberalism proves fruitful. Classical liberalism came into being in the 17th and 18th centuries as European intellectual culture adapted to the realities of the formation of colonial empires across the world. The cultural dominance of medieval Christian conservatism and even Renaissance humanism were increasingly displaced by social philosophies that emphasized labour, liberty, private property and productivity. A critical problem for early liberalism was how to make the pursuit and possession of private property a virtuous path, since it would seem to threaten to deprive the poor of their share of God's gifts to humanity. The solution was to emphasize that human science and industry's ability to improve the productive use of resources combined with the sheer abundance of the new colonial frontier meant that the acquisition of private property need not be antithetical to Christian values. A perhaps unintended consequence of this new ethical formation was concentrated attention on the individual as a subject of reason, action, freedom and virtue. As liberalism developed in conjunction with the rise of capitalism and its modern ways of life, the individual became an increasingly important figure in Western culture. At first, the individual sought to harmoniously counterbalance the restrictive forces of "society," but increasingly individuality was positioned as an end in itself where all social and economic relations ultimately served to develop and enable robust, productive, self-sustaining individuals. These individuals were imagined as being ideally free of social determination and instead free to think and act as they wished. I describe this model of individuality, following anthropologist Elizabeth Povinelli, as "autological" in its working ideological assumption that individuals to a great extent are capable of "making themselves," a proposition that remains cherished across the liberal political spectrum today.

What does all this have to do with computer screens you might ask? It is true that the first great ventures in analogue and digital computation took place in the 1930s as the Keynesian social democracies of the mid-20th century readied themselves for war. But the development of personal computation that was the more direct forerunner of contemporary screenwork developed during the 1970s and 1980s at the same time that neoliberalism rose to political and philosophical dominance as Keynesian social democracy seemed to collapse under the weight of the multiple geopolitical crises of the late 1960s and 1970s (the Vietnam War, the Arab–Israeli conflicts, the formation of OPEC, among others). Where liberalism had long believed that the best way to pursue public interests was by empowering private interest, one might describe neoliberalism as ruthlessly autological in its empowerment of private interests at the expense of public investments and institutions. The neoliberal turn in politics and policy had a profoundly negative impact on the kind of public interest news journalism that accompanied Keynesian mid-20th-century norms even as it propelled massive new investments in communication and information infrastructures like the Internet, satellite broadcasting and cellular telephony around the world. The imagination and creation of these infrastructures originally had very little to do with news media. The Internet, as is widely known, came into being through the shared interests of military defence and research science. Less well known, but equally important, was the usefulness of fast-time transnational communications for financial practices like arbitrage. Nevertheless, the new information and communication infrastructures impacted all areas of social communication including, of course, news-making. Their net effect was the radical strengthening of point-to-point lateral messaging capacities as well as the pluralization and retemporalization of hub-to-spoke broadcasting such that even though radial messaging still exists, it is increasingly transnational and asynchronous. The model of the nation sitting down to listen to the evening news together simply does not exist in any practical sense in most parts of the world, even in Europe and Asia where stronger public broadcasting traditions have endured.

Our contemporary news ecology does not actually guarantee robust individualism even though it has made finding community and trusted information a more precarious venture. But where the rubber hits the road for digital liberalism, so to speak, is in the individualizing experience of screenwork (and screenplay for that matter). The evolution of personal computation, the Internet and social media were deeply shaped by the social importance of neo/liberal principles of maximizing individual capacities for action, communication and ideation. Over the past decade, an increasing percentage of the population (over 70% of the United States, for example) carries with them an all-purpose portable media device operating like a fifth limb of the body. That limb allows access to multiple information flows, the possibility of curating those flows to reflect personal interests and desires, and myriad ways to message personal views and thoughts and to constitute self-centred micropublics. It is both the inheritor of centuries of liberal epistemology as well as the crucial device for enabling the reproduction and intensification of that epistemology in what we have come to call "the digital era." You have seen the images of strangers in a bar or on a train, everyone glued to their screens. The smartphone did not invent social estrangement of course. What it invents is a communicational interface that allows us to experience active, productive individuality, while minimizing social connectedness and accountability, even when we are crowded among strangers in any given place in the world. In other eras those strangers might have found greater occasion and opportunity in their co-presence to become unneighbourly with one another.

In short, I remain convinced that autological individuality is being reinforced by the proliferation and intensification of screen interfaces even as the fact those interfaces exist in the first place has much to do with technologies developed to materialize liberal worldviews and priorities over the course of the past few centuries. To paraphrase Marshall McLuhan, we assume we work our screens but we should recognize that our screens also work us. This juncture of mobile portable screen-based media and liberal perceptions of autological individuality is what I term "digital liberalism," and it will be interesting to see how that liberalism further evolves in the future. What if all the strangers on that train car were wearing VR headsets that allowed them immersive access to virtual worlds? How might such new media interfaces elicit new modes of individuality and sociality? Although data journalism is often suspected to share kinship with surveillance technologies and algorithmic authoritarianism, I would submit that the evolution of digital liberalism is actually data journalism's deeper history.

Works Cited

Boyer, D. (2013). *The life informatic: Newsmaking in the digital era*. Cornell University Press.

Williams, R. (1974). *Television*. Wesleyan University Press.

About the Author

Dominic Boyer is an anthropologist, filmmaker and podcaster who founded the Center for Energy and Environmental Research in the Human Sciences (CENHS) at Rice University.

Index

Note: entries given in italics refer to figures.

Printed in the United States
By Bookmasters